Philosophy of Death & Dying

Philosophy of Death & Dying

by M.V. Kamath

Published by
HIMALAYAN INTERNATIONAL INSTITUTE
OF YOGA SCIENCE AND PHILOSOPHY

Library of Congress Card No.: 78-67174

ISBN: 0-89389-046-4

Copyright 1978

HIMALAYAN INTERNATIONAL INSTITUTE
OF YOGA SCIENCE AND PHILOSOPHY
Honesdale, Pennsylvania

All Rights Reserved

Vayur-anilam-amrtam-athedam bhasmantam shariram,
Om Krato smara krtam smara krato smara krtam smara.

Now let my breath return to immortal prana,
and my body to ashes.
Remember, O Mind, remember OM and remember my deeds,
Remember my deeds.

Ishopanishad

ACKNOWLEDGMENTS

A book of this nature would not be easy to write without recourse to original sources. The author who has quoted directly or indirectly from various authors wishes to acknowledge with grateful thanks his indebtedness especially to the following: *Self Knowledge*: Swami Nikhilananda, Ramakrishna Vivekananda Center, New York; *The Mystics of Islam*: Reynold A. Nicholson, Routledge & Kegan Paul Ltd., London; *Indian Philosophy*: S. Radhakrishnan, The MacMillan Co., New York; *A Source Book of Indian Philosophy*, edited by S. Radhakrishnan and Charles A. Moore, Princeton University Press, Princeton; *The Reconstruction of Religious Thought in Islam*: Sir Mohammad Iqbal, Oxford University Press, London; *The Koran*, translated with notes by N. J. Dawood, Penguin; *Great Dialogues of Plato*: translation by W. H. D. Rouse, The New American Library Inc., New York; *The Judaic Tradition*: texts edited and introduced by Nahum N. Glatzer, Beacon Press, Boston; *Moses Maimonides: The Guide for the Perplexed*, translated by M. Friedlander, Dover Publications, New York; *The Question of God*: Protestant Theology in the 20th Century: Heinz Zahrnt, Harcourt Brace, Jovanovich, New York; *A History of Christian Thought*: Paul Tillich, edited by Carl Braeten, Simon and Schuster, New York; *The Ocean of Theosophy*: William Q. Judge, Theosophical University Press, Pasadena, California; *A Handbook of Christian Theology*: A Meredian Book, New American Library, New York; *Death, The Riddle and the Mystery*: Eberhard Jungel, The Westminster Press, Philadelphia; *Sri Aurobindo or the Adventure of Consciousness*: Satprem, Harper & Row, New York; *Death, The Final Stage of Growth*: Elisabeth Kubler-Ross, Prentice-Hall, Inc., Englewood Cliffs, New Jersey; *The Meaning of Death*: edited by Herman Feifel, McGraw Hill Book Co., New York; *Man Is Not Alone*: Abraham Joshua Herschel, The Noonday Press, New York; *The Saviors of God*: Nikos Kazantzakis, Simon & Schuster, New York; *Man's Search for Meaning*: Viktor E. Frankel, Beacon Press, Boston; *Man In The Universe*: W. Norman Brown, University of California Press, Berkeley; *Tragic Sense of Life*: Miguel de Unamuno, Dover Publications, Inc., New York; *The Spirit of the East*: The Sirdar Ikbal Ali Shah, E. P. Dutton & Co., New York; *The Kabir Book*: Robert Bly, Beacon Press, Boston; *Many Mansions*: Gina Cerminara, The New American Library, Inc., New York; *Life After Life*: Raymond A. Moody, Jr., Mockingbird Books, Inc., Atlanta; *Labyrinths*, Jorge Luis Borges, New Directions Publishing Co., New York; *Vedanta for the Common Man*: edited by Christopher Isherwood, New American Library, New York; *The Perennial Philosophy*: Aldous Huxley, Harper & Row, New York; *Sadhana: The Realization of Life*: Rabindranath Tagore, The Omen Communications, Inc., Tucson; *Only In America*: Harry Golden, The World Publishing Co., New York. Other books consulted are detailed in the bibliography to all of whom thanks are hereby offered.

Contents

Author's Note xi
Introduction xiii
Part I
Life to Death: The Questionable Pursuit. 1
Savitri and Satyavan: The Power of Love 5
The Story of Nachiketa: The Quest for Meaning 7
The Bhagavad Gita: The Interpretation of Death 15
Theory of Rebirth: The Endless Chain of Life and Death 18
The Doctrine of Lokayata: There Is No Life But This 22
Is There Life After Death?: New Evidence to the Fore. 25
Reincarnation: Life, Death and the Question of Rebirth. 32
Karma Revisited: Shaking One's Own Hand in Another Life 36
Nirvana: The Deliverance of the Soul. 40
The Way of the Buddha and the Order of the Universe. 45
Bardo Thodol: A Traveler's Guide to Other Worlds. 53
The Theosophist: Understanding Life and Death 57
Reincarnation and the Life Eternal. 60
The Pervading Influence of the Reincarnation Doctrine 62
Sri Aurobindo on Death and Reincarnation 68
The Socratic Concept: Death and the Nature of the Soul 74
Osiris and His Forty Two Assessors. 80
Zoroastrianism and the Concept of Future Rewards and Punishments. 81
The Three Great Semitic Religions: Judaism, Christianity and Islam. . . . 84
Judaism and the Doctrine of Free Will 87
Man Can Control His Passions and Be a Force for Good 89
The Purpose of Creation and the Relevance of Man 91
Jewish Attitude Toward Death 93
Islam and the Idea of a Future Life. 95
Iqbal's Theory: Koranic View of the Destiny of Man. 97
Islamic Concepts of Heaven and Hell. 100
Sufism and the Mystics of Islam. 102
Christian Faith and the Concept of Personal Responsibility. 105
Immortality, Life Eternal and Everlasting Life 109
Destiny, Fate and Predestination 110
The Roman Catholic Understanding of Sin 112
The Doctrine of Justification by Faith Alone 114
The Sacraments and the Attaining of Salvation 115
Karl Barth and the Humanity of God. 118
Dark Night of the Soul: Toward Perfect Union 120
The Question of Being: Between Finitude and Infinity 122
The Need for an Everyday Philosophy of Death 123
A Personal Philosophy 129
References. 150

PHILOSOPHY OF DEATH & DYING

Part II 157

- The Lord, Krishna 161
- The Buddha 163
- Socrates 165
- Cicero 168
- Jesus Christ 170
- Alexander 176
- Ramakrishna Paramahansa 178
- William Shakespeare 181
- St. Francis of Assisi 184
- Sigmund Freud 187
- Albert Einstein 189
- Aurangzeb 193
- Lenin 196
- Mahatma Gandhi 198
- Leo Tolstoy 202
- Anne Boleyn 206
- Ivan Turgenev 209
- Voltaire 211
- Thomas More 214
- Muhammad 216
- Dag Hammarskjold 219
- Napoleon 223
- Martin Luther King Jr 227
- Oliver Wendell Holmes 230
- General Tojo 233
- John, Duke of Marlborough 235
- Swami Vivekananda 237
- Thomas Jefferson 241
- Pope John XXIII 245
- Henrik Ibsen 248
- Goethe 250
- Akbar 253
- Isaac Newton 256
- George Gordon Byron 258
- John Keats 262
- Percy Blysshe Shelley 264
- Queen Christina 267
- Gogol 269
- H. G. Wells 272
- Abraham Lincoln 274
- Thomas Alva Edison 277
- Samuel Johnson 279
- Joseph Stalin 281
- Chinghis Khan 284
- George Washington 287
- Benito Mussolini 289
- Adolf Hitler 292
- Ludwig van Beethoven 296
- Victor Hugo 298
- Queen Elizabeth 301
- Marie Curie 304
- Lord Nelson 306
- William Butler Yeats 310
- Henry David Thoreau 312
- Wolfgang Amadeus Mozart 315
- Summing Up 317

Bibliography 326

Index 333

Author's Note

What? One more book on death? But why not? The subject is so vast, so inexhaustible, that it can do with dozens of books more. Mysterious is man's passing away. Death holds terrors to many, for a variety of reasons; it is hard for them to conceive of suddenly—or even gradually—ceasing to be. In a sense, sudden death is preferable; at least it gives no time to be introspective and maudlin and to be frightened.

Facing death comes hardest for those who linger in bed, wondering what is in store for them. Death itself may not be frightening to them as what may come thereafter. It is, then, not the fear of the known, but of the unknown that is cause for anxiety and misery.

If there is certainty that death is the end of it all, a total annihilation, it is at least sufferable. But man's conscience does not permit him this luxury. He is afraid that such an annihilation will not meet the ends of justice. He argues that there *must* be some life after death. But exactly what *sort* of life? And for *whom?* It is obviously not for the corporeal body; that quickly becomes dust unto dust. Is there something in man apart from body? A soul? What is the nature of the soul? Whence did it come and where would it go and what would become of it when man dies?

These are fabulous questions and the history of philosophy is the history of man's attempts to answer these questions. They have been answered in a variety of ways. That, indeed, is what religions are all about.

This book is a study of how the great religions of the world have handled these questions. It does not claim to be a comprehensive study; it does not even claim to come to any conclusions, though I have added a brief chapter on what I myself feel about the subject. They embody thoughts for today. They are liable to be changed tomorrow. To live is to change.

Writing a book of this kind is by no means easy; where I have been stumped by some abstruse argument, I have borrowed the language of the authorities freely. I express my apologies to them in advance.

This book is in two parts. Part I deals with the philosophic aspects of the hereafter. Part II deals with the last days of some of the most distinguished people in the world, down the centuries. One suspects that these are no different from the last days of many of us, plain, ordinary people. Like all mortals, they too, have thought, felt and suffered before facing death. What Part II of the book brings out, if anything, is the commonality of man. Suffering is the badge not only of the poor, the meek and the humble. It is the hallmark of all mankind.

The lives and deaths of some fifty-five distinguished men and women chosen at random from history tell us what we ought to know or intuite: that those who are well integrated die bravely, calmly and at peace with themselves. That is the only moral we can draw and that is the only moral worth appreciating. Whether it is George Washington or Swami Vivekananda, William Butler Yeats or Henry David Thoreau, Oliver Wendell Holmes or Socrates, Cicero or Tojo, these are men whose deaths tell us how to die. In the manner of their dying, we have an object lesson. And that is what this book is for to draw.

I want to thank my friend, O. N. Nagaratnam, for his selfless and informed help in taking time to find me the books I needed to read and for his constructive suggestions at all times.

I am especially grateful to Sri Swami Rama for offering to publish this brief study.

M. V. Kamath
Washington, D.C.
September 7, 1977

Introduction

"Oh, my death, come and whisper to me." — Tagore

Tagore, the famous poet of the East, wanted death to reveal a secret to him. So did Tilak, a great scholar and commentator of the Bhagavad Gita. It is true that the mystery of life here and hereafter is revealed to a fortunate few. The great sages of the ancient lore knew that this birth is but one bend of the eternal stream of life. In its continuity the stream of life rushes through many avenues and finally meets the ocean. Coming out of one avenue is called death and going through another avenue is called birth. So is the case of human life. After many rounds of births and deaths, when the human being liberates itself from the self-created bondage of karma, he finally attains emancipation and perfection.

In the Bhagavad Gita it is said, "learned is he to whom the mystery of birth and death is revealed." When the body, senses, conscious mind and the two breath guards (inhalation and exhalation) separate from the unconscious mind and the individual soul, this separation is called death. Therefore death is but a separation and not complete annihilation. Death is a habit of the body and not of the soul. Death is not painful; the fear of death is painful. Death is but a momentary disappearance which is revived again in another form. It is merely a game of hide and seek which can never mystify the wise one who knows how to look to himself and beyond.

Egotism, pride and vanity can only appear when we move around our own orbits and refuse to believe that our real orbits are not around ourselves in narrow circles, but on the widest line which goes around us all. Truth consists in the reality of that whole of which we are individual constituents. This does not mean the sacrifice of individuality. It merely means that the true individual, when properly and systematically interpreted, extends further and further, wider and wider, until it permeates through all things in the world and loses itself in the infinite completeness of the whole.

The chasm of death only obstructs our view. Our sorrow is due to our foolish refusal to see and believe that what comes next is but that which is not seen at the moment. The individual soul is self-existent, unborn, and not subject to change, death and decay. Life is like a manuscript whose beginning and end is missing. But by properly analyzing, practicing and realizing the middle portion of that manuscript, one can search for the missing pages of this manuscript of life. Who am I? From where have I come? What is the purpose of life? Where shall I go? These are the prime questions waiting for answers. You are here because you were somewhere else. You move from the known to the unknown, from visible to invisible and from seen to unseen.

The three Sanskrit words, *janma, sristhi,* and *udpatti* explain the mystery of birth and death. Birth and death are like two commas in the sentence of life. The sentence of life begins from eternity and is everlasting and never ending. The word *janma* means that which was hidden came forward. The word *sristhi* means that which was already behind the curtain came forward to the visible world. *Udpatti* means that which already existed in seed form came into manifestation in the plant. For a wise man, death is like a long sleep—probably for several hundred years. All the memories of our lifetimes are stored in the unconscious. That storehouse is used as a vehicle by the individual soul. Anything that is stored in the infinite library of the unconscious mind is called *samskaras.*

To properly understand the meaning of birth and death is to comprehend the entire cycle of human evolution by understanding the twin laws of life called karma and reincarnation. These two laws should be understood first. In the cycle of the universe, a stage comes when a human being is born and thus becomes responsible for his karma. The law of karma means cause and effect mingled together. A human being can attain liberation here and now if he understands that all bondages, miseries and delusions are self-created. There is a way of obtaining freedom from these self-created miseries—it is skillful action done selflessly for others.

If we all learn to do our actions or duties selflessly, we will be doing our karmas but others will be reaping the fruits. Actually karma does not bind but the fruits therein. No human being can live without doing karma, but when he performs the karmas he has to reap the fruits. If he learns to surrender all the fruits of the karma he will be free forever. Karma in its essential nature is a desire to perform action. Therefore, the world of desire should be understood carefully.

Desire is the motivation for our rebirth. A strong and intense desire to be reborn is the main reason for our birth. Human beings leave their mortal bodies with many desires in the unconscious mind and those desires motivate them to come to this platform again and again. So the rounds of births and deaths depend on the human motivations called desires. If we learn to reduce all our desires to a point of zero, all our motivations will be over and there will be no karma. There will be no bondage and the human being will not be in bonds for the fruits of his karma.

We live in a world of fear, anxiety, stress and strain but these are all self-created. The delusion and ignorance that are created by not realizing the true nature of the self is the main cause of all miseries. When one learns not to identify oneself with the objects of the world and constantly becomes aware of the reality or center of consciousness within, one considers birth and death voluntary actions.

As one changes one's pillow cover or book cover, so one casts off one's body. Casting off the body is called death and assuming a new garment is called birth. Attachment seems to be the mother of all miseries. When a human being gets attached to the body, he brings pain to his individual soul. But this pain and attachment can be removed by understanding that the body, breath, senses and mind are like instruments of the individual soul. He should learn the technique of living in the world yet remaining out of it.

When one knows that all the things of the world, even his body, breath, senses and mind, are his instruments, and learns how to use them by realizing that all the things that he has are for him, but are not his, then the strong sense of attachment disappears and the light of wisdom dawns. Such a fortunate one attains enlightenment and freedom from worldly fetters, as well as from the rounds of births and deaths.

Mr. M. V. Kamath, a prominent U.N. journalist, philosopher and author beautifully expresses himself and describes various ways and methods adopted by the great religious groups of the world. He gives a glimpse of the philosophy of the ancients and presents many modern writers' viewpoints on the subject. A tremendous task was accomplished. It is my sincere hope that this book will be useful, informative and enlightening to students and that they will understand the two ends of the same lifeline called birth and death.

Swami Rama of the Himalayas
June 20, 1978

Part I

LIFE TO DEATH: The Questionable Pursuit

The most natural thing for man—*homo sapiens* is for him to take an intelligent interest in death. Death, as he knows, is inevitable. It has to come, sooner or later. It may come instantaneously, as after a massive heart attack, or as the result of an accident, a plane crash or a train wreck, or it may come after days and weeks of suffering and pain. It may come at birth, soon after birth, in early childhood, youth, manhood or middle age. But come it must.

We all have our rendezvous with death and whether it is in the relative comfort of our beds when the sun is rising and all the world is astir, or, as Alan Seeger would say, "at midnight in some flaming town," the meeting is inevitable and surely to be welcomed.

As a physical fact, death is easily understood. It is the departure of the life force from the body. What has animated a handful of earth, as it were, is gone. What is left is dross. Is that the end of man?

This question has haunted philosophers. Indeed, the history of philosophy is the history of the search for an answer to this question. One way to look at it is to concede that that indeed is the end of man and that there is no need to pursue the matter further. It is a short and simple answer but one that apparently has not satisfied the many in search of the truth.

What, then, is the truth? Put that way, the question assumes a hundred forms. What is man? How did he come to be? What is the purpose of his existence? Who created him? Why? If somebody created him, who is his Creator? What should be the proper relationship between him and his Creator? Is death, as we know it, truly the end of man? If not, is there "life" after death? If there is, what sort of "life" is it? Besides, how does one define "life"? Is "life" the same thing as what we commonly refer to as "soul"?

What is the relationship between man, his soul and his Creator?

Animals do not ask these questions; man, the thinking animal, does. An animal is born, it lives, it dies. Man is not satisfied with living without knowing. He is ever in quest for knowledge. He wants to know who he is and where he goes, if he goes, after he dies. If death is not the end, what is? Man's mind, like Shelley's "dome of many-colored glass" stains the white radiance of eternity with questions. In fact, to be human, to be alive, is to ask questions.

We may have begun with the simplest of all questions: "Is death the end of man?" but that, as we shall quickly see, is like opening a different kind of Pandora's Box for other and more complex questions to fly out. And it is these questions that philosophers down the ages have addressed themselves to.

We know some of these philosophers. Others we don't. Some of their cumulative wisdom has come to us in the shape of the Upanishads, the Socratic dialogues, the sayings of the Buddha and of Mahavira and other writings. These, subsequently, have been embellished, commented upon and enlarged by men who followed them. We have, too, the received wisdom of Christ and Zoroaster, Muhammad and Maimonides, Sankara, Madhwa and Ramanuja. Some of it is claimed as revelation. No matter. What is important, surely, is not *how* the wisdom has been revealed, but *what* it is. If the questions are many, so too, are the answers. What shall be our response to a world where the only certainty is uncertainty? Shall we stick to one set of answers and reject the rest as untrue at best and unworthy at worst? Shall we reject *all* answers and like Fitzgerald's Omar Khayyam "leave the wise to talk" on the grounds that the only thing certain is that life flies?

The uncertainty, we may well admit, can be horrendous. Some believe that there is nothing more beyond death. Others argue that death is not the end but the beginning. Some believe that there is no such being as God; others would argue, just as passionately that not only does He exist, but that the goal of life is to finally attain Him.

The purpose of this brief study is to examine all these

propositions. One thing stands clear: we cannot discuss death in isolation, as if it has no connection with a whole set of values, and value systems. Death is irretrievably linked with such issues as the nature of God, the nature of the soul, the relationship between God, man and soul, what happens to the soul after the body perishes, does it return to God, does it have a habitation elsewhere, if it has, where is it and what is the duration of its stay there?

Just as there cannot be a door without rooms and walls, similarly, death is inconceivable as an event that stands apart without supporting cast. If we must discuss death, we must *pari passu* discuss associated ideas, for then alone will death have any meaning. We may, at the end of all our study, still not get a satisfactory answer. Indeed, of death it can be said, as has been said of Brahma: *Naham manye suvediti no na vedeti vedacha*, I think not that I know him well, or that I know him, or even that I know him not. No matter how deeply one dwells on the subject, death may to the end still remain a mystery. But that is not to say that we should not try to pierce the veil. True, as Omar Khayyam said, "there was a door to which I found no key, there was a veil past which I could not see," but the joy is in the search for answers, not in the answers themselves. The door may ever remain locked, the veil may ever stay inpenetrable, but not to search for the key or seek to penetrate the veil is to deny ourselves our human heritage.

And yet it is a fact that too often, and for a variety of reasons, from mental sloth to fear of the unknown, man declines to search for the key. It is as if he presumes that he will never die, that the end will never come, that he will last forever. An episode in the *Mahabharata*, the great Hindu epic brings this out in stark relief.

The story is of the five Pandava brothers,[1] who, driven to exile in a forest and losing their way, get very thirsty. Yudhishtira, the eldest and noblest thereupon bids his youngest brother, Nakula, to go look for water and fetch some for the rest. After some search, Nakula finds a lake, but even as he is about to drink from it, he hears a voice from nowhere, imperious, demanding: "Young man, stop. Answer first my questions before you take a sip." But Nakula is in no mood to stop, let alone answer questions from any disembodied voice. He drinks and promptly falls down dead. Minutes pass and Yudhishtira sends the next oldest, the twin Sahadeva to find out what has happened to Nakula and also to bring back some water. The story is repeated.

As he is about to stoop to take a drink from the placid waters, he hears the same, persistent voice and the same question: "Young man, stop. Answer first my questions before you take a sip." But so great is Sahadeva's thirst that he fails to respond. He takes a sip and drops down dead.

Now Yudhishtira is plainly in a quandary. With no word either from Nakula or Sahadeva, Yudhishtira first sends Arjuna, third of his brothers, in search of the last two and when he, in turn, fails to return, sends his second brother, Bhima, with the same instructions. When Bhima fails to return, Yudhishtira himself sets out in search of his lost brothers and it is not long before he finds them all by the lakeside, dead. His heart is full of grief and great is his lament.

Now he hears that voice again, but this time the demand is couched after an explanatory statement. "Do not, I ask you, act rashly. I am a Yaksha, living, as a crane, on tiny fish. It is by me that your younger brothers have been brought under the sway of the Lord of the Departed Spirits. If thou, O Prince, answer not the questions put by me, even thou shall die. But if you answer well my questions not only yours is life, but that of your brothers as well."

Yudhishtira wisely consents to answer the questions satisfactorily to the Yaksha. Then comes the last—and crucial—question: What is the most wonderful fact in the world? Yudhishtira has the answer ready. "O Yaksha," he says, "we see our fellow beings dying around us every moment and yet the living think they never will die. That, surely, is the most wonderful fact of all!" Yudhishtira had hit the bull's eye. Pleased is the Yaksha who declares himself to be none other than Dharma, the God of Justice and promptly restores the four Pandava brothers to life.

There is a moral here. Like the four younger Pandava brothers, most of us are too avid to slake our thirst at the well of life to answer questions. The result is spiritual death.

SAVITRI AND SATYAVAN: The Power of Love

In our quest for the meaning and riddle of death, we may take a few detours in order better to appreciate the philosophic landscape. Such a detour is the story of Savitri[2] who asked of Yama, the Lord of Death—we shall come across him in another context—the gift of life.

Savitri has come down to us as the princess who brought her husband from death back to life through the power of her unshakeable love. Savitri was the daughter of King Ashvapati and was famed for her goodness and beauty. When she came of age, her father, as was the custom in those days, asked her to choose for herself a husband. Ashvapati provided her with a retinue of courtiers and guards and set her off on a journey to different courts.

So Savitri traveled from court to court, mounted in a golden chariot and met all the eligible princes; but none won her heart. None, that is, until she and her party came across a holy hermitage, in one of those forests in ancient India where no animal was permitted to be killed. Here Savitri met the deposed King Dyumatsena, stricken with old age, blind and served only by his loving queen and her ever-loyal son, Satyavan.

For Savitri, it was love at first sight. It was as if this was the prince she had waited for and her longing for him was great. Quickly she returned to her parents to seek their permission to marry Satyavan. Marry Satyavan, a pauper, a prince without any patrimony? Ashvapati was understandably aghast. What had Satyavan to offer her but roots and herbs, fruits and water and a life of ceaseless toil in the service of an old and dying king? In his despair Ashvapati turned to the wise men in his court. Their advice was firm and to the point. They advised against the marriage. For one thing, they said, the stars predicted that Satyavan had only a year more to live. To marry him was for Savitri to invite widowhood. And to what purpose? But Savitri was not to be deterred. She had made up her mind. A maiden, she told her father, chooses only once and she had chosen. Reluctantly, Ashvapati had to give his consent to his daughter's marriage to her beloved, knowing only too well that disaster was round the corner.

So the marriage was celebrated and Savitri went off to the forest to live with her husband and to assist him in his daily chores. Her happiness knew no end. Days passed and weeks and Savitri heroically kept the thought from out of her mind that the day of days was coming closer.

Finally the appointed day arrived. Satyavan, as usual, set out on his daily round of gathering roots and herbs but now Savitri insisted on accompanying him. This was no day to leave him alone. As the noonday sun crept up in the heavens, Satyavan began to complain to tiredness and a desire to sleep. Savitri knew in her heart that the moment had come for Satyavan to die.

Sitting under the shade of a tree, holding her husband's head on her lap, Savitri waited for the coming of the messenger of death to take Satyavan's soul away. But they had reckoned without Savitri's prayers which now surrounded Satyavan in a zone of fire. Satyavan had become unapproachable. It was left for Yama himself finally to come to earth to lead Satyavan to his new abode.

But Yama had not counted with Savitri's devotion either. As he gently led Satyavan away Savitri followed them through briar and bush, across rivers and mountains until Yama had to take cognizance of her presence. "Daughter," he told her, "desist from following me. Your husband's fate is merely the fate of all mortals." But Savitri was not about to accept that explanation; she had a higher vocation. A wife went where her husband took her; the eternal law did not separate loving man and faithful wife. If Yama insisted on taking Satyavan he might as well let Savitri accompany him, too, on the journey. There could be no separation of the two. In vain Yama remonstrated. In vain he promised Savitri any boon she might ask. Did she ask for the restoration of her father-in-law's eyesight? It was granted. His happiness? That, too, was granted. But as for herself, Savitri had nothing to ask but the right to follow her beloved. Where the soul of Satyavan was, there was her soul also.

Yama was willing to grant more boons. He would restore to King Dyumatsena his wealth, his kingdom. Only he could not let a living mortal walk with him. Besides, Yama asked, in one last but futile effort to dissuade Savitri, what if Satyavan had been a sinner and was to go to hell? No matter, replied Savitri, she would go there too. Where her husband was, there was her rightful place. In desperation Yama promised yet another boon to Savitri, short of her husband's life. "Well then," she replied, "since you so permit me, grant that my father-in-law's line not be terminated; let his kingdom descend to Satyavan's sons."

Yama had given his word; it had to be fulfilled. He would release Satyavan's soul. Even he, he declared, was helpless against the power of true love. Where there is true love there is eternal life. The word "savitri," incidentally, is derived from the word "savitur" which is the name of a sacred prayer of the Hindus.

THE STORY OF NACHIKETA: The Quest for Meaning

One of the earliest attempts to inquire into the meaning of life and death—what is it all about?—is to be found in the Upanishads.[3] Of the twelve Upanishads, the *Katha Upanishad* is the most philosophical, the one most concerned with the nature of the eternal Self. It is a metaphysical work concerned with the immortality of the soul and the means of achieving that immortality.

The story of Nachiketa is in the form of a dialog between a young boy whose strength lies in his faith and Yama, the King of Death, but it could well be a dialog between the inquiring mind and the highest form of intelligence, the doubter and the knower. Nachiketa was the son of Vajasravasa, who, desirous of heavenly rewards attempted to surrender at a sacrifice all that he possessed. But the surrender was only partial. Vajasravasa would not part with the best of his cattle; he would give away only those cows that were old or dry, blind or diseased. This hurt Nachiketa who went over to his father and said, "Father, to whom will you give me?" Vajasravasa did not reply. Nachiketa asked again and still getting no reply, asked for the third time. Angered, his father replied, "I shall give you to Death!"

The words were uttered in anger, but a promise made called for fulfillment. Nachiketa's heart was pure and the thought of entering the abode of death did not frighten him. On the contrary he was only too eager to go so he could learn at first hand the mystery of death. But his time had not yet come and when he entered the abode of Yama Vaivasvata (the Ruler of the Departed) there was no one to receive him. When Yama returned from his appointed rounds after an absence of three nights, during which time Nachiketa had received no hospitality as befitting a Brahmin, the Ruler of the Departed was most upset. The first rule of hospitality had been unwittingly broken. A guest had remained uncared for. There had to be recompense and Yama promised Nachiketa three boons, one for each night that he had been left alone to fend for himself.

The first boon was easily granted. Nachiketa asked that his father's anger pass away from him so that when he returned to earth he would be received with loving kindness. It showed a dutiful son's concern for his father's well-being and happiness and Yama, quite pleased, granted the boon.

Now Nachiketa wanted to know the nature of the sacrifice that leads a mortal to heaven. Yama obliged and taught him of the flame "that is the world's beginning" and of how the sacrificial fire was built and ever a bright student, Nachiketa repeated the instructions he had received so diligently that Yama, mightily pleased granted yet one more supplemental boon to the boy. He also honored Nachiketa by naming the fire-sacrifice after him and promising that whoever lighted the three fires—Nachiketagni—and came to union with the three, they would be beyond birth and death, and leaving sorrow behind, rejoice in heaven.

Now came the time for Nachiketa to ask his third boon. "There is that doubt," he said, "when a man is dead; some say he is, others, he is not. This I should like to know, taught by thee.

This is the third boon of the boons of my choosing." Yama, the Ruler of the Dead was in a quandary. He alone had the key to the knowledge of the mystery of death. That mystery had been debated even by the gods of old. But it was not to be imparted to anyone, not even to Nachiketa who had been promised a boon in good faith. Yama hemmed and hawed. Couldn't Nachiketa ask for another boon? He could have all the good things he could ever want: sons and grandsons who would live a hundred years, cattle, elephants, gold and horses, a mighty reach of earth, delectable women with their chariots and bugles, in fact, anything a mortal could desire. Anything, except the key to the mystery of death. That was not easy of knowledge.

But Nachikata was not so easily dissuaded. Surely, Yama could not be serious? The things he had promised, Nachiketa reminded the Ruler of the Dead, lasted only until tomorrow. No man could be made happy by wealth. As for long life, he said, "what mortal, slowly decaying here below, and knowing, after having approached them, the freedom from decay enjoyed by the immortals, would delight in a long life after he has pondered on the pleasures which arise from beauty and love?" And he added, "this thing whereon they doubt, O Death, what there is in the great passing-on, tell us that! This boon which enters into the secret that is hidden from us, no other boon than that does Nachiketa choose."

Yama was impressed by Nachiketa's persistence, his purity of heart and his refusal to accept nothing less than the "better knowledge." Complimenting him for not entering "into the net of riches in which many men sink to perdition" Yama proceeded to impart to Nachiketa the Truth. He had found the perfect seeker; he would impart the perfect answer.

The Wise One is Not Born, Neither Does He Die

"The Wise One," said Yama, "Is neither born, nor does he die. He is unborn, constant, eternal, primeval."[4] Yama was describing the nature of the immortal Self. How could this immortal self die or be slain when the Self had neither birth nor death? Such was its nature that it was more minute than the minute, greater than the great. It was all pervasive. It was *atman*.

Yama might have been referring to the atom which is all pervasive, which is part of all matter organic or inorganic, which is in Yama's own words, "soundless, touchless, formless, imperishable, likewise tasteless, constant and odorless." It had no beginning and could not possibly have any end. To know this was to know the truth about immortality. But to know this was no easy task. The path, Yama told Nachiketa was "sharp as a razor's edge and hard to traverse." The senses, which were like wild horses, had to be controlled, the mind steadied and knowledge sought. He who used the mind as reins, knowledge as driver of the chariot which was the body could ultimately reach the end of the road which was knowledge of the Absolute. It required effort. Yama gave Nachiketa an idea of what the Absolute could be. Man understood senses. Now higher than the senses are the objects of sense. Higher than these was the mind. But higher than the mind was the intellect and higher than the intellect was the greater Self. Higher than this was the Unmanifest and higher than the Unmanifest was the *Purusha*—the person. There was nothing higher than the Person. The journey to understand ended there. That "Person" was the secret Self in all existence and yet He could not be seen. But He pervaded the universe. He corresponded in form to every form. He was unsullied, beyond stain, manifested Himself in many forms. Again and again Yama says, "This is That thou seekest."

The ignorant, of course, could hardly understand this. Like children they pursued the objects of desire and pleasure. But the wise realized that Death is not the end, that the aim of life was to understand the Self—call it Brahman if you like—and thus seek true liberation. It was only when man was liberated from the senses that bound him that he became immortal. What was this Brahman and how is one to attain Him? We have here two tasks awaiting us: one to understand what Brahman is and then to find a way of knowing him.

Brahman has been defined as pure intelligence, what is behind the Unmanifest, the Inner Self, the universal principle of nature, the *antaratman* (the innermost Self). The *Chandogya Upanishad,* one of the oldest and best known of the Upanishads seeks to present the idea of what Brahman is, in the form of a simple dialogue.[5] The dialogue is between Uddalaka Aruni and his son Svetaketu. Uddalaka Muni is trying to explain to his son that which is not to be seen but which is the essence of all and pervades the universe.

"Bring hither a fig from there."
"Here it is, sir."
"Divide it."
"It is divided, sir."
"What do you see there?"
"These rather fine seeds, sir."
"Of these, please divide one."
"It is divided, sir."
"What do you see there?"
"Nothing at all, sir."

Then said Uddalaka Muni to his son Svetaketu, "Verily, O Svetaketu, that finest essence which you do not perceive, verily from the finest essence, this great Nyagrodha (sacred fig) tree thus arises. Believe me, that which is the finest essence—this whole world has that as its self. That is reality. That is *atman*. That art thou *(tat tvam asi)* Svetaketu. . . "

It does not require much stretching of our imagination in this day and age for us to believe the power of the atom or to accept the fact that whatever exists is made up of atoms—and in the final analysis, electrons, protons and neutrons, in a word, energy. What does require imagination is to accept the fact that organic and inorganic matter, human and animal life all are one in essence and that essence is, once again, Brahman.

The *Svetasvatara Upanishad,* one of the later Upanishads in point of time, takes us further into an understanding of Brahman. What is perishable—the body, for example—is primary matter, says the Upanishad. What is immortal and imperishable is Hara (the

Self) and over both the perishable and the Self, the one God rules.

If this was understood and taken wholly to heart, there could then be no scope for distress. To know that the Eternal (the *atman*, Brahman) was present in the Self, to acknowledge that there was nothing higher than that to be known, was to know all. Running through all the Upanishads like a golden thread is the single theme that man is not to be distinguished from all other things, animate or inanimate, that within man is the great principle of the universality of the Self, that in the understanding of the Self lies the understanding of what life is all about. The Upanishads go a step further. They teach us how to achieve the ultimate goal, Brahman; knowing what Brahman is, is one thing. It has been beautifully explained in, among other works, the *Mundaka Upanishad*, the most poetical of all the Upanishads. But how is one to achieve Brahman? The *Mundaka Upanishad* suggests meditation.[6]

> Not by sight is It (Brahman) grasped, not even by speech,
> Not by any other sense organs, austerity or work.
> By the peace of knowledge, one's nature purified
> In that way, however, by meditating, one does behold Him,
> Who is without parts.

So then, we have one answer: meditation. But meditation on what? The *antaratman*, the innermost Self, of course. And how does one go about it? The seer in the *Mundaka Upanishad* says, one must do away with desire. Desire holds back the mind and imprisons it. He who cherishes desire is by his desires born again. Only he who is freed from desire can concentrate and through concentration ultimately achieve Brahman. The early Indian philosophers have prescribed a way to meditate, to liberate the mind from all disturbing thoughts, emotions and desires, to attain what they called *dhyanam nirvishayam manah*. It consists of eight steps,[7] each leading to the next.

The first step is called *yama*. It consists of non-injury, truthfulness, non-covetousness and chastity and non-acceptance of gifts from others. To be truthful in thought, word and deed obviously is the first step in self-purification. How can a covetous mind ever possibly concentrate? How can a person in conflict with the world be at peace with himself? The act of meditation is in principle an act of surrender. In order to meditate, the person perforce has to learn and practice the simple virtues. *Yama* leads to the purification of the mind and gives it its independence.

The second step is called *niyama*. *Niyama* calls for austerity *(tapas)*, study *(svadhyaya)*, contentment *(santosha)*, purity *(saucham)* and the worship of God. Austerity does not necessarily mean the punishing of the flesh; one does not have to wear a hair shirt to practice meditation. Indeed it may even be a distraction! Though the study referred to is of the Vedas, one might as well include all great literature that is ennobling and purifying; the aim, again, is to condition the mind to receive good thoughts. Purity is of two kinds: mental purity, that acquired by adherance to truth and non-injury and physical purity, by cleansing the body of external dirt. Anger, jealousy, hatred—in fact any emotional disturbance can be as much a distraction as physical dirt. A cleansing bath, external and internal, is a pre-requisite for continued meditation.

The third step is *asana* or right posture. Obviously a person curled up in bed or sitting in a chair with his legs dangling is in no fit position to meditate. Even as the mind is in need of concentration, so too, the body must be so positioned as to give it unity. Then alone can it function at its most efficient, permitting smooth and easy breathing. The spine has to be erect, the head held straight, every muscle now in its place, to facilitate the fourth step, *pranayama*, or right breathing. *Prana* means the vital life force, *ayama* means control and *pranayama* merely means the control of breathing. Breathing consists of inhaling, retention and exhaling and the meditator or *sadhaka* can carry on the process in twelve seconds or a multiple of it, depending on how much mastery he has attained in the control of that simple exercise. It is during *pranayama* that the meditator must seek to control his will, to turn inwards, to concentrate his awareness on the here and now. This is the fifth step, *pratyahara*, when the aspirant seeks to withdraw from the world, from all sense experiences and perceptions, ever telling himself: "I am the *atman*, the infinite." The further apart the mind wanders, the more the aspirant seeks to bring it gently back to the center. Right breathing greatly helps in the process.

The sixth step is among the hardest. It is *dharana* or the fixing the mind at one spot, the penultimate in concentration. Here the body is at peace; breathing is controlled. The wandering mind has been tethered. The aspirant is ready for the seventh step, *dhyana*, or true meditation. Here there is no wandering of thought, no distraction of any kind. The mind is concentrated on unity, on the space within the heart and all is quiet. The aspirant is in tune with the universal principle, and ready for the last step, *samadhi*. This is attained when the whole mind has become one wave and is bereft of all association with places and centers. At this point the mind goes beyond the plane of self-consciousness to super-consciousness. *Dhyana* has been taken to its logical conclusion: the exclusion of external perceptions and the concentration on the internal part, the meaning.

Those who practice Raja Yoga—the eight steps—are rightly cautioned against involuntarily stumbling upon this state, since there is the danger of the brain itself getting damaged. The attainment of *samadhi* is not lightly to be undertaken. It calls for training and guidance under a master. Indeed in the practice of meditation, it helps to have a *guru*, a teacher, to give right guidance at all times. Meditation is more than prayer or a private devotional act. It is a specific means to a specific end. It is not undertaken lightly. In his famous lecture on Raja Yoga, Swami Vivekananda gave a lesson on how to meditate.[8] He said:

> Imagine a lotus upon the top of the head, several inches up, with virtue as its center and knowledge as its stalk. The eight petals of the lotus are the eight powers of the yogi. Inside, the stamen and pistils are renunciation. If the yogi refuses the external powers, he will come to salvation. Inside the lotus, think of the Golden One, the Almighty, the intangible, whose name is Om, the inexpressible, surrounded with effulgent light. Meditate on that.

Similarly, another way is shown:

> Think of the space within your heart and think that in the

midst of that space, a flame is burning. Think of that flame as your own soul. Inside the flame is another effulgent light and that is the soul of your soul, God. Meditate upon that in the heart.

It is important not to get too enmeshed in the technicalities of meditation and forget that the aim, first of all, is to understand the self and what we are. It is necessary not to mistake the wood for the trees lest we presume that meditation is all. Meditation, it may be remembered, is only a means to a greater end. That end is self-knowledge. We may learn the ways of yoga and yet not be yogis. To confuse the one with the other is to confuse means for ends.

Samadhi, incidentally, can be better appreciated in terms of another state, *turiya*, discussed in the *Mandukya Upanishad*, named after Mandukya, the sage-teacher who has given to Indian thought the famous theory of the four states of consciousness. These are: waking, dreaming, profound sleep and the fourth state—*turiya*—which alone is claimed to be real.[9]

This fourth state, *turiya*, is in fact what the ultimate in yoga is all about. It is that state in which the self is in total communion with the greater Self and therefore with God. The *Mandukya Upanishad* defines the four states as follows: First, the waking state, outwardly cognitive. This is what we are aware of most of the time when we are awake. Second is the state of dreaming when the individual is not aware of the external world but is only inwardly cognitive. Third is the state of deep sleep when there is neither external or internal cognition and the mind is at complete rest, which is bliss. The fourth, says the *Mandukya Upanishad*, is the "lord of all," the "all-knowing, the inner controller, the source of all, for this is the origin and end of all beings." It is during this state, *turiya*, that the mind is attuned to the Supreme, the one without a second.

THE BHAGAVAD GITA: The Interpretation of Death

Whether one interprets the *Bhagavad Gita* (Song of the Lord) as a religious classic or as a philosophic treatise, it is clearly a masterpiece of spiritual literature. In essence it is a dialog between Krishna, the teacher and Arjuna, the warrior-disciple. The scene is set on a battlefield, in a war between the Kauravas and the Pandavas, cousins by birth. Arjuna, third of the five Pandava brothers is aghast at the thought of fighting his own kin. His charioteer is Krishna, God incarnate, on whom falls the task of instructing Arjuna in the verities of life. We can imagine Arjuna's grief. He is confronted with a host of his own near and dear relatives arrayed against him; fight he must and in the course of the battle kill many. At stake is a kingdom but of what avail is a kingdom if it has to be won after needless carnage?

This is the central question. To fight or not to fight, that is Arjuna's dilemma. Not to fight would be against the warrior's *dharma*, his code of conduct. To fight would mean killing one's own kith. Their blood would be on his hands. And yet the war is a just one; the kingdom really belonged to the Pandavas and had been wrongfully wrested from them. But was that sufficient cause to go to battle? In other circumstances Arjuna would have delighted in warfare; indeed, he had fought other wars and come out victorious. He had no doubts that in this one, too, he would emerge victor. He was not opposed to fighting, then. What he was opposed to was the killing of those he held dear, for a cause not sufficiently redeeming. This is the dilemma that Krishna is called upon to resolve. On the battlefield he discourses on the meaning of death and existence.

Krishna had to convince Arjuna that he had no alternative but to fight, that indeed fighting was his *dharma*, that the universe moved according to the laws of *dharma*, that as long as Arjuna fought for a right cause he was freed of attachment, that as long as he was freed of attachment he was doing well and that death, in any event, was not for him to ordain as it had already been ordained for mortals. Krishna went a step further. Death was not something to be grieved over, but to be accepted as the natural course of events. In the first place death was as inevitable as birth and as constant as the pole star. There was no escape from it. It was unavoidable. In the second place, there was no such thing, really, as death. Just as a person casts off worn-out garments to put on others, so did the embodied soul cast off worn-out bodies to take on new ones.

There was something eternal in man that was not destructable, that fire did not burn, water did not wet. In that sense he who thought this slays or that this was slain failed to perceive the truth. The truth was that this one neither slayed nor was he slain. What was perceived by the naked eye was not necessarily true. The argument of the Gita is four-fold: on the physical plane, the death of the body is certain and irrelevant and hence there should be no grief over what is inevitable, even necessary. Secondly, there is no such thing as the death and destruction of the eternal Self or the universal Self, wherefore, grief is obviously foolish. Thirdly, the Self, or the true principle, does not die but merely goes on to take a new body and start the process all over again, whence it is pointless to worry about the discarding of the present body. Lastly, he who realizes that he is part of the universal Self, the eternal principle, the Brahman, has no cause for grief, for Brahman does not die.

Krishna goes to great length to explain the nature of the eternal principle and the importance of appreciating it as the means for release from ignorance. It is only when Arjuna continues to have doubts that Krishna reveals himself in his *viratarupa*, the form infinite, to convince him of the source of wisdom. The Gita is not merely a call to action; it defines and sustains action. Action had to be detached from desire if it was to be relevant. We will come to this later when we discuss *karma*. In this context it suffices to say that only when man is freed from attachment in the course of undertaking action will he be free from the eternal cycle of birth and death.

The Gita is in truth an elaboration and amplification of the *Kathopanishad* with its stress on the universal Self and its indestructability. As a guide to human behavior it has few rivals. Its relevance is the strength it gives to man in facing up to the inevitable, in explaining that death is not something to be shunned but an event to be understood and in suggesting that there is an escape from the eternal wheel of life and death through right action. It is the definition of right action that is the core and pith of the Gita.

THEORY OF REBIRTH: The Endless Chain of Life and Death

The Gita speaks of the endless series of births and deaths. It is not a new theory. In the *Satapatha Brahmana*, one of the earliest Hindu writings, we have the notion of being born again and again after death in an endless cycle coupled with the doctrine of retribution. The theory is that those who have right knowledge and perform their duties are born again after death for immortality, a state of being man aspires to achieve, while those who do not have such knowledge and neglect their duties are reborn, only to die.

In the Upanishads, however, we have a new concept. Good and evil actions experience a two-fold retribution, once in the "other" world and again in a renewed life on earth. It is said that the soul, after it has journeyed to heaven in a radiant form on the burning of the corpse, returns thence immediately through the three regions to a new existence. The fully realized soul attains *moksha*, liberation, an idea we shall examine later. But the partially realized soul is subject to birth and death and has to work out its destiny until it is fully eligible to *moksha*. In that sense *moksha*, true immortality is for the fully liberated, survival in time is for the bound.

Some questions inevitably arise in regard to the theory of rebirth. The theory itself may sound logical but does not fully explain the multiplication of human lives. If there were X number of souls when human life came into existence, we will have to presume that every time a child is born, God creates a new soul. So it is not necessarily so that a new child is only a soul from one previous life taking on another birth. Mathematically speaking it has never been proved that there is a balance between the number of those who died and those who were born. Indeed more babies are born every year than the number dead. Theology has therefore to invent the notion that God creates new souls continuously, though why he should do so, unless the whole thing is an illusion in the first place, is not sufficiently explained.

Rebirth is considered a discipline by which the soul perfects itself. The soul is given a chance, an opportunity, to march onward to its goal of perfection through birth after birth. Why God, if there is a God, in His infinite grace does not spare the soul its endless births and deaths and gives it peace is not, again, explained in any meaningful way. Why, having created a soul, should God turn it over to a treadmill-like future? Why should God create man and then endow him with senses and tell him not in the gratification of the senses, but in his disciplining them, lies salvation? This is either a cosmic joke or godly cruelty. Neither makes sense, unless it is not for man to question what God decides.

There was a reference, earlier, to *moksha*. What is *moksha*? Is it mere vanishing into nothingness? Is that what happens when man dies? The question was put to Yajnavalkhya by Arthabhaga,[10] in the *Brihadaranyaka Upanishad*. "Does the soul survive bodily death? Yajnavalkhya, if after the death of the man his spirit goes into fire, his breath into wind, his eyes into the sun, his mind into the moon, his ear into the direction of space, his body to earth, his self into the ether, the hair of his body into plants, the hair of his head into trees, the blood and semen into water—what then becomes of the man?"

Almost all Indian thinkers are agreed that *moksha* is release from birth and death. There is a disintegration of individuality, a giving up, as Dr. Radhakrishnan has described it,[11] of selfish isolation, but *moksha* is not a mere nothing, or death. The *Mundaka Upanishad* put it this way: "As the flowing rivers disappear in the sea, losing their name and form, thus a wise man, freed from name and form, goes to the divine person who is beyond all."

Thus, the goal of man is not annihilation of the self, but rather fulfillment, the final merging with the Brahman. Fulfillment consists of the attainment of *moksha*, described as "a state of rapture and ecstasy, a condition of *ananda* (ineffable joy) where the creature as creature is abolished but becomes one with the creator or, more accurately, realizes his oneness with him."

That is how the philosopher Dr. Radhakrishnan describes it, but there cannot possibly be any way of describing what is indescribable. What Dr. Radhakrishnan argues is that there is hope after physical death. "After all our troubles in the sea of life," he says optimistically, "we do not reach a desert shore where we are obliged to die of hunger. The liberated condition must be looked upon as the fullest expression of the self."[12]

The trouble is that the soul's immortality cannot be experienced in advance of death. For immortality, death is a precondition, contradictory though it may sound. Only after death does the soul join and become one with the immortal Brahman, provided, of course, that the soul is truly fulfilled. Yajnavalkhya explains this in a most ingenious way. Even as a lump of salt when thrown into water dissolves and cannot be gathered up again but wherever water is drawn it is salty, he explains, even so, it is when man dies and goes back to the "endless, the unlimited." There is no consciousness after death. When Maitreyi, his wife and disciple observes that she is perplexed with this explanation, Yajnavalkhya replies that there is no need to be perplexed for the explanation was quite comprehensible. Where there was a duality of existences (the one and the other), one could see the other, smell the other, hear the other, think of the other, apprehend the other. "But where everything has turned into *atman*, by whom shall he see, by whom and whom shall he smell, by whom and to whom shall he speak . . . through whom shall he apprehend him the apprehender?"[13]

But is fulfillment, a union of the soul with the Brahman, where all activity ceases? One theory is that propounded in the *Chandogya Upanishad*, that immortality is lifting oneself up to the region of the deity. That indicates not unity, but togetherness and apartness. The *Mundaka Upanishad* suggests companionship with God. Absolute likeness with God is also suggested. Dr. Radhakrishnan says, "Whatever differences there might be about the exact nature of the highest condition, one thing is clear, that it is a state of activity, full of freedom and perfection." But freedom to do what? What does it imply? To be reborn, knowing full well that life on earth, or for that matter, elsewhere, can only be imperfect? Why should perfection seek imperfection? We have no answer.

Now fulfillment comes through liberation; liberation through detachment and detachment is prescribed to free us from the aftereffects of action. For action without detachment has its inevitable effects. This is the law of *karma*. According to the principle of *karma*, there is nothing uncertain or capricious in the moral world. We reap what we sow. Action and reaction are equal and opposite which is the same as the second law of dynamics. In that sense, every little action—any action—has its effect. When does that effect, reaction, as it were, cease to operate? With death? If there is a life after death as is vouched for by the Gita as well as by the *Kathopanishad*, is there a carryover of the reaction? Or is death the end of all calculations?

If death means total annihilation as the doctrine of Lokayata maintains and which has been affirmed in our own times by so distinguished a scientist as Nobel Laureate Jacques Monod, then the law of *karma* must operate during one's brief life span. There cannot be any carryover for the simple reason that there is no future life. But if there is future life, if the soul is indeed reborn, if the chain of life-death-life continues without end, then it is possible to assert that whatever we do in our present life will have its natural and inevitable repercussion in a later life and that the only way in which to stay the reaction is to reduce the chances of reaction to zero. But is that possible?

The *Bhagavad Gita* says it is possible. One must act in such a manner that we do not desire the fruits of our action, says Krishna. The Gita does not say man should not act out of fear that it will produce reaction. Man must of necessity act, but action must be devoid of desire. Between actor and action there should be no attachment. As Krishna says, "To action alone hast thou a right and never at all to its fruit. Let not the fruits of action be thy motive, neither let there be in thee any attachment to inaction." Again, "Not by abstention from work does a man attain freedom from action; nor by renunciation does he attain to his perfection." The implication is that action and reaction are separated by desire or attachment to the fruits of action. It is the desire for the fruit of action that causes reaction. If no desire is attached to action, then it stands by itself. It can be expressed in two formulae:

Man + Action + Desire = Man + Reaction

Man + Action - Desire = Man + Action

There is no way in which man can live without performing action. Action is essential for sustenance of life itself. There is no such thing as renunciation, since renunciation is an act by itself. The prescribed process to gain freedom, liberation, *moksha*, oneness with Brahman or God—however it is defined— is to so act that it does not carry with it the concommitant of reaction.

THE DOCTRINE OF LOKAYATA: There Is No Life But This

We shall discuss *karma* in a different context when we discuss Buddhist concepts but we may pause here to note what Jacques Monod said and what Charvaka, who antedated Monod by at least 2,500 years said about prospects of future life. Monod who believed with Democritus that "everything existing in the universe is the fruit of chance and necessity" (we hear that refrain in the *Svetasvatara Upanishad:* What is the cause: Brahman? Whence are we born? And on what are we established? Time, or inherent nature, or necessity, or chance?") would have agreed with Charvaka that there is but one life and it is the one we live and that once it ends, nothing remains.

The Charvaka doctrine is also known as the doctrine of Lokayata, as it holds that only this world *(loka)* exists and there is no beyond, nor any future life. Perception is the only source of knowledge. What is not perceived plainly does not exist. Since perception is the only form of valid knowledge what is perceived, namely, matter, becomes the only reality.

It is possible to dismiss the Lokayata philosophy as being too materialistic, which it indeed is. Thus it holds that the soul is only the body qualified by intelligence and that when the original principles—earth, water, fire, air—are transformed into the body, intelligence is produced. Soul, then, is body with intelligence. When the body perishes, intelligence automatically perishes as it cannot survive by itself. To speculate about God, then, is beside the point. All postulates of religion, such as God, freedom, immortality, *moksha*, *karma*, are illusions. There is something cynical about this approach, however intellectually enticing it is. Lokayata bravely holds that nature is indifferent to good and evil and that, in any event, history does not bear witness to divine providence. Lokayata admits of no God, dismisses the concepts of heaven and hell as downright silly and has no use for sacrificial ritual. The only facts of life are what are observable: pleasure and pain.

The Lokayata philosophy is discussed in three works, [14] the *Sarvadarshanasangraha* (14th century, A.D.), the *Sarvasiddhantasarasangraha* and the *Tattvopaplavasimha* (7th century A.D.) and the ancient Sanskrit drama *Prabhoda Chandrodaya* (The Rise of the Moon of Intellect).

The *Sarvadarshanasangraha* has some biting things to say about faith in God or in afterlife or sacrificial rituals. It emphatically asserts that there is no heaven, no final liberation or souls in another world and it mocks at the very concept of sacrificing a beast so it can go to heaven. If that is so, mocks the work, why then does not the sacrificer forthwith offer his own father?

The *Sarvasiddhantasangraha* is just as nihilistic in many ways and its bitterness can be overwhelming. It equates heaven with eating delicious food, keeping company of young women, using fine clothes, perfumes and garlands and hell with the troubles that arise from enemies, weapons and diseases. And it dismisses other concepts such as the realm of Siva as the inventions of "stupid imposters." Jacques Monod is less caustic though not less assertive. His theory, as propounded in his book, *Chance and Necessity* is that mankind owes its existence to nothing but a roll of some cosmological set of dice and at least has the virtue of making some sense out of our dilemma. "When one wonders," writes Monod, "on the tremendous journey of evolution over the past three billion years or so, the prodigious wealth of structures it has engendered, and the extraordinarily effective teleonomic performances of living beings, from bacteria to man, one may well find oneself beginning to doubt again whether all this could conceivably be the product of an enormous lottery presided over by natural selection, blindly picking the rare winners from among numbers drawn at random."[15]

But, on the weight of evidence before us, there is no reason to doubt. A detailed review of the accumulated modern evidence permits us the conclusion that the miracle of life is compatible with the known facts about the molecular mechanisms of replication, mutation and translation. A thinking man evolving from out of the pre-biotic "soup" by the structuration of complex particles is an idea that is not so hard to accept, though it may run counter to our concepts of a supreme being who endows each new human being with a soul.

Monod, it is only fair to say, does not concern himself with explaining how matter originally came into being or the nature of the First Cause. He provides an answer to how life would have evolved from the basic materials available on earth (water, ammonia, methane), also how, over the billions of years that it took to "perfect" man, the system of evolution and natural selection worked and one almost gets the feeling that given the complex, rich cybernetic network in living beings, the evolution of man was solely a matter of chance and necessity.

There is scientific evidence that a living cell can be produced from off-the-shelf inorganic chemicals. It is then not hard to follow Monod's thesis that life originally sprang from the basic materials available at the beginning of history on earth, that the first living beings were microscopic, fortuitous "and utterly without relation to whatever may be their effects upon teleonomic functioning" and that, once those living beings were incorporated in the DNA structure, mechanical and faithful replication automatically followed. The first living cells came about from pure chance; once that happened, the accident of creation entered the realm of necessity, of the most implacable certainties. If we accept this theory, it is possible to conceive of man as a little machine, made possible by an accidental arrangement of atoms and a naturalistic evolutionary process, the end product of years of selectivity. Pain and suffering, then, can be explained away as the result of the dysjunction of the atoms. Life, in the circumstances, ceases to have any other "meaning" and it would be patently illogical to project a "purpose" to it.

IS THERE LIFE AFTER DEATH? New Evidence to the Fore

For all the scientific theorizing of Jacques Monod, new evidence is available to indicate that there is some kind of existence after death. What it is that exists—obviously it is not the body—beyond death? How is it to be defined? Is it the soul? If it be that, what is the nature of that entity? Is it memory? How can memory be materialized?

Most of the explorations on the subject conducted in recent times by many scientific inquirers independently of each other, involve interviewing people who have experienced a clinical form of defined death. Major impetus to the study was supplied by the well-known psychiatrist, Dr. Elizabeth Kubler-Ross. According to Dr. Kubler-Ross, her talks with hundreds of people who had been resuscitated had convinced her "beyond a shadow of doubt" that there is life after death.

In an address to Earlham College in Richmond, Indiana, in 1975, Dr. Kubler-Ross described three components common to these "death" experiences: a sense of the soul floating out of the body; feelings of peace and wholesomeness (wholeness) and a meeting with someone who had previously died. "None of the patients who have had a death experience and returned are ever afraid to die" she told her audience.

Dr. Kubler-Ross' report has been independently corroborated by Mrs. Barbara Pryor, the wife of Arkansas Governor, David

Pryor in a newspaper interview. Mrs. Pryor suffered a pulmonary embolism—a blood clot in her lungs—following an emergency hysterectomy in a Washington hospital on Thanksgiving Day 1971. The physician in attendance was one Dr. Donald Payne. Before Mrs. Pryor slipped into unconsciousness she saw 'a look of fear come over the doctor's face" and then, she says, it happened: "My spirit started rising in the air. I was so at peace. The feeling was magnificent. I could see my body on the bed and knew it once belonged to me. But I felt completely detached from it. I really didn't care what happened to my body."

Dr. Payne was shouting at his nurses. "Code Blue! Code Blue!"—an emergency code which meant that a life was at stake. Later Dr. Payne recalled that he was beating on Mrs. Pryor's chest and giving her an external cardiac massage. Mrs. Pryor said she watched the frantic activity while her spirit floated above the room which was rapidly filling up with nurses and other doctors.

Let her now tell her own story: "I remember thinking, 'Why are you working so hard? I am completely and utterly happy.' A man I had never seen before came to my body and administered a shot to the heart. When he finished, a nurse rushed to the bed and in her haste knocked over the pole holding the bottles of intravenous fluid. I watched the pole fall on the bed and saw one of the bottles hit the side of my body's face. But I didn't care. I was free of all pain. Everything that was going on below me in the room seemed to have nothing to do with me. Then I had the strangest feeling that at any second I would find my brother, who had died the year before of leukemia, right next to me. I was just about to see my brother when I looked down again and saw Dr. Payne massaging my body's chest. In a pleading voice, he said, 'Breathe, Barbara, breathe.' I remember saying to myself, 'Oh no, I won't. You can't make me breathe. You can't make me leave this paradise.' Just as I said that, a searing pain rushed through my chest and instinctively I knew that I had returned to my body. I felt trapped and angered for being forced to return. If there had been any way to stop the doctors, I would have done it. When I woke up, life-supporting machines were all around me and there was a painful black and blue welt around my eye. The nurse confirmed what I already knew—another nurse had knocked over the intravenous bottle which had struck the side of my head. My out-of-body experience was wonderful. Now I know there is nothing to fear from death. I know there is really something else—peace and tranquility like I've never known on earth."

Now how much of this is the subconscious mind working under anaesthesia and how much of this can we take as scientifically accurate? There is no way of knowing. Dr. Eugene Kennedy, a well-known Catholic psychologist and author believes life beyond death will remain an "untameable mystery"—a conviction, incidentally, that is shared by many. Referring to the testimony from those who have been resuscitated, Dr. Kennedy has said that he believes those experiences are "psychological and that they don't prove there is an afterlife."

Or take this report about Dr. George Ritchie, a respected Charlottesville psychiatrist who has said that after he was declared clinically dead back in 1943, he underwent a "life after life" experience for a full nine minutes. (*Washington Post*, June 3, 1977, B1, "Nine Minutes of Death" by William Gildea).

There is apparently no question that Ritchie was pronounced dead. He has the hospital staff's sworn testimony on that, including one doctor's additional opinion that Ritchie's "virtual call from death and return to vigorous health has to be explained in terms other than natural means." As the story has been told, this is what happened: In December, 1943, Ritchie, then a private in the U.S. Army, was hospitalized with pneumonia. His condition worsened day by day. After a week in bed he finally collapsed with a 106.5 degree fever. Twenty-four hours later he was discovered showing no signs of life and was pronounced dead.

About nine minutes later, the hospital ward boy who discovered Ritchie "dead," thought he was the young enlisted man move. But the doctor again declared him dead but just to be sure gave him a shot of adrenalin. At that instant, Ritchie's vital signs returned.

What happened to Ritchie during those intervening nine minutes has been described in great detail. He had feelings of peace, hearing noise, leaving the human body, seeing a being of light, seeing a panoramic review of one's life and approaching a border or limit. Before he fell ill, Ritchie had been scheduled to go to Richmond to complete medical studies at the Medical College of Virginia and now "dead," his instinct was to rush to Richmond. This is how he related his experience:

"I sat up on the side of the bed in this little isolation room. In the process of trying to find my uniform I looked back on the bed and there was this body lying there. But I didn't have time to think about that. I had one thing on my mind. I knew I had missed my train. I knew I had to get back to Richmond. So I came on out, I'm going back to Richmond and I see this ward boy coming up with a tray. I turned to tell him to watch where he's going and he either walked through me or I through him. I didn't have time to think about that either. Now I know this sounds ridiculous. I got outside and swoosh, man, I'm traveling at something approaching the speed of sound, about a hundred to 500 feet above the trees. And suddenly I'm crossing this large river and I see this little town. There's this lone guy coming down the street; there's this all-night cafe on the corner. So I sit down on the sidewalk to ask him where I was and he could neither hear nor see me. So I thought, well, I'll tap him on the side of his cheek to get his attention. And I went through him. (A year later I was going through this town and I recognized it. I told the guy driving the car, 'If you go down one block further on this street, you'll find an all-night cafe.' He went one block further down the street and there was an all-night cafe. Guess what town it was? Vicksburg, Mississippi.) Suddenly it hit me that I had left the body back there in the bed. I knew there wasn't any sense of going any further.... Just as fast as I left, I got back there...."

But before he could "re-enter" the body, Ritchie was confronted with a light, the intensity of which was so great, it was like turning on "a million welder's lights." Out of that light stepped another "form of sheer light" and at that point, the hospital walls disappeared "and every single thing that had ever happened to me from the time I was born was there in panoramic view."

As Ritchie put it, every detail was there. "Everything I had ever done in public, in private, in light, in darkness." But Ritchie did not find that frightening, because, as he put it, "I have never been in the presence of such total and absolute love, a Being that totally knew everything about me and totally accepted me and totally loved me. A moment before, desperately alone and frightened, awful gloom. Now to be in the presence of this Being, I didn't want to leave Him under any circumstances." The form itself, according to Ritchie, was an "easily recognizable form, but not human." It was light all over. The form then took Ritchie on a conducted tour through "different realms of life" which he described in some detail. Then back he was again, in the hospital room, and into his body . . . . Believable? And why not?

A book that has been running into several editions and which has a bearing on this subject is Dr. Raymond A. Moody's *Life After Life* which is based on his study of several instances such as that of Mrs. Barbara Pryor. Dr. Moody says [16] that the experiences he studied fell into three distinct categories: 1. The experiences of persons who were resuscitated after having been thought, adjudged, or pronounced clinically dead by their doctors. 2. The experiences of persons who, in the course of accidents or severe injury or illness, came very close to physical death and 3. The experience of persons who, as they died, told them to other people who were present. In all he examined about 150 cases.

According to Dr. Moody, despite the wide variation in the circumstances surrounding close calls with death and in the types of persons undergoing them, there is still a striking similarity among the accounts of the experiences themselves. In fact, he asserts, the similarities among various reports are so great that one can easily pick out about fifteen separate elements which recur again and again in the mass of narratives he has collected.

The experiences roughly follow along these lines: a person is dying; at the point of greatest physical distress he hears himself pronounced dead by his doctor. He "hears" a loud ringing or buzzing, then finds himself moving rapidly through a long, dark tunnel. He realizes that he is now outside his own body, but still in the immediate physical surrounding of that body. This gives him an odd feeling. But by now he senses that friends and relatives long dead have come to meet him and he also finds himself in the presence of a loving, warm spirit in the form of light.[17] He finds himself asked, non-verbally, to evaluate his life. There is an instant replay of his life's major events. But soon he finds himself approaching some sort of barrier. There is a struggle inside him. On the one hand he is intensely happy in his new surroundings; at the same time there is an earthward pull which becomes very powerful and he is "reunited" with his body that not too long ago he had forsaken.

We must presume here that Dr. Moody's witnesses gave an accurate account of their "after death" events. Dr. Moody himself has examined possible psychological, physiological, pharmacological and neurological explanations. He is not satisfied with them and concludes, as well we, too, might: "Let us at least leave open the possibility that near-death experiences represent a novel phenomenon for which we may have to devise new modes of explanation and interpretation."[18]

We may follow this up further to see what other scientists think. Critics of after-life research can't see how a control group can be set up to examine the subject scientifically, but some, at least, seem willing to wait and see. Thus, Dr. Charles Garfield of the Cancer Research Institute of the University of California says that while he does not at all agree with Dr. Kubler-Ross when she says that her experiences with the dying absolutely guarantee life after death, he will not also take the extreme scientific-materialistic position that the utterances of the dying are those of deranged persons. He is quoted as saying: "I don't really know what is happening and I am willing to tolerate the ambiguity."

Psychologist Karlis Osis of the American Society for Psychical Research in New York City has tabulated by computer, interviews with 877 physicians who have reported deathbed visions by their patients. Most of them involve dying patients who see benign apparitions coming for their souls. As reported by *Newsweek* [19] Dr. Osis has determined, at least to his own satisfaction, that patients whose brains were impaired by high fever or disease reported fewer visions than those who were fully alert at death.

Moreover, Dr. Osis asserts, powerful drugs such as morphine and demerol actually decrease the coherence of such visions. "The sick-brain hypothesis we considered do not explain the visions and so far it looks as if patterns are emerging consistent with survival after death" is Dr. Osis' explanation. He sees rapidly increasing evidence "for something in the human personality which can be called 'soul' which can exist outside of the human organism and also after death." One dominant finding, Dr. Osis has reported, was the recurrence of apparitions who seemingly come to "take away" the dying patient. He said these "take-away" figures appeared to come, whether or not the dying patient was anxious to die or expected to recover. The apparitions also were not determined by the religious background or culture of the patient. "We found the take-away cases were essentially similar in the U.S. and India. They had characteristics which neither the Bible nor the Gita suggests."

According to Dr. Osis, if these deathbed visions were true "religious experiences," that is, an awareness of "another world," an emotional reaction of peace and serenity would be expected. "And indeed, " he noted, "we did find that at death, many patients do "light up" even while their relatives are weeping." One suggestion of what happens to the soul after a person's physical death has been provided by an Indian Yogi, Swami Rama, in his book *Life Here and Hereafter*. According to Swami Rama [20] when the soul, *jiva*, departs, it is followed by the vital energy, *prana*, and when the *prana* departs, all the other organs follow. "The soul with its particular consciousness goes into the body which is best suited to that consciousness. It is followed by knowledge, actions and past experiences."

REINCARNATION: Life, Death and the Question of Rebirth

One case has been made that there is some sort of life after death. There is also a strong case to suggest that not only is there such disembodied life, but that the soul is reborn and is part of another body and that, in very special circumstances the new body can recall past lives.

In South Wales today lives a young housewife who saw the Roman Emperor Constantine learning swordsmanship in the year A.D. 286. Her husband was his tutor. She remembers meeting King Henry VIII before he married any of his wives. She remembers under hypnosis, dying in 1190, in a massacre at York and recalls meticulous details about a medieval French merchant of whom, when wide awake she has never heard. This woman and her six previous "lives" are among the weird cases related in a new BBC-TV documentary and a book *More Lives Than One?* published by Souvenir Press (*Washington Post*, Nov, 13, 1976).

Both the TV series and the book were based on 20 years of work by Arnall Bloxham, a "hypnotherapist" in Cardiff, Wales. Jeffrey Iverson, BBC producer, learned that Bloxham had tape-recorded trance sessions in which more than 400 people "regressed" to previous lives. Iverson is quoted as saying: "If true, then that single famous case of regression, published in 1954 in *The Search for Bridey Murphy* was just a tune on an Irish fiddle compared to his symphony of voices."

Swami Rama asserts that through proper spiritual discipline, yogis can easily learn about their past lives. As he states, the inward act of meditation is the only possible method for reaching the deeper levels of inner being. Once the conscious mind is controlled, the subconscious mind remains to be dealt with. And "one who reaches the depth of the hidden portion of mind can know one's previous births easily." To know the *atman* and the truth of rebirth, it is essential for the aspirant to study carefully the vast portion of the mind: without knowing it, the doctrine of rebirth cannot be fully fathomed.

There have been many instances of the very young reporting

that they remember their past lives and the National Institute of Mental Health and Neuro Sciences in Bangalore, India has investigated 16 cases, but has withheld its opinion pending further inquiry and collection of data. According to Dr. R. M. Varma, Director of the Institute and Dr. H. N. Moorthy, Professor of Clinical Psychology, although the cases are baffling, no scientific verdict can be given at the present stage of investigation.

Among the cases investigated by the Institute was a five-year-old girl who recalled that she was a night-soil carrier in her previous birth. Another was a 38-year-old Maharashtrian from India who spoke fluent Bengali of the last century—a language that she could not possibly have picked up in her native town. The Institute has minutely checked each case of "re-incarnation," sending experts to visit the places of their previous births suggested by the cases and subjecting to scrutiny the vivid details recalled by the "patients" about their earlier life, including articles owned by them and money they thought was due to them. So far, no frauds have been detected. Scientists at the Institute have asked themselves whether these cases could be owing to "cryptomenesia" (recapitulation of somebody else's words), hysteria, extra-sensory perception, telepathy, clairvoyance (genetic memory) or "possession syndrome" but it has been stated that facts are against all these possibilities.

Dr. Ian Stevenson, chairman of the Department of Pathology, Virginia University, who has worked in the Institute has been quoted as saying, "Scientists feel that these are genuine cases of reincarnation."

One of the most remarkable studies made on reincarnation is Gina Cerminara's book *Many Mansions* and concerns a psychic, Edgar Cayce, who was born in 1877 and who became famous for his life-readings based on clairvoyance. Cayce first discovered his powers in 1923 and by the time he died in 1945, he had given some 2,500 life-readings. Cayce gave his readings when he was under hypnotic sleep. It has been said of the readings that they have been consistent and "accurate" and that when a reading of the same person was given sometimes months apart, they never contradicted each other. Most readings contained some background information about past eras of history, such as Egypt and Atlantis. And, according to Dr. Cerminara, the Cayce readings agreed in many respects with the facts of recorded history, no matter how obscure. Dr. Cerminara says that one of Cayce's early readings referred to a man's previous incarnation as a stool-dipper, though Cayce himself apparently had no idea what a stool-dipper was and only learnt about it on consulting an encyclopedia. The term referred to the early American custom of strapping supposed witches on stools and dipping them into a pool of cold water.

Cayce's readings customarily gave the exact name borne by an individual in previous lives and in several instances also told the individual where he might find records of his former personality. These records in fact were found in books, old registries or on tombstones. It would have called for extraordinary leg work to fake the facts. One must presume, for lack of evidence to the contrary that Cayce was telling it as it is. According to Dr. Cerminara, in addition to the curious historical confirmations of past life data, there were innumerable confirmations in Cayce's readings of present life material.

The sceptic may not give credence but the claim has been made that on the basis of his reading into the individual's past life, Cayce could accurately predict what course a child would take almost immediately after its birth. The claim has also been made that in all known cases, his predictions turned out to be correct. Even in reading adult minds, apparently, Cayce, under hypnosis, could get in touch with the unconscious levels of those minds. The unconscious mind, according to Cayce, retained the memory of every experience through which the individual—should we call it the individual's soul?—had passed, not only from the time of birth, but also before birth, in all its previous experiences.[21] As Dr. Cerminara put it: "These pre-birth memories exist below what might be called a trap door, and at deeper levels of the unconscious mind than those commonly tapped by modern psychotherapists; but they are there, nonetheless."[22] This generally bears out with Swami Rama's own thesis that to know one's previous lives, one must be able to know one's entire mind. The conscious mind that we are aware of is only the minutest tip of the whole mind, like the tip of an iceberg.

Dr. Cerminara has some intelligent explanations to offer about the nature of genius. She takes her cue from Ralph Waldo Emerson's essay on the Gita in which he refers to the experience of being on a stairs, ascending. Dr. Cerminara's conclusion is that human capacities seem to advance upward as lifetimes progress, birth by birth. She refers to the growth of traits, notices in Cayce's data a kind of continuity "that is stairlike in nature." We may call it the Continuity Principle.

What this principle suggests is that if an entity starts in lifetime 1 to use a rudimentary musical instrument, say a reed, in lifetimes 2, 3 and 4 that same entity would use other musical instruments—obviously belonging to later cultural epochs—but with greater and improved control over the faculties of pitch, rhythm or melodic memory, components of what we might call musical talent until at some distant lifetime—say lifetime 40 or 50—that entity would be born with extraordinary talent amounting to genius.

As a theory, it is fascinating. But then what becomes of a Bach, a Beethoven, a Mozart or a Brahms? Did their souls fade away because they had reached the ultimate heights of musical perfection or can we expect vast improvements in, for example, the Ninth Symphony and the "Ode to Joy"?

Basic to the Continuity Principle, of course, is the tacit and total acceptance of the principle of rebirth and the theory of karma. As you sow, so you reap. What the explanation does not quite concern itself with is why any entity should have started to play on the reed in lifetime 1 in the first place and why any entity, for example, should take to crime, also in lifetime 1. Some answers to these and other questions are provided by other philosophies which we shall examine later on and if they are raised at this stage, it is because they provide a counterpoint to what seem alluring explanations.

KARMA REVISITED: Shaking One's Own Hand in Another Life

Rebirth, in a sense, is meeting oneself in another life and if there is no sense of immediate recognition, presumably it is because most of us have not learnt to do so in the manner of Cayce. There is, according to this thesis, no getting away from karma. It is like a boomerang that comes back to one who throws it. It is not an arrow let fly. Karma, besides, has nothing to do with heredity. Two perfectly healthy entities can bring forth a sick child, as we see too often in day-to-day life. When Cayce was once asked from which side of a family an individual inherited most, his answer was: "You have inherited most from yourself, not from your family! The family is only a river through which the soul flows."[23]

Dr. Cerminara disposes of another issue concerning karma: the ethical one. Is a person blind because in some past life the person has blinded another entity, as we must presume on the theory of as we sow, so we reap? To this the answer is that not the act itself, but the inner consent given to it, is the determining factor. A hangman in one life need not necessarily end up by himself being hanged in another life if, in the course of his duties, the hangman merely carried out his duty—his *dharma*, as it were—without giving his inner consent to what was asked of him to do. This is clearly a case of doing one's duty, without having any attachment to the task.

What is postulated here is that while it is not possible to dodge the results of one's past actions, man still has the will to create his own destiny and that the mind of man has formative power. The answer to all problems is within the Self. Even as a hangman, an individual can escape the fruits of his overt action, provided he has consciously separated himself, by the power of his will, from that action. It is, as the Gita clearly says, with the severance of attachment from the act that the chain of karma is broken. The theory of karma gets circumlocuitous confirmation from St. Paul as when he says, "Be not deceived; God is not mocked; for whatsoever a man soweth, that shall he also reap."

In fact it has been argued that the law of karma is the application of the law of cause and effect in the moral world. No action is exhausted without producing its effect both on the body and on the mind. The suggestion has been put forward that at the time of his death, the actions of a man remain in seed form and the seeds develop when he assumes a new body either on earth or any other plane of existence. Every man is born in the world fashioned by himself. He who has done good in a past life will be born as good in his next life. He who does evil will be born as evil. Karma and rebirth are indubitably intertwined. A man's happiness and suffering are the inevitable consequences of the actions of his previous life and the actions performed in his current life will determine those of the next.

It is amazing how much thought and ingenuity has gone into the conception of the triple entities—body, mind and soul—and what happens to them when the body disintegrates or, as we call it, dies. Entire philosophies have been woven round the relationship between these three and God and any study of death will have to take account of these philosophies. The texts of Vedanta, to start with Hindu philosophy, have in the main given birth to two sub-systems of philosophy, namely, the non-Dualism of Sankara made explicit in that unrivalled classic *Vivekachudamani* and the Theism of philosophers like Ramanuja and Madhva.

According to Sankara, Brahman, or pure consciousness, is the only reality, the universe of names and forms is unreal and man, in his true essence, is one with Brahman. Now the Theists have a different understanding of reality. They accept a personal God as ultimate reality. He is related to the universe and embodies souls in varying degrees. According to Madhva, for instance, the universe and the living souls are separate from God. The universe is a material entity, but the souls are spiritual in nature. But the souls, though separate from God, cannot exist independently of God or without Him. Their existence is entirely dependent on God. Indeed, Madhva speaks of living beings as the servants of God. This is known as the philosophy of Dualism. Ramanuja, the founder of the philosophy of Qualified Non-Dualism, known as

Vishishtadvaita propounds still another theory. According to him, the reality is the Brahman. But the individual souls and the universe are also real, being parts of Brahman or modes of his manifestation. Brahman, with the universe and the individual souls, constitutes the whole of reality. This theory has been illustrated with the metaphor of the pomegranate fruit. The seeds are the living souls, the rind is the universe but the seeds and the rind together make the pomegranate; one cannot think of the fruit without the seeds or the rind.

The Jains have come up with yet another theory. Tradition has it that the philosophy of Jainism was taught by a succession of saints *(Thirthankaras)*, the last of whom was Vardhamana, called Mahavira (the great hero) and Jina, the victor. It is after Jina that we get the derivative, Jainism. According to Jainism, everything in the world, fire, wind, and plant, insects and leaves have a spirit in them.[24] Living things—*jiva*—consist of a body and soul, of which the soul, understandably, is the active partner. The liberated *jiva* freed from matter is called the *atman* which is pure consciousness, untainted by matter. We might dwell a little bit on Jaina philosophy.

Though *jiva* is defined as the combination of body and soul, the word has been variously used to denote life, vitality, soul and consciousness, also, living experience. *Jivas* are, in number, infinite and are sharply differentiated according to their character. There are, for example, the *nityasiddhas*, or the ever-perfect, the *mukta* or the liberated and the *baddha* or the bound. The *mukta jivas*, or the liberated souls will not be embodied. Having achieved purity, they dwell in a supramundane perfection, unconcerned with worldly affairs. Those condemned to an infinite succession of lives are the *baddha* who are prey to illusion and are condemned to submit to the yoke of matter. As long as the *baddha jivas* continue in the cycle of life and death, the soul persists throughout all changes, always connected with matter, except in the final release, the link between soul and matter being karma.

The Jains propound that there is no creation of a new

substance or destruction of the old; it is only an endless fusion of elements in different forms. Birth and death are seen as *paryayas*, or modifications of the soul. The soul is also defined as being free from the dialectic process of evolution and capable of maintaining an existence independent of the body.

Jain philosophy, it may be remembered, was drawn and refined in a Hindu milieu and often uses the same vocabulary to be found in Vedanta. As in Vedanta philosophy, so in Jainism, the goal of all human endeavor is the absolute liberation of the soul from the body, of the *jiva* from the *ajiva*. And the prescribed way for this liberation is the shedding of karma.

So once again we come to our old friend, karma. According to the Jains, karma works in such a way that every change which takes place leaves a mark which is retained and built into the organism, as in a computer, to serve as the foundation for future action. Jainism classifies karmic conditions in five categories: *audayika, aupasamika, kshayika, kshayopasamika* and *parinamika.*

In the usual course of events, karma takes effect with its clear certainty and in this situation the soul is said to be in the *audayika* state. By proper effort karma may be prevented from taking effect for some time, but not for all time, the simile employed being that of fire covered by ashes. In such a condition the soul is said to be in the *aupasamika* state. The third condition is when karma is not only temporarily neutralized but is destroyed altogether when the soul is said to be in the *kshayika* state which leads to *moksha* or liberation. *Kshayopasamika* or the fourth state of the soul partakes of the nature of all the preceding ones. In this condition some karma is destroyed, some neutralized and some still active. The last state, *parinamika*, is unconditioned by karma.

The Jains hold that when a particular karma—action—prduces its effect, it is purged from the soul. It is as if a debt has been paid and so written off from the books. The process of paying off could go on and if this discharge takes place uninterruptedly, all taint of matter will be wiped out from the soul thus qualifying it for liberation. Unfortunately for a *jiva* the problem is not as simple as all that, for along with purging of past karma, man accumulates new karma, thus making for the endless chain of *samsara*—life. What is the process that binds the body and soul? The Jains attribute it to wrong belief *(mithyadarsana)*, non-renunciation *(avirati)*, carelessness *(pramada)*, passions *(kashaya)* and vibrations set up in the soul through mind, body and speech.

The outstanding aspect of Jainism is its belief that everything in the solar system from a mountain to a dewdrop has a soul. The universe, indeed, is filled with *jivas*. Each plant may be the body of one soul or may possess a multitude of embodied souls. Thus souls are infinite and available to take new forms of life in hand. Another feature of Jain philosophy is the belief that souls have dimensions and the capacity to expand and contract. At the end of each earthly life, the soul contracts again into the seed of the next birth which it has to undergo.

NIRVANA: The Deliverance of the Soul

What is *nirvana*, which the Jains prescribe as the most desirable goal of all human endeavor? Is it the annihilation of the soul? Is it its final extinction? Not so. Dr. Radhakrishnan has described it as the soul's entry "into a blessedness that has no end."[25] The soul does not cease to exist. It is merely separated from the body with the energy of its past karma finally and totally extinguished, the spirit thus freed from the prospect of reembodiment. It is thus in a state of perfection, free from action and desire, in a rest that knows no change or ending. *Nirvana*, thus, is not a negative state of non-existence but a positive state of utter and absolute quiescence; the gears, one might say, are in the neutral position.

The soul that has attained *nirvana* can now perceive and know, since perception and knowledge are functions of the soul and not of the sense organs. In *nirvana* the soul gains infinite consciousness, pure understanding, absolute freedom and eternal bliss. But how is one to attain this state? Jainism prescribes the apparatus of morality. The way to *nirvana* lies through the three jewels *(triratna)* of faith in Jina, knowledge of his doctrine and perfect conduct. What is right faith? Belief in real existence or *tattvas*. What is right knowledge? This is knowledge of real nature without doubt or error. What is right conduct? This is an attitude of neutrality without desire or aversion toward the objects of the external world. By following these three principles, together and simultaneously, the claim is made, the individual can inhibit the formation of fresh karma and thus pave the way for the soul to liberate itself from *ajiva*—matter—to attain *nirvana*.

We shall see later how another great *sadhak*, aspirant to truth, the Buddha, looks at the question of attaining *nirvana*. Both Buddha and Mahavira antedate Christ by five centuries and more. The sixth to fifth century B. C. was a period of great flowering of philosophy in India. The spirit of inquiry into the nature of man flourished freely. That spirit is evident in one of the great works of that period, *Yoga Vasishta*. It is in this work that the sage Vasishta explains to Rama the significance of death and what happens to the soul after the event.

Death, argues Vasishta, does not bring about complete annihilation. It merely brings about the temporary withdrawal of the thought process of the individual. The soul, laden with desires, goes to another space and time. This is the *jiva*, the atomic vital, that is freed of the body, following the illusory insensibility of death. What happens then is that the entity has experience of the "other world" in the same manner as in life he experiences dreams, daydreams and illusions, except that the order and contents of the afterlife experience are in accordance with the desires of the "dead."

In this state the entity undergoes the consequences of one's actions during his lifetime and once this is over he enters the heart of man and associating with his spermatozoa, enters the uterus of a fit mother. With all his faculties dormant (unconscious) the entity becomes the seed in which capacity he enters the uterus of a female and then grows as a fetus. Thus it is, according to Vasishta, that the entity goes from one body to another, bound by hundreds of desires and hopes, like a bird flying from one tree to another. Those who, in their previous life, had attained some spiritual progress were born in the family of good, pure and virtuous people and so took off from where they had ended their past life, recollecting their past stages of spiritual progress and proceeding to attain greater heights.

Mention is made in the *Yoga Vasishta* as in other works of that transitional period between death and rebirth and the Vedic mystics have charted the courses that individuals follow during that time. These are determined by one's actions and thoughts while still alive. Thus, those individuals who lead an extremely righteous life and practice the various spiritual disciplines but who still have not succeeded in attaining complete self-knowledge before death go to *Brahmaloka* (or the plane of Brahma) or heaven and from there, in due course, attain liberation.

But not all. Some return to earth and are born again. Their journey lies through a path known as the *devayana*, or the Passageway of the Gods. Those among the returnees, so to speak, who led good and virtuous lives and intensely cherish a desire to reap the fruits of their good deeds, go after death to *Chandraloka*, or the lunar sphere. This journey to *Chandraloka* lies through a path known as *pitriyana* or Way of the Fathers. Here in *Chandraloka* they enjoy immense happiness as a reward for their meritorious acts, but they too come back to earth as they hanker for worldly joys. Then there are those individuals who have led evil lives. These, after death, assume sub-human bodies and live in hell. After expiating for their evil, they too are reborn as human beings on earth. Lastly are those whose evil is immeasurable and these spend many births in lower forms of life such as mosquitoes and fleas. But even they, in the long run, return to human form. It is when the entity recovers human form that the soul again takes up the thread of spiritual evolution and works upwards towards perfection. What divine computer works out what Sir William Gilbert has called the punishment to fit the crime will always remain a mystery. What are those crimes that condemn an entity to turn into a flea, a lizard or an earthworm in lives to come? And how many such lizard-lives is an entity to live to qualify for a return to the human form divine? We never will know.

According to Hindu tradition, there are seven heavens: *Bhuh, Bhuvah, Swah, Mahah, Janah, Tapah* and *Satyam*. *Bhuh* is the world we live in. *Swah* or *Swargah*, is a celestial world where people, after death, enjoy material happiness as a reward for the good that they did in their lifetime. *Bhuvah* is the in-between region, between *Bhuh* and *Swah*. *Mahah* again is another intermediary region between the first three and the last three. The last three, *Janah, Tapah* and *Satyam* constitute the plane of Brahma, or *Brahmaloka*, corresponding to the highest heaven where fortunate souls go after death there to be in permanent communion with God.

Just as there are seven heavens, Hindu tradition has it that there are seven nether worlds as well. These are: *Atala, Vitala, Sutala, Talatala, Rasatala, Mahatala* and *Patala*. It is to these that the wicked are consigned to pay for their evil deeds. But their souls do not dwell there forever. No soul is eternally damned. Rebirth on earth is ordained as an intermediate station there to seek perfection and thereafter, through the process of self-knowledge, to attain God.

But what exactly is meant or sought to be conveyed by the word *jiva*—soul? What is the nature of its being? How does it relate to the body?[26] What we see of a person is the gross body—skin, bones and muscle, the nervous system, the brain, whatever, in fact, in known and perceived by the anatomist and the physiologist. This is known as the *sthoola sharira*. This is the food-formed sheath of man, known as *annamaya kosha*. The *annamaya kosha* encloses what is known as the *sookshma sharira*—the subtle body. This is the coating that accompanies the soul—*jiva*—in all its many wanderings from one gross body to another. It sticks to the *jiva* through all its journeys, until it is ready for final release.

What is the nature of the *sookshma sharira*? It is composed of five organs of knowledge (*jnanendriyas*), the five organs of action (*karmendriyas*), the five breaths (*prana, apana, vyana, udana* and *samana*) and the mind. The *sookshma sharira*, in turn, embraces three other sheaths: the *pranamaya kosha*, the *manomaya kosha* and the *vijnanamaya kosha*. Finally is the last inner coating, the one next to the *jiva* itself, which is the *karana deha*, forming the sheath of bliss or the *anandamaya kosha*.

To look at it in the reverse order, the *jiva's* immediate sheath is the *anandamaya kosha*—the sheath of bliss. Covering this are three other sheaths, *vijnanamaya kosha* (the sheath of knowledge), *manomaya kosha* (the mind sheath) and the *pranamaya kosha* (the sheath of the life force). These three subtle sheaths form the *sookshma sharira*—the subtle body, that which is not seen but whose processes are intensely felt. It is this *sookshma sharira* that travels with the *jiva* from one physical body to another.

What happens when man "dies" is that first, the *sookshma sharira* (the subtle body) is separated from the *sthoola sharira* (the gross body), leaving the latter a lifeless, inert mass. The *jiva* continues to remain in the *sookshma sharira*, but very soon it shakes off the *pranamaya kosha* and then has the denser part of the *manomaya kosha* as its outer garment. At this stage it is called a *pretha*. If the entity has led a good life the *jiva* is in a condition of joy; but if the entity has been evil, the *pretha* craves for the pleasures denied in a lifetime. According to the strength of these cravings, the *pretha* exists in the *pretha-loka* (the region of its being) for an appropriate period of time. This is time for the cravings to cease and when cessation of all cravings is complete the densest part of the *manomaya kosha* simultaneously withers away, freeing the *jiva* to go to the *Pitr-loka* (the world of the fathers).

Here in *Pitr-loka* more time is spent in purging the *manomaya kosha* from all elements unfit for *swarga* (heaven). This achieved, the *jiva* with a blemishless *manomaya kosha* goes to heaven there to enjoy the fruit it has stored up. This, however, is not everlasting. The stay in heaven is in direct proportion to the accumulation of merit and when this is played out, the purified *manomaya kosha* dissolves away now leaving the *jiva* in the *vijnanamaya kosha*. It is said that the *jiva* thereupon takes on a new *manomaya kosha*, acquires a fresh *pranamaya kosha* and is reborn.

Endless is this chain of life in the visible world, death, life in the invisible worlds, rebirth until the *jiva* grown weary and longing for higher, subtler experiences turns away from the joys of the materialist world, discards the lures of self-gratification and seeks through selfless service, the breaking of its bonds. That is the time for final union with Brahman.

THE WAY OF THE BUDDHA and the Order of the Universe

The Buddha was born around 563 B.C. when vedic concepts were already several centuries old and were beginning to lose their spiritual luster. Attention was being given more to the outer form than to the inner content. Rituals were being performed for the sake of ritual.

As a young man the Buddha—or Siddhartha, as he was known, a price of the Saka clan—lived as young princes of his period lived, tasting the pleasures of life which, however, brought him no sense of satisfaction. On the contrary, he was weary of them and eager to know the answers to life's mysteries, the way and wherefore of death, disease, sorrow and endless suffering. At the age of 29, Siddhartha forsook his wife, his only child, his kingdom and his inheritance to seek enlightenment. The perceived wisdom in those days laid down a life of grim austerity for the seeker after enlightenment and this Siddhartha followed with true grit and unflinching determination. But six years of austerities led Siddhartha nowhere; he grew weak in body but no wiser than he began until one day, as he sat in deep meditation under a bodhi tree, he received enlightenment. At that moment he became the Buddha, the truly enlightened. (The Mahayana—the northern branch of the Buddhist philosophy—speaks of *the* Buddha, meaning the fully enlightened man, but when the word Buddha is used without the article, it refers to the transcendent, spiritual Buddha, the essence, the divine source, as distinct from the historical person.)[27]

All his education was in the Vedas, the Brahmanas and the Upanishads, the available knowledge of his times. These he fully imbibed; but much he discarded. There were far too many inconsistencies in what he had learned, too much speculative chaos. In the *Brahmajalasutta* alone there were as many as sixty-two theories about the nature of God. From these the Buddha must have drawn the futility of metaphysical thinking. What was left was the immutable nature of suffering. Disease, death, pain, these were perennial as the hills. The Buddha's immediate concern was suffering and how to overcome it. The first thing about Buddhism that strikes with refreshing force is the Buddha's apparent unconcern with God and soul. The immediate reality was suffering in all its varied faces. This, the Buddha said, could be overcome by the perfection of character and devotion to the good. His approach was empirical. It has been said that he was spokesman of an age where thinking men were trying to harmonize the ineradicable aspirations of human nature with the obvious data of experience.

So God, in the circumstances, did not figure in Buddha's scheme of things. In a conversation with Anathapindika, the Buddha is said to have argued that if the world had been made by Isvara (God) there should be no change nor destruction and that there should be no such thing as sorrow or calamity, as right and wrong, seeing that all things, pure and impure, must come from Him. The Buddha's argument was that if sorrow and joy, love and hate which are part of the normal makeup of all conscious beings be the work of Isvara, He himself must be capable of those emotions and if He was, how then can He be said to be perfect, which is the attribute of God? But if it was argued that it was not God who was responsible for sorrow and suffering then there would be something else of which Isvara was not the cause. Why, then, should not all that exists be uncaused too? Again, if Isvara was all-powerful and all beings were to submit silently to Him, what would be the purpose of practicing virtue? The Buddha further argued that the Supreme Creator, as was then conceived, acted either with or without purpose. If He acted with a purpose, that implied that He was satisfying a want and was tainted with desire and to that extent imperfect. If, on the other hand, He acted without purpose, it was no less a taint on God as perfect.

Either way the concept of Isvara was riddled with contradictions.

The theistic systems of *Nyaya Vaisesika* were attacked by later Buddhism on much the same grounds, namely, that no God would lead individuals to practice unrighteousness; if He was agent only for the virtuous, then He was not infinite and that in any event the existence of God made man helpless. It may be remembered that the attack was on dogma then extant and then perceived as illogical and not necessarily directed against the kernel of Upanishadic teaching. The Buddha neither affirms nor denies the existence of the soul which is the subject of the Upanishad. Claims were made both in behalf of its existence and its non-existence. What the Buddha does is to exhort us to be philosophical enough to recognize the limits of philosophy. Would a man hurt by an arrow ignore pain to inquire into the origins of the arrow or the direction from which it came or would he concern himself with the immediate problem of alleviating suffering? Pragmatic as he was, the Buddha concerned himself with the immediate problem of understanding suffering and through that understanding, the alleviation of pain. Central to the Buddha's teachings are the Four Noble Truths: that there is suffering; that suffering has a cause; that it can be suppressed; and that there is a way to accomplish it.

When the Buddha speaks of sorrow and suffering it embraces a wide spectrum of experience: pain, anxiety, frustration, grief and loss; again, when he speaks of the cause he is referring to spiritual ignorance that, in turn, gives rise to anger, passion, jealousy, desire and attachment. There was, insisted the Buddha, a way to end sorrow and suffering. He called it, appropriately enough, The Middle Way. It dismissed a life of pleasure as contrary to the spiritual life. At the same time it was wary of the life of ceaseless austerities. The Buddha, it may be remembered, had lived both. They were obvious hindrances to the acquisition of illumination. So the Buddha proclaimed the Four Noble Truths.

The First Noble Truth is the existence of pain. Life is suffering. In his very first sermon after he had received enlightenment, the Buddha said: "Now this, O monks, is the noble truth of pain: birth is painful, old age is painful, sickness is painful, death is painful, sorrow, lamentation, dejection and despair are painful. Contact with unpleasant things is painful, not getting what one wishes is painful. In brief, the five aggregates which spring from attachment are painful." Was there any escape from pain from our weary round of existence? The Buddha said, yes, there was indeed. And this was the Second Noble Truth, which was knowing the cause of pain. At the root of all suffering was desire stemming from ignorance. If man was to be rid of pain, he had to be rid of desire; from desire came clinging. Bondage lay in clinging to things. Release from earthly bondage, from the schema of suffering and sorrow, lay in overcoming desire. If there was no desire there could be no suffering either.

The Buddha did not halt there. It was not enough for him to lay down that desire was at the root of all evil and misery. There was always a way out. And this is his Third Noble Truth, that sorrow can be brought to an end, that the *taan*—the thirst—for pleasures that led to rebirth could be got rid of, set aside, in man's quest for *nirvana*. This is the affirmative aspect of Buddhism. It shows a way out. And that way out is the Fourth Noble Truth. It is called the Eight-fold Path and it consists of Right Views, Right Aspirations, Right Speech, Right Conduct, Right Livelihood, Right Effort, Right Mindfulness and Right Contemplation. There is a strong resemblance between the Noble Eight-fold Path and the Ten Commandments[28] though the Noble Eight-fold Path is more than an exhortation: it is a systematization of ethics; more, it is a practical guide to wisdom.

Right View is to know suffering and the cause of suffering as originating from *avidya*—ignorance. It is also to know and accept as a fact that suffering can be brought to an end. It is the first step failure to appreciate which could lead the individual astray.

Right Aspirations consisted of the will to attain *nirvana* through self-discipline and the resolve not to do any hurt or harm to all living beings as well as to cultivate the inner, intuitive vision.

Right Speech was to shun, abstain from lies and slander, from reviling others and always to speak the truth. Though the Buddha could have stressed the importance of adhering to the truth as a necessary vehicle on the road to enlightenment, he could not also have been unmindful of what the *Mundaka Upanishad* said: *Satyameva Jayate*—Truth conquers.

Right Conduct lay in abstaining from taking life, from stealing and from lechery and by being guided in all our day-to-day living by the inner law of love, compassion and wisdom.

Right Livelihood was a sum of many things. All wrong modes of livelihood were to be excluded so that no shadow was cast on the disciple of the Noble One.

Right Endeavor was to ceaselessly strive to foster good qualities in oneself, to suppress wrong qualities and renounce those that have already manifested themselves while simultaneously seeking to enlarge and develop and perfect those good qualities which already are there.

Right Mindfulness is the development of insight through discipline and training of the discursive mind. This can indeed be considered the key to Buddhist practice and has been elaborated in *Satipatthana*—the Way of Mindfulness—by the Buddha himself. It is one of two "ways" of Buddhist meditation practice, the other being the development of tranquility.

Last comes Right Rapture or Right Concentration wherein the individual discards lust, enters into a state of peace and self-illumination through proper meditation. In this state the individual develops and dwells in inward serenity. For the beginner it is suggested that he choose an appropriate part of the day and a quiet place and make a willing effort to radiate loving kindness. There are many degrees of concentration, leading to first, second, third and lastly, fourth ecstasies.

The Second Noble Path explained the cause of suffering. How does misery and sorrow arise? This is set forth in the *Nidanas*, the Causal Wheel, which is the core and pith of the whole doctrine of the Buddha. In it the Buddha traces the steps that begin with ignorance and end in grief and despair. There is an awesome logic

in the tracing of cause and effect but the *Nidanas* comprise a wheel and so there is no starting point and if ignorance is placed first, it is merely because it is the primary root of existence and its deletion is considered the sine qua non for release from the endless chain of birth-death-rebirth. As the Buddha saw it, this is the sequence:
On ignorance depends karma;
On karma depends consciousness;
On consciousness depend name and form;
On name and form depend the six organs of sense;
On the six organs of sense depends contact;
On contact depends sensation;
On sensation depends desire;
On desire depends attachment;
On attachment depends existence;
On existence depends birth.
On birth depends old age, death, sorrow, lamentation, misery, grief and despair. In a word, *dukkha*.
If this cause-and-effect sequence is properly understood, then, the Buddha stated, it was possible to put an end to suffering. The logic, again, is clear:
When there was a cessation of ignorance, karma ceased.
When karma ceased, consciousness ceased.
When consciousness ceased, name and form ceased.
When name and form ceased, the six organs of sense ceased.
When the six organs of sense ceased, contact ceased.
When contact ceased, sensation ceased.
When sensation ceased, desire ceased.
When desire ceased, attachment ceased.
When attachment ceased, existence ceased.
When existence ceased, birth automatically ceased.
With the cessation of birth ceased old age and death and *dukkha*.
It will be seen that the Buddha traces all our suffering to the root cause: ignorance. But who planted ignorance in man in the first place; why should not man be born with innate knowledge of his true nature and the nature of the world around him? The

beginning of the circuit is nowhere apparent in the Buddha's teachings. We do not know the cause of *avidya*—ignorance—and it is begging the question to say that that is where it all starts. As Dr. Radhakrishnan pithily observes: "It *(avidya)* seems to be a blind end or an incomprehensible reality which we must accept unthinkingly."[29]

Whether we accept the premise or not, so far as the Buddha is concerned, it all starts from *avidya* and everything that lives, moves and displays individual existence does so through the power of *avidya*. There is nothing prior to it. The Buddha does not blame God or Satan for man's fall; he blames ignorance. The answer of the early Buddhists to the question, ignorance of what? is direct. It is ignorance of the true nature of "I" and of the Four Noble Truths. Ignorance is attested by the fact of its existence. It is only by presuming its existence that the Buddhist circuit can be completed. It is like the eighteenth elephant.

In accepting the existence of *avidya* as the mysterious element in the solution of the riddle of life and the cessation of birth, we may hark back to the story of the eighteenth elephant.

Once upon a time there was a rich man who had three sons. Before he died he willed that all his possessions should be distributed among the three in accordance to a set formula. The eldest son was to get one half; the second son was to get one sixth and the youngest of all was to get one ninth. Everything went off well until it came to the elephants. The rich man had left seventeen elephants behind him and there was no way in which they could be divided among the sons as their father had specifically willed. The sons thereupon called on a learned Brahmin to settle the dispute. There was, said the Brahmin, no difficulty at all in the matter. Why, said he, should not the sons presume that he has donated an elephant to their welfare and to add to their inheritance? But, argued the sons, you do not have an elephant to donate; you are as poor as nay Brahmin can be. What kind of a joke was that? To avoid further argument, however, the sons acceded to the Brahmin's wishes in order not to offend him, which was bad form anyway. So the eighteenth elephant was deemed as accepted and the division took place forthwith. The eldest son received nine elephants, the second son three and the last, two. The equation had been resolved. The eighteenth elephant was not needed.

It is in that sense that *avidya* must be treated as a "cause by courtesy." It has no substratum; and yet it cannot be considered unreal for in that case it cannot lead to anything. It is there; it is the source of all existence. Existence automatically implies transformation. What is, grows; what grows undergoes change; and whatever undergoes change must, in the end, perish. "I will teach you the *dharma*" says the Buddha, "that being present, this becomes; from the arising of that, this arises. That being absent, this does not become; from the cessation of that, this ceases."

Life, then, is a story of ceaseless flux and change and death is not the end. It is merely the beginning of another life. This need not be disheartening. *Nirvana* is not attained in one life. But it is possible; man is not punished for his karma but by it. The more he understands the nature of his being, the greater his chances of working out his own salvation. Buddhism is a religion of hope. It is also a humane religion. And it helps to approach it with due reverence and submission. This is the significance of the Three Venerations:

Buddham sharanam gacchami.
Dhammam shararam gacchami.
Sangham sharanam gacchami.

In an insecure world they are a source of strength:

I take refuge in Enlightenment;
I take refuge in the Eternal Law;
I take refuge in the Fellowship of Virtues.

There is a story told of the Buddha's compassion and it is a story that illustrates his enlightenment too. The Buddha was traveling in the upper regions of India when there came to him a woman in great distress. She had lost her only child, a son, and she was disconsolate. Long she had sought someone who could bring her child back to life and always she was told to seek out the

Buddha, the Enlightened One. Now she had found him. The Buddha listened to her sad story as her tears rolled down her cheeks. Filled with compassion the Buddha said: "Bring me a mustard seed from a house in which neither parent, child, relative nor servants ever died and I shall bring your child back to life."

Filled with hope, the mother immediately went out in search and from door to door she went with the same question on her lips and received the same answer. There was no such home where someone had not died. At last she returned, empty handed, to the Buddha. "My daughter," said the Buddha, "have you brought the mustard seed I asked for?" And the woman understood.

BARDO THODOL: A Traveler's Guide to Other Worlds

Bardo Thodol, the Tibetan Book of the Dead, provides a fascinating account of what could happen after the individual dies. The book deals with the period (longer or shorter according to circumstances peculiar to each individual) which commences immediately after death and ends with "rebirth."

In the Buddhist view, life consists of a series of successive states of consciousness. The first state is birth-consciousness; the last is the consciousness existing at the moment of death or the death-consciousness. We know what happens to man from the time he is born to the time he dies. What *Bardo Thodol* seeks to tell is what happens from the moment a man dies to the time he is reborn. This interval between the two states of consciousness, during which the transformation from the "old" to the "new" is being effected is called the *Bardo* or intermediate state *(antarbhava)*. It is divided into three stages called the *chikhai, chonyid* and *sidpa bardo* respectively.[30]

Chikhai Bardo: When an individual dies his soul-complex is "disincarnated"; the empiric consciousness or consciousness of objects by the "knower" is lost in the process and the dying person glimpses the Clear Light. Among Tibetans the dying person is adjured to recognize the Clear Light and thus liberate himself. If he does so, it is because he is himself ripe for the liberated state which is presented to him. This is the *dharmakaya*. If he does not, as is commonly the case with most mortals, it is because the individual is so attached to worldly matters that their pull *(samsara)* draws him away. He is then presented with the secondary Clear Light, which is the first, but somewhat dimmed by *maya*.

If the mind does not find its resting place here, the first or *chikhai bardo* which may last for several days or just a brief, glorious moment ("for the time it takes to snap a finger") according to the state of the deceased, comes to an end.

Chonyid bardo: Now comes the second stage. In this, there is a recovery of the death consciousness of objects. The "soul-complex" emerges from its experience of the Clear Light into a state much like that of a dream. During this *bardo*, the deceased is in the *mayik* world (or world of forms) and if liberation is then attained, it is with form *(roopavan)*. The consciousness of the deceased is presented two pathways: a *nirvanic* line, symbolized by various dazzling colors, with certain divinities (both peaceful and wrathful) emanating from them and a *samsaric* line, consisting of six *lokas*. With the *lokas* are given their "poisons" which are the sinful characteristics of their inhabitants. The "soul-complex" of the deceased is then adjured, on the one hand, to seek liberation through the compassionate grace of the *nirvanic* line and on the other, to shun the particular *loka* (world) which is concomitantly presented to the deceased's mental vision. The six *lokas* consist of *devas, asuras* and men, of *pretas* (ghosts), brutes and hell.

If the "soul-complex" accepts the *nirvanic* line, it is in the *sambhoga kaya* (the body of bliss) and is accompanied on the sixth and seventh day by the peaceful divinities, followed on the eighth and subsequent days by the wrathful divinities which so terrify the deceased that he flees from them and sinks more and more into such a state as will eventually bring him birth in one or other of the *lokas*.

Sidpa bardo: About the fifteenth day, passage is made into the third *bardo,* in which the deceased, if not previously liberated, seeks "rebirth." His past life has now become dim. The "soul-complex" takes on the color of the *loka* in which it is destined to be reborn. If the deceased's karma leads him to hell, thither he goes after the judgment in, we are assured, "a subtle body which cannot be injured or destroyed" but in which atrocious pain is inevitable. But if the karma is good, the deceased could go to the world of *devas* or gods or some other *loka* as befitting his past karma, to return, at length, and in all cases, to earth where alone can new karma be established. Neither heaven, nor hell, nor any other *loka* is a permanent habitat for the "soul-complex." And it is on earth alone that one performs karma; it is the earth-life that determines future lives. It is on earth that the individual carves out his post-death future.

Whatever the period the "soul-complex" spends in any *loka*, if the lot of the deceased is immediate rebirth on earth in human form, then he sees visions of mating men and women. If the deceased is to be reborn as a male, the feeling of its being a male comes upon the knower and, says the *Tibetan Book of the Dead*, "a feeling of intense aversion for the father and attraction for the mother is begotten" and vice versa, as regards birth as a female.[31] At length the choice is made, the deceased passes out of the *bardo* dream world into a womb of flesh and blood, issuing out of it once more into the waking state of earth experience and birth conscience. In the circumstances, there is no breach of consciousness, but a continuity of transformation. Death is not the end but the beginning of another cycle. We can recall here the poignancy of a remark made by Dr. Radhakrishnan that "in this world of unresting change and eternal becoming, there is no firm resting place for man."

There has been reference made to *maya* and *mayik* world above. What does *maya* really mean? And what has it got to do with death? Simply put, the diversity that we encounter in our daily life is *maya*.[32] *Maya* is a mirage that puts off the truth, that masks it. The Vedanta does not precisely define it; it is *anirdesyam*—impossible to define—of which we cannot say it is, for it is an illusion. And yet we cannot say that it is not, for we see it in action. It is intellectually envisaged, as Sri Aurobindo would say, a subjective necessity. *Maya* starts where duality begins, when *Purusha* differentiates from *Prakriti*, spirit from matter, force from energy, ego from non-ego. When we confuse the multiple forms of life with Brahman that is *maya*. *Maya* is what prevents us from seeing the ultimate truth. The *Ishopanishad* tells us that "the face of Truth is veiled with a golden disc." We have to see beyond the veil to seek the truth. *Maya* is synonymous with *avidya*, nescience or *ajnana*, ignorance. It is our ignorance that tells us that we are separate from God. On account of this man is not conscious of his real Self. To know one's true self, then, one must again pierce the veil of *maya*.

Brahman used *maya* as the material of creation. *Maya*, if it had any birth, took place on the other side of phenomena, before the origin of time, space and causality, and is not recognizable by the intellect which can only think in terms of these three factors. *Maya* prevents us from seeing Brahman. All souls are free from bondage and are pure by nature, but it is *maya* which makes the ignorant person think of himself as bound. To be free from the bonds of *maya* and to see ourselves whole, the keys are meditation and knowledge.

The *Ishopanishad* states this clearly enough. Knowledge and illusion, it says, he who knows both, overcomes death through illusion and through knowledge enjoys immortality. We weep for the dead because we do not understand death. We are attached to the dead by *maya*. When we see beyond death, as the Gita adjures us to do, and uncover Reality, we cease to weep; for now we know. *Maya* is false knowledge; and like all false knowledge it is very alluring. Far too many of us are comfortable with it, when we should not be. Its characteristic has indeed been aptly described by the *Ishopanishad*. It is *hiranmaya*—luminous, golden, attractive and therefore causing attachment. That is its basic attraction.

When we have discovered the allure of *maya* and learned to discard it through the acquisition of knowledge by meditation, then we see it for what it is. St. Paul may have had it in mind when, in his first Epistle to the Corinthians he wrote: "When I was a child, I spoke as a child, I understood as a child; but when I became a man, I put away childish things. For now we see through a glass, darkly, but then, face to face; now I know in part; but then I shall know even as also I am known." He who is blinded by *maya* sees as through a glass, darkly. But when he pierces the veil of *maya*, then he is face to face with truth. He will come to appreciate what has been said in the Gita:

> I am the *Atman* dwelling in the heart of every being;
> I am the beginning and the middle and likewise the
> end of all beings.

THE THEOSOPHIST: Understanding Life and Death

Before we go to other religions and religious philosophy in our search for the meaning of death, we may briefly study what the Theosophists have to say on the subject. Theosophy holds that the course of evolution is the drama of the soul and that nature exists for no other purpose than the soul's experience. Its exponents claim that Theosophy is a scientific religion and a religious science and "is a knowledge of the laws which govern the evolution of the physical, astral, psychical and intellectual constituents of nature and of man."

One of the early Theosophists, William O. Judge, put it this way: "That man possesses an immortal soul is the common belief of humanity; to this Theosophy adds that he is a soul; and further that all nature is sentient, that the vast array of objects and men are not collections of atoms fortuitously thrown together and thus without law evolving law, but down to the smallest atom all is soul and spirit ever evolving under the rule of law which is inherent in the whole."[33]

In many ways the Theosophists stay close to the Upanishadic-Buddhist doctrines. Thus A. P. Sinnett in his book *Esoteric Buddhism* classifies the nature of man as follows: there are seven constituents to what we know as man: the body or *roopa*, vitality or *prana-jiva*, astral body or *linga sarira*, animal soul or *kaama-roopa*, human soul or *manas*, spiritual soul or *buddhi* and finally spirit or *atma*. The real man is the trinity: *atma-buddhi-manas*.

The body is the most transitory, impermanent and illusionary of the whole series of constituents in man. Not for a moment is it the same. How can it be when it is made up of gross elements? Constantly changing, its parts continuously interacting with each other, the body truly never remains finished, but is subject to continued change—*nitya pralaya*.

Many names have been assigned to the astral body: *linga sarira*, meaning design body, is one; others are ethereal double, phantom, wraith, apparition, doppelganger, personal man, perispirit, irrational soul, bhoota, spook, devil. Some of these designations, of course, apply only to the astral body when devoid of the corpus after death. As Mr. William O. Judge puts it, the astral body is made of matter of very fine texture as compared with the visible body, and has a great tensile strength, so that it changes but little during a lifetime while the physical alters every moment, as it were. Also, says Mr. Judge, it is flexible, plastic, extensible and strong and is composed of electrical and magnetic matter, "just what the whole world was composed of in the dim past, when the processes of evolution had not yet arrived at the point of producing the material body for man."[34]

When the body dies, the astral man is released and as at death, the immortal man—the Triad—flies away to another state, the astral becomes a shell of the once living man and requires time to dissipate. According to Theosophy, the astral body retains all the memories of the life lived by the man and thus reflexly and automatically can repeat what the dead man knew, said, thought and saw. It remains near the deserted physical body nearly all the time until that is completely dissipated, for it has to go through its own process of dying. It may become visible under certain conditions.

In sum, this is what happens when man "dies":
First the life force leaves, the physical frame is cold, the eyes are closed; all the forces of the body and mind rush through the brain and by a series of pictures the whole life just ended is imprinted indelibly on the inner man not only in a general outline, but down to the last detail. In this sense a man can be pronounced "dead"

only after the work of the real man is ended in the brain. When that work is over, the astral body detaches itself from the physical, the latter being left to decompose in a grave or be destroyed on a pyre. The astral body, made up of the astral body and the passions and desires has a life period of its own and exists in *kama loka*, purgatory, the place of desire. The astral man in *kama loka* is a mere shell, devoid of soul and mind, without conscience and also unable to act unless vivified by forces outside of itself. The astral man may stay in *kama loka*, passing the period in great suffering, or in a dreamy sort of sleep, each according to his moral responsibility, his particular karma while on earth.

Here in *kama loka* come into operation the *skandhas*, the aggregates that make man and which are created day by day under the law that every thought combines instantly with one of the elemental forces of nature, becoming to that extent an entity which will endure in accordance with the strength of the thought as it leaves the brain, all of them inseparably connected with the being who evolved them. During his stay in *kama loka*, the real man has to struggle to divest himself from the lower *skandhas*; as he sheds them, the being falls into a state of unconsciousness which precedes the change into the next stage:*devachan*. It is, says Mr. Judge, "like the birth into life, precluded by a team of darkness and heavy sleep." From this the real man, the triad of *atma-buddhi-manas* emerges into the state of *devachan*, which means "the place of the gods" where the soul enjoys felicity. The self in *devachan* is devoid of mortal body. It exists in that state "for years of infinite number," though Mr. Sinnett puts it at fifteen hundred years "in general," but by logic "proportionate to the unexhausted psychic impulses originated in earth life."[35] According to one authority "those whose actions were preponderantly material will be sooner brought back into rebirth by the force of *tanha. Tanha* is the thirst for life.

Devachan, then, is an interlude between births in the world. The law of karma which forces us to enter into the world being ceaseless in operation and also universal in scope, acts also on the being in *devachan*, for only by the force or operation of karma are we taken out of *devachan*. Says Mr. Judge: "The whole period allotted by the soul's forces being ended in *devachan*, the magnetic threads which bind it to earth begin to assert their power. The Self wakes from the dream, it is borne swiftly off to a new body and then, just before birth, it sees for a moment all the causes that led it to *devachan* and back to life it is about to begin, and knowing it to be all just, to be the result of its own past life, it repines not but takes up the cross again—and another soul has come back to earth."[36]

REINCARNATION and the Life Eternal

What is reborn is the eternal triad—*atma-buddhi-manas*—and whether rebirth is considered strictly in this context or not, the belief that man is born again and again in an endless cycle has been held by philosophers, scientists and ordinary mortals throughout history.

Indeed, even the Christian Church, no doubt under the influence of Eastern philosophies, held to the doctrine of rebirth until the year 553. That year, the doctrine was rejected by the Second Council of Constantinople, one third of the bishops present voting for the retention of the doctrine and the rest voting against; one assertion is that the doctrine was voted out because it conflicted with the assumed powers of the priest class to "remit sins"; clearly, the priest class would not let mere philosophical assertions come in the way of temporal power.[37]

That the concept of reincarnation cannot be lightly dismissed was conceded by George Foot Moore (1851-1931), professor of History in Religion, Harvard University, in his Ingersoll Lecture on Immortality. "A theory (metempsychosis) which has been embraced by so large a part of mankind" he said, "of many races and religions, and has commended itself to some of the most profound thinkers of all time, cannot be lightly dismissed . . . If man's earthly existence be conceived as a probation, it must be admitted that in any one life men are put upon this probation under very unequal conditions of every kind, and that the theory of a series of embodiments in which the soul is tested under various conditions accords better with our opinions of justice in the order of things. Finally if an end of perfection is set for the soul, metempsychosis affords the opportunity for a progressive approach to that infinite attainment . . . . " Writing in the *Aryan Path*, John Middleton Murray (1889-1957) gave his own explanation:[38] "The doctrine of reincarnation," he wrote, "is one of the great historical solutions to the problems of life which life sets to the human imagination. It is an answer to the deep desire of the spiritually awakened soul for divine justice . . . for an order of existence in which the suffering and the apparent injustice of this world shall be abolished and . . . for an opportunity of self-redemption and self-purification, not so much for what is generally called "sin," as from the spiritual lethargy which appears to be a condition of continued physical existence itself. The doctrine of reincarnation," Murray added, and he provides one of the most logical explanations to it, "as I understand it, is an attempt to declare the final triumph of the spiritual life. If we imagine . . . that no human soul is perdurably doomed, we must needs have a religious system which offers the opportunity of redemption to all and continues to offer it until the redemption of all is accomplished. Those who are now blind to the necessity of the spiritual life must journey on till their eyes are at last opened. And there is no denying that the doctrine of reincarnation declares this in a form acceptable to the ordinary imagination." It is well to remember that the doctrine of reincarnation is in direct conflict with accepted Christian doctrine of what happens to the soul, which will be discussed later on.

Thoughts very similar to those expressed by Murray have been expressed by Aldous Huxley in his *The Perennial Philosophy*. Huxley examines both the Christian and Eastern propositions and comes to the conclusion that Hindu or Buddhist logic, in the circumstances, is self-consistent. "The eschatologists of the Orient," he wrote, "affirm that there are certain posthumous conditions in which meritorious souls are capable of advancing from a heaven of happy personal survival to genuine immortality in union with the time-less, eternal godhead. And, of course, there is also the possibility (indeed, for most individuals, the necessity) of returning to some form of embodied life, in which the advance toward complete beatification, or deliverance through enlightenment, can be continued . . . .

"Orthodox Christian doctrine does not admit the possibility, either in the posthumous state or in some other embodiment, of any further growth towards the ultimate perfection of a total union with the godhead. But in the Hindu and Buddhist versions of the perennial philosophy, the divine mercy is matched by the divine patience; both are infinite. For Oriental theologians there is no eternal damnation; there are only purgatories and then an indefinite series of second chances to go forward toward not only man's but the whole creation's final end—total reunion with the Ground of all being . . . .

In the Vedanta cosmology there is, over and above the *atman* or spiritual self, identical with the divine Ground, something in the nature of a soul that reincarnates in a gross or subtle body, or manifests itself in some incorporeal state. This soul is not the personality of the defunct, but rather the particularized I-consciousness out of which a personality arises . . . . Either one of these conceptions (Hindu or Buddhist) is logically self-consistent and can be made to "save the appearances"—in other words to fit the odd and obscure facts of psychical research."[39]

THE PERVADING INFLUENCE of the Reincarnation Doctrine

Murray and Huxley are only two of a long list of scientists, psychiatrists, poets and philosophers who have examined the concept of reincarnation for its logical consistency and its inner structure and given it varying degrees of understanding and support. What seems to appeal to them is the sense of justice implicit in the doctrine and the acceptance of the role of the psyche. After carefully defining five main types of rebirth, namely, metempsychosis, reincarnation, resurrection, rebirth within one's life and transformation, Carl G. Jung (1875-1961) in his work *Archetypes and the Collective Unconscious* noted that rebirth is not a process that we can in any way observe. It was entirely beyond perception. However, he said, "we have to do here with a purely psychic reality, which is transmitted to us only indirectly through personal statements." Jung evidently is loth to dismiss the theory of reincarnation as scientifically implausible. "One speaks of rebirth" he wrote, "one professes rebirth; one is filled with rebirth. This we accept as sufficiently real . . . I am of the opinion that the psyche is the most tremendous fact of human life . . . . The mere fact that people talk about rebirth and that there is such a concept at all, means that a store of psyche experiences designated by that term must actually exist.

"Rebirth is an affirmation that must be counted among the primordial affirmations of mankind. These promordial affirmations are based on what I call archetypes . . . There must be psychic events underlying these affirmations which it is the business of psychology to discuss—without entering into all the metaphysical and philosophical assumptions regarding their significance."[40] It is not an endorsement of the doctrine, to be sure. Neither is it a denial. The scientist is ever cautious about committing himself. It is interesting to note in this connection that the distinguished artist, Salvador Dali, believed not only in reincarnation but felt that he was the reincarnation of St. John of the Cross, an assertion that, had it come from some less well-known person, might have only raised a titter.

In an interview published in *Today's Living*, Dali said: "As for me, I am not only a mystic; I am also the reincarnation of one of the greatest of all Spanish mystics, St. John of the Cross. I can remember vividly my life as St. John, of experiencing divine union, of undergoing the dark night of the soul of which he writes with so much feeling. I can remember the monastery and I can remember many of St. John's fellow monks."

Albert Schweitzer, himself a great theologian, thought the idea of reincarnation contains "a most comforting explanation of reality by means of which Indian thought surmounts difficulties which baffle the thinkers of Europe." Writing in *Indian Thought and Its Development*, Schweitzer said: "If we assume that we have but one existence, there arises the insoluble problem of what becomes of the spiritual ego which has lost contact with the eternal. Those who hold the doctrine of reincarnation are faced by no such problem. For them that non-spiritual attitude only means that those men and women have not yet attained to the purified form of existence in which they are capable of knowing truth and translating it into action."

Another believer in reincarnation was Victor Hugo (1802-1885). Writing in his *Intellectual Autobiography* he said: "I am a soul. I know well that what I shall render up to the grave is not myself. That which is myself will go elsewhere. Earth, thou art not my abyss . . . the whole creation is a perpetual ascension, from brute to man, from man to God. To divest ourselves more and more of matter, to be clothed more and more with spirit, such is the law. Each time we die we gain more of life. Souls pass from one sphere to another without loss of personality, become more and more bright . . . . " Hugo held that the tomb was not "a blind alley" but that it was a "thoroughfare." It "closes on the twilight; it opens on the dawn."

John Masefield, the British Poet Laureate got into the spirit of the idea in one of his poems:

> I hold that when a person dies
> His soul returns to earth;
> Arrayed in some new flesh-disguise,
> Another mother gives him birth.
> With sturdier limbs and brighter brain
> The old soul takes the road again.
>
> Such was my belief and trust;
> This hand, this hand that holds the pen,
> Has many a hundred times been dust
> And turned, as dust, to dust again;
> These eyes of mine have blinked and shone
> In Thebes, in Troy, in Babylon . . .
>
> So shall I fight, so shall I tread
> In this long war beneath the stars;
> So shall a glory wreathe my head,
> So shall I faint and show the scars,

> Until this case, this clogging mould,
> Be smithied all to kingly gold.
>> "A Creed"

It is a remarkable poetic statement of the concept of reincarnation. Life goes on in endless births and deaths, until, and though Masefield does not elaborate the thesis, he clearly means it, the soul purifies itself and finally attains salvation, *mukti*.

It is interesting to note that William Ernest Henley (1849-1903) deals with a similar theme in his *Ballade of a Toyokuni Colour-Print:*

> Was I a Samurai renowned,
> Two-sworded, fierce, immense of bow?
> A histrion angular and profound?
> A priest? A porter? — Child, although
> I have forgotten clean, I know
> That in the shade of Fujisan,
> What time the cherry orchards blow,
> I loved you once in old Japan . . .
> Dear, 'twas a dozen lives ago;
> But that I was a lucky man
> The Toyokuni here will show:
> I loved you — once — in old Japan.

Indeed, backward and forward in the history of literature, we see instances of the thought of reincarnation intruding in the minds of thinkers. In *Cato* (Act V, Scene 1) Joseph Addison (1672-1719) makes the point about the soul immortal:

> . . . . I shall never die.
> The soul, secure in her existence, smiles
> At the drawn dagger, and defies its point.
> The stars shall fade away, the sun himself
> Grow dim with age, and Nature sink in years;
> But thou shall flourish in immortal youth,
> Unhurt amidst the war of elements,
> The wreck of matter, and the crush of worlds.

Rudyard Kipling (1865-1936) who spent many fruitful years in India and no doubt was steeped in Indian folklore, if not philosophy, could say the same thing in his own inimitable way:

> They will come back, come back again, as long as the red Earth rolls. He never wasted a leaf of a tree. Do you think He would squander souls?

Or again, in his poem "When Earth's Last Picture is Painted":

> When earth's last picture is painted

> And the tubes are twisted and dried,
> When the oldest colors are faded,
> And the youngest critic has died;
> We shall rest, and faith, we shall need it
> Lie down for an aeon or two,
> Till the Master of all Good Workmen
> Shall put us to work anew.

Take Thomas Bailey Aldrich (1837-1907) whose poem "The Metempsychosis" provides a clearer picture of the theory of rebirth:

> I know my own creation was divine . . .
> I was ere Romulus and Remus were;
> I was ere Niniveh and Babylon;
> I was, and am, and evermore shall be,
> Progressing, never reaching to the end . . . .
>
> A century was a single day.
> What is a day to an immortal soul?
> A breath, no more. And yet I hold one hour
> Beyond all price,—that hour when from the sky
> I circled near and nearer to the earth . . . .
>
> We weep when we are born, not when we die!
> So was it destined; and thus came I here,
> To walk the earth and wear the form of Man,
> To suffer bravely as becomes my state,
> One step, one grade, one cycle nearer God.

Aldrich is both pessimistic—the soul, he says, may never reach the end—and hopeful: every life is one step, one grade, one cycle nearer to God.

Oliver Wendell Holmes (1809-1894) similarly wrote about the evolution of the soul through successive lives in "The Chambered Nautilus":

> Build thee more stately mansions, O my soul!
> As the swift seasons roll!
> Leave thy low-vaulted past!
> Let each new temple, nobler than the last,
> Shut thee from heaven with a dome more vast,
> Till thou at length art free,
> Leaving thine outgrown shell by life's unresting sea!

In his "Song of Myself" Walt Whitman (1819-1892) comes on strong on the subject of rebirth and the deathlessness of the soul:

> I know I am deathless,

I know this orbit of mine cannot be swept by a carpenter's
    compass . . .
And whether I come to my own today or in ten thousand
    or ten million years,
I can cheerfully take it now, or with equal cheerfulness I can
    wait . . .
To be in any form, what is that?
I tramp a perpetual journey (come listen all!) . . .
This day before dawn I ascended a hill and look'd at the
    crowded heaven,
And I said to my spirit, when we become enfolders of those
    orbs, and the pleasure and knowledge of everything in them,
    shall we be fill'd and satisfied then?
And my spirit said, No, we but level that lift to pass and
    continue beyond . . . .
And as to you, Life, I reckon you are the leavings of many
    deaths,
(No doubt I have died myself ten thousand times before . . .)

Benjamin Franklin (1706-1790) was certain that the soul could not possibly be annihilated. At the age of 22, he wrote an epitaph for himself which Carl Van Doren has called "the most famous of American epitaphs" in which Franklin states his belief:

> The body of B. Franklin
> Printer,
> Like the Cover of an Old Book
> Its Contents Torn Out
> And
> Stripped of Its Lettering and Gilding
> Lies Here
> Food for Worms,
> But the Work Shall not be Lost,
> For it Will as He Believed
> Appear Once More
> In a New and more Elegant Edition
> Revised and Corrected
> By the Author.

"When I see" Franklin explained, "nothing annihilated (in the works of God) and not a drop of water wasted, I cannot suspect the annihilation of souls or believe that He will suffer the daily waste of millions of minds ready made that new exist, and put Himself to the continual trouble of making new ones. Thus, finding myself to exist in the world, I believe I shall, in some shape or other, always exist; and, with all the inconveniences human life is liable to, I shall not object to a new edition of mine, hoping, however, that the errata of the last may be corrected."

SRI AUROBINDO on Death and Reincarnation

One of the profound thinkers of our age, Sri Aurobindo, has given much thought to death, the necessity of death, its meaning and significance. According to him, death is imposed on the individual life both by the conditions of its own existence and by its relations to the All-Force which manifests itself in the universe.[41]

As Sri Aurobindo sees it, the individual life is a particular play of energy, specialized to constitute, maintain, energize and finally to dissolve when its utility is over, one of the myriad forms which all serve, each in its own place, time and scope, the whole play of the universe.

Sri Aurobindo holds that there is one fundamental necessity of the nature and object of embodied life and that is to seek infinite experience on a finite basis. But how is infinite experience possible on a finite basis, since the body, the basis, by its very organization, limits the possibility of experience? Sri Aurobindo answers this by saying that this can be done by dissolving the form and seeking new forms. As he puts it, "for the soul, having once limited itself by concentrating on the moment and the field, is driven to seek its infinity again by the principle of succession, by adding moment to moment, and thus storing up a Time-experience which it calls its past."[42]

In that Time, it moves through successive fields, successive experiences or lives, successive accumulations of knowledge, capacity, enjoyment and all this it holds in subconscious or superconscious memory as its fund of past acquisition in Time. "To this process," adds Sri Aurobindo, "change of form is essential, and for the soul involved in individual body change of form means dissolution of the body in subjection to the law and compulsion of the All-life in the material universe, to its law of supply of the material of form and demand on the material, its principle of constant intershock and the struggle of the embodied life to exist in a world of mutual devouring." That, he calls, is "the law of Death."[43] And he adds, "This then is the necessity and justification of death, not as a denial of life, but as a process of life;

death is necessary because eternal change of form is the sole immortality to which the finite living substance can aspire and eternal change of experience the sole infinity to which the finite mind involved in living body can attain."

Sri Aurobindo's comments on rebirth—on karma—is even more significant. The true foundation of the theory of rebirth, according to him, is the evolution of the soul, or rather "its efflorescence out of the veil of matter and its gradual self-finding." And if this gradual efflorescence is true, he argues, then the theory of rebirth is an "intellectual necessity, a logically unavoidable corollary." But what is the aim of that evolution? Not, says Sri Aurobindo, conventional or interested virtue and the faultless counting out of the small coin of good in the hope of an apportioned material reward, but the continual growth of a divine knowledge, strength, love and purity.

Sri Aurobindo has patently no use for the theory that doing good in this life will necessarily bring suitable rewards in another life, in the shape of fortune, prosperity and general happiness. Indeed, he states, prosperity could often be a worse ordeal than suffering, no doubt in the manner of Christ's parable of the rich man and the camel passing through the needle's eye. As he puts it: "Indeed, adversity, suffering, may often be regarded rather as a reward to virtue than as a punishment for sin, since it turns out to be the greatest help and purifier of the soul struggling to unfold itself. To regard it merely as the stern award of a Judge, the anger of an irritated Ruler or even the mechanical recoil of result of evil upon cause of evil is to take a most superficial view possible of God's dealings with the soul and the law of evolution."[44]

This is a revolutionary way of looking at the theory of karma and in some ways Sri Aurobindo literally stands it on its head, since he makes us examine with a new freshness the significance of sorrow and adversity. In regard to rebirth, too, Sri Aurobindo has little use for those, like Jung, who would want experimental evidence. The soul, according to Sri Aurobindo, needs no proof of its rebirth, any more than it needs proof of its immortality "for there comes a time when it is consciously immortal, aware of itself in its eternal and immutable essence." Once that realization is accomplished, he argues, "all intellectual questionings for and against immortality of the soul fall away like a vain clamor of ignorance around the self-evident and ever-present truth."

Sri Aurobindo, however, warns that to view ourselves as such and such a personality getting into a new case of flesh "is to stumble about in the ignorance, to confirm the error of the material mind and the senses." And why? Replies the savant: "The body is a convenience, the personality is a constant formulation for whose development action and experience are the instruments; but the Self by whose will and for whose delight all this is, is other than the body, other than the action and experience, other than the personality which they develop. To ignore it is to ignore the whole secret of our being."

The Self is not born and does not exist in the body; rather, the body is born and exists in the Self. For the Self is everywhere, in all bodies. Even what we call the individual soul, says Sri Aurobindo, is greater than its body and not less, more subtle than it and therefore not confined by its grossness. At death it does not leave its form, but casts it off.

In his teachings, Sri Aurobindo points out that obviously then, there is no soul that reincarnates, but only karma that persists in flowing continuously down the same apparently uninterrupted channel. It is karma that incarnates; karma creates the form of a constantly changing mentality and physical bodies that are the changing composite of ideas and sensations which one calls "myself." The identical "I" is not, never was, never will be.

This poses an interesting question. If there is no such thing as an identical "I," what then, are we? What we are, says Sri Aurobindo, is a soul of the transcendent Spirit and Self, unfolding itself in the cosmos in a constant evolutionary embodiment of which the physical side is only a pedestal of form corresponding to its evolution to the ascending degrees of the spirit, but the spiritual growth is the real sense and motive. What is behind us is the past terms of the spiritual evolution, the upward gradations of the spirit already climbed, by which through constant rebirth we have developed what we are, and are still developing this present and middle human term of the ascension . . . . What is in front of us is the greater potentialities, the steps yet unclimbed, the intended mightier manifestations.

Even as he dismisses the doubters, Sri Aurobindo does not believe that we are but end products of chance and necessity as suggested by Jacques Monod. Sri Aurobindo, indeed, is positive about why we are here on earth. We are here, he believes, because this is the means of the spirit's upward self-unfolding. There is here a clear reason and purpose. And what we have to do with ourselves, Sri Aurobindo further suggests, is to grow and open the means to greater significance of divine being, divine consciousness, divine power, divine delight and multiplied unity. "And what we have to do with our environment is to use it consciously for increasing spiritual purposes and make it more and more a mold for the ideal unfolding of the perfect nature and self-conception of the divine in the cosmos." Few philosophers have been more positive and affirmative in defining the purpose of our existence as of its meaning.

Death, obviously, is not then the end. Besides, this universe is nothing else but a continuum of consciousness-force or, as Sri Aurobindo himself phrases it, a gradation of planes of consciousness, which range uninterruptedly from pure matter to pure spirit, as in a cosmic spectrum. We can envisage such a spectrum ranging from subtle physical, vital, mental, supramental. In Sri Aurobindo's theory, everything takes place in the midst of these planes, our life, our sleep, and our death. There is nowhere to go outside this. Life, death, sleep are simply stations of the consciousness amidst this same gradation.[45]

This proposition has been stated in all its simplicity by a contemporary student of Sri Aurobindo, Satprem. According to Satprem, when we are awake, we receive mental or vital vibrations, which are translated into certain symbols, certain ways of seeing or understanding or of living. This, of course, is self-evident. But Satprem says that when we are asleep or "dead," we receive the same symbols, other ways of seeing, understanding or living the same reality! Satprem suggests that to become aware of these various degrees of reality is then our fundamental task. He says: "And when we have done this work integrally, the lines of artificial demarcation which separate our diverse modes of living will crumble and we shall pass without break or without a gap in the consciousness from life to sleep to death. Or, more precisely, there will no longer be death or sleep as we understand it, but various ways of perceiving continuously the total Reality, and perhaps finally an integral consciousness which will perceive everything simultaneously. Our evolution is not over. Death is not a denial of life but a process of life."[46]

In one of his poems Sri Aurobindo puts it more succinctly:

I with repeated life death's sleep surprise;
I am a transcience of the eternities.

Sri Aurobindo returns to the subject again and again in his *Last Poems*. Thus defining man, he says:

A trifling unit in a boundless plan
Amidst the enormous insignificance
Of the unpeopled cosmos' fire-whirl dance,
Earth, as by accident engendered man.

A creature of his own grey ignorance
A mind half-shadow and half-gleam, a breath
That wrestles, captive in a world of death,
To live some lame brief years.

There is reference, earlier, to integral consciousness. Most people are not "integrated." It is usually one part of their being that functions most of the time, a tiny fraction of themselves. Man is constituted of an incongruous mass of mental, vital and other fragments which have an independent existence, on their particular planes. When one is asleep and the body is no longer under the tyranny of its mental mentor, these fragments turn "free" of man's true psychic center. According to Satprem, if all the fragments are not fully integrated, they have no recourse of re-precipitating themselves into the body for protection, when one is dead. And, he adds, the unintegrated fragments suffer much unpleasantness. However, he explains that the unpleasantness is suffered only by the lower fragments of our nature (here we may hark back to the Theosophists' explanation) corresponding to the navel and sex regions, the most difficult to integrate naturally, which are peopled by famished forces.

Satprem recounts the story of a young disciple at Sri Aurobindo's ashram in Pondicherry who, prematurely dead, had come to relate to his friend in sleep what had happened on the journey. He said: "Just behind your world there is no law and order. I had with me (the Master's) light and I crossed over."[47] Explains Satprem: "As the experience is typical of many deaths, perhaps it should be made clear that the meeting of the two friends took place in the higher vital regions (which correspond to the heart center), in the midst of those beautiful colored gardens which are often met with there and which constitute one of the innumerable so-called "paradises" of the other world—they are paradises which hang low. Generally, the disembodied one remains there as long as he wishes, then gets tired and goes to the place of true rest, into the original Light, with his soul awaiting the hour of return. To say that an individual goes to "eternal hell" is a cruel absurdity; how could the soul, the Light, ever be a prisoner of those low vibrations? As well say that the infra-red is master of the ultra-violet. The similar goes with the similar, always and everywhere, down here or elsewhere. And what could be "eternal," truly, except the soul, except joy?" And he quotes Sri Aurobindo as saying: "If there were an unending hell, it could only be a seat of unending rapture, for God is Joy, *Ananda* and than the eternity of His bliss there is no other eternity."[48]

Sri Aurobindo invites us to understand this in his *Last Poems.* Writing about the journey of the soul, he says:

> I made an assignation with the Night;
> In the abyss was fixed our rendezvous;
> In my breast carrying God's deathless light
> I came her dark and dangerous heart to woo.[49]

Then:

> Alone with God and silence
> Timeless it lived in Time;
> Life was His fugue of music,

Thought was Truth's ardent rhyme.

The Light was still around me
When I came back to earth
Bringing the Immortal's knowledge
Into man's cave of birth.

As would have been seen by now there is a common strain of thought, varied though its interpretation, in the Indian philosophical tradition and its approach to death. That tradition stretches from the Vedas to our own times and includes the teachings of the Upanishads, of the Buddha, Mahavira and the Tirthankaras, the interpretations of Sankara, Madhva and Ramanuja, the Theosophists and of Sri Aurobindo. There is a consistency in the approach to death as only a station in eternity that the soul must of necessity pass before reunion with the Godhead. This approach is sharply different from those of the great Semitic religions, Islam and Christianity and their predecessor, Judaism, which will be discussed later.

THE SOCRATIC CONCEPT: Death and the Nature of the Soul

Socrates, the Greek philosopher, was born in Athens circa 469 B.C. and died in 399 B.C. and came a hundred years after the Buddha. Considering that there was a great deal of intellectual traffic between the great civilizations of the times, there is no reason to doubt that Buddhist ideas traveled to the Greek city-states and that there was a two-way traffic between Greece and northern India. It comes as no surprise, then, that there is considerable similarity between Socratic concepts of the nature of the soul and its relationship to the body and those of Indian philosophers. The similarities, indeed, are striking. The views of Socrates come to us in the nature of a dialog[50] between the philosopher and his friends, especially Simmias and Cebes, in the account left to us by Plato. The dialog takes place on the day Socrates is to take poison, as decreed by the courts, and die. On hand are Phaidon, Apollodoros, Criton, Hermogenes, Epigenes, Aischenes and Antisthenes, Ctesippos the Paianian and Menexenos,

Simmian the Theban and Cebes and Phaidondes as also Eucleides and Terpsion from Megara. Socrates, it may be remembered, is in the shadow of death. His views were made known not in a theoretical context, but in the knowledge that in a few hours he would be no more. What he has to say, therefore, is all the more remarkable for its clarity and insight.

The conversation inevitably led to the purpose of philosophy, the meaning of death and the nature of the soul. The timing of the conversation could not have been more relevant as much to Socrates as to his listeners. Socrates held that those who tackle philosophy aright "are simply and solely practicing dying, practicing death, all the time, but nobody sees it." Death, Socrates contended, was nothing more than the separation of the soul from the body. After death, the body separated from the soul and the soul, separated from the body, existed by itself apart from the body. As Socrates saw it, the "true philosopher" should have as his concern not the body which was just a prison and a corrupting prison at that, but the soul which needed to be set free. The body was a hindrance and a poor companion for the philosopher in search of true wisdom, who was sensible in trying to keep aloof from it as far as was possible. The soul reasoned best when it was left undisturbed by the senses, sight or hearing, pleasure and pain, when, indeed, it was completely by itself and had no dealings of any kind whatsoever with the body. In the circumstances, the philosopher's soul held the body cheap and escaped from it while it sought to be by itself. We can hear echoes of Upanishadic wisdom in what Socrates says, especially in the stress he lays on controlling desires.

Desires, indeed, were the hurdles the philosopher had to cross in his quest for wisdom. The body, with its loves and hopes and fears provided a thousand distractions that kept interfering with the soul in its efforts to see the truth. There was no way a man could see anything "purely" except by getting rid of the body. Socrates is very clear on this point. Socrates strongly held that it is impossible for the soul, in company with the body, to know anything "purely." If this was acceptable as a proposition, then one thing of two followed: either knowledge is possible nowhere or only after death for then alone would the soul be quite by itself, unbound by the body and free to communicate with the Absolute.

Socrates conceded—if the elucidation of ideas in the course of a dialog can so be construed—that the philosopher, while still alive, can yet come nearest to knowing the truth, if, as far as possible, he held no commerce or communion with the body. What remains a mystery is why, having come so near to the truth about the distracting nature of the body, Socrates gave no further thought to the question of mastering the body, as did the Vedic philosophers. Socrates believed that once man was rid of the body's demands and was pure, he would probably be in the company of those like himself and know through his own self "complete incontamination."

The contempt for the body that Socrates held is the key to his own contempt for death. Death held no fear for him for the simple reason that he saw it for what he thought it to be: release from the body's bondage, for a chance to be free, pure, uncontaminated. Death provided the soul with a chance that life continually denied it: the chance to be alone, to collect itself together, to communicate with God. So we hear Socrates telling his friends that those who rightly loved wisdom, practiced dying and death to them was "the least terrible thing in the world." A man who fretted about death was not really a philosopher, but a philosoma, not a wisdom-lover, but a body-lover.

Socrates thought that when a man died, the soul departed, but it had "some power and sense." The souls of the dead went to Hades and were continually arriving there from this world. At the same time, souls already in Hades were returning to the world. This, said Socrates, confirmed his view that the living were born from the dead, no less than the dead from the living and that there seemed to be sufficient proof that the souls of the dead must of necessity exist somewhere, whence they are born again.

Socrates' conception that a man's learning was simply his recollection jibes with some of the theories propounded by

Theosophists and among others, by Cayce. Socrates held that what man learned in one life was just a recollection of what had been learned before in some past life. From this the presumption was that souls were immortal but returned to earth time and time again. Souls, besides, existed before they were in human shape, apart from bodies. When souls returned to earth they naturally had to function through bodies and that meant being controlled by the senses as well. Imprisoned as the soul was by the body, it was dragged by the body towards what was always changing; thus the soul went astray and was confused.

Socrates' understanding of what happens to the soul when a man dies is vivid; the body, the corpse, of course, properly dissolved and disappeared. But the soul, the "unseen" part of man, went to another place "noble and pure and unseen like itself," to the presence of the good and wise God. The soul did not perish when the body did. There was, however, the question of how pure the soul was. If it was pure when it separated from the body and was free of the blemishes one normally associates with the body, the soul could be said to have become truly free at last to be associated forever with the gods.

If, on the other hand, the soul left the body polluted and unpurified and contaminated with desires unfulfilled and pleasures unsatisfied, it was inevitably weighed down and was likely to cruise about restless among tombs and graves. Its destiny was to wander until such time it could once again enter into a body and carry on with the desires and pleasures of a life past. Gluttons went on to more gluttony and—here do we hear the echoes of the teachings of Mahavira?—likely, those who practiced gluttony and violence and drunkenness and did not take heed of their ways entered the bodies of asses and suchlike beasts. Those who indulged in injustice and tyranny entered the bodies of wolves and hawks and kites. "Or where else do we say they would go?" Socrates asked. Logic, he seemed to say, was on his side. In a sense, Socratic wisdom seems to be a compound of the wisdom of the Upanishads and of Jainism and Buddhism, but this can only be inferred; nowhere in the dialogs does Socrates refer to other philosophies and if he ever did, it is not so recorded. But as did the Buddha and the Vedic seers before him, Socrates, too, enjoined on men "who truly seek wisdom steadfastly" to abstain from all bodily desires and refuse to give themselves over to them. Here he is categorical. The body, in the final analysis, is the enemy to be shunned if not discarded. Socrates does not go to the extent of suggesting suicide as a way of escape for the soul. But he clearly states that the soul's aspirations to the higher wisdom suffer delimitation because of its imprisonment in the body. The body is an abomination and even so are the senses. And even as the Upanishads tell us to control our senses in order to obtain release from rebirth, Socrates conveys a similar admonition.

Yet while he is tantalizingly close to the Upanishadic seers in seeing the co-relationship between body, soul and rebirth, Socrates does not follow through with a methodology such as the Buddha suggested, for freeing the soul of its worldly attachments. In other words, Socratic diagnosis is credible, but Socratic prescription is incomplete.

That the diagnosis is on all fours with that made by his Vedic predecessors in another time and place is understandable. The soul was imprisoned in the body and welded to it and saw things through it and often, as a prisoner was chief helper of its own imprisonment. Each pleasure and pain was a nail and nailed the soul to the body and pinned it down to such an extent that the soul did not see itself as separate from the body, but compelled to adopt the ways of the body and grow on the same nourishment, often was identified with its vulgar component. It was thus deprived of its chance to hold communion with the divine.

Repeatedly Socrates suggests that the true philosopher should not oppose deliverance but should abstain from pleasures and desires and griefs as much as possible. That way alone led to the company of the gods. Socrates held that since the soul was immortal there was no getting away from the fact that it needed care and tending, not only during the time of life, but for all time. It just could not be neglected. And death certainly did not disoblige man of his responsibilities towards the soul. For if death were a release from everything, Socrates pointed out, a great blessing it would be for evil men to be rid of the body and their own wickedness along with the soul. For evil could not thus be easily gotten rid of. It accompanied the soul wherever it went. It was there with the soul when it went to Hades. Forever the soul was accompanied with its education and training, and rejoiced or suffered depending on the state of its purity.

As in other systems, Socrates, too, has his own concepts of what happens to the soul after a man dies. To the soul of each man, he says, a guardian spirit is allotted. When man dies and his spirit is released, the guardian spirit takes charge of it and leads it to a certain place where those gathered must first stand their trial and then pass on to the house of Hades under the guidance of the spirit. The guidance of the spirit was absolutely necessary as there were many "breaks and branches" on the road to Hades. The wise and decent soul had no difficulty making the journey to Hades where, in any event, it found itself in the company of like souls. But the unpurified soul suffered along the way and had to be dragged along unwillingly. But no soul stayed in Hades forever. The time came to each soul to return to the world, which it did, in due course.

Towards the end of his dialog with his friends Socrates gives a highly imaginative picture of the soul's journey to Hades, of the rivers it has to cross, like Acheron, the River of Pain, Pyriphlegethon, the River of Burning Fire, Stygian, the River of Hate and Cocytos, the River of Wailing. There were lakes, too, like Acherusian to which came the souls of the dead to remain there for certain ordained times and a chasm, Tartaros into which were cast those who had committed crimes of violence.

Socrates, however, is careful to point out that things may not happen exactly as he had described. No sensible man, he told his listeners, would think it proper to rely on things such as he had described, but then it was just possible that something along the lines he had suggested could happen to souls. Ever the pragmatist, Socrates was not going to demand that he be believed explicitly.

OSIRIS and His Forty Two Assessors

The Egyptians are said to be the first to recognize the doctrine of the future life, or, at least, to base the principles of human conduct on such a doctrine. As the ancient Egyptians conceived it, man descended into the tomb only to rise again. After his resurrection, he entered on a new life, in company with the sun, the principle of generation, the self-existent cause of all.

The soul of man was considered immortal like the sun and as accomplishing the same pilgrimages. The belief, however, was that all bodies descended into the lower world but they were not all automatically assured of resurrection. The deceased were judged by Osiris, the Great Teacher, and his forty two assessors.

Those judged guilty were annihilated; the righteous, purified of venial faults, entered into perfect happiness and, as the companions of Osiris, were fed by him with delicious food. Very obviously, in ancient Egypt, the availability of "delicious food" for the majority of the people was rare. Hence, obviously, the promise of that gastronomic fare to the good and the pure in a life after death. If there was nothing much to live for in this world, at least the good life gave assurance of something worthwhile in the next.

There was the further belief that there was a periodic rebirth amongst men of wise benefactors. In his *Treatise on Providence*, Synesius, one of the fathers of the Christian Church thus records the instructions received by Osiris: "Yet you must not think that the gods are without employment or that their descent to this earth is perpetual. For they descend according to orderly periods of time, for the purpose of imparting a beneficent impulse in the republics of mankind . . . . For there is indeed in the terrestrial abode the sacred tribe of heroes who pay attention to mankind, and who are able to give them assistance even in the smallest concerns . . . . This heroic tribe is, as it were, a colony from the gods established here in order that this terrene abode may not be left destitute of a better nature . . . . "

The concept of "the sacred tribe of heroes" paying attention to the better needs of mankind is, curiously enough, reflected in the Gita where Lord Krishna promises that the Lord will be reincarnated, time and time again for the succour of the good and the noble and the annihilation of the wicked and the evil.

ZOROASTRIANISM and the Concept of Future Rewards and Punishments

Zoroastrianism is considerably older than even Buddhism. Zoroaster or Zarathushtra was born in 628 B.C. and died in 551 B.C. and his teachings have come to us in *Zend Avesta*. Originally Zoroastrianism was a reformed type of Persian nature worship but dualism was strong. Ahura Mazdah headed the gods of goodness and Ahriman, the gods of evil. Wars between these two forces was the motive power of the universe, in which good will finally triumph.

The Zoroastrianism that has come down to us in the Bundehesh (composed probably towards the close of the fifth century, A.D.) holds that after a man's death the demons take possession of his body, but that, on the third day, consciousness returns. According to the Bundehesh,[51] for three nights after death, the soul waits near the head of the body, hoping to re-enter the body. On the third night after dawn, the souls of good men find sweet winds blowing toward them. The good soul is approached by a beautiful maiden—the *Din* (ethical symbol) evolved during a lifetime of good works—who leads it to the realm of bliss. The evil soul is met by an ugly woman who lead it to a treeless garden.

The good man is first led by the fair maiden to *setar-payak* (star paradise), then to *Mah-payak* (moon paradise) and at last to *Khurshid-payak* (sun paradise). The sinful soul is taken by the ugly woman to walk on sharp edges. Then the symbol of the soul's deeds assumes the form of a ferocious wild beast and the soul, in its attempt to flee from it, falls into hell. Those souls whose wicked deeds are equal to their virtuous deeds are taken to Hamistegan, a place said to resemble the earth. All souls have to pass the terrible bridge Chinevad. The good souls successfully pass it and entering the realm of bliss, join Ormuzd and the Amshaspands in their abode, where, seated on thrones of gold, they enjoy the society of beautiful fairies (*Hooran-i-Behisht*) and all manner of delights. The wicked fall over the bridge or are dragged down into the gulf of *duzakh* where they are tortured by the *daevas*. The duration of the punishment is fixed by Ormuzd and some are redeemed by the prayers and intercessions of their friends. Toward the end of the world, a prophet is to rise, who is to rid the earth of injustice and wickedness and usher in a reign of happiness—the Zoroastrian millennium, Ormuzd's kingdom of heaven.

The concept of a prophet rising to deliver final judgment squares with man's need for justice to be done. This is a time for friends and relatives to meet again to be judged before the prophet. After the joys of recognition comes the sadness of separation, when the good are separated from the evil, to whom grievous punishment is meted out. But that is not the end. A blazing comet falls on earth, igniting the world. Mountains melt and flow like liquid metal and in this all souls, good and bad alike, pass, coming out purified. Even Ahriman is changed and *duzakh* cleansed. Evil, thenceforth remains annihilated; mankind continues to live in the enjoyment of ineffable delights.

To the twentieth century student all this might sound highly imaginative, if not simplistic an understanding of what happens to the soul after death. Zoroastrianism has so few followers today that it is not even among the recognized great religions of the world which it ought to be, considering its impact on Judaism, Christianity and Islam.

The first and earliest impact was on Judaism at the time of the second Isaiah. Zoroastrianism talked about the war between the two great cosmic forces, that of light and darkness, good and evil. But no sooner did the dualism of Zoroastrianism come to the attention of Jewish leaders than they countered it with their own monism: "I am the Lord and none else, that forms light and creates darkness, makes peace and creates evil. I am the Lord that does all this" (45:6-7).[52]

But there were ways that Zoroastrianism crept into Judaism as in the notions of the resurrection of the dead and the Last Judgment. Could it be that the notions of God and Satan were also borrowed from Zoroaster? Judaism is not entirely free of dualism, for toward the end of the Law of Moses we find this summing up: "See, I have set before you this day life and good, death and evil. If you obey the commandments of the Lord your God which I command you this day, by loving the Lord your God, by walking in his ways, and by keeping his commandments and his statutes and his ordinances, then you shall live and multiply . . . . But if your heart turns away, and you will not hear, but are drawn away to worship other gods and serve them, I declare to you this day that you shall perish . . . . I call heaven and earth to witness against you this day, that I have set before you life and death, blessing and curse; therefore choose life . . . . " (Deuteronomy 30: 15-19).

The theme was taken up in a different form in Christianity and Islam, the other two Semitic religions. The central concern of the Gospels, it may be remembered, is with salvation and the basic question of what one must do to be saved. The Devil—just another word for the force of Zoroastrian darkness, Ahriman—is a far more powerful figure in Christianity than Satan is in the Old Testament. In that sense, the dualism of Zoroastrianism gets transfigured into the dualism of Christianity much more effectively than would have been thought possible. As Walter Kaufmann has said: "The position of the Christian is even worse than most Christian writers on this subject realize: there is yet the doctrine of hell and damnation."[53]

As for the influence of Zoroastrianism on Islam, one has only to read the Koranic concept of what happens to the soul after death which is described in the most awesome terms. "When the sun shall be folded up and the stars shall fall and when the mountains shall be set in motion . . . . and the sea shall boil . . . . then shall every soul know what it hath done" (lxxxi). Or again, "On that day of judgment each individual will be accountable for the way he has lived. Every man's actions have we hung round his neck and on the last day shall be laid before him a wide-open book" (xvll:13). Powerful ideas do not fade away. They merely get transmuted into others.

THE THREE GREAT SEMITIC RELIGIONS: Judaism, Christianity and Islam

We may now examine how the three great Semitic religions, Judaism, Christianity and Islam deal with the issue of death and thereafter. Of the three, Judaism is the oldest and Islam the most recent in terms of chronology. They have their similarities and their profound dissimilarities and yet, in regard to certain aspects they show their debt to a common tradition.

Easily the most remarkable aspect of Judaism is its influence on Western thought. In terms of time span, Judaism itself is a comparative newcomer. By 3000 B.C. Egypt already had its pyramids and Sumer and Aked were world empires. By 1400 Phoenicia was colonizing. During all this time the Jews were minor tribes of no consequence. And yet they have left their mark on civilization as no other body of people has or is ever likely to have.

One reason was the basic monotheism of the Jewish people at a time when the peoples of the then civilized world were pantheistic. "Hear, O Israel, the Lord our God, the Lord is One."[54] That was a bold assertion to make. When other people could think of the Sun God and the Moon God and the Rain God, the Jews were claiming that there was only one God and that it was that God who made everything else. "The heavens declare the glory of God; and the firmament showeth his handiwork."

The Jewish God, the only One, Yahweh, again, was different from gods conceived by other cultures, such as the Hellenic. Yahweh was just and righteous—and not amoral. With such a God as an anchor, Jewish philosophers could then adjust their concepts of individual souls and their relationship to Yahweh. One of the earliest such philosophers was Leone Modena, a late Renaissance figure in Venice (1571-1648) and a noted Rabbi.

Writing in his *Shaagat Arya* (The Lion's Roar) Modena

said that when man contemplated his present existence, reason inclined him—if it did not altogether compel him—to believe that the soul continued on after his physical death.[55]

This belief, he claimed, was logical. Nature did nothing in vain. If then nature implanted in the human mind a desire for eternal life that was not realized in the life of the body, surely there was cause to believe that the soul continued to exist after death?

Then there was the evidence from the increase in our mental powers at the very time when old age brought with it a weakening of the body. If the connection between body and mind were absolute rather than incidental, we should have expected the opposite to be true: the mind becoming weaker in proportion to the body's enfeeblement. Furthermore, argued Modena, what he considered to be the decisive proof that the soul continued after man's death was derived from the basic assumption that man is *sui generis*, neither like the angels nor like the beasts. Man was created for the purpose of giving God pleasure by his wide range of intelligent actions. Modena's argument is that man, *homo sapiens*, who by dint of his intellect, built cities, moved mountains, changed the course of rivers, knew the path of the stars in the skies and recognized his God, cannot just come in the end to perish like a mere animal. He had to have a different destiny.

For if there was nothing more to a man's death than his physical extinction, what could be said for man's consciousness? Animals were not troubled by it. They lived for the actual experience of the moment. They were not troubled by thoughts of life and death. But man's consciousness, on the other hand, increased his pains by anticipating troubles yet to come and dwelling on those already present. In this he was unique among all life on earth. His anticipation of trouble was more painful at times than the actual trouble. The trouble of death was the thought of it before it came.

Modena concluded that man, in the circumstances, must have a soul, that God, having joined the soul to the body took pleasure in, or abhorred, man's deeds and bestowed His rewards or punishments accordingly. And to do so, it was imperative that the Creator make it possible for a man at his death to have his soul separated from the body, so that the former could remain to receive the pleasure or the pain of which, in his lifetimes, the man was judged deserving in accordance with his deeds.

So much about what could happen to the soul after man dies. What is the Judaic conception of the creation of man? According to Moses Maimonides, the religious philosopher, talmudist and mystic of the thirteenth century, God created man *ex nihilo* (out of nothing) only on the first day and that from then on He used the elements (which He had also created on the first day) for the continuance of man.[56] Out of the earth came forth the material elements to make up the body of man, except that God blew "the soul of life" into his nostrils.

In the circumstances, man's soul did not originate in the material elements of his body, as is the case of all lower living creatures. Nor was it even a substance evolved from the Separate Intelligences. Man's powers of learning and understanding came directly from God. Man was created for the prime purpose that he recognize his Creator.

Both the Talmud and the Midrash record popular tales about the Angel of Night and Conception and the dramatic story of the soul has been compiled in *Midrash Yetzirat ha-Velad* (The Midrash of the Creation of the Child).[57] It recounts how a child receives a soul.

It is the time when a man approaches his wife. At that instant, the Holy One summons His messenger in charge of pregnancy and asks him to get the man's seed. This brought, the Holy One determines at once whether it shall be male or female, tall or short, strong or weak, foolish or wise, rich or poor. In fact at that moment, the Holy One determines the seed's future, except whether it would be just or wicked. That is left to it.

Having determined the seed's future, the Holy One summons His messenger who holds sway over souls to bring Him a soul which is now enjoined to enter the seed. Here, there is reluctance on the part of the soul to do as it is bid. The soul claims that it is holy and pure and quite content where it is and does not want abode in a mortal seed. The Holy One, however, is insistent and informs the soul that it was created, in the first place, for mortal seed. The soul has no alternative but to obey the Holy One's instructions. The soul is then asked to enter the womb of the mother where a light is kindled over it.

The next day the messenger returns to lead the soul first into the Garden of Eden where those who in their previous lives had all obeyed the laws and ordinances of the Holy One, now dwelt in glory and informs it of its destiny if it also obeyed the Holy One's laws.

The soul is also shown a place where souls that in past lives had erred and sinned and broken the Holy One's commandments were in deep agony. The moral is clearly drawn: the soul had a choice. It could live a saintly life and be rewarded or it could live a life of sin and pay for it.

The messenger then leads the soul from morning till night to all the places it will futurely dwell in as also its final resting place, awhile showing it the world of the good and the evil. At nightfall the messenger returns the soul to the womb of the mother. There the child stays for nine months.

Now comes the time for the child to emerge and the messenger visits it with summons to emerge from the womb but once again the soul is unwilling to do so. It is comfortable where it is. Once again the messenger has to cajole the soul to obey the summons.

So the child is born, crying. As it issues forth, the messenger strikes it under its nose and extinguishes the light that shone over its head. The soul now forgets its past. Meanwhile, the messenger parades before the child its life to come in full detail. The child sees itself as a toddler, an adolescent, youth, householder and finally as the decrepit old figure awaiting death.

JUDAISM and the Doctrine of Free Will

Biblical laws and the call to "choose life" (Deut. 30:19)

tacitly presuppose man's free will. The prophets postulate man's moral responsibility, implying his freedom. There is no talk of karma; every time a child is born, it is born with a brand new soul, not a soul "recycled" as it were, to continue as a result of past karma. The Talmud is explicit: "Everything is in the hand of Heaven, except the fear of Heaven" (Berakhot 33b) the latter being in the realm of human decision and action. Divine omniscience is assumed, but no attempt is made to resolve the contradiction between freedom of will and divine foreknowledge.

In fact, Saadia Gaon, one of the Medieval Jewish philosophers maintained God's full knowledge of events, including those in the future, but denied that this knowledge is the cause of human action. Man was free; he began on a new slate when he was born, with no past karma clinging to him, but what he would do, how he would end, all these were known to God before hand and God would do nothing to stop or encourage his actions. According to Saadia, freedom of will was among the three central teachings of Judaism, the others being God and immortality.

However, Gersonides (13th - 14th century) who accepted natural causality as the principle regulating the affairs of the world, had no difficulty separating divine foreknowledge from the realms of human action. But the soundest Judaic statement on the issue is conceded to be the one put out by Moses Maimonides, author of *Guide to the Perplexed*. In his *Mishneh Torah*, Maimonides noted that free will was bestowed on every human being.[58] If he desired to turn towards the good path and be just, man had the power and the free will to do so. If he wished, instead, to turn toward the path of evil and be wicked, then, too, he was at liberty to do so. The Holy One did not decree one way or another on what a given individual should be when he took birth. There was no one that coerced him into either the path of goodness or of evil. Every person turned to the way he desired, with the free consent of his own mind and of his own volition. Accordingly it followed that it was the sinner who inflicted the harm on himself—not an outside agency.

Maimonides argued that if God had decreed that a person

should be either just or wicked, or if there were some force inherent in his nature which irresistably drew him to a particular course, or to any branch of knowledge, as to a given view or activity, how would God have charged men through the prophets: "Do this and do not do that, improve your ways, do not follow your wicked impulses?" Furthermore, if, from the very beginning, man's destiny had already been decreed or his innate constitution drew him to that from which he could set himself free, what room would there be for the whole of the Torah? By what right could God punish the wicked or reward the just, if He Himself had decreed that wicked should be wicked and the just, just?

So this is how Maimonides saw the situation: man was born with a free will. He could exercise it whichever way he liked. But God knew beforehand what man would do, but would not interfere. It was in man's hands to be good or evil; the choice was his and there was no coercion, one way or the other. Man was judged according to his deeds which he committed of his own volition, guided by his own mind and with no direction from God.

MAN CAN CONTROL HIS PASSIONS and Be a Force for Good

Maimonides held that transient bodies are only subject to destruction through their substance and not through their form; nor, he maintained, can the essence of their form be destroyed. Form could only be destroyed accidentally, i.e., on account of its connection with substance, the true nature of which consisted in the property of never being without a disposition to receive form.

That was the reason why no form remained permanently in a substance; a constant change took place, one form was taken off and another was put on. The same was the case with matter. Whatever form it had, it was disposed to receive another form; it never left off moving and casting off the form it had in order to receive another.

The same took place when this second form was received. It was therefore clear that all corruption, destruction or defect came from matter. Thus, man's deformities, weaknesses or disorder of his actions, whether innate or not, originated in the transient substance, not in the form. All other living beings likewise died or became ill through the substance of the body and not through its form.

The knowledge of God, the formation of ideas, the mastery of desire and passion, the distinction between that which is to be chosen and that which is to be rejected, all these man owed to form. But eating, drinking, sexual intercourse, excessive lust, passion and all vices had their origin in the substance of the body. It was impossible, according to the wisdom of God, that substance should exist without form, but then, the Creator gave the form of man, power, rule and dominion over the substance: the form could subdue the substance, refuse the fulfillment of its desires, and reduce them, as far as possible, to a just and proper measure. The station of man varied according to the exercise of this power.

Intelligent persons, said Maimonides, must, as much as possible, reduce wants, guard against them, feel grieved when satisfying them, abstain from speaking of them, discussing them and attending to them in company with others. Man's aim must be the aim of man as man, viz., the formation of ideas and nothing else. Such men were always with God.

This is a highly puritanic approach to what a man should be and how he should disport himself. Maimonides does not lay down an elaborate system for the control of desire and passion. In insisting that wants, etc., must be reduced "as much as possible," he even concedes that there are limits to what can be expected of human beings. He does not demand the impossible. At that same time he makes a clear distinction between matter and form, substance and form. Matter and substance were subject to deterioration and destruction and had nothing whatever to do with form. Form continued.

Furthermore, there is no question here of explaining man's present ills to the aftereffects of a previous birth and the carryover of *samskara*. The numerous evils to which individual persons were exposed were due to the defects existing in the persons themselves. Men complained and sought relief from their own faults. They suffered from the evils which they, by their own free will, inflicted on themselves and ascribed them to God, who was far from being connected with them.

Man, in the circumstances has no alibi. He is the captain of his fate and the master of his soul. If his life is wrecked he has no one but himself to blame; and he is warned sufficiently in advance by the messenger of the Holy One.

THE PURPOSE OF CREATION and the Relevance of Man

Intelligent persons, concedes Maimonides—and well he might—are much perplexed when they inquire into the purpose of the creation. We know creation; what could be its object? The question, asserts Maimonides, is absurd. The question: "What is the purpose thereof?" cannot be asked about anything which is not the product of an agent.[59] Therefore, we cannot ask what is the purpose of the existence of God.

God, in the first place, Himself was not created. We seek a purpose only for things produced intentionally by an intelligent cause; that is to say, a final cause must exist for everything that owes its existence to an intelligent being. But for that which is without a beginning, a final cause need not be sought, and, in the circumstances, there can be no occasion to seek the final cause of the whole universe. Maimonides, however, is clearer about the purpose for the existence of every species. He approvingly quotes Aristotle to indicate that the ultimate purpose of the genera is the preservation of the course of genesis and destruction, for the production of the best and the most perfect being formed of matter "because the ultimate purpose is to arrive at perfection." In this regard Maimonides antedates both Darwin and Sri Aurobindo by centuries.

So one answer to the question of why the universe has been created is that it was created for the sole purpose of enabling man to reach perfection, that he might serve God. But what could be the end of serving God? He did not become more perfect even if all His creatures served Him and comprehended Him. Could it be then that the service of God was not intended for God's perfection, but for the perfection of man himself?

The question, of course, could also be asked: what was the purpose of man being perfect? Maimonides quickly gets out of this impasse by suggesting that "we must in continuing the enquiry as to the purpose of the creation at last arrive at the answer: it was the Will of God, or His wisdom decreed it." That, he adds somewhat unconvincingly, is the correct answer.

Though Maimonides may not lay down an elaborate system of yoga for the perfection of the body and thereafter of the soul, both of which, he holds, are objects of the Law, he is clear that perfection is not only desirable, but possible. Perfection of the body was possible when man had all his wants supplied, like food and shelter; this, in turn, was possible only in organized society. So man had a duty to society.

The second perfection of man consisted in his becoming an actually intelligent being. But this second and superior kind of perfection could only be attained when the first—bodily—perfection had been acquired. A person suffering from great hunger, thirst, heat or cold could hardly be expected to grasp an idea, even if communicated by others, much less could he arrive at it by his own reasoning. But when a man was in possession of the first perfection, then he might possibly acquire the second perfection which was undoubtedly of a superior kind and was alone the source of eternal life. But how was one to attain the second perfection, granted that he had attained the first?

Maimonides prescribed that man must turn his thoughts away from everything while he read *Shema* or during the *Tefillah* and not content himself merely with being devout. Having successfully practiced that for many years the individual should try, in reading the Law or listening to it, to have all his heart and thought occupied with understanding what he was reading or listening to. In other words he had to learn to concentrate.

The third step was for the individual to accustom himself to empty his mind of all extraneous thoughts and to direct attention exclusively to the perception and understanding of what he was uttering. Finally it became the individual at all times of solitude to indulge in nothing but the intellectual worship of God. Maimonides asserted that Divine Providence was constantly watching over those who had obtained that blessing which was prepared for those who endeavored to obtain it. If man freed his thoughts from worldly matters, obtained a knowledge of God in the right way, and rejoiced in that knowledge, it was impossible that any kind of evil should befall him while he was with God and God was with him.

Maimonides' final words of exhortation are some of the most beautiful: "God is near to all who call Him, if they call Him in truth and turn to Him. He is found by every one who seeks Him, if he always goes toward Him and never goes astray. Amen."

JEWISH ATTITUDE TOWARD DEATH

The Jewish attitude towards life is reflected in the attitude towards death. Both come from God and therefore, both are reaffirmed as good. As life is lived in the consciousness of the Divine Presence, so the Jew hopes to die in full consciousness of the divine. He prays in life to express his communion with God and so he prays when death approaches and dies with the affirmation of God on his lips. His body is returned to dust, but death and destruction are transcended in the glorification of God and the vision of a perfect world.

Take, for example, the death of Eleazor whose speech to the defendants of Masada Fort has something deeply moving and profoundly liberating about it.[60] When Rome conquered Judaea and Jerusalem fell (A.D. 70) there still remained three fortresses, strongly defended by the Jewish rebels, to be taken over. The last of them, defended by Eleazor, stubbornly resisted the concentrated Roman attack. But as it became clear that defense was no longer possible, Eleazor and his men resolved never to serve the Romans nor any master other than God and unable to offer further resistance, decided to commit mass suicide. Some of his men were ready to follow Eleazor, others, moved by emotions too powerful to be easily overcome, not. Eleazor renewed his proposal for mass death in a second speech, recorded by Flavius Josephus, in the seventh book of his *The Jewish War*.

Eleazor argued that it was death that sets the soul at liberty and permits it to depart to its "proper and pure" abode, where it will be free from every misery. But as long as it was imprisoned in a mortal body and infected with its pains, it was, so to speak, truly dead. Association with what was mortal did not befit what was divine. It was only when the soul was freed from the body that it assumed its proper sphere and enjoyed a blessed strength and a power wholly unrestricted, even though, like God Himself, it remained invisible to human eyes.

Eleazor pointed out that the soul was not seen when it was in the body which it entered unperceived and unseen. The soul was one and uncorruptible though what it touched, lived and flourished, whatever it was removed from, withered and died. So much was there in it of immortality. Eleazor then referred to sleep, during which the soul "converses with God because of its relationship to Him" and gave—amazingly enough!—a discourse on the Indian view of death as the release of the soul from the body. "Should we hold baser notions than the Indians?" he asked. He continued: "But even had we from the first been educated in opposite principles and taught that to live is the supreme good and death a calamity, the occasion still is one that calls upon us to bear death cheerfully, since we die by the will of God and out of necessity."

There are other stories about what should be considered a truly Jewish approach towards death.[61] There is thus the story of Rabbi Susya who lived up to a great age. For seven years before his death, he was bedridden and in pain, in atonement, it was said, for the sins of Israel. His gravestone is inscribed: "Here lieth he who served God in love, rejoiced in pain and turned many away from guilt." Just before he died, Rabbi Shneur Zalman of Ladi asked his grandson: "Dost thou see aught?" The grandson looked at the rabbi in surprise. Thereupon the dying man said: "I see as yet only the Divine Nothing that gives life to the universe."

When Rabbi Bunam was lying on his deathbed, his wife wept bitterly. Thereupon he said: "Why dost thou weep? All my life has been given me merely that I might learn to die."

In the hour of his death, the Baal Shem said: "Now I know the purpose for which I was created."

There is here no fear of death. Death is not considered a calamity to be shunned or to be afraid of. Death liberates the soul and there is the promise of the life eternal. "Exalted and sanctified be His great name" says the *Kaddish,* the Jewish prayer for the dead, "in the world that is to be created anew where He will quicken the dead and raise them up unto life eternal." The *Kaddish* was originally intended as a closing prayer at study sessions but because of its reference to the "quickening of the dead" and to life eternal, has become part of the burial liturgy. It summons peace from heaven for the dead and the living.

ISLAM and the Idea of a Future Life

Islam was born in the deserts of Arabia, where water is scarce, where any vegetation is a source of delight and a well-watered garden can indeed be considered something close to paradise. If, therefore, paradise is indeed described in these terms, it should come as no surprise. Islamic scholars have often warned against taking some of the Koranic descriptions too literally. The Prophet, it is well to remember, had to address himself not only to the advanced minds of a few idealistic thinkers of his age, but to the wide world around him engrossed in materialism of every type. He had to adapt himself to the comprehensions of all and not only of the elite of his times.

For the world in which Muhammad, the Prophet, was born was barbaric. Starved of material possessions, bereft of any intellectual direction, the Bedouin of the desert followed what might be described as a religion of animistic polytheism that did not provide him with any spiritual anchor. In the sixth century A.D., life in Arabia's leading city, Mecca, was anything but serene.

Drunken orgies were common, bloodshed an everyday affair and at nights, dancing girls flitted from tent to tent inflaming the passions of the nomads. It was this world that Muhammad set out to instruct and to reach. He had to speak the emotional language of the people to capture their hearts.

If, therefore, Islam speaks of paradise in visual terms, it has to be understood in the context of the day. As one scholar, Ameer Ali has stated: "To the wild famished Arab, what was more grateful, or what more consonant to his ideas of paradise than rivers of unsullied incorruptible water, or of milk and honey? Or anything more acceptable than unlimited fruit, luxuriant vegetation, inexhaustible fertility? He could conceive of no bliss unaccompanied with these sensuous pleasures. This is the contention of that portion of the Moslem world which, like Sanai and Ghazzali, holds that behind the descriptions of beautiful mansions with fairy attendants, lies a deeper meaning; and that the joy of joys is to consist in the beatific visions of the soul in the presence of the Almighty, when the veil which divided man from his Creator will be rent and heavenly glory revealed to the mind untrammelled by its corporeal, earthly habiliments."[62]

But the concept of paradise is the least of the Islamic concept of what follows after death. The chief and predominant idea of Islam respecting a future life is founded, according to Syed Ameer Ali, upon the belief that, in a state of existence hereafter, every human being will have to render an account of his or her actions on earth and that the happiness or misery of individuals will depend upon the manner in which they have performed the behests of their Creator.

On the day of the resurrection, when "all shall return to your Lord" as says the Koran, there is no escape. "On that day man shall be informed of all that he has done and all that he has failed to do. He shall become his own witness; his pleas shall go unheeded." And the sinner will pay the penalty for his sins.

And yet the mercy of Allah and his grace are unbounded and are to be bestowed alike upon His creatures. "By the light of the day, and by the fall of night, your Lord has not forsaken you, nor does He abhor you. The life to come holds a richer prize for you than this present life. You shall be gratified with what your Lord will give you," says the Koran. Elsewhere it says: "O thou soul which art at rest, return unto thy Lord, pleased and pleasing Him, enter thou among my servants and enter thou my garden of felicity." According to Ameer Ali, this is the pivot on which the whole doctrine of future life in Islam turns and "this is the only doctrinal point one is required to believe and accept."

This is upheld by the words of the Koran as well as the authentic sayings of the Prophet. "The most favored of God" said the Prophet, "will be he who shall see his Lord's face (glory) night and morning, a felicity which will surpass all the pleasures of the body, as the ocean surpasses a drop of sweat."

IQBAL'S THEORY: Koranic View of the Destiny of Man

The Koranic view of the destiny of man, according to Sir Mohammad Iqbal, the poet-philosopher, is partly ethical, partly biological. The Koran, for instance, mentions the fact of *Barzakh*, a state, perhaps, of some kind of suspension between death and resurrection. Resurrection, too, appears to have been differently conceived, says Iqbal. Thus, the Koran does not base its possibility, like Christianity, on the evidence of the actual resurrection of an historic person. On the contrary, it seems to take and argue resurrection as a universal phenomenon of life, in some sense true even of birds and animals (6:38). Iqbal calls attention to three things which he argues are perfectly clear from the Koran and regarding which there is, or ought to be, no difference of opinion.[63]
1) That the ego has a beginning in time and did not pre-exist its emergence in the spatio-temporal order.
2) That there is no possibility of return to this earth.
3) That finitude is no misfortune.

Point No. 2 surely is clear from these verses:
When death overtaketh one of them, he saith: "Lord! send me back again that I may do the good that I have left undone!"

> By no means. These are the very words which he shall speak. But behind them is a barrier *(Barzakh) until the day when they shall be raised again.* (23: 101, 102).
>
> And by the moon when at her full, that from state to state shall ye be surely carried forward. (84:19).
>
> The germs of life—is it ye who created them? Or are we their Creator? It is We who have decreed that death shall be among you; yet are we not thereby hindered from replacing you with others, your likes, *or from creating you again in forms which ye know not?* (56:59-61).

Point No. 3 is evident in the following verse:

> Verily there is none in the heavens and in the earth but shall approach the God of Mercy as a servant. He hath taken note of them and remembered them with exact numbering: *and each of them shall come to Him on the day of Resurrection as a single individual."* (19:95,96).

It is clear from this that the Koran has a definite understanding of the meaning of salvation. It is with irreplaceable singleness of individuality that the finite ego will approach the infinite ego to see for himself the consequences of his past action and to judge the possibilities of his future.

> And every man's fate have We fastened about his neck; and on the day of Resurrection will We bring forthwith to him a book which shall be proffered to him wide open: "Read thy book: there needeth none but thyself to make out an account against thee this day." (17:14).

Thus, argues Iqbal, whatever may be the final fate of man, it does not mean the loss of individuality. The Koran, he says, does not contemplate complete liberation from finitude as the highest state of human bliss. The "unceasing reward" of man consists in his gradual growth in self-possession, in uniqueness and intensity of his activity as an ego. Even the scene of "Universal Destruction" immediately preceding the Day of Judgment cannot affect the perfect calm of a full-grown ego, as the following verse would testify:

> And there shall be a blast on the trumpet, and all who are in the heavens and all who are in the earth shall faint away, *save those in whose case God wills otherwise.* (39:69).

Iqbal says that the subject of this exception can only be those in whom the ego has reached the very highest point of intensity. And the climax of this development is reached when the ego is able to retain full self-possession, even in the case of a direct contact with the all-embracing Ego; such was the case of the Prophet's own vision of the Ultimate Ego:

"His eye turned not aside, nor did it wander" (53:17). That, notes Iqbal, is "the ideal of perfect manhood in Islam" and nowhere, he adds, has it found a better literary expression than in a Persian verse which speaks of the Holy Prophet's experience of divine illumination:

> Moses fainted away by a mere surface illumination of Reality:
> Thou seest the very substance of Reality with a smile!"

Iqbal dismisses the theory of the materialists that man is a creature of chance and necessity and that, when he dies, that is the end of him. "It is highly improbable" he notes, "that a being whose evolution has taken millions of years should be thrown away as a thing of no use." What, then, is man's relevance? Iqbal argues that it is only as an ever-growing ego that man can belong to the meaning of the universe. Says the Koran:

> By the soul and He who hath balanced it, and hath shown to it the ways of wickedness and piety, blessed is he who hath made it grow and undone is he who hath corrupted it. (91: 7–10).

It is interesting to consider that Iqbal thinks it is natural and perfectly consistent with the spirit of the Koran to regard the question of immortality as one of biological evolution. Rumi, it may be remembered, wrote how first man appeared in the class of inorganic things and passed therefrom into that of plants, animals and such like until the great Creator "drew man out of the animal into the human state."

> Thus (writes Rumi) man passed from one order of nature to another
> Till he became wise and knowing and strong as he is now.

One may compare this with Jain philosophy which believes that even inanimate objects have a soul and with Hinduism which speaks of 8,400,000 graded kinds of births culminating in man (*Brihad Vishnu Purana*).[64] Greek and Roman writers, too, have written about thousand-year periods of transmigration into plants, animals, and defective human beings, prior to rebirth in a human body free from karmic blemishes.

Muslim philosophers and theologians, however, have expressed divergence of opinion as to whether the re-emergence of man involves the re-emergence of his former physical medium. Most of them, including Shah Wali Ullah, the last great theologian of Islam are inclined to think that it does involve at least some kind of physical medium suitable to the ego's new environment.

ISLAMIC CONCEPTS OF HEAVEN AND HELL

In Islam God gives man the freedom to choose his own ways. In this regard Islam is like Judaism; man cannot blame God for his misfortunes. He is a free entity to make his own mistakes. On the other hand, God is to be adored for He is full of mercy and compassion. The very first *sura* in the Koran begins with *hamd*, adoration. God is not awesome and terrifying.

Neither is God one who arbitrarily dispenses with rewards and punishment. Man creates his own reward and punishment. If man on the basis of knowledge and understanding of himself and his environment finds the "straight path of rectitude" he merits suitable award. According to the Koran, the ego's re-emergence brings him a "sharp sight" (50:21) whereby he clearly sees his self-built "fate fastened round his neck." There is no such thing as heaven and hell. Heaven and hell, asserts Iqbal, "are states, not localities." [65] Their descriptions in the Koran are visual representations of an inner fact, i.e., character. Hell in the words of the Koran is "God's kindled fire which mounts above the hearts"—the painful realization of one's failure as a man and heaven, by contrast, is the joy of triumph over the forces of disintegration.

But hell and heaven are not everlasting. They are time-limited. In Islam there is no such thing as eternal damnation. There is a good deal of similarity between the Koranic and Judaic conceptions of what happens to the dead. There is a Day of Resurrection when the dead shall be judged. There is the sound of trumpet; the world lies shattered. Each individual will be asked to account for himself. The righteous will be upheld, the unrighteous destroyed. The similarity between "The Day of Judgment" and "The Victory of the Righteous" described in the Book of Enoch and the chapters in the Koran entitled "The Inevitable" and "That Which is Coming" is too striking to go unnoticed. In Islam, the righteous are those who follow the five basic duties to God which are known as the pillars *(arkan)* of Islam.[66] The first is *Iman*, (faith) which is essential for salvation *(najat)* in the next world, the second, *salat* (prayer), which is the most important of all duties to God, next only to *Iman* and in the words of the Prophet is the point of distinction *(al-fariq)* between faith and disbelief, the third is *Zakat* (charity), the fourth *Sawm* (fasting) and the last, *Hajj* (the pilgrimage to Mecca).

But not all right actions are *salih*. A *salih* action is that which merits reward by God in the life hereafter. There are two necessary conditions of a *salih* action. First, it should conform to the rules laid down in the Koran and second, it should be done with a view to pleasing God. Faith is therefore an essential condition for a *salih* act. Devoid of that, an act may be right, but not *salih*:[67]

While similarities can be stretched too far, the stress on right action, however it is defined, is also reminiscent of Buddhism. Islam, like Buddhism, again lays stress on the moral aspects of life. Also, while there is a place for healthy asceticism in Islamic ethic, it does not make renunciation of desires or reduction of material needs an end in itself. Islam never makes too much of anything: the secret of righteous living lies in avoiding the extremes, in choosing, as it were, the Middle Path. Worldly goods are not to be shunned: rather, they are to be shared, whence the emphasis on charity. The Islamic list of the things which are good is very comprehensive. Life, comfort, friendship, social intercourse, remembrance of Allah and his worship, pleasure and satisfaction are all explicitly mentioned in the Koran. They are not things to be ashamed of, but wonders to be enjoyed, though they are not all equally valuable but have a definite scale of preference among them.

Duties to other fellow human beings are as important in Islam as religious duties.

SUFISM and the Mystics of Islam

As in other religions, so in Islam, there is a strong strain of mysticism which is nothing more than the eternal yearning of the human soul to have direct experience of the Ultimate Reality.

Mysticism, it has been said, has no genealogy; its roots are in all religions. The Prophet defined *ahsan* (the earliest term used for mystic experience in the Traditions of the Prophet) as follows: "You pray God in a way that you have a feeling that you are looking at Him; if that be not possible, then you feel as if He is looking at you." No better explanation is possible.

Whether extraneous influences inspired the mystical movement in Islam or not—the beginnings of the movement can be traced back to the Koran itself—the fact remains that it has had a profound impact on the religion itself. The two bedrocks on which the entire structure of mystic ideology in Islam rests are love of God and personal contact with Him.

Of the mystic cult of love Sufism, described as "the apprehension of divine realities" is best known around the world. Islamic mystics are fond of calling themselves *Ahl- al-Haqq*—the followers of the Real. What is the Real that we must learn to follow? Allah is the One Reality. Seventy thousand veils separate Allah from the world of matter and of sense. When a child is born, the soul is imprisoned in his body, separated from Allah by the thick curtains. The whole purpose of Sufism is to give the soul an escape from this prison, a recovery of the original unity with the One, while still in the body. The body is not to be put off; it is to be refined and made spiritual—a help and not a hindrance to the spirit.

In some ways the Sufi conception of the passing away *(fana)* of individual self in Universal Being is almost Upanishadic. But *fana* is not the same as *nirvana*, though both terms imply the passing away of individuality. *Fana* is accompanied by *baqa*—everlasting life in God. *Fana* involves the extinction of all passions and desires—the holding back of the senses, as it were, advocated by the Upanishads. Indeed, Sufism has been described in such terms as, it is wholly self-discipline, it is to possess nothing and to be possessed by nothing, it is the control of the faculties and observation of the breaths.

Sufism, like the Upanishads, calls for the giving up of desire as a means to attain God. This calls for the eradication of self-will. The story is told of the dervish (the Sufi mendicant) who fell into the Tigris. Seeing that he could not swim, a man on the brink called out: "Shall I call on someone to help you?"

"No" said the dervish.

"Then do you wish to be drowned?"

"No."

"What, then, do you wish?"

The dervish replied: "God's will be done! What have I to do with wishing?" To attain *fana*, certain steps are prescribed, even as they are in Raja Yoga. The first step is a moral transformation of the soul through the extinction of all its passions and desires. The second step is a mental abstraction or passing away of the mind from all objects of perception, thoughts, actions and feelings through its concentration upon the thoughts of God. (Here, the thought of God signifies contemplation of the divine attributes). The third step is the cessation of all conscious thought. The highest stage of *fana* is reached when even the consciousness of having attained *fana* disappears. This is what the Sufis call "the passing away of the passing away" (*fana al-fana*). The mystic, who like the Hindu in *samadhi*, is now rapt in contemplation of the divine essence. The final stage of *fana*, the complete passing away from self, forms the prelude to *baqa* which is continuance or "abiding" in God. The Sufi who seeks the goal of union with ultimate Reality (*fana'l-Haqq*) calls himself a traveler (*salik*) and advances by slow "stages" (*maqamat*) along a path (*tariqat*) to his final goal. The stages bear a resemblance to those prescribed in Raja Yoga.

There are seven stages to the ultimate goal: repentance, abstinence, renunciation, poverty, patience, trust in God and finally, satisfaction. These seven stages constitute the ascetic and ethical discipline of the Sufi and must be carefully distinguished from the so-called "states" *(ahwal,* plural of *hal)* which form a similar psychological chain. There are ten such "states": meditation, nearness to God, love, fear, hope, longing, intimacy, tranquility, contemplation and certainty.

The "stages" can be acquired and mastered by one's own efforts, but the "states" are spiritual feelings over which man has no control: they descend from God into his heart. This calls for comparison with *Dark Night of the Soul* by St. John of the Cross.

In sufism, as in the Upanishads, the holding back of the senses is the essence of man's search for the Ultimate. This is illustrated by the story of the man who has just returned from the pilgrimage *(Hajj)* and calls on Junayd of Baghdad, the Sufi mystic.

Junayd puts the man through his spiritual paces. Did the pilgrim when he first journeyed away from home, also journey away from his sins? Did he, at every stage where he halted for the night, also traverse a station on the way to God? Did he as he put on the pilgrim's garb at the proper place also discard the qualities of human nature as he cast off his clothes? Did he when he stood at Arafat stand one moment in contemplation of God? And so, all down the line, he was questioned until he was asked whether, when he threw the pebbles, he also threw away whatever sensual thoughts that had accompanied him. The pilgrim could, in his honesty, only say "no" to all questions. In that case, said Junayd, the pilgrim had simply not performed the pilgrimage.

For the Sufi, there is no fear of death because he does not see death as the end of man. As Reynold Nicholson put it, impersonal immortality of the human soul kindles in the Sufi an enthusiasm as deep and triumphant as that of the most ardent believer in a personal life continuing beyond the grave. The great mystic Jalaluddin Rumi, after describing the evolution of man in the material world and anticipating his growth further in the spiritual universe, utters a heartfelt prayer for self-annihilation in the ocean of the Godhead:

> I died as mineral and became a plant,
> I died as plant and rose to animal,
> I died as animal and I was man.
> Why should I fear? When was I less by dying?
> Yet once more I shall die as man, to soar
> With angels blest; but even from angelhood
> I must pass on: all except God doth perish.
> When I have sacrificed my angel soul,
> I shall become what no mind e'er conceived.
> Oh, let me not exist! for Non-existence
> Proclaims in organ tones: "To Him we shall return."

CHRISTIAN FAITH and the Concept of Personal Responsibility

When we come to Christian faith and the afterlife of man, we come to an entirely new set of value systems that are only partly—and often tangentially—encountered in other philosophies.

Christian values encompass such concepts as evil and sin, finitude, grace, redemption, predestination, resurrection, sacraments, the Kingdom of God and the Holy Spirit, many of which we do not encounter in Hinduism or Buddhism, or in Islam.

We might start with the Christian concept of death. The Bible teaches that God created man by breathing His Spirit into the dust of the earth and so bringing into existence the *nephesh* or living personality. When God withdraws His Spirit, man dies and returns to the dust. Thus man's life is lived by favor of God.[68]

Nowhere in the Bible, however, is the human soul regarded as naturally immortal. The only way in which man can live again after death is by resurrection—a miracle. Interestingly enough, death does not necessarily mean utter extinction. It may be pointed out that the departed Israelite was thought to be in Sheol, where (as in the Greek Hades) the bloodless wraiths kept a joyless existence. Sheol was not originally conceived to be a place of retribution. It was simply a place of exile from God. It lay beyond the frontiers of His realm and its inhabitants were just denied the opportunity of worshipping Him. The question could be asked: If God created man in His own image—as the Bible says— in order that man might glorify Him and enjoy Him forever, why should it be decreed that he should die? In the context of the statement, death is a contradiction, not only of man's hopes and longing for life, but also—by implication—of God's gracious purpose in creating him.

To this the answer is that man must die because of his sins. "The wages of sin is death." Death is not an arbitrary penalty which is imposed on man by God for transgressing His laws, but a penalty which is self-imposed.

But what is sinning? We will come to it later. Suffice it to say at this point that the root of all sinning is unbelief, which, by the way, is not an intellectual scepticism but man's deliberate refusal to acknowledge God by trusting Him and obeying Him. Sin, in the circumstances, disrupts what should be a straightforward relationship between God, the source of life and man, the receiver of life. By unbelief, man brings death unto himself. The only hope for man, then, is the grace of a forgiving God; he can be saved only by being raised from the dead. Not a natural immortality of the soul, then, but resurrection from the dead by the power of God, is the message of the Bible.[69]

But why do even those people who are ardent believers in God and who cannot, by any manner of means, be accused of being sinners in the sense of being unbelievers, also die like the rest of sinners?

The answer to that is that there is no way he can escape from man's original sin, the state he finds himself in because of the fall of Adam. This is the interpretation of Christian faith as given by Augustine (354-430 A.D.) Bishop of Hippo in North Africa that has stood the test of time. Adam's fall cut the relationship of communion and fellowship with God. Man was thus alienated from Him. That alienation was transmitted to all of Adam's descendants. This meant that man was deprived of the grace of God. As a consequence man was helpless to "save" himself, since his will was perverted at its very root. Death, then, was inevitable.

So, even a true believer must die a "natural" death. But happily, this is not the end. For when Christ died, he took the sting of death, which is sin. In dying on the cross, Christ, the second Adam, died for all men and thereby made death the gateway into eternal life.

In the light of the Christian gospel, death appears both as the penalty of sin and simultaneously as the means of salvation. When the believer dies, he begins a new life in the Spirit. He lives "unto the Lord." The Apostle Paul put this in a noteworthy phrase: "Ye died, and your lives are hid with Christ in God." And as Christ is quoted as saying in the Fourth Gospel: "He that believeth hath eternal life."

As we shall see later, there are many contradictions in this regard. There is, for instance, the question of the final judgment. We cannot expect our entrance into eternal life, which is prepared for us by God's grace, in any other way than by going through the final judgment. That is the moment of truth, the point at which the final decision about man's right to eternal life is made.

As St. Augustine sees it, God acts to give His "fallen" creatures—sinning men—a new beginning through Christ, the embodiment of divine charity. It is in Christ, the new and perfect man, that God, the father, has established the principle of grace. If man wants to seek and benefit from God's grace, he has to respond in faith, by surrendering his will to His. And yet, this is no automatic guarantee that he will necessarily receive grace. According to Augustine, man's surrender is itself made possible only because God elects those who shall respond and Himself creates both the conditions for that response and the possibility of the response itself. So, only those who are "elected" shall be "saved."

This is a most tantalizing prospect; it provides man no incentive to be good and to believe. He has to be good and a believer not because he may derive any benefit from it but only because it may make him feel better. Augustine, it may be remembered, derived his views from his reading of the Epistle to the Romans. As a theologian, W. Norman Pittinger has remarked, "whether Paul himself, in that Epistle, intended to teach what Augustine understood him to teach, is a much-debated question."

Now grace is a very special Christian concept. Indeed, it was St. Paul who was the first to make grace—*charis*—a central theological word. St. Paul credits grace with his new existence as an apostle, in contrast to his former existence as an enemy of the Church, in one of the most beautiful submissions to God ever made. Consider his statement (I Corinthians 15:9–10) "For I am the least of the Apostles, unfit to be called an apostle, because I persecuted the Church of God. But by the grace of God, I am what I am, and his grace toward me was not in vain. On the contrary, I worked harder than any of them, though it was not I, but the grace of God which is with me."

Grace, then, is God's personal attitude toward man and for Christians this is concretely manifested in, and communicated through, the historical person, Jesus Christ.[70] Man stands in grace because faith binds him to Christ, in his death, his burial and his resurrection. Without that faith in Christ, grace is not attainable. We have to take grace with forgiveness. Grace is impossible without the prior act of forgiveness. Forgiveness in itself is an act of grace which brings sinful man into a right relationship with God through Christ, the intermediary.

Among the values central to Christianity is one of eternal life. According to the gospel of St. John, the grace of God in Jesus Christ transplants everyone who has faith into "eternal life," except that that life remains "hidden with Christ in God" (Cor. 3:3) because of the veil of sinfulness which covers man's empirical life.

When man dies, his earthly form as a person is naturally destroyed. But that does not mean his identity is destroyed as well. Man sins as a whole being and dies as a whole being and is called to account as a whole being so that God can fulfill what He has begun. (I Cor. 1:9 and Phil. 1:6.) Christian faith takes man as a whole, ontologically as well as ethically. Body and soul are taken as one. There is no dualistic distinction between body and soul (or the spirit). When resurrection takes place, the arisen man has both his body and soul together in him. The resurrection, therefore is a transformation of the whole human being, maintaining the identity of the person and his personal history before God. This, of course, differs from the Platonic concept of an "immortality of the soul" which supposedly is free from evil. It is closer to the Islamic concept of the unity of body and soul.

IMMORTALITY, Life Eternal and Everlasting Life

It is interesting to note that "immortality" is a relatively rare concept in biblical thought and occurs only in Rom. 2:7, Cor. 15:53-54, I Tim. 6:16 and II Tim. 1:10.[71] The idea of immortality is primarily of Hellenistic origin and it came into the mainstream of Christian thought from early contacts with Greek culture. Again, Christianity received the concept of resurrection this time from Hebraic culture. This is also true of Islam. Indeed, the Apostles' Creed, for example, which is the early Christian confession of faith, affirms belief in the "resurrection of the body," but the "body" should be taken to mean the total personality which dies and is then raised by the power of God—much as Allah would do. It is construed that because the phrase was liable to be misconstrued, for many centuries it became acceptable in Christian theology to speak of the "immortality of the soul" when in fact there is really no dichotomy between "body" and "soul." The two are taken together.

Immortality, in the circumstances, is what happens after resurrection and is a convenient synonym for "everlasting life," "life eternal," etc. What is stressed is that man having lived his three score years and ten does not disappear after death and equally, does not exhaust the meaning of his existence. What God began in him, He continues and completes in His own mysterious way, beyond the confines of earthly life. Man's life on earth is a preparation for a life to come to be lived in the presence of God. But congenital sinner that man is, his deliverance is dependent on his receiving grace. He can receive it but only "through Jesus Christ, our Lord" (Rom. 7:24-25.) In the words of St. Paul "God was in Christ reconciling the world unto himself." For man to establish the right relationship between himself and God, he has to atone.

DESTINY, FATE AND PREDESTINATION

One thing comes out clearly in Christian theology: there is no such thing as destiny or fate within the terms of man's existence which is not at the same time determined by his own free decision.[72] Man is solely responsible for himself and his actions. He can resort to no subterfuge, give no excuse for sinning. Man is not the product of certain inescapable conditions and circumstances such as karma, but, on the contrary, he is constantly confronted with the necessity of deciding how he is to live in the situation in which God, in His providence, has placed him.

There is no re-birth, so he can work out past sins. The life he has on earth is the only life he ever will have; he gets no second chance. There is resurrection, of course, if God wills. When the day of judgment comes, man is answerable to his sins. If there is at all any "destiny," it is the destiny to be free to make his own mistakes, to commit his sins—but also to seek refuge in God.

We must take this, however, with the Roman Catholic idea of predestination, in which God is said to foresee the future faith and merits of believers and to predestine salvation according to what He thus knows to be their free choice. What this amounts to saying is that man may be free to do what he pleases, but God in His omniscience already knows what man will do in his freedom.

There is another issue: whom does God "elect" to save? St. Thomas Aquinas has affirmed the gracious election by God of the smaller number of mankind, without respect to human merit. St. Augustine affirms the double predestination of a fixed number of souls to salvation and the remainder to damnation. Men are not all created with a similar end in view. Eternal life is fore-ordained for some and eternal damnation for others.

This is a somewhat frightening thought. It is confirmed by Calvin. His definition of predestination goes as follows: "We call predestination the eternal decree of God by which he has determined in Himself what He would have every individual of mankind to become, for they are not all created with a similar destiny; but eternal life is foreordained for some and eternal damnation for others. Every man, therefore, being created for one or the other of these ends, we say is predestined either to life or death."

It seems an irrational definition. Why should some individuals be destined for eternal life and not others? Why this preference or partiality? Why should some suffer and others not? Calvin has an easy answer. "If, therefore, we can assign no reason why He grants mercy to His people but because such is His pleasure, neither shall we find any other cause but His will for the reprobation of others." The seeker is asked, in other words, to shut up and not question God's will. Commenting on this, Paul Tillich, in his *History of Christian Thought* remarks: "The irrational will of God is the cause of predestination. This introduces us to an absolute mystery. We cannot call God to account. We must accept it purely and simply and drop our own criteria of the good and the true. If someone says this is unjust, Calvin would say that we cannot go beyond the divine will to a nature which determines God, because God's will cannot be dependent on anything else, not even in Him.[73]

Calvin himself felt the horrible aspect of this doctrine. "I inquire again how it came to pass that the fall of Adam, independent of any remedy, should involve so many nations with their infant children in eternal death, but because such was the will of God . . . it is an awful decree, I confess!"[74]

The problem for Calvin was how to be among the "elect" that God would choose for eternal life, having decided that God indeed would do some choosing of His own in this matter. Since Calvin was not God, he could only think of what he himself would choose for his criteria to separate those "elected" for eternal life and those condemned to eternal damnation. The first and most decisive criterion was obviously the inner relationship of man to God in the act of faith. Then there was the high moral standing of a person. The individual, theorized Calvin, could gain some certainty of eternal life by producing the marks of election in terms of a moral life. The Buddha suggests the moral life—he called it the eightfold path—as a means of salvation. Calvin suggest the moral life as a means of getting eternal life in the hereafter by being accepted as one of God's "elected." There is here no scope for divine love. In Calvin's thinking, there is God in his divine glory. When Calvin speaks of divine love, it is a highly selective love towards those who are elected. The universality of the divine love is denied. There is, however, some logic in all this. If one accepts the theory that some are going to be eternally damned, divine love will have to be discounted, except conditionally. For, if something is created by divine love, how can it be eternally damned?

THE ROMAN CATHOLIC UNDERSTANDING OF SIN

It was stated earlier that sin consisted of unbelief. But the Council of Trent saw sin as a transformation of man into something worse—*in deterius commutatum*—commuted into something worse, or deteriorization.[75] The Council of Trent, it may be remembered, was held to counter the theories of the Protestant reformers. The reformers had held that man has completely lost his freedom by his fall. That freedom was the freedom to contribute to one's relationship to God. To this the Council of Trent countered by saying that man's freedom was not lost or extinguished, but merely diminished or weakened. The sins before baptism were forgiven in the act of baptism, but after baptism, concupiscence remained. The Roman Catholic Church argued that this concupiscence should not be called sin. Conceded that concupiscence came from sin and was inclined to sin, but that was not the same thing as saying that it was sin itself.

In this, the Roman Catholic Church differs vitally and meaningfully from Prostestantism. For the former, man is completely corrupted; even his natural drives are not sin. Furthermore, from the time of the Council of Trent, sin was understood in the Catholic Church in terms of particular acts that could be forgiven, given contrition. When Catholics confessed their sins to a priest, they received absolution and were liberated from them.

Again, the reformers saw sin as unbelief—separation from God. "Sins"—or infractions—were secondary. To overcome sin, something fundamental had to happen like a complete conversion, a transformation of being and reunion with God. But the Catholic Church held that sin was neither unbelief nor separation from God, but acts against the law of God.

The quintessence of Protestant understanding of sin is that laid down by Martin Luther. "Unbelief is the real sin." "Nothing justifies except faith and nothing makes sinful except unbelief." "Unbelief is the sin altogether." "The main justice is faith and so the main evil is unbelief." "Therefore the word "sin" includes what we are living and doing besides the faith in God." Luther could not have been clearer or more explicit. Luther did not make gradations in sin into "sins." Everything which separated man from God was sin and had equal weight.[76]

We may pause here for a moment to examine Luther's idea of God. That idea, Paul Tillich has said, "is one of the most powerful in the whole history of human and Christian thought." Luther's idea of God is not a Being beside others. It is a God whom we can have only through contrast. "Which are the virtues of God?" asks Luther and replies: "Infirmity, passion, cross, persecution: these are the weapons of God." Or again: "The power of man is emptied by the cross, but in the weakness of the cross the divine power is present."[77]

Luther denies everything which can make God finite—and in this, he comes close to the Vedic thinkers. Nothing is so small but God is ever smaller. Nothing is so large but that God is larger. We hear Upanishadic overtones when Luther proclaims: "Who knows what that is, which is called God? It is beyond body, beyond spirit, beyond everything we can say, hear and think." And he makes the great statement that God is nearer to all creatures than they are to themselves, a statement unequalled in its magnificent concept of God's all-pervasiveness. "God has found the way that his own divine essence can be completely in all creatures, and in everyone especially, deeper, more internally, more present that the creature is to itself, and at the same time nowhere and cannot be comprehended by anyone, so that he embraces all things and is within them. God is at the same time in every piece of sand totally and nevertheless in all, above all and out of all creatures."

But God can be comprehended even better in terms of man. About the state of man, Luther says: "Being man means non-being, becoming, being. It means being in privation, in possibility, in action. It means always being a sinner, a penitent, a just one." Luther speaks of creatures as the "masks" of God. Do we here have a mirror image of the theory of "maya"—illusion? God, says Luther, is hidden behind these masks. "All creatures are God's masks and veils in order to make them work and help Him to create many things." [78] In other words, everything moves through and because of, divine purpose. All natural orders and institutions are filled with divine presence. So, adds Tillich, is the historical process. The great men in history, the Hannibals, Alexanders, the Timurlanes, the Goths, the Vandals, the Nazis, all are driven by God to do their work. Through them and their action, God is speaking to us. It is for us to figure out what God's message is.

THE DOCTRINE OF JUSTIFICATION BY FAITH ALONE

Can sins be forgiven by God's grace alone? The question has relevance in terms of man's desire to be one of God's "elected," worthy of eternal life. With his sins forgiven, man can hope for that life eternal following death.

But to receive grace, man has to have faith in the atoning work of Christ as revealed in scripture. So, in a sense, grace could be received through faith. The simple act of faith practically compelled God to give his forgiveness. Forgiveness thus could be attained by faith alone—*sola fide*.[79]

The reformers held therefore that grace could be received only by faith. Here they parted company with the Roman Catholic Church. For the Catholic Church held that the *remissio peccatorum*—the forgiveness of sins—is not *sola gratia*, by grace alone. The Church spoke of a preparation for the divine act of justification whereby a *gratia praeveniens*, a prevenient grace, is effective in man which can either be accepted or rejected whichever way a man decides. Thus, it was necessary that man cooperated with God in his prevenient grace. Man received grace to the extent and degree of his cooperation. The more man cooperated with God, in his prevenient grace, the more was the grace of justification given to him.

The point was made that justification as a gift contained two things: faith on the one hand; hope and love on the other. Faith alone, then, was not sufficient. The Council of Trent held that a Christian, through a mortal sin, might lose justification, though his faith remained intact. Faith was an intellectual and moral act.

But for the reformers, faith was the act of accepting justification and the two could not be separated. On this issue, what the reformers called the *articulus stantis aut cadentis ecclesiae*—the article by which the Church stands or falls—the Church and the reformers parted company. There was no reconciliation between the two.

THE SACRAMENTS and the Attaining of Salvation

The most beautiful—and classic—definition of sacraments is contained in the catechism of the Anglican Book of Common Prayer. Sacraments, it states, are "an outward and visible sign of an inward and spiritual grace."[80] This definition summarizes the teachings of the early Fathers of the Church, notably St. Augustine. It is said that this definition, beautiful as it is, will be acceptable to most Christian theologians, with the following amendments:

> A sacrament is distinguished from other sacred signs by its express institution, whether by word or by exemplary action, of Christ Himself. A sacrament is efficacious only when it is performed in and by the Church acting through recognized ministers or by agents who intend to act for the Church.[81]

It is important to bear in mind the involvement of the Church in this matter. The point is made that apart from the context of corporate church life, a sacrament is meaningless, if not, more extremely, a superstitious piece of magic. As one theologian has put it: "To be a Christian involves more than a personal faith in the redeeming act of God in Christ. It demands an incorporation into the community where the effects of Christ's redemption in reconciliation and charity may be actualized and nurtured. A sacrament cannot be performed by an individual for himself alone; it requires at least another party. Thus a sacrament is more than a visible token of God's free favor and grace offered to one who accepts his redeeming love in faith and devotion. It is an instrument whereby the individual is made a member of a covenant-community and ordered by its disciples and responsibilities."[82]

What this implies is that an individual cannot have the benefit of sacraments outside the Church. He has to be part of it. He cannot claim to sacraments as a right just because he accepts, as a matter of personal faith, the redeeming act of God in Christ.

Down the ages, Catholics and Protestants have differed in their emphases upon the way in which sacraments conveyed divine grace. Catholics (in the Reformation era) stressed the objective efficacy of sacraments when duly performed with sincere intention by authorized ministers using the proper form (words) and matter (elements or actions) of a sacrament. Protestants tended to emphasize the subjective conditions of penitence and faith in the recipients of sacraments as a condition of receiving beneficially the promise of grace proclaimed by the word of Christ and offered with the sacramental signs.

There were other differences between Catholics and Protestants. The Protestant reformers, for example, were unanimous in rejecting the Medieval dogma of transubstantiation: that the substance of bread and wine were miraculously changed by consecration into the substance of Christ's body and blood, the accidents of the elements only remaining.

At the same time, the reformers were not quite agreed among themselves in their interpretations of how the body and blood of Christ were conveyed in or with the blessed elements, whether substantially, spiritually or virtually. However, it is well to remember that none of the reformers opposed, as an objective, effectual presence of Christ in the supper offered to those who would receive Him by faith.

Again, the Protestant reformers were unanimous in rejecting the medieval doctrine that in the Mass, Christ was offered anew, albeit mystically, for the remission of sins of the living and the dead on the logical grounds that this was a derogation of the once-and-for-all character of Christ's sacrifice for sin upon the cross. There is one other difference between Catholics and Protestants concerning the number of sacraments.

Catholics, following Peter Lombard and Thomas Aquinas, claimed there were seven sacraments, although it is clear that the early Fathers of the Church had settled upon no determined number. Most Protestants accepted only two sacraments as instituted by Christ and, therefore, generally necessary for salvation: baptism and the Lord's Supper. Followers of Luther have been inclined to receive also the sacrament of Penance. Many Anglicans have come to acknowledge not only Penance to be a sacrament, but also the other four: Confirmation, Matrimony, Unction and Holy Orders, though they would not place them in the same rank as the gospel sacraments of Baptism and the Lord's Supper. But whether one accepts only the two or all seven, they are the core and pith of Christian belief, mysteries in which the limitations of time are transcended.

But what does salvation mean? It means liberation or release. What is man released or liberated from? Release, of course, is from his sinful selfhood.[83] To be a man at all is to be involved in pain, loss, estrangement from God. Man is forever being attacked from within and without by dark destructive forces. To be liberated from these forces is to attain salvation. Salvation, then, has decisive importance in the vocabulary of theology because it points to an experience that is utterly central to faith itself. But there is no salvation without the sacraments. The sacraments are saving powers, not merely strengthening powers. They have a hidden force of their own and they are available to anyone who does not resist the grace.

To achieve salvation, one does not have to die. Salvation can be obtained when one is still alive. But salvation takes place "through Jesus Christ, our Lord," since in Him, God takes man's condition upon Himself, moves to bridge the gap between what man's sin has caused and what He intends him to be.

Seeking salvation is to put one's faith in Jesus Christ; hence, salvation, it has been argued, is "by faith alone," for if man does not have faith in Jesus Christ, he cannot possibly be receptive to His grace. One definition of salvation is "accepting God's acceptance of us in Christ."

Salvation belongs to God. Man can contribute to his salvation, but that he must "work out by fear and trembling." The initiative is God's but that does not contradict the place of human freedom; on the other hand, it assumes it, addresses itself to it and builds upon it. The argument has lasted whether salvation can be obtained by "faith alone" or also by faith and works. There is no good reason to continue the argument. Faith, it may be argued, is itself work.

KARL BARTH and the Humanity of God

Karl Barth is one of the greatest Protestant theologians of the twentieth century and has his own interpretation of faith, grace and redemption. Barth's definition of Christian faith is "awe in the presence of the divine incognito . . . the love of God that is aware of the qualitative distinction between God and man." As Barth put it, only "those who stand in awe in the presence of God and keep themselves from revolt live with God."[84] This is a very negative definition. Consequently, faith signifies "the end of all idealist assaults upon heaven," "the end of all perceptibility and comprehensibility." Faith is "not a ground to stand on, not a system to follow, not an air to breathe," rarher it is, when it is true faith, nothing but a "void" and "vacuum," sorrow, waiting and deprivation, openness, a sign and a sign-post "a standing place in the air." [85] This is an extraordinary definition.

According to Barth, faith has no form or beauty. Rather than humanity, it reveals the limits of humanity. The borderlines between faith and unbelief cannot be defined in human and sensible or historical and psychological terms. "The hands of all of us are and remain perceptually empty."

This was a younger Barth speaking. As Barth grew older, his thoughts mellowed. Always, of course, he had asserted the absolute priority of the grace of God. We see this in the way he defined the realtionship between creation and covenant, that is, between the order of nature and the order of grace. Creation, he held, was the external basis of the covenant, the covenant, the internal basis of creation. Man was not to look first on creation, turning his eyes to the redemption afterwards, but from the start to regard the creation from the point of view of the grace of God in Jesus Christ. Barth opposed the concept of an independent creation. The mystery of creation could only be known and understood on the basis of atonement, of redemption. He reversed the conventional order in which redemption followed creation and grace followed nature. No, he said, in God's plan, redemption was willed first, and creation second. God created the world for the sake of grace and did not institute grace for the sake of the world.[86]

As Heinz Zahrnt puts it in his *The Question of God*: "Thus grace does not represent something which was later added to creation, as though it were only the subsequent reaction of God to the "incident" of sin which he had not provided for; rather, based on the eternal purpose of salvation, the divine "original decree," grace was attendant to creation from the first as its goal, and is therefore antecedent to creation. God does not first will and create the world and man, in order to destine them afterwards to salvation; the reverse is the case." [87]

This is a very logical thesis. Zahrnt adds: "Because God has resolved by his free love, before all time, to exercise grace, and in order to provide an object and recipient of this grace and a partner for himself, he creates, sustains and rules man and the world for this reason alone, with this sole aim and for this purpose." God made the world to be the theatre of his glory and man to be the witness of this glory. And—here we have the final fruit of Barth's logic—"for the purpose for which God made the world, it is also good."[83]

The world then, is the *theatrum gloriae Dei*—the theater of the glory of God. In many ways Barth's theology of grace is the theology of hope. "God is gracious," he argues, "and continues gracious even when there is no grace. And it is only by grace that the lack of grace can be recognized as such"[89] —and the paradox provides its own answer. Barth proclaims this with all the emphasis he can muster in *Church Dogmatics*. God's decision to be gracious, made in eternity, is irrevocable. Man cannot alter or reverse it; he cannot bring into being any fact which would abrogate God's election in grace. Here faith is the sole possibility, and unbelief "the excluded possibility." Man, claims Barth, can dishonor the divine election of grace; he cannot overthrow or overturn it.

To bring home his point, Barth describes the parable of the King who awards a decoration to a subject. The subject may not accept it but did not that mean he had not received the award from the King? He who did not believe in God was like some one behind times—his subjective knowledge had not yet caught up with objective reality.[90]

One more point: Barth does not deny that God punishes man, but he avers that even in the matter of punishment, grace prevails. "Even the wrath and judgment of God which may overtake man do not indicate any retraction, but only a special form, and in the last analysis the most glorious confirmation of the permission and promise given to him."[91] Clearly, Barth's God is different from Calvin's.

DARK NIGHT OF THE SOUL: Toward Perfect Union

Few works better delineate the trials and tribulations of the soul's journey toward unity with God as *Dark Night of the Soul* written by St. John of the Cross. It is more than a classic in the literature of mysticism; it is about the clearest delineation of what pitfalls await the individual in his journey toward perfection. St. John of the Cross speaks of two nights of purgation—cleansing. The first night is of the sensual part of the soul; the second is of the spiritual part. In his treatise he also speaks of the third part, with respect to the activity of the soul and yet one more part, with respect to its passivity. This last part is the dark night. Of it, the saint writes:

> And the second night, or purification, pertains to those who are already proficient, occurring at the time when God desires to bring them to the state of union with God. And this latter night is a more obscure and dark and terrible purgation . . .

The saint outlines the step by step approach that is to be undertaken in the soul's approach to perfect union with God. It is a hard and difficult journey. Every step is hounded by imperfections such as spiritual pride, spiritual avarice, spiritual wrath and spiritual gluttony.

The saint describes their symptoms to help the beginner to understand himself better. When the beginner has overcome them all, comes the second night. But the saint administers a warning. The soul, he says, which God is about to lead onward is not led by His Majesty into the second night as soon as it goes forth from the aridities and trials of the first purgation and night of sense; "rather it is wont to pass a long time, even years, after leaving the state of beginners." The beginner needs divine aid more abundantly. "However greatly the soul itself labors" he writes, "it cannot actively purify itself so as to be in the least degree prepared for the divine union of perfection of love, if God does not take its hand and purges it not in that dark fire."

Here is a principle of dogmatic theology; that by himself and with the ordinary aid of grace, man cannot attain to that degree of purgation which is essential to his transformation in God. The soul, it may be remembered, will not come to have the capacity of God, for that is impossible.

St. John says that all that the soul is "will become like to God, for which cause it will be called, and will be, God by participation."[92] But it is a long struggle and not many souls are up to it. But for any who are willing to embark on that adventure, *Dark Night of the Soul* is a beacon in the darkness.

THE QUESTION OF BEING (man): Between Finitude and Infinity

Man asks for the meaning of his life, says Paul Tillich, one of the great theologians of our times, because he is "a mixture of being and non-being." He partakes in being and at the same time is separated from it. In this, his finitude is revealed. Man, according to Tillich, exists on the boundary between finitude and infinity. He is miserable because he is finite, imperfect, transitory and mortal. He experiences that he is finite, but he would not experience it if he did not know or have some foreknowledge of infinity. He experiences that he is imperfect but he would not experience it if he did not have some foreknowledge of perfection. Unconsciously, then, man always measures himself against the dignity of his origin and his true being. Admittedly, this dignity is lost, but that only points to the fact that he once possessed it.

We can examine Tillich's thinking further. The separation of man from being, he says, points to the fall of man. Tillich interprets the fall as the transition of man from essence to existence. First there is essence; out of essence comes existence. But it is not an event in space and time. Tillich says the transition from essence to existence is "the trans-historical quality of all events in space and time." The result of that transition, of course, is estrangement. The nature of that estrangement consists in man's being estranged from that to which he essentially belongs. He is separated from the ground of being and therefore from the origin and goal of his life.

Tillich says that the state of estrangement in which man exists implies a three-fold separation: from the ground of his being, from his fellow men and from himself. Tillich defines this as sin—sin, singular, not plural. To live under the circumstances of existence means to live in sin—a new definition of the word. Tillich is of the opinion that it is no longer possible for us to make use of the concept of "original sin," although he retains its content. Before all acts, sin is in an ontological state; it is the "state of estrangement" of man from God. So there is only one sin, man's separation from God. That has nothing to do with particular moral failings.

In sum, Tillich describes man's existence as his separation from the ground of being. But only because he is separated from his true being can he ask the question of his being at all. Non-human beings don't ask the question; neither does God who is beyond the gap between essence and existence, and so has no need to ask the question. Only man asks, for only he knows that he is finite, separated from the ground of being and yet not completely apart from it, however much he might like it to be.

THE NEED FOR AN EVERYDAY PHILOSOPHY OF DEATH

When one comes to think of it, the central concern of all philosophies is not life, but death. If man did not die, he would in all truth, not philosophize either. What would be there to philosophize about?

It is because man knows in his heart of hearts that life is finite and the future is unknown that his natural inclination is to ask what comes after death: is there life after death? If so, what sort of life will it be? And life for whom? Obviously it would not be the sort of physical life that he is accustomed to; it has to be a life for something else apart from the body. Hence the speculation about what it could possibly be.

Again, if man had no conscience, there would be no need to be sorry either. He has a conscience. He distinguishes between what he feels is right and wrong. It bothers him. Not all his wrongs, his "sins," his "inequities" are recognized by society. They may not surface at all, if ever. And yet man knows that he has committed them. His sense of justice tells him that some day he has to pay for them. When? Where? If not in this life, will he pay for them in another?

Again, not all the good things he has done get rewarded. The poor man, alas, too often stays poor. The ill in health stay ill in health, no matter how good they are and how well-disposed they may be to their relations, family and friends. Surely, if goodness and decency and rectitude are not paying in this life, one may hope for payment in another? Hence man's conception of heaven and of hell and of purgatory; it is hard to think of total annihilation as the result of death. Man's sense of justice cannot accept the idea.

If man's conscience goads him to think of what may come in the hereafter, his senses (*indriyas*) goad him to desire everlasting life. It is good to be living, his senses tell him. Life is to be enjoyed. Food, drink, sex, travel, the companionship of like-minded people, the accretion of knowledge all seem worthwhile goals to pursue endlessly. Why die, when there is so much to live for? Will man ever grow tired of living, presuming that by some alchemy his life span can be expanded?

Simon de Beauvoir dealt with this theme in one of her novels: *All Men are Mortal.* The story is of Raymond Fosca, a ruler of thirteenth century Caromina, who does not want to die, or even grow old. He has plans to build his city and achieve many other things and life, he felt, was too short. Happily he meets an old apothecary who has just the right elixir of life to assure him immortality. The apothecary himself dared not drink it, somewhat disconcerted with the thought of life without end. But for Fosca this was what he had long sought. He had wanted everlasting youth, virility, strength and now he had an assurance of being guaranteed all of them.

It was indeed the elixir of life. Life eternal was not something to come after death, but it was here for him, in the very world so dear to him. Now there was nothing to fear. Fortified by the thought he governed his city for two centuries, fought wars, built a great many buildings, loved many women and begot sons and daughters and in turn saw them provide him with grandsons and granddaughters *ad infinitum.* He then discovered, much to his surprise, that he did not seem to accomplish any more in those two hundred years than he could not have accomplished in a reign of a few years.

Focsa learned a few more things that were getting at him: that instead of eliciting admiration from his subjects, he was only getting their contempt. Few wanted to accept their leader's grandiose ideas. Even his own children, and after them his grand and great-grand children went their own way, planning their lives and hopes in terms of their limited lifetimes, unaffected by what their sire said he would do.

Tired of Caromina, the city that was once his pride and for which he wanted so much to do, Fosca left it for fresh fields, but always it was the same. He became a confidante of Emperor Charles V but soon Emperor and Foxca fell out. In the seventeenth century, still very much alive and still very young, Fosca participated in the discovery of Canada; in the eighteenth century he was the darling of Paris and active in its salon life. In 1789 he was a participant in the Revolution, side by side with one of his descendants. Fosca, ever the builder and innovator, was on the side of the rebels; the happiness of the people remained his bright and burning ambition.

He paid for some of his daring. He spent years in prison and in exile and on one occasion slept for sixty years! And in all this time, he loved and married and had children, scores of them. They would get old and grey and die, but Foxca, he remained very youthful. But after all those years of striving and achieving, Foxca began to ask whether it made any sense any more. It did not. Boredom began to set in and women who loved him soon got to realize that he was incapable of giving himself fully and totally.

It was then that Fosca finally came to realize that it was not longevity that mattered but what one did in a comparatively short life that was important. But it had taken Fosca centuries to know that he was playing a meaningless game.

There is the other side of the coin: those who courted death voluntarily because of their hope that eternal life awaited them once they crossed the threshold. During the early years of Christendom, men who accepted the faith of Paul died fearlessly, hopefully and joyously when the Romans made martyrs of them. "The desire for martyrdom became at times a form of absolute madness, a kind of epidemic of suicide and the leading minds of the Church found it necessary to exert all their authority to prevent their followers thrusting themselves into the hands of the persecutors." Tertullian mentions how, in a little Asian town, the entire population once flocked to the pro consul, declaring themselves to be Christians, and imploring him to execute the decree of the emperor and grant them the privilege of martyrdom! "These wretches" Lucian wrote," persuade themselves that they are going to be altogether immortal and to live forever, wherefore they despise death and many of their own accord give themselves to be slain."

There is indeed no knowing what man would do to gain immortality. But side by side with this desire to gain immortality is gnawing disbelief in the tenets of most religions. Could this be true? Could that be true? Or is all this a dream from which we may never truly get out? Remember what Shakespeare said:

> The cloud-capp'd towers, the gorgeous palaces,
> The solemn temples, the great globe itself,
> Yea, all which it inherit, shall dissolve;
> And, like this insubstantial pageant faded,
> Leave not a rack behind. We are such stuff
> As dreams are made on, and our little life
> Is rounded with a sleep.

Many would like to think of life as an unpleasant dream and only hope for pleasanter ones, as when William Cullen Bryant (1794-1878) wrote:

> So live, that when the summons comes to join
> The innumerable caravan, which moves
> To that mysterious realm, where each shall take
> His chamber in the silent halls of death,
> Thou go not, like the quarry slave at night,
> Scourged to his dungeon, but, sustained and soothed
> By an unfaltering trust, approach thy grave
> Like one who wraps the drapery of his couch
> About him, and lies down to pleasant dreams.
> *(Thanatopsis)*

But others would say that life is not a dream, that, in the words of Longfellow, life is real, life is earnest and the grave is not the goal. What, then, is the goal? To the living, this is the only relevant question. All else comes out of fear of the unknown. As John Dryden said: "Death, in itself, is nothing; but we fear, to be, we know not what, we know not where."

Need we fear the unknown? Fear most often arises out of a

bad conscience, out of a sense that we have done the wrong things, that indeed, we have not done well with the world around us. Those who have a clear purpose in life fear no death. When Socrates was charged with impiety and corruption of youth, for which the punishment meted out was death, his answer was simple and it is an answer, one may add, that stands out for all men in all times:

> . . . if you say to me . . . you shall be let off, but upon one condition, that you are not to inquire . . . in this way any more, and that if you are caught doing so again , you shall die—if this was the condition, on which you let me go, I should reply: ". . . while I have life and strength I shall never cease from the practice and teaching of philosophy, exhorting anyone whom I meet . . . . Are you not ashamed of heaping up the greatest amount of money and honor and reputation, and caring so little about wisdom and truth? . . . . The unexamined life is not worth living . . . . If you suppose that there is no consciousness, but a sleep like the sleep of him that is undisturbed even by dreams, death will be an unspeakable gain . . . . Eternity is then only a single night.[93]

What does Socrates say that is so important? The unexamined life is not worth living. If there is one exhortation that can be made, it is that the examination of our life must go on, on a day-to-day basis, not morbidly, not in a spirit of breast beating, but in a free spirit of inquiry that leads us to purposefulness and freedom from death's fear. Jovenal (AD 30-130) had the right advice to give:

> *Orandum est ut sit mens sana in corpore sano.*
> *Fortem posce animum mortis terrore carentum,*
> *Qui spatium vitae extremum inter munera ponat*
> *Naturae.*
>
> (Your prayer must be that you may have a sound mind in a sound body. Pray for a bold spirit, free from all dread of death; that reckons the closing scene of life among Nature's kindly boons.)

This is the Vedic prayer, that prays for the bold spirit:

> *Asatoma sadgamaya*
> *Tamaso ma jyotirgamaya*
> *Mrityurmamamritamgamaya.*
>
> (From untruth lead me to truth
> From darkness lead me to light,
> From death to immortality.

It is when the search goes on, purposefully, for the Truth, for the

Light that when death finally comes it can be accepted as among "Nature's kindly boons." It is only when life is spent in aimless pursuits that death holds us in its endless terror. It is not, as Keats would say, that those whom the gods love die young; rather it is the young who have achieved that fear no death and can accept it with serenity, with a sense of fulfillment, as when Keats says:

> Darkling I listen; and, for many a time
> I have been half in love with easeful Death;
> Call'd him soft names in many a mused rhyme,
> To take into the air my quiet breath;
> Now more than ever seems it rich to die,
> To cease upon the midnight with no pain,
> While thou are pouring forth thy soul abroad
> In such an ecstasy!
>
> *Ode to a Nightingale*

How many thousands have been the young, down the climes, who have, in Rupert Brooke's immortal words "poured out the red sweet wine of youth" on the battlefields! Of them it was that Lawrence Binyon said "They shall not grow old, as we that are left grow old, age shall not weary them, nor the years condemn." In our memory, collectively, they have already achieved immortality.

Death may be inevitable, but purposelessness is not. And it is given to anyone—even the least among us—to have a sense of purpose. Obviously it is not given to everyone to write Schiller's *Ode to Joy*, or a Beethoven Symphony, or a Shakespearean play or to discover the law of gravity. Our talents are limited but what we can do is to relate our purposefulness to our talents so that there is no need to despair that we haven't climbed Mount Everest or discovered penicillin. There are things each one of us can do: teach a class, chop wood, dig coal, run the railways, sell tickets at the counter, take down letters, each a job to do that done well, not only could bring us the satisfaction of a job well done, but fulfill the purpose of our existence.

For there is, as Browning would say, nothing big or small:

> All things rank the same with God.

It is when we reach out, in whatever station we are in, for

something still beyond us (A man's reach should exceed his grasp, or what's a heaven for?) aspire and ever act that life assumes meaning and death loses its sting. And in the end, that is all there is to it. We need never ask the question: What will happen after death? The more relevant question we need ask is: What am I doing right here? When we have got the question right, the answer is bound to be right, too. In the question is the answer.

A PERSONAL PHILOSOPHY

Sometime or other in the course of his life, man must ask himself the questions: Who am I? What am I here for? Where do I go from here? And why? Is there really a hereafter, a hell, a heaven, a purgatory?

Some time in the mid-seventies, when two dear friends and contemporaries died—and when I myself was in my early fifties, the thought of death and what it could mean hit me hard. Others, much closer—a brother, a sister, a nephew, a niece, my father, my grandparents—had died, but life, it seemed, would continue. Death ever present, was still distant. I could contemplate it with some degree of equanimity. Sometimes the very young died before they could etch their mark on one's memory. And then the very old died and that seemed a blessing. But death in one's middle years is different. To the friends of the dead that leaves time for reflection and contemplation.

So, when two friends died, one after another in fairly close succession, it occurred to me that surely there is more to life than living. There were these two bright young men, full of hopes and desires, wanting to make their mark in life, struggling, striving, and then—phut!—the light was snuffed out of their lives. What was life all about? A four-days' wonder? A moveable feast at the end of which the flowers lay withered?

I had always fought shy of seeking teachers—gurus. And I told myself that I had no time to sit at the feet of the master to hear of his wisdom. And even if I had the time, from where I was living—Washington, D.C.—it was impossible to expect the wise man to be available to me, when I wanted, as I wanted. But one way was still open to me: reading.

In truth, reading is not enough. In the end only a good teacher can show the way. But in the physical absence of a teacher, a library was a happy substitute. And I spent many educative hours reading up on philosophy. I had started with the simple question about life: what does it all mean? Does life have any meaning at all beyond the immediate demands of daily survival? If there was a meaning, what was it? If there was no meaning, how should one disport oneself? I soon found, however, as I progressed with my studies, that the issue was not as simple as I had posed for myself. Involved in my being was the question of who brought me into being, in the first place. And what would and should be my relation to him.

I had started with the concept of death and what was to come after. But I found that if I had to have any meaningful answer to that, I had to know the meaning of life, of the origins of life, of the significance, if any, of a creator, if there was one and whether if there was a creator, it was ever possible to know Him or understand Him.

So there were questions within questions. Who was this He, the creator? The Vedic philosophers called Him *swayambhu*—the one who created Himself. Why did He create Himself? All the literature on the world provides no satisfactory answer. We have to accept the fact that He did—because we see the creation around us and that is for real. The world is not an illusion; one can see it, feel it, sense it; it is not a figment of one's imagination.

Sri Madhava, the exponent of the philosophy of dualism sums up the relation between God (the He, the creator), the individual soul and the world thus:

Srimanmadhavamate haree paratarara satyam jagat tatvato Bhedau jivaganaa hareranuchara nichochchabhavam gathah muktirnaija sukhanu bhutiramala bhaktischa tatsadhanam hyaksha dhitrithayam pramanamakhilamyayaikavedhyo hari.[94]

(In Sri Madha's theology, Hari (God) is supreme, the world is real, separateness is true, the individual souls are infinitely graded as superior and inferior, and are dependent on God, liberation is self-realization, consisting in the enjoyment of such bliss as remained latent in the soul. Pure devotion is the means to this end. Perception, inference and testimony, are the sources of knowledge (measures of proof), mundane and heavenly. Hari (God) is knowable in the entirety of the Vedas and the Vedas alone.")

But could it be that the world is unreal and that the true Reality lies in our acceptance of the unreal? God, by definition was infinite; man, finite. How can the finite understand the infinite? Over and over again, the philosophers say: don't ask questions. The questions have no answers. The only answer is the one you are willing to accept. If you are willing to accept an answer, it means that you are willing to suspend reason. Reason, then, is the enemy of faith. If you have faith, you can accept any answer; it does not necessarily have to be based on logic.

Down the years, ever since, in fact, man began to ask himself the why and wherefore about himself, he has raised questions and the history of philosophy is the history of questions asked, the reason sought. To each his own answer. I began with death. How was death to be defined? The end of life? The beginning of life? The junction between two lives? A nodal point in a series of live, life without end? Is there any way out of this "series," what the Buddhists would call "chain" and if so, how is one to get out of it and, more importantly, what is the destination? How can what is, cease to be? The philosophy of Monism towers high in speculative flights upon this point. It holds absorption into Brahman as the goal, an absolute merger and identity with the Supreme Being. This is the highest heaven, from which there is no return. As the *Brahma Sutras* say:

nacha punaravarthathe, nacha punaravarthathe.

"He does not revert, does not revert."

The Hindus call this *mokshya*—final release.

As I started to contemplate on death, to my surprise, I began contemplating on life and ultimately on myself—the "I." And it occurred to me: am "I" that important in the scheme of things? Who am I that I should think so highly of myself as to think of all the possible relations between me and the creator? And I remembered a passage in Harry Golden's book *Only in*

America which he started with an essay on why he never bawls out a waitress in a restaurant for either serving bad food or taking a long time to serve it.

> ... because I know that there are at least four billion suns in the Milky Way—which is only one galaxy. Many of these suns are thousands of times larger than our own, and vast millions of them have whole planetary systems, including literally billions of satellites, and all of this revolves at the rate of about a million miles an hour, like a huge oval pinwheel. Our own sun and its planets, which includes this earth, are on the edge of this wheel. This is only our own small corner of the universe, so why do not these billions of revolving and rotating suns and planets collide? The answer is, the space is so unbelievably vast that if we reduced the suns and the planets in correct mathematical proportion with relation to the distances between them, each sun would be a speck of dust, two, three and four thousand miles away from its nearest neighbor. And mind you, this is only the Milky Way—our own small corner—our own galaxy. How many galaxies are there? Billions. Billions of galaxies spaced at about one million light-years apart (one light year is about six trillion miles). Within the range of our biggest telescopes there are at least one hundred million separate galaxies such as our own Milky Way, and that is not all, by any means. The scientists have found that the further you go out into space with the telescopes, the thicker the galaxies become, and there are billions of billions as yet uncovered to the scientist's camera and the astrophysicist's calculations ... [95]

When you think of all this, wrote Golden, it's silly to worry whether the waitress brought you string beans instead of limas.

We are not just part of that small space in space called earth, or of that conglomeration we know of as the solar system, but literally billions upon billions of solar systems. When one contemplates this, the utter insignificance of man becomes apparent at once.

This, surely, is what the Psalmist meant when he said:

> When I consider Thy heavens, the work of Thy fingers; the moon and the stars, which Thou hast ordained; what is man that Thou art mindful of him? and the son of man, that Thou visitest him?
>
> Psalm 8:3-4

There are two ways of looking at this: one, that man is so insignificant, that surely God, if there is One, could hardly be bothered with him; two, that if God indeed created man, as he created everything in the expanding universe, surely He is as much interested in man as in everything else of His creation? Yes, but what does "caring" mean? It means, in its simplest meaning, goodness. Does a good God destroy what He has made? Or alternately, should man in his own rationalization of God's goodness maintain that whatever God does is, by definition, good and that, therefore, whatever is construed as "destruction" in man's books is only the carrying out of God's will?

It seems a strange rationalization of God's will that He who gives life so freely should take it away too often in the cruellest of fashion. Consider this: the number of man-made deaths in the twentieth century alone is about one hundred million.[96] These people did not die a natural death. They died violently in the hands of their fellowmen or out of privation. Anything from 5 to 9 million Jews died in Germany at the hands of the Nazis. This is a strange way for God to deal with his chosen people and can hardly be dismissed by the notation that God's ways are strange indeed.

True enough, seeking an answer to death is perhaps the greatest wild-goose chase of human existence, as Gil Elliot, author of *Twentieth Century Book of the Dead* remarks after his painful cataloguing of deaths in this, our bloodiest century. But if there is no answer, both the question and the questioner become absurdities. Abraham Joshua Heschel, that lovable Jewish philosopher who died in 1972 understood this delemma when he recounted the story of the Hasid who once started to recite the thirteen principles of Maimonides:

> "I firmly believe that the Creator, blessed be His name, is the Creator and Ruler of all created things" . . . . Suddenly he paused: "Can I say that I firmly believe? If I did, I would not be so fretful, so profane; I would not pray so half-heartedly . . . . But if I do not, how dare I tell a lie . . . . No, I will not say it; a liar is worse than a non-believer . . . . Yet this would mean I do not believe. But I do believe! . . . . " Again he paused, until he found a way out. He decided to say: "Oh that I might firmly believe . . . "[97]

The truth of the matter is that the thinking man wants an answer. Conditioned as the religious man is to accept what his particular religious dogma dictates, he may compromise, like our good Hasid and wish he could believe. To demand of man that he accept on faith what his reason tells him is unacceptable is to perpetrate a monstrous joke. Heschel has his answer. "Neither reason nor faith is all-inclusive" he says in his book *Man Is Not Alone, A Philosophy of Religion* "not self-sufficient. The insights of faith are general, vague and stand in need of conceptualization in order to be communicated to the mind, integrated and brought to consistency. Reason is a necessary co-efficient of faith, lending form to what often becomes violent, blind and exaggerated by imagination. Faith without reason is mute; reason without faith is deaf."[98]

As a statement it is very clever; faith demands the subservience of reason. The reasoning man can only revolt at this imperious demand. Some philosophers attempt to provide an answer to the unanswerable by the introduction of a novel idea: fate. Thus and thus it is fated and since fate, by definition, brooks no appeal, we resolve one dilemma with a stroke of the pen.

The thinkers of old in India—as thinkers elsewhere in the civilized world—concocted a story, a fable which is recounted in the *Mahabharata*, the great Hindu epic. According to this story, Brahma created so many beings that the earth began to be overpopulated to the point that "there was no room to breathe." Death had not yet entered the world. Creation alone was going on at full speed. Overburdened as a result, mother earth could only appeal to the creator—Brahma—to somehow lighten her load by "removing" a reasonable number of His own progeny.

Thereupon, he repressed a portion of His creative energy, in order to provide for both creation and destruction. From His repressed energies emerged Kali, dressed in scarlet robes and with eyes blazing red. Her, Brahma named death and enjoined on her to carry out His vision of lightening mother earth's load.

But Kali would not comply. Compassion seized her and her tears of grief fell copiously. Confounded, Brahma transformed those tears into diseases. Brahma also instructed Kali to visit his creatures with the vices of desire and wrath before inflicting on them the diseases that destroy. In that way death could be said to have been brought on the unrighteous. Note the name Kali. It stems from the word *kal*, "time." And time has a special place in Hindu eschatology.

In the *Atharva Veda*, time is a theme of philosophic speculation. Everything exists in time.

> Time begot yonder heaven, time also (begot) these earths. That which was, and that which shall be, urged forth by time, spreads out.
>
> Time created the earth, in time the sun burns. In time are all beings, in time the eye looks abroad.
>
> In time mind is fixed, in time breath (is fixed), in Time names (are fixed); when time has arrived all these creatures rejoice.
>
> In time *tapas* (creative fervour) is fixed; in time the highest (being is fixed); in time brahman (the mystic power in the universe) is fixed; time is the lord of everything . . . .
>
> By him this (universe) was urged forth, by him it was begotten. Time, truly, having become the brahman supports Paramesthin (the highest lord).[99]

Or again:

> From time the waters did arise, from time the brahman, the tapas, the regions (of space did arise).
>
> Through time the wind blows, through time, the great earth. The great sky is fixed in time. In time the son (Prajapati) begot of yore that which was, and that which shall be . . . [100]

In the Upanishads, however, Brahman has two forms, namely time and beyond time, the timeless form. Time is not the first cause, it is Brahman. Time is also charged with the task of destruction. Nothing can last except time. Time alone prevails. And just as, earlier, we measured man's insignificance in terms of creation— the billions and billions of universes that make the expanding space beyond us—so can we measure man's insignificance in terms of time.

Think now of the *Brahmarandhra*—the Hindu conception of the complete life of Brahma, the creator:

360 (odd) mortal days make 1 mortal year.

360 mortal years make 1 year of the gods, or a divine year.

Krita Yuga (The Golden Age) has 1,728,000 mortal years.

Treta Yuga (The Silver Age) has 1,296,000 mortal years.
Dwapara Yuga (The Copper Age) has 864,000 mortal years.
Kali Yuga (The Iron Age) has 432,000 mortal years.

One *Maha Yuga* (or the four preceeding) thus has 4,320,000 mortal years.
71 *Maha Yugas* form the reign of one *Manu* or 306,720,000 years.
14 *Manus* make, in all, 4,294,080,000 mortal years.
Adding the dawns or twilights between each *Manu* make 25,920,000 mortal years.
These reigns of *Manu*, along with dawns make 1,000 *Maha Yugas*, a *Kapla*, or Day of Brahma amounting to 4,320,000,000 mortal years.
Brahma's Night equals his Day and thus his Day and Night make 8,640,000,000 mortal years.
360 of them make Brahma's Year of 3,110,400,000,000 mortal years.
100 of these make Brahma's Life or 311,040,000,000,000 mortal years.[101]

How insignificant seems man when one contemplates time. Well might the Psalmist say: "The days of man are but as grass for he flourisheth as a flower in the field. For as soon as the wind goeth over it, it is gone; and the place thereof shall know it no more." We can think of time then as God. Indeed, in the Bahgavad Gita, there is a passage where Krishna, the god Vishnu incarnate, proclaims his universality, in the course of which he asserts that of measurers, those things which reckon by parts, he is time and again that he is imperishable time. Another view of time is that it constitutes the great dissolution of the universe in an all-consuming fire at the end of an eon.

We do not, of course, understand ourselves, or the why and wherefore of the world one whit the better by telling outselves that time is God or that God is time. It is begging the question, intended, in the final analysis, to cover our ignorance. We presume that there should be God because He is the best explanation of what exists. If there is a watch, there should be a watchmaker. If there is time there should be a timemaker. As Miguel de Unamuno argues, in strict truth we deduce the existence of the creator from the fact that the thing created exists, a process which does not justify rationally His existence. "You cannot deduce a necessity" as Unamuno so charmingly puts it, "from a fact, or else everything were necessary."[102]

In many ways Unamuno is an excellent guide to the seeker after God. In his book *Tragic Sense of Life* he says that when, in his early youth, he begn to be puzzled by "external problems" and read in a book that "God is the great X placed over the ultimate barrier of human knowledge" and that "in the measure in which science advances, the barrier recedes," he wrote in the margin: "On this side of the barrier, everything is explained without Him; on the further side, nothing is explained either with Him or without Him; God, therefore, is superfluous."[103]

Is He though? If He indeed was superfluous, then there is no need to think of Him. Superfluities are expendable. The trouble is that whether we dismiss Him as superfluous or accept Him as necessary, we still do not know the answer. Carducci, in his *Idilio Maremmano* writes:

Meglio oprando abliar senza indagarlo,
Questo enorme mister del universo!

"Better to work and to forget and not to probe into this vast mystery of the universe!"[104] It is the last resort of despair. In his poem "The Ancient Sage" Lord Tennyson says:

> Thou canst not prove the Nameless, O my son,
> Nor canst thou prove the world thou movest in,
> Thou canst not prove that thou art body alone,
> Thou canst not prove that thou art spirit alone,
> Nor canst thou prove that thou art both in one:
> Nor canst thou prove thou art immortal, no,
> Nor yet that thou art mortal, nay, my son,
> Thou canst not prove that I, who speak with thee,
> Am not thyself in converse with thyself,
> For nothing worthy proving can be proven,
> Nor yet disproven; wherefore thou be wise,
> Cleave ever to the sunnier side of doubt,
> Cling to faith beyond the forms of faith!

That, of course, is the ultimate answer: faith. In another sense, it is the ultimate in frustration. What you cannot understand, you have to believe. Listen to Unamuno: "Not by way of reason, but only by the way of love and suffering, do we come to the living God, the human God. Reason rather separates us from Him. We cannot know Him in order that afterwards we may love Him; we must begin by loving Him, longing for Him, hungering after Him, before knowing Him. The knowledge of God proceeds from the love of God and this knowledge has little or nothing of the rational in it. For God is indefinable. To seek to define Him is to seek to confine Him within the limits of our mind, that is to say, to kill Him. Insofar as we attempt to define Him, there rises before us—nothingness."[105]

Further along Unamuno says: "To believe in God is, in the first instance, as we shall see, to wish that there may be a God, to be unable to live without Him."[106] God then exists, when we wish Him to exist. "And He is in us by virtue of the hunger, the longing, which we have for Him; He is Himself creating the longing for Himself." Elsewhere, Unamuno says that faith is our longing for the eternal. Man aspired to God by faith and cries to Him: "I believe—give me, Lord, wherein to believe!" There is the charming story in the ninth chapter of the Gospel according to Mark of the man who brought unto Jesus his son who was possessed by a dumb spirit and wanted Jesus to cure him. And Jesus said unto him: "If thou canst believe, all things are possible to him that believeth!" To which the man replies: "Lord, I believe, help thou mine unbelief!"[107] Immortal words. There is, one suspects, no real contradiction here. The man wishes to believe; wherefore he needs assistance to overcome his unbelief. That, indeed, is the cry of saints down the centuries. That was the cry of August Hermann Francke, who resolved to call upon God, a God in whom he did not believe, or rather, as Unamuno says, in whom he believed that he did not believe, to take pity upon him, if perchance He really existed. That is the Athiest's Prayer, as noted by Unamuno himself in his *Rosario de Sonetos Liricos:*

    Sufro yo a tu costa
    Dios no existiente, pues si tu existieras
    existieria yo tambien de veras.

> Thou art the cause of my suffering
> O non-existing God,
> For if Thou didst exist,
> Then should I also exist.[108]

But then the eternal is already in us, whether we realize it or not. It is the DNA—de-oxyribonucleic acid—which maintains its headquarters in the nucleus of each living cell. With its celebrated "double helix" architecture, DNA is the master molecule of heredity—in fact of all life. As Albert Rosenfeld in his book *Prolongevity* puts its, "DNA is the molecule from which all life on earth seems to have sprung, from its dawn in prehistory through all the millennia of evolution, from protozoa to dinosaurs to people, all of whose 'genetic codes' have been surprisingly alike."

DNA, in fact, is millions of years old, yet shows no signs of old age. "As far as we know" writes Rosenfeld, "DNA is the only organic substance in the universe that possesses the information to ensure its own virtual immortality."[109] The cells may grow old and die, but the DNA continues by renewing itself in the mother's egg and the father's sperm. It is as if DNA used us to keep itself going! Adds Rosenfeld: "It discards individuals as blithely as a snake sheds its successive skins after they have outlived their usefulness and simply continues its own life in the next generation. We like to think that we use DNA (but) one might just as readily speculate that the purpose of human life is to perpetuate DNA!"[110]

The reference to the immortality of DNA is not as irrelevant or irreverent in this context as it may momentarily seem. Gerontologists are agreed that man's life can be prolonged—exactly how long depending upon the acquisition of man's knowledge of the mechanics of aging. Theoretically speaking, prolongation of man's life should not be an impossibility. Rosenfeld says it is now possible to come to the following conclusions:
1) That there does exist within ourselves an identifiable "clock of aging," a genetically determined program which dictates that we will age and die, and the rate at which this will occur;
2) That we have an excellent chance of discovering the location

(there may be more than one) of the clock of aging, as well as the nature of its operating mechanisms—and how to interfere with them to our own advantage:

3) That, moreover, all this can begin to happen, not centuries from now, but now, if only the research can be carried out;

4) That senescence may thus be started on its way to obsolescence.[111]

The implication is that man may yet discover, not the elixir of eternal life, but the means of structurally changing the clock of aging to keep man eternally young.

Should such a thing happen, will that basically change man's attitude towards God? We think of God primarily because we know our finitude; man, by definition, is mortal. But if science can help him become immortal, then where is God's place in man's world? If suffering is banished from the world, as we have succeeded in banishing small pox or to a lesser extent, tuberculosis, how can we know God whom man calls for in his suffering? Like so many other questions, this too will have to wait for an answer. Faith and doubt are two sides of the same coin. Faith, indeed, is not without its incertitudes, illogical as it may seem. We may well say with Robert Browning:

> All we have gained, then, by our unbelief
> Is a life of doubt diversified by faith
> For one of faith diversified by doubt.
> "Bishop Blougram's Apology"

The truly happy, of course, are the truly ignorant; blessed are the ignorant, for they don't have to argue about the existence of God; they just accept Him. I am endlessly struck by the simple faith of old Strepsiades who asks of Socrates in *The Clouds* of Aristophanes: "Who is it that sends the rain? Who is it that thunders?" To which the philosopher matter of factly replies: "Not Zeus, but the clouds." "But" questions Strepsiades, dissatisfied with the answer, "who but Zeus makes the clouds sweep along?" Says Socrates again: "Not a bit of it; it is atmospheric whirligig." "Whirligig?" muses Strepsiades, "I never thought of that—that Zeus is gone and that Son Whirligig rules now in his stead!"[112] It would have been patently pointless for Socrates to go on.

Strepsiades' mind had been made up already: there had to be Zeus—a god. If perchance, He was away, what more sensible for Him than to appoint His son to carry on His work in His absence? Reason, where is your victory, faith, where is your defeat?

Earlier, I had said that when I thought of death, my thoughts, by necessity, had gone to life and to life's creator and the creator, by definition, was self-created or as the Aryans would say *Swayambhu*. The creator may have started life, but did He ordain death as well? Isn't there any prospect of man perpetuating himself not through his children but in the prolongation of his life? The question should not, again, be dismissed as far-fetched. Immortality, as the scientist F. M. Esfandiary has written in *Optimism One* "is only another phase in evolution. It is no more spectacular than the evolution of the upright position or the attainment of speech. Certainly it is far less spectacular than the emergence of life from matter." Put that way, it certainly is. I am even more impressed by what Dean F. Juniper of the University of Reading School of Education in England has to say in *Man Against Mortality*. Man, he writes "may be designed to make himself and life immortal, the necessary skills and motivations having been built into him. If this is the case then all his myths and fantasies of immortality may be in the nature of necessary rehearsals for an as yet unrealistic, but eventually to be realized, ultimate transformation."

The point to note here is that a good deal—probably all—of our thinking about God and ways to attain Him is conditioned by our thoughts on death. Would we be thinking about God if there was no death? If it is theoretically possible to attain immortality— and let it be remembered, the science of cryonics has still to be developed—could it be that our concept of God will undergo a deep and qualitative change? We are afraid of God because we are afraid of death, and even more, we are afraid of the hereafter. Death itself would lose its terror if man knew what came after it. All that we know of what will come after is pure speculation; intelligent speculation, perhaps, even convincing speculation, but nevertheless speculation. No one has returned from death to tell us what is there in the Great Beyond. But knowledge of what comes after—the only knowledge worth having, as Nachiketa would have us believe and which is true—could make God irrelevant, for it is the mystery of what comes after death that makes us turn to God in life. In that sense may it be said that knowledge of the afterlife is knowledge of god. Presto, if there is no afterlife, that is to say "life" or continuity after physical death, there can be no god.

Why is it that man who has been vouchsafed so much knowledge is not vouchsafed knowledge of what comes after death? Why is it that it has to be surmised? Could it be that there is no God but thinking brings him into existence? Can the principle of *cogito ergo sum* be extended to God as well? I think, therefore I am; I think God exists; therefore God exists. God is there only to the extent man wills Him to be. If God created man, man surely created Him as well. As Unamuno would put it: "God and man, in effect, mutually create one another."

It is, alas, not necessarily a satisfactory answer. It does not take us one whit further along our quest for the knowledge about after-death to say that man created God. That knowledge remains elusive as ever for all that we have pondered on the subject. Abraham Herschel has one answer. Man, he says, more, one suspects, by way of providing consolation than innate knowledge, is not an innocent bystander in the cosmic drama. "There is in us more kinship with the divine than we are able to believe. The souls of men are candles of the Lord, lit on the cosmic way, rather than fireworks produced by the combustion of nature's explosive compositions and every soul is indispensable to Him. Man is needed, he is a need of God."[113] As a thought, this one is undoubtedly beguiling. Man is a need of God! Well, we might exclaim what do you know!

The truth, of course, is that it is not God who is in need of man, but man who is in need of God and it pleases him to think that perchance God is in need of him as well. But it would be in keeping with the essence of creator-createe relationship to argue that what is created has been needed by the creator. A watchmaker, to go back to the old simile, would not make a watch if he did not need it. A potter would not make a pot if he, in turn, did not need it. If, then, God created man, surely it is because He needed him?

But the analogy can be carried too far, as Unamuno warns. The traditional analogy of the watch and the watchmaker, he argues, is inapplicable to a Being absolute, infinite and eternal. It is, moreover, only another way of explaining nothing. As Unamuno put it: "For to say that the world is as it is and not otherwise because God made it so, while at the same time we do not know for what reason He made it so, is to say nothing. And if we knew for what reason God made it so, then God is superfluous and the reason itself suffices."[114]

Acceptable as the answer is that God made man because He needed him, the question arises: needed for what? To satisfy God's ego? To say that would be to define God who is indefinable. So we come back to square one, no wiser than before. Perhaps we should not attempt to ask why but rather treat God in a different way, in such a way as saints often do, to accept Him as real and even finite and even to argue with Him. Or, like Nikos Kazantzakis to treat God not like someone high up on the altar to be worshipped and prayed to, but as a companion in one's joys and sorrows, a fellow-traveller, a general.

To Kazantzakis God comes in innumerable ways. "I believe" he says in his book *The Saviors of God* "in the innumerable, the ephemeral masks which God has assumed throughout the centuries, and behind His ceaseless flux I discern an indestructable unity." Kazantzakis' concept of God is best described as passionate. He sees God as man in action, a powerful description and not less valid because God is made more human. "Our love for each other" he writes, of his love for God, "is rough and ready, we sit at the same table, we drink the same wine in this low tavern of life. As we clink our glasses, swords clash and resound, loves and hates spring up."[115] And when Kazantzakis prays, it is "not the whimpering of a beggar nor a confession of love" but rather it is "the report of a solider to his general: this is what I did today, this is how I fought to save the entire battle in my own sector, these are the obstacles I found, this is how I plan to fight tomorrow."116

I find this a refreshing attitude toward God. It is the kind of attitude that Francis of Assisi who was a gay rake and prodigal before he took up his staff and sandals would have understood. Then there was the Portuguese John of God who was a gambler, drunkard and a mercenary soldier until he was forty who also became a saint. And what about Mary of Egypt who was a harlot like Magdalene before her or Saint Augustine whose famous cry of the heart, "God, make me chaste, but not yet" has that authentic note of humanity?117 These saints, as Phyllis McGinley writes in her charming book *Saint-Watching* had their own ways. They lost their tempers, got hungry, scolded God—and why not?—were egotistical or testy or impatient in their turns, but went doggedly blundering toward heaven. Or so, one likes to believe.

Those saints! They don't make them anymore. They were so many in the medieval ages and even later and their names strew the hagiographic history of Europe, the Middle East and India. Nivritti, Jnandev, Sopana, Muktabai, Eknath, Namdeo, Tukaram, Tulsidas, Kanakadas . . . their name is legion. The thread that binds them is the thread of love. Thomas Aquinas may have been a great intellectual, but most saints were anything but. They loved God, man and beast with equal abandon and not necessarily in that order. They desired. Teresa of Avila could say: "I have no defense against affection. I could be bribed with a sardine." When someone remonstrated with her for her zest in enjoying food she said: "There is a time for partridge and a time for penance." And how right she was.

Perhaps that is the best way to know God. To love. Ramakrishna, the Saint of Dakhshineshwar was known for it. When Kanakadas sang of his love for Krishna, it has been said, his idol in the famous Udupi temple turned towards his devotee, who, because he was an untouchable, had been unable to enter it. The authorities had to make a hole in the wall so Kanakadas could feast his eyes upon his Lord. Indeed, there is no pain here, no cause for doubt, no need for intellectual debate, no necessity for philosophical carping. To love is all.

The Hindus have a word for it. They call it Bhakti Yoga, the yoga of devotion. It calls for no intellectual gymnastics. It makes no demand on one's body as would asceticism with its praying and fasting. All it asks for is total devotion. And what is devotion, but love?

Miss McGinley tells us of Bridget, the Irish saint who gave away everything in her own house and in the house of her father and eventually of the king himself, to any beggar passing by. So great was her love, that she even managed to make the forces of nature cooperate with her in giving. When all the food in the convent where she lived had been given and word suddenly came that the Seven Bishops of Cabinteely were about to visit her she could tell the nuns: "Go out and ask the hens kindly to lay more eggs. And speak to the trees—see whether they have anything left in the way of fruit. Talk gently to the cows and beg them for a little milk" and sure enough the hens cackled and laid eggs, the trees shook their branches and apples and pears fell into the nuns' aprons and the Seven Bishops that evening vowed they never had a richer repast in their lives. That is saintliness.[118]

One suspects that God need not have to exist in order to love Him and thereby to be happy. For surely, the aim of all seekers of God is not so much to find Him—as if he is lost property—but to be, in the first place, at peace with themselves and be happy. The aim, then, is not so much the abstract God as the concrete peace that comes out of understanding. And if that can come from a song, as was the case with Mirabai, or service, as in the instance of Francis Xavier, why not? To know God one does not have to define Him. God can be known, as has been testified time and again by hundreds, just by living.

That is the only meaning there is to life and it should be good enough. In his book *Man's Search for Meaning*, the distinguished physician Viktor E. Frankl says that ultimately, man should not ask what the meaning of life is, but rather must he recognize that it is he who is asked. In a word, each man is questioned by life and he can only answer to life by answering for his own life; to life he can only respond by being responsible.[119]

Writes Dr. Frankl: "The meaning of life differs from man to man, from day to day and from hour to hour. What matters, therefore, is not the meaning of life in general, but rather the specific meaning of a person's life at a given moment . . . One should not search for an abstract meaning of life. Everyone has his own specific vocation or mission in life to carry out a concrete assignment which demands fulfillment. Therein he cannot be replaced nor can his life be repeated. Thus, everyone's task is unique as is his specific opportunity to implement it."[120]

So simple an answer that its very simplicity has the ring of audacity to it, not to speak of the aura of truth. We should not dwell too much on whether life has any meaning especially considering that meaning denotes a condition that cannot be reduced to a material relation and grasped by the sense organs. If life has no meaning, is it to be thrown away? Throwing away does not fulfill life's meaninglessness. Inasmuch as one has control over it, life has to be used. Where one has no control over life, death is the true meaning. Whether one accepts the possibility of life after death or not, insofar as one accepts death as a fact of life, that should suffice as a meaning. No further probing need be made, no questions asked.

Elisabeth Kubler-Ross puts it another way: she calls death as the final stage of growth and it should be an acceptable definition. And one can approach that final stage by learning to die just a little every day. And how does one die just a little every day? By suppressing one's ego or, alternatively, by living just that little bit extra to give our day that additional dimension which is as much taking something from life as giving it to it.

Elisabeth Kubler-Ross put it this way: "In order to be at peace, it is necessary to feel a sense of history—that you are both part of what has come before and part of what is yet to come. Being thus surrounded, you are not alone; and the sense of urgency that pervades the present is put in perspective: do not frivolously use the time that is yours to spend. Cherish it that each day may bring new growth, insight, and awareness. Use this growth not selfishly, but rather in service of what may be, in the future tide of time. Never allow a day to pass that did not add to what was understood before...[121]

This, of course, does not guarantee us an answer to the meaning of life except in terms of making life meaningful. Indeed, the answer to the meaning of life is the making of a meaningful life. Meaningful in terms of love, devotion and service. The ultimate meaning, says Dr. Frankl, necessarily exceeds and surpasses the finite capacities of man. "What is demanded of man" as he so rightly says, "is not, as some existential philosophers teach, to endure the meaninglessness of life, but rather to bear his incapacity to grasp its unconditional meaningfulness in rational terms." How better can the question be answered?

The Indian epic, *Mahabharata* says it in a different way:

> Do good today, time passes, death is near.
> Death falls upon a man all unawares
> Like a ferocious wolf upon a sheep.
> Death comes when his approach is least expected;
> Death sometimes seizes ere the work of life
> Is finished or its purposes accomplished.
> Death carries off the weak and strong alike
> The brave and timourous, the wise and foolish,
> And those whose objects are not yet achieved.
> Therefore delay not. Death may come today,
> Death will not wait to know if thou art ready
> Or if thy work be done. Be active now
> While thou art young, and time still thy own
> This very day, perform tomorrow's work.
> This very morning, do thy evening's task
> When duty is discharged, then if thou live
> Honor and happiness will be thy lot
> And if thou die, supreme beatitude.[122]
>
> *Mahabharata XII, verse 6534*

One of the great devotional saints in India is Kabir who was born in the fifteenth century—a century rich in saints. Kabir's songs are justly famous and Robert Bly provides a beautiful translation of one of them that is in the same spirit of the *Mahabharata*. Kabir speaks of God as the guest and believes that it is "the intensity of the longing for the guest"—an assertion with which no doubt all saints would subscribe to—"that does all the work."

To seek God, not, as the English poet Thompson said, in "the labyrinthine ways of my own mind" but everywhere, in the hovels of the poor, in the crowded streets of any city, anywhere . . . that is Kabir's message.

> Friend, hope for the Guest while you are alive.
> Jump into experience while you are alive!
> Think . . . and think . . . while you are alive.
> What you call "salvation" belongs to the time before death.
>
> If you don't break your ropes while you're alive,
> do you think
> ghosts will do it after?
>
> The idea that the soul will join with the ecstatic
> just because the body is rotten—
> that is all fantasy.
> What is found now is found then.
> If you find nothing now,
> You will simply end up with an apartment in the city of death.
> If you make love with the divine now, in the next life
> you will have the face of satisfied desire.
>
> So plunge into the truth, find out who the teacher is,
> Believe in the Great Sound!
>
> Kabir says this: When the Guest is being searched for,
> it is the intensity of the longing for the Guest
> that does all the work.
>
> Look at me and you will see a slave of that intensity.[123]

The Guest, God, the soul, life, death—can they all be for real? What, in fact, are we all talking about? I am sometimes reminded of the story of Vishnu's *maya*. The story is about the mystery of *maya*, the cosmic power of illusion in Indian philosophy which envelops all of creation and gives us the sense of what we are. It begins with the sage Narada, asking his teacher, Vishnu, who is one of the three primary aspects of God in the Hindu pantheon, to explain the secret of his *maya*. Vishnu is most reluctant to do so, realizing that *maya* cannot be intellectually explained and that once a person understands what it is, he will no longer be ensnared in the illusive power of the world.

Narada, in search of knowledge, persists in his questioning

and Vishnu finally relents, promising an answer after the sage had brought him some water to drink from a nearby village.

So Narada goes to the village, meets some villagers and gets so involved with them that he forgets why he had gone there in the first place. What should have been a stay of a few minutes becomes a permanent stay, with Narada eventually marrying and raising a family.

During his twelfth year in the village there are heavy rains and floods and in an attempt to escape Narada and his family try to ford a swollen river. First his children and then his wife are swept away in the swirling current and Narada alone survives. Tired and frightened and unable to grasp his personal tragedy, Narada falls exhausted on the bank of the river, whereupon he suddenly sees Vishnu standing by his side, gently asking: "Narada, Narada, where's my water? I've been waiting half an hour."

Foolish, foolish man, to want to know what can't be known. To know is not to ask.

REFERENCES

1. There are several versions to this story. I have taken the version given by Swami Vivekananda in *Vivekananda: The Yogas and Other Works*; Ramakrishna Vivekananda Centre, New York, NY 1953, p. 851.

2. *Ibid.* pp. 848-850.

3. See Swami Rama: *Life Here and Hereafter*, Himalayan International Institute, Honesdale, Pennsylvania; also *Sri Aurobindo: The Upanishads*, Vol. 12, pp. 237-265.

4. S. Radhakrishnan and Charles A. Moore: *A Source Book of Indian Philosophy*; Princeton, N.J., 1957, p. 45.

5. *Ibid.*, p. 69.

6. *Ibid.*, p. 54.

7. Vivekananda: *The Yogas and Other Works:* Ramakrishna Vivekananda Centre, New York, NY, 1953. For a detailed discussion see chapter on Raja Yoga, pp. 586-621.

8. *Ibid.*, p. 620.

9. S. Radhakrishnan and Charles A. Moore: *A Source Book on Indian Philosophy*; Princeton, N.J., p. 55.

10. *Ibid.* p. 82.

11. S. Radhakrishnan: *Indian Philosophy*, Vol I, p. 209.

12. *Ibid.*, p. 237.

13. *Ibid.*, p. 240.

14. For a fuller discussion, see S. Radhakrishnan: *Indian Philosophy*, Vol. I, The McMillan Co., New York, pp. 227-249.

15. Jacques Monod: *Chance and Necessity*, Vintage Books, Random House, New York, p. 138.

16. Raymond A. Moody Jr., *Life After Life*; Mockingbird Books, Atlanta, 1975, p. 19.

17. *Ibid.*, p. 23.

18. *Ibid.* p. 120.

19. *Newsweek*, July 12, 1976.

20. Swami Rama: *Life Here and Hereafter*, Himalayan International Institute, Honesdale, Pennsylvania, p. 109.

21. Compare this with Swami Rama's comments (p. 109) in *Life Here and Hereafter*: ("When the inhalation and exhalation cease to function, it is called death; but with the help of subtle *pranas* all the former impressions or *samskaras* are preserved.")

22. Gina Cerminara: *Many Mansions*, The New American Library, Inc., p. 42.

23. *Ibid.*, p. 211.

24. S. Radhakrishnan: *Indian Philosophy*, Vol. I, p. 293.

25. For a fuller discussion, see S. Radhakrishnan: *Indian Philosophy* Vol. I, pp. 446-453.

26. For a diagrammatic study, see Swami Rama, et al., *Yoga and Psychotherapy: The Evolution of Consciousness*, Himalayan International Institute, Honesdale, Pennsylvania, p. 98.

27. Dorothy C. Donath: *Buddhism for the West*, McGraw-Hill Paperbacks, New York, 1971, pp. 10-11.

28. *Ibid.*, p. 35. (Ms. Donath points out that while there is a similarity between the Precepts and the Ten Commandments, there is one important difference. "Here we are not commanded to do anything under the threat of punishment from any outside power. The law of karma takes care of that eventually and inevitably good follows good thoughts and actions. . . ")

29. S. Radhakrishnan: *Indian Philosophy*, Vol. I, p. 416.

30. W. Y. Evans-Wentz: *The Tibetan Book of the Dead*, Causeway Books, New York, 1973, pp. 28-30.

31. *Ibid.*, introduction p. xl.

32. For a fuller appreciation, see Swami Rama: *Life Here and Hereafter*, pp. 111-121 and *Sri Aurobindo*, Vol. 12, Sri Aurobindo Ashram, Pondicherry, pp. 23-44.

33. William Q. Judge: *The Ocean of Theosophy*, Theosophical University Press, Pasadena, California, 1973, p. 2.

34. *Ibid.*, p. 44.

35. *Ibid.*, pp. 126-127.

36. *Ibid.*, p. 131.

37. Dorothy C. Donath: *Buddhism for the West*, McGraw-Hill Paperbacks, New York, 1971, p. 42.

38. *The Aryan Path*, (June, 1938)

39. Aldous Huxley: *The Perennial Philosophy*, Harper & Row, Publishers, New York, 1945, pp. 214-215.

40. Also see Carl G. Jung in *The Meaning of Death*, McGraw-Hill Book Co., New York, 1959, pp. 3-15.

41. Sri Aurobindo: *The Life Divine*, Books I and II, Sri Aurobindo Ashram, Pondicherry, pp. 188-197.

42. *Ibid.*, p. 193.

43. *Ibid.*, p. 193.

44. For a fuller discussion on karma, see Sri Aurobindo: *The Life Divine*, Vol. 19, Sri Aurobindo Ashram, Pondicherry, pp. 804-823.

45. Satprem: *Sri Aurobindo or the Adventures of Consciousness*, Harper & Row, Publishers, 1968, p. 123.

46. *Ibid.*, pp. 123-124.

47. *Ibid.*, p. 139.

48. *Ibid.*, p. 139.

49. Sri Aurobindo: *Collected Poems*, Vol. 5, Sri Aurobindo Ashram, Pondicherry, p. 132.

50. W. H. D. Rouse, (Trans): *Great Dialogues of Plato*, New American Library, Inc., New York, 1956, pp. 461-521.

51. The Sirdar Ikbal Ali Shah: *The Spirit of the East*, E. P. Dutton & Co., Inc., New York, 1975, p. 274.

52. Walter Kaufman: *Existentialism, Religion & Death*, New American Library, Inc., New York, 1976, p. 125. See also Ameer Ali Syed: *The Spirit of Islam*, Christopher's, Longon, 1949, pp. 190-198.

53. Walter Kaufman: *Existentialism, Religion and Death*, New American Library, Inc., New York, 1976, p. 127.

54. Huston Smith: *The Religions of Man*, Harper & Row, Publishers, New York, 1965, p. 258.

55. Nathan N. Glatzer (ed). *The Judaic Tradition*; Beacon Press, Boston, 1969, pp. 329-331.

56. *Ibid.*, pp. 327-329.

57. *Ibid.*, pp. 332-335.

58. Moses Maimonides: *The Guide to the Perplexed*; Dover Publications, New York, 1956, p. 285.

59. *Ibid.*, p. 272.

60. Natha N. Glatzer (ed). *The Judaic Tradition*; Beacon Press, Boston, 1969, pp. 154-159.

61. *Ibid.*, pp. 456-458.

62. Ameer Ali Syed: *The Spirit of Islam*; Christopher's, London, 1949, pp. 198-199.

63. Sir Mohammad Iqubal: *The Reconstruction of Religious Thought in Islam*; Shaikh Muhammad Ashraf, Booksellers, Lahore, 1954, pp. 116-121.

64. W. Y. Evans-Wentz: *The Tibetan Book of the Dead*; Causeway Books, New York, 1973, p. xlii, ff.

65. Sir Mohammad Iqbal: *The Reconstruction of Religious Thought in Islam*; Shaikh Muahmmad Ashraf, Booksellers, Lahore, 1954, p. 123.

66. Dr. M. Abdul Haq in *Islam: Faith and Practice*; Punjab University, Patiala, 1969, p. 22.

67. *Ibid.*, p. 24.

68. H. F. Lovell Cocks in *A Handbook of Christian Theology*; New American Library Inc., New York, 1958, pp. 70-73.

69. *Ibid.*, p. 72.

70. A. T. Molligan in *A Handbook of Christian Theology*; New American Library Inc., New York, 1958, pp. 154-156.

71. Robert McAfee Brown in *A Handbook of Christian Theology*; New American Library, Inc., New York, 1958, pp. 183-185.

72. Shubert M. Ogden in *A Handbook of Christian Theology*; New American Library Inc., New York, 1958, pp. 77-80.

73. Paul Tillich: *History of Christian Thought*; Simon & Shuster, New

York, 1968, p. 268.

74. *Ibid.*, p. 268.
75. *Ibid.*, p. 212.
76. *Ibid.*, p. 245.
77. *Ibid.*, p. 247.
78. *Ibid.*, p. 248.
79. *Ibid.*, pp. 213-218.
80. Massey H. Shepherd Jr., in *A Handbook of Christian Theology*; New American Library Inc., New York, 1958, p. 331.
81. *Ibid.*, p. 331.
82. *Ibid.*, p. 331.
83. Roger Hazelton in *A Handbook of Christian Theology*; New American Library Inc., New York, 1958, pp. 336-339.
84. Heinz Zahrnt: *The Question of God;* Harcourt Brace Javanovich, New York, 1966, p. 31.
85. *Ibid.*, p. 31.
86. *Ibid.*, p. 96.
87. *Ibid.*, p. 96.
88. *Ibid.*, p. 96-97.
89. *Ibid.*, p. 109.
90. *Ibid.*, p. 110.
91. *Ibid.*, p. 110.
92. St. John of the Cross: *Dark Night of the Soul*, Doubleday & Co., (Image Books), Garden City, New York, 1959, p. 175.
93. Quoted by Walter Kaufmann in *Existentialism, Religion and Death*; New American Library Inc., New York, 1976, p. 161.
94. C. M. Padmanabhacharya: *Life and Teachings of Sri Madhvacharya*; Sri Palimar Mutt, Udupi, 1970, p. 108.

95. Harry Golden: *Only in America*; The World Publishing Co., New York, 1958, p. 21.

96. Gil Elliot: *Twentieth Century Book of the Dead*; Charles Scribner's Sons, New York, 1962, p. 1.

97. Abraham Joshua Heschel: *Man Is Not Alone; A Philosophy of Religion;* Farrar, Strauss and Giroux Inc., New York, p. 173.

98. *Ibid.*, p. 173.

99. W. Norman Brown: *Man in the Universe: Some Cultural Continuities in India*; University of California Press, Berkeley and Los Angeles, California, 1966, p. 72.

100. *Ibid.*, pp. 72-73.

101. William Q. Judge: *The Ocean of Theosophy*; Theosophical University Press, Pasadena, 1973, pp. 142-143.

102. Miguel de Unanumo; *Tragic Sense of Life*; Dover Publications, New York, 1954, p. 161.

103. *Ibid..*, pp. 160-161.

104. *Ibid.*, p. 102.

105. *Ibid.*, pp. 167-168.

106. *Ibid.*, p. 168.

107. *Ibid.*, pp. 119-120.

108. *Ibid.*, p. 121.

109. Alfred Rosenfeld: *Prolongevity*; Alfred A. Knopf, New York, 1976, p. xvi.

110. *Ibid.*, p. xvii.

111. *Ibid.*, p. 15.

112. Miguel de Unanumo: *Tragic Sense of Life*; Dover Publications, New York, 1954, p. 145.

113. Abraham Joshua Heschel: *Man is Not Alone, A Philosophy of Religion*; Farrar, Strauss and Giroux Inc., New York, p. 215.

114. Miguel de Unanumo: *Tragic Sense of Life*; Dover Publications, New York, 1954, p. 162.

115. Nikos Kazantzakis: *The Savior of God*; Simon & Schuster (A Touchstone Book), New York, 1960, p. 108.

116. *Ibid.*, p. 107.

117. Phyllis McGinley: *Saint Watching*; The Viking Press, New York, 1969, p. 6.

118. *Ibid.*, p. 12.

119. Viktor E. Frankl: *Man's Search for Meaning*; Beacon Press, Boston, 1962, pp. 110-111.

120. *Ibid.*, p. 110.

121. Elisabeth Kubler-Ross: *Death: The Final Stage of Growth*; Prentice-Hall Inc., Englewood Cliffs, New Jersey, 1975, p. 167.

122. C. M. Padmanabhacharya: *Life and Teachings of Sri Madhvacharya*; p. 169.

123. Robert Bly: *The Kabir Book*; Beacon Press, Boston, 1977, p. 24.

Part II

To know how a man dies is to know the man. Man can die in many ways; he may have foreknowledge of his impending death, as in the instance of a man who is condemned to die for crimes or by cancer. It may be lingering illness the end of which can only be death. Or death may come like a thief, by stealth, catching the man unawares. And then there is death by accident—and by design. We call the latter suicide. Death has many faces.

Not all of us are prepared for death even knowing that it is the only certainty about life. Most of us cast aside the very thought, as if, by so doing, we postpone the evil day. Many, no doubt, see it coming, but refuse to acknowledge the fact. We deny death by not accepting its reality. The rare few have faced death with courage and equanimity, happy in the thought that their time has come. For most, however, the difficulty is not of facing death, but of being concerned by the feeling that they have not completed their mission or attained their goals. The father who has growing children and who feels that he must live long enough to see his son through college or his daughter married. The scholar who has begun work on a major project and who thinks life owes it to him to finish it. The profligate who hopes to have his debts repaid . . . they all have set goals and want to achieve them before they turn in.

The death of the very young is particularly painful. There is the promise cut short, the tasks that never will be done. But when is a task ever gotten done? When do we say, enough?

Mahatma Gandhi used to say that he wanted to live up to a hundred and twenty five years to complete his self-appointed duties but toward the end of his life he had begun to despair—not of his life, but of his task. Perhaps death came timely. His task was never to end.

And so we come to the question: when is the right time to die? At twenty? Thirty? Fifty? Seventy five? After the son has been seen through college and the daughter married? After the great tome has been completed and the reviews garnered? After the discovery of the century has been made? After the highest mountain has been climbed, the widest desert crossed, the most turbulent sea swum? Do we know when to die?

Would Christ have done more for the world by living the biblical three score years and ten? Would the Buddha's life have been more meaningful if he had lived another twenty years? Would Einstein's greatness been enhanced with the addition of a few more years to his distinguished career? Abhimanyu was not yet a youth when he died in battle. One wonders whether we would have acknowledged his courage if he had lived up to hoary old age. History is full of names of men and women who died young and attained glory, early achievers, one might well call them. Whether God loved them or it was just that their time was up, they had carved out for themselves a quiet niche in mankind's memory.

As age goes, Shakespeare was only 52 when he died, but no greater bard ever lived or wrote. Lord Byron was 36, Shelley a bare 30 and John Keats an absurd 26 when they died. And think of some others: Franz Kafka, the Czech writer whose name has been associated with a literary scenario, was 41 at the time of his death. Gerald Manley Hopkins, the poet, was 45, O. Henry, 48, Baudelaire 46, Apollinaire 38. There is something to be said, perhaps, for old age, but, except for a favored few who flowered late, many had reached their peak when they were in the thirties or forties. After that the going was mostly downhill.

There is, then, no particular virtue in living long and unlaborious lives unless it is held that not labor but life is precious. Churchill's last days were miserable; he had almost become a vegetable, a burden to himself and his family. Happier, undoubtedly, the man who goes to his death with all his senses gloriously intact, his body whole, his mind functioning, his spirit undimmed. And yet, how many would want to? How many, given the choice, would call it a day when they still can enjoy a sunrise, appreciate great art and beautiful music, rather than linger on to become caricatures of themselves, sans eyes, sans teeth, sans everything?

It is hope that keeps us going, long after we know that any meaningful achievement is beyond our grasp. If the children are married, we want to see our grandchildren—and then our great grandchildren. If the great discovery has been made we would want to make just one more discovery, climb just one more mountain, swim one more sea, not realizing that it is the first mountain climbed that is the heart of achievement and the first book written. But it is only the Psalmist who says, "vanity of vanities, all is vanity." We keep going until we drop dead, struggling, complaining and to the end, hoping. And till then, living in constant terror. Need we? There is a way to die as there is a way to live. And what follows is an account of how some of the great—and not so great—died. Hopefully, in it is a moral.

THE LORD, KRISHNA

We know of Krishna, Arjuna's great charioteer, to whom is ascribed the luminous thought of the Bhagavad Gita, as the incarnation of Vishnu, the Godhead. It was Krishna, again, who saw the Pandavas through the battle of Kurukshetra and the rehabilitation of the five brothers as the rightful rulers of Hastinapura. The battle had been won but Krishna had called on himself the curse of Gandhari, mother of the Kauravas who had been slaughtered. "O Krishna," Gandhari had said in lamentation of the fallen heroes, "you remained indifferent while my sons and relations slew each other. Wherefore, you shall be the slayer of your own kinsmen. Thirty six years hence, you shall, after causing the death of your kinsmen, friends and son, perish by ignoble means in the wilderness."

Thirty six years thus passed and Yudhistira, eldest of the Pandava princes, began to see many unusual portents. One day, the heroes of the Vrishni clan, to which Krishna belonged, saw the sages Vishwamitra, Kanva and Narada who had arrived at Dwaraka, the Vrishni capital. Foolishly, they decided to play a prank on the holy men.

Disguising Samba, one of their own, as a woman, the heroes approached the ascetics and said: "This is the wife of the illustrious Vabhru who wishes to have a son. Tell us, O sages, whether the child she is bearing will be a boy or a girl." The sages who saw through this all, felt insulted and enraged. In their anger, they now uttered a curse on the proud Vrishnis.

"This kinsman of Krishna, Samba, will produce a dreadful iron bolt for the destruction of all of you as well as the Andhakas. Through that iron bolt you will be the exterminators of your family, with the exception of Balarama and Krishna. The blessed Balarama will enter the ocean, renouncing his body, while a hunter by the name of Jara will strike the great Krishna while he is lying on the ground," the sages said as they departed.

And now the curse slowly began to take hold. The Vrishnis and the Andhakas, on a pilgrimage, had arrived at Prabhasa where they intended to rest a while. But soon they set to drinking and the drinking turned into an orgy; words flowed, and so did insults. The Vrishnis attacked the Andhakas and the latter returned the compliment. Words came to blows. Blows to death. One of those killed was Krishna's own son, Pradyumna.

This was too much for Krishna who had been watching the insane battle of words and swords. Seeing his own son killed right in front of him, Krishna, unable to contain his anger, took up a handful of the eraka grass which grew around him, and transforming it into a terrible bolt of iron infused with the energy of thunder, hurled it at all those engaged in the orgy. Thus was the curse of Gandhari, as of the three sages, partially fulfilled.

Thereupon Balarama and Krishna together with Vabhru, left the scene of wholesale destruction. Balarama retired to a solitary place and even as Krishna watched him, spew out from his mouth a powerful snake. The snake, which had a thousand heads, a body as large as a mountain, and a red visage proceeded toward the ocean. Thus ended the life of Balarama.

Krishna was now all alone. He knew his time had come; absorbed in thought, he wandered for a while in the nearby forest. After a time, he decided to rest. He would concentrate his mind in yoga, to await the end. There, under a tree, lying on the earth in splendid yoga, Jara, the fierce hunter, found him and mistaking him for a deer, struck him in the heels with a deadly arrow, from a respectable distance. Rushing forward to capture his quarry however, Jara found that what he had misjudged to be a deer was a yogi wrapped in his ochre robe. Filled with fear, Jara asked for forgiveness as he reverently touched Krishna's feet. But the high-souled Krishna thanked Jara and comforted him and then, the curse of Gandhari finally fulfilled, ascended upward, filling the skies with splendor.

THE BUDDHA: "All component things must grow old and be dissolved again."

The Buddha was well in his eighties as he moved from village to village, grove to grove, staying at one place for a while and then moving on, ever preaching to his devoted followers.

After he stayed a long time at Ambapali's Grove, he went to Beluva, near Vaisali, there to take up abode for the rainy season. He fell ill there, recovered, but realized that his journey was drawing to a close. "I am now grown old, O Ananda" he told his favorite disciple, "and full of years." Like a wornout cart, he said, that cannot be made to move along without additional care, so was the Tathagata's body. The time for him to go had come. "Therefore, O Ananda" he said, "be ye lamps unto yourselves. Hold fast to the Truth."

He asked that all the brethren as reside in the neighborhood of Vesali be summoned once more, which was done. To them he gave another sermon. Practice, he told them, the earnest meditations he had taught them. And he ended his talk with an exhortation: "Behold, O brethren, the final extinction of the Tathagata will take place before long. I now exhort you, saying, All component things must grow old and be dissolved again. Seek ye that which is permanent and work out your salvation with diligence."

From Beluva, the Tatagatha went to Pava and once again he fell sick. He was staying in the mango grove of Chunda, the ironsmith, and had partaken of a meal prepared by the poor man that consisted of rice cakes and a dish of dried boar's meat. It was to be his last meal.

Sick, but anxious not to show it, the Tatagatha decided to push on to Kusinara and felt thirsty on the way. On his instructions, Ananda fetched him a bowl of water from a nearby streamlet that had been muddied by passing carts, but when the Buddha held it, clear as crystal became the water.

Now the Buddha warned Ananda against stirring up remorse in Chunda for feeding the Tatagatha rotten meat. Tell Chunda, said the Buddha, that it was good of him and gain to him that the Tatagatha died having eaten his last meal from Chunda's provision.

The Buddha thereon proceeded to the sala grove of the Mallas, on the further side of the river Hiranyavati near Kusinara and there asked Ananda to make a bed for him, with the head to the north, between twin sals trees. But Ananda was sorely troubled and started to weep. The Buddha admonished him. "Have I not already, on former occasions, told you that it is in the very nature of things that we must separate from them and leave them? The foolish man conceives the idea of "self," the wise man sees there is no ground on which to build it!"

And the Buddha added: "For a long time, Ananda, thou hast been very near to me by thoughts and acts of such love as is beyond all measure. Thou hast done well, Ananda! Be earnest in effort and thou too shalt soon be free from evils, from sensuality, from selfishness, from delusion and from ignorance!" But Ananda was inconsolable. He asked: "Who shall teach us when thou art gone?" There will be other Buddhas who will arise in the world, said the Tatagatha, endowed with wisdom, knowing the universe, who will reveal the same eternal truths that he has taught. Even as he was conversing with Ananda, the Mallas, with their families came streaming to the sala grove to be blessed by the Buddha. Then, the Blessed One received with joy, saying: "Seeking the way, ye must exert yourself and strive with diligence. It is not enough to have seen me! Walk as I have commanded you; free yourself from the tangle of sorrow. Walk in the path with steadfast aim. He who obeys the *dharma* will always enjoy the bliss of the Tatagatha's presence." Then the mendicant Subhadda was received by the Buddha and was accepted as a disciple and true believer.

Now the Buddha asked his audience to have their doubts on anything cleared when they were still face to face with him. Convinced that there were no doubters, the Buddha once more began to speak. "Behold now, brethren" said he, "I exhort you by saying: decay is inherent in all component things, but the truth will remain forever! Work out your salvation with diligence."

Those were his last words. Then the Tatagatha fell into deep meditation, and having passed through the four *jhanas,* entered Nirvana. When the Buddha entered Nirvana, it is said, there was a mighty earthquake and thunder rumbled in the skies. From the assembled Mallas rose the cry: "Too soon has the Blessed One died! Too soon has the Happy One passed away from existence! Too soon has the Light of the world gone out!"

SOCRATES: "We owe a cock to Asclepios: pay it without fail."

The Buddha lived about 500 years before Christ. Socrates came a little later (469-399 B.C.) and lived in the great age of Greece after the two Persian invasions had been repulsed and the Carthaginians overcome. Socrates lived in Athens, by today's standards a small country town, where everybody was known to everybody else. When the Athenians wanted to exchange ideas, they gathered at the market place and there, in the halls, or under the colonnades, or in the open air parliament (of which every grown man was automatically a member) they talked and argued, tried law suits and generally enlightened themselves.

Socrates was a stonemason and carver who believed that he had a divine mission to test all statements. So he delighted in questioning public and private citizens, arguing with them at length to test the validity of anything they said. This was the Socratic dialogue.

Socrates wrote nothing himself, but his most brilliant and noteworthy pupil, Plato (427-347 B.C.) who had set up a school of philosophy in an olive grove on the outskirts of Athens, known as Academy, remembered the words of Socrates and set them down into a more or less complete system. It is to Plato that we owe an account of the last days of his mentor.

By his constant challenging of the thoughts of others in his reckless pursuit of truth, Socrates had made himself unpopular with many Athenians, until, in 399 B.C., when the sage was nearing 70, he was accused of impiety and of corrupting the young men, by three citizens, Meletos, Anytos and Lycon.

The court which tried Socrates was composed of 501 men who were a subdivision of a larger court of 6,000 citizens and were chosen by lot. There was no judge or jury. The majority opinion among the 501 prevailed. Socrates argued his own case but to no avail. He was pronounced guilty. The law required him to propose his own penalty, as an alternative to the death penalty demanded by his chief accuser, Meletos. The law itself did not prescribe any penalty. The court was free to choose between what Meletos proposed and any alternative put forward by Socrates.

After an elequent defence by Socrates, the court by a vote of 281 to 220 adjudged Socrates guilty as charged. Socrates said he was surprised at the close vote but added that he was not resentful; indeed if only thirty votes had changed, he might well have been let off. The question was: what alternative should he propose to Meletos' demand for death? What was proper for him to suffer or to pay? Socrates said that what he deserved for making people happy was free board and lodge in the town hall. He was not asking for pity, but he was convinced that he had wronged no man. In any event he had no money to pay as a fine. Banishment, perhaps? Not, said Socrates, at his age. A fine life it would be for him to be constantly on the run. Could he stop talking as he perennially did, in seeking what he thought was the truth? Alas, a life without enquiry was not worth living for a man and if he said that he would henceforth cease talking, nobody would believe him anyway. But if pay he must, he would propose as a penalty, thirty *minas* of silver and his friends Criton, Critobulos and Apollodoros would stand as sureties.

Having heard him, the court again went into session and voted to condemn Socrates to death. Not for a moment did that faze Socrates, nor did he bear any grudge against those who voted against him. The difficult thing, he told them, was not to escape from death, but to escape from wickedness. And he could say one thing: if they believed that by putting men to death they would stop everyone from reproaching them because they were wrong, they made a great mistake. For himself, he was willing to die many times. For what a pleasure it would be to meet those who had gone before him, men like Ulysses and Homer. There would be an infinity of happiness there! And in that place where he would go they wouldn't put anyone to death for asking questions! He was quite philosophic as he took his accusers' leave. "And now it is time to go, I to die and you to live: but who of us goes to a better thing is unknown to all but God."

In prison his friends called on him on the day of his death. It was a poignant scene. Present were Echecrates, Phaidon, Apollodoros, Cebes, Simmias, Criton. Socrates continued to discourse on philosophy, the nature of the soul, of truth, until it was nearing sundown. Then he got up from his seat and retired to an adjoining room for his bath. He then returned to his friends and asked to see his two sons and the women of his house. Plato does not tell us what he told the women, or his sons, one of whom was little, but he soon sent them away before turning to his friends again, who were near tears.

About this time, his prison ward appeared to remind Socrates that his time was up and to thank him for his courtesy. As the man left, tears in his eyes, Socrates observed to his friends: "See what a nice fellow he is! See how generously he is shedding tears for me! Let's obey him"—and he summoned the prison boy to bring the poison potion.

Socrates' friends reminded him that it was not sundown yet and he need not hurry; but the philosopher was in no mood to tarry. He would gain nothing, he said, by drinking the poison a little later, only that he shall be thinking himself a fool for clinging to life. So the cup was brought and Socrates drank from it cheerfully, without a tremble, change in color or looks. He was worried though that he may not have offered the gods a proper libation.

Was it allowed, he wondered, but when told that just enough potion had been ground to suffice for the death, he said he understood and would only offer a prayer "for good luck in the migration from here to there."

Now his friends could bear the scene no more and began to weep. Socrates was obviously upset. "What a scene!" he reminded them. "You amaze me. That's just why I sent the women away, to keep them from making a scene like this. I've heard that one ought to make an end in decent silence. Quiet yourself and endure."

Saying so, Socrates began to walk about as instructed until unable to do so, he laid down, as the potion began to take effect and first his feet and legs and gradually the lower parts of his body grew cold and stiff. As the stiffness neared the abdomen, Socrates threw off the covering from his face and addressing himself to Criton, he whispered: "Criton, we owe a cock to Asclepios; pay it without fail." "That indeed shall be done" answered Criton, "have you anything more to say?" From Socrates there was no reply. He was dead.

CICERO: "I shall die in the country I have so often served."

Marcus Tullius Cicero of Rome (106-43 B.C.) was an orator, statesman and writer, a humanist considered the greatest master of Latin prose style who wrote extensively and was revered in the Middle Ages and Renaissance as one of the luminaries of classical culture.

He wrote his philosophic works very quickly, almost all of them in less than two years from 46 to 44 B.C. Of them he wrote: "They are mere transcriptions; they cost me very little labor; all I provide is words, of which I have plenty!" Well educated in law, oratory, Greek literature and philosophy, he did military service under Strabo, then Sulla. Cicero held several government positions as Quaestor in Sicily, as Praetor and as Consul. As Consul, he crushed Catiline's conspiracy to seize government and accused later by the First Triumvirate of executing Catiline without trial, went into voluntary exile (58-57 B.C.).

On return he became spokesman for preservation of the republican form of government against Caesar's idea of popularly supported dictatorship, though, it is said, the oligarchic senators never trusted Cicero fully because he advocated compromise in the form of *concordia ordinum* (harmony among the classes).

After Caesar's death, Cicero turned from political to literary activity. He had at his disposal the libraries of friends—too often the fruits of booty from the East. The first public library in Rome was yet to be founded. He wrote fairly extensively on philosophy, *The Academic Treatises* or *Academia*, then *Hortensius* (a dialogue based on Aristotle's *Protrepticus*) and then *De Vinibus Boni et Mali* (On Supreme God and Evil).

Other books followed. Philosophy, Cicero wrote, is the medicine of the soul. He taught readers to despise death, endure pain, moderate sorrow, avoid other disturbances of the mind and believe virtue is sufficient for happiness. His words on theology were impressive such as *De Natura Deorum* (On the Nature of the Gods). Do the gods exist, he asked. If so, how and when? Why should God suddenly create the world, as Plato held?

Cicero knew Caesar well. Indeed Caesar once complimented Cicero by saying that it was a greater thing to have advanced the frontiers of the Roman genius than to have enlarged the frontiers of the Roman Empire. But Cicero was not invited to join the plot to murder Caesar: he was considered too old and too nervous. Nevertheless he was in his place in the Senate on the Ides. After Caesar's assassination, Cicero led republicans against Mark Antony through his speeches, the famous fourteen Philippics. In his second Philippic, Cicero wrote: "Remember for once, I beg you, Mark Antony, the State; think of your ancestors, not your associates; do with me as you please, but with the State, make your peace!"

It was enough to anger Antony. He could not make up his mind. Should he run away, stay, capitulate to Antony's thugs or hide? Having embarked, he quickly disembarked and finally decided to go to Caieta, where he had property. Thither his servants carried him in a litter. His assassins were now after him.

Led by Herennius, a centurion of Popillius, a military tribune, they broke down the doors of his house and not finding him inside questioned his servants.

On being told that he was being taken toward the sea, Popillius took a few men with him, while Herennius hurried along the paths. Cicero saw him coming and quietly ordered his servants to put down the litter. He had been on the run and now the time had come to face death. His neck and hair were unkempt and his face was worn with anxiety. But now he looked steadfastly upon his murderers and as Herennius lifted his sword, most of those present covered their faces. Cicero stretched his neck out of the litter as if in offering and Herennius thereupon beheaded him at one stroke as the blood flowed freely and mixed with the dust. Cicero was then sixty four years old.

Cicero's head and his hand were severed and taken back to Rome where Antony had them nailed up on the rostrum in the Roman Forum. His hands had been cut "because they had written something against Antony." But before he died, Cicero had told his servants: "I shall die in the country I have so often served."

JESUS CHRIST: "Father, forgive them for they know not what they do."

The death and resurrection of Jesus Christ has been recorded by four of his Apostles: Matthew, Mark, Luke and John, but all of them gloss over the agony of Christ on the cross. We have to piece together the accounts left by them to get a composite picture of the event for history does not record elsewhere the crucifixion.

The four men make a remarkable quadrumvirate. Matthew worked in the internal revenue service of Herod Antipas when Jesus called him to be one of His disciples. This background no doubt explains the many references to tax collectors and the many incidents relating to money in his gospel. Matthew was a Jew writing to other Jews.

Ancient tradition associates the gospel of Mark with Peter and Rome. Mark was Peter's companion in Rome and recorded

Peter's recollections of what Jesus had said and done. In Mark's gospel, we find a reflection of Peter's style: impulsive, sympathetic and full of energy. The emphasis is on what Jesus did rather than on what He said. Luke was a Greek, making him the only Gentile among the New Testament writers. A physician by profession, he was a companion of Peter and Paul and accompanied the latter to Rome about the year 60 A.D., where he also came in contact with Mark. He wrote in the style characteristic of Greek historians in the early Roman period. Luke is a careful researcher, but even his account of the last moments of Jesus is not complete.

John is quite different from the rest. He gives no account of the birth, baptism or the temptations of Jesus. He dismisses Jesus' work in Galilee in only a few paragraphs. He says almost nothing of the Last Supper with the disciples and nothing at all about His agony in Gethsemane or His ascension to heaven. Most surprising of all, John relates no parables by Jesus.

But John knew Jesus at close quarters. One explanation is that the story of Jesus had already been written about by others and he did not want repetition. What John wanted was the world's acceptance of Jesus as Christ, the Son of God, the Savior. In His person, Jesus had challenged the times and men among whom He lived. He was perceived as a threat and the penalty was death. It is important to remember that it was not the Roman rulers who saw in Him a threat to their empire. It was His own people who saw in Him a challenger to the established order of things.

So these people, the priests and officers of the Temple and the Elders had Him seized and placed in a guardroom to await a trial. But He was left unprotected, one suspects deliberately, so that the mob could get at Him. It did.

The moment the Sanhedrin declared that Jesus was worthy to die, the mob rushed upon Him like wild beasts and would have probably torn Him to pieces had not the Roman soldiers intervened and pushed them back. But the mob would not be easily kept away. They threw an old garment over His head, struck Him in the face, and cried out mockingly: "Prophesy unto us, thou Christ, who is he that smote thee?" And when the garment was removed, they spat in His face.

From the guardroom, Jesus was taken to the Roman governor Pilate's judgment hall, know as the Praetorium, there to have the Sanhedrin's death sentence confirmed as a legal face to be put on what had been a legal farce. But Pilate, it is clear, saw no wrong-doing on Jesus' part.

The whole company of priests, elders and scribes had earlier tried in their council to get Jesus to admit to heresy, but they had been baulked. "If you are the Christ, tell us" they had asked. But the reply Jesus gave was clear. "If I tell you, you would not believe; and if I ask you, you will not answer. But from now on, the Son of Man shall be seated at the right hand of the power of God." And the priests had said, "Are you the Son of God, then?" To which Jesus had replied, "You say that I am." With this, the priests and scribes asked Him about His teachings. But Jesus had no reason to repeat Himself. He said, "I have spoken openly to the world; I have always taught in synagogues and in the temple, where all Jews come together; I have said nothing secretly. Why do you ask me? Ask those who have heard me, what I said to them; they know what I said." At this, one of the temple officers standing by struck Jesus with his hand, saying, "Is that how you answer the high priest?" Replied Jesus, "If I have spoken wrongly, I bear witness to the wrong; but if I have spoken rightly, why do you strike me?"

Finding Jesus a difficult man to pin guilt on, the priests led him to the Praetorium and Pilate came out to receive them. "What accusation do you bring against this man?" he asked. "If this man were not an evil-doer, we would not have handed him over" they replied.
Pilate replied, "Take him yourselves and judge him by your law." But the priests said, "It is not lawful for us to put any man to death."
So Pilate called Jesus and asked, "Are you the King of the Jews?" Jesus answered, "Do you say this of your own accord, or did others say this about me?"
Pilate answered, "Am I a Jew? Your own nation and the chief

priests have handed you over to me. What have you done?"
Jesus replied: "My kingship is not of this world. If my kingship were of this world, my servants would fight that I might not be handed over to the Jews; but my kingship is not from the world."
"So you are a king?" queried Pilate, half amused.
But Jesus answered, "You say that I am a king. For this I was born and for this I have come into the world to bear witness to the truth. Everyone who is of the truth hears my voice."
And Pilate said, "What is truth?"

According to Luke, Pilate, on learning that Jesus was from Galilee and hence properly under the jurisdiction of Herod, sent Him over to his colleague to be tried by him. But Herod was interested only in seeing a miracle performed and with Jesus remaining silent, sent Him back to Pilate. Pilate now had to pronounce judgment. Calling the priests and the rest of the council he told them what he thought.

"You brought me this man as one who was perverting the people; and after examining him before you, behold, I did not find this man guilty of any of your charges against him. Neither did Herod, for he sent him back to us. Behold, nothing deserving death has been done by him. I will therefore chastise him and release him." Thereupon Pilate had Jesus scourged, a painful punishment. The Roman soldiers stripped Jesus to the waist and lashed him. The Roman lash consisted of leather strips to which sharp pieces of metal or bone were attached. Jesus suffered deep and painful wounds and blood came pouring out of them.

Then, according to Mark, the soldiers led Jesus to the Praetorium and clothed him in purple and plaiting a crown of thorn, placed it on his head, saluting him meanwhile in mock seriousness, "Hail, King of the Jews." They also struck his head with a reed and spat upon him and knelt down in homage to him. Then the mockery over, the purple cloak was taken away, Christ clothed in his own rags and led out. But Pilate tried one more ploy to save Jesus. In prison was a hardened, infamous criminal called Barabbas and Pilate now offered the screaming mob a choice. There was a custom that on the day of Passover, holy to the Jews, the governor should release one man. "Will you," asked Pilate, "have me release for you the king of the Jews?" But the mob had been worked up by the priests to fever pitch. "Not this man," they cried, "release Barabbas."

"What shall I do with Jesus which is called Christ?" asked Pilate, tired of the whole show.

"Let him be crucified!" came the answer.

Pilate now ordered Jesus to be brought before the mob and said to it, "See, I am bringing him out to you, that you may know that I find no crime in him." And still the cry went forth, "Crucify him, crucify him." So Pilate said to the assembled then, "Take him yourself and crucify him, for I find no crime in him."

To that the priests said, "We have a law and by that law he ought to die, because he has made himself the son of God."

When Pilate heard the words, he was bothered. Turning to Jesus, he asked, "Where are you from?" But Jesus, standing there, bleeding profusely from his lacerated body, gave no answer. Irritated, Pilate asked, "So you will not speak to me? Do you not know that I have power to release you, and power to crucify you?" To which Jesus now replied, "You would have no power over me unless it had been given you from above; therefore, he who delivered me to you has the greater sin." Pilate still had second thoughts about having an innocent man crucified. But the priests cried out, "If you release this man, you are not Caesar's friend. Everyone who makes himself a king sets himself against Caesar."

When Pilate saw that he was making no headway with the mob which seemed to be in a riotous mood, Matthew says that he took water and washed his hands before the crowd, saying, "I am innocent of this man's blood; see to it yourselves." And the mob answered, "His blood be on us and on our children!"

The judgment was over; the case finished. Only the crucifixion remained. Barabbas was released and Jesus was now led out. It was ordinarily the custom for the condemned man to carry his own cross. But Jesus was weak with loss of blood. He had been scourged and there was hardly a place on his shoulders where he could let his cross lie. So the soldiers pressed a passer-by, Simon of Cyrene, who was coming in from the country, to carry the cross for Jesus.

The procession now marched slowly through the winding streets of Jerusalem until it came to a place called Golgatha—the place of a skull. Here, the cross was laid on the ground; Jesus was stripped of his bloodied garment which was divided among the soldiers, by casting lots. Then the Roman soldiers stretched Jesus on the cross as it lay on the ground, driving the nails through his hands and feet and the agony can only be imagined. Jesus' lips moved and he was heard to say, "Father, forgive them, for they know not what they do."

As soon as Jesus was nailed to the cross it was lifted by strong men and with great violence thrust into the hole prepared for it. On either side the soldiers also crucified two robbers. At the head of the cross was the inscription: The King of the Jews.

Some among the assembled crowd jeered. One said, "Aha, you who would destroy the temple and build it in three days, save yourself and come down from the cross." A priest said, "He saved others; he cannot save himself. Let the Christ, the King of Israel, come down now from the cross that we may see and believe." Even one of the criminals hanging beside him on his cross said, "Are you not the Christ? Save yourself and us!" But the other criminal silenced him, "Do you not fear God since you are under the same sentence of condemnation? And we indeed, justly; for we are receiving the due reward of our deeds; but this man has done nothing wrong." And he turned to Jesus and said, "Jesus, remember me when you come into your kingdom." And Jesus promised him that. "Truly" he said, even in the midst of his physical agony, "I say to you, today you will be with me in Paradise." The hot afternoon passed. The crowds began to melt. But standing by the cross were Jesus' mother, Mary, and his mother's sister, Mary, the wife of Clopas and Mary Magdalene. And when Jesus saw his mother and the disciple whom he loved standing near, he said to his mother, "Woman, behold your son!" And he said to his disciple, "Behold your mother!"

The sixth hour had come and there was darkness over the land until the ninth hour. At the ninth hour, Jesus cried in a loud voice, *"Eloi, Eloi, lama sabacthani?"* which means "My God, my God, why hast thou forsaken me?" One of the bystanders thereupon filled a sponge full of vinegar and with the help of a reed pushed it towards Jesus' lips, to quench his thirst. When Jesus had finished the vinegar, he cried out in a loud voice, "Father, into thy hands I commit my spirit!" Then he was heard to say, "It is finished." The head sagged. The agony was over.

ALEXANDER: "It is a lovely thing to live with courage and die leaving everlasting fame."

Alexander, than whom no other deserves to be called The Great, born in Macedonia in 336 B.C. died 32 years later in Babylon, a legend in his own time. He had fought the great Porus in India and with his travel-weary soldiers returned to set up headquarters in Babylon which he had selected to be his capital because it was practically midway between his Eastern and Western dominions.

Its climate was unhealthy, it was surrounded by swamps, but his ambition was limitless. He set about improving the city's internal conditions and first drained the malarious swamps. He could hardly have known that death was near.

First his beloved friend Hephaestion died. It was a cruel blow. Now there were many ominous signs and omens that were recognized as sinister at that time. His throne had been occupied, during his brief absence, by a demented man who was later killed for the capital offence. On another occasion he lost his hatband as well as the royal diadem, the symbolic mitra, while sailing. It had to be retrieved by a sailor who made the mistake of wearing it on his own head, so it would quickly dry. Then one day, as he was dressing for dinner, he felt the first shivers of fever. He was giving a splendid entertainment in honor of Nearchus, one of his generals. Earlier in the day he had held ceremonies, on his soothsayer's advice, to ward off ill omens. The party to Nearchus over, he went to a late-night party given by Medius of Larissa, a close friend. The party went on, two days running. At the end of the first night, Alexander slept most of the day. He was clearly fatigued, feeling tired and off-color. Yet he returned to the second party, knowing he was running a mild fever. It could have been malaria. The fever, however, has been attributed to the water he had drunk, water obviously taken from the polluted river that carried the sewage of an overgrown army camp.

On the second night he left before the end, though still late. He had many things on his mind. He was planning to start on a major expedition within two weeks. A lot of work had to be put in. But the fever was telling. Foolishly he had a bath and for the first time he really felt ill. He had a bed made up for him right near the bath house by a pool and spent the rest of the night there.

In the morning he had to be carried in a litter to perform the daily offering at the household altar, so sick he had become. It was a June day and the sweltering heat forced him to another bath after which he felt much worse. He was in high fever. Medication did not help. By the ninth day he could scarcely make the offering when he was carried to the shrine. Yet with thoughts of the expedition on his mind, he continued to brief his officers. On the tenth day the sickness was seen to be fast advancing. He ordered all his chief officers summoned before him and the junior ones were told to wait outside his doors. We never know what he planned to say for before he could address them he had a stroke, and was in great pain. He could barely manage to whisper a word or two to those immediately near him.

He was too ill to be moved from the royal bedchamber. Meanwhile, word spread in the army camp and there was a clamor from the soldiery to see their dying leader. He must have given permission. A door was opened at the far end of his room and the men now passed by, in single file. As the first man entered, Alexander turned himself towards them and held himself in that stance, till the last man left—a heroic feat. "He greeted them all" the historians tell us, "lifting his head though with great difficulty, and signing to them with his eyes." He was in evident agony.

Alexander is credited with remarking ironically that he foresaw a great contest at his funeral games. That is very unlikely. He was too ill for jokes. However, he took off his royal ring and handed it to Perdiccas, as if to appoint him temporary Regent. The generals standing around him knew that his time had come. "To whom do you leave your kingdom?" they asked him. His wives were pregnant and conceivably they could bear sons. Replied Alexander, *"Hoti to kratisto"*—to the strongest, or the best. The next day his friends returned from the healing shrine where they had asked the God whether it would help Alexander if he were carried into the sanctuary. The oracle would not recommend it. Perdiccas asked Alexander at what times he wished to have his divine honors paid him. Replied the conqueror, "When you are happy!" Those were his last words.

"A dark mist" it is recorded, "crossed the sky. A bolt of lightning was seen to fall from heaven into the sea, and with it a great eagle. The bronze statue of Arimazd in Babylon quivered and the lightning ascended into heaven and the eagle went with it, taking with it a radiant star. And when the star disappeared in the sky, Alexander had shut his eyes." Long before Alexander had said, "It is a lovely thing to live with courage and die leaving an everlasting fame."

RAMAKRISHNA PARAMAHANSA: "Pain is unavoidable so long as there is form."

In India's long history of saints, Sri Ramakrishna Paramahansa shines like a radiant star. It was his disciple, Narendranath—afterward to be known all over the world as Swami Vivekananda—who set up the monastic order after his teacher and guru and established the Ramakrishna Mission.

A beloved ascetic, Ramakrishna could spend hours in meditation and worship of the goddess Kali, whom he would address as Mother. He was born on February 18, 1836 in Bengal and by the time he was in his forties, his saintliness had won him disciples who flocked to hear him at his residence in Calcutta.

Around 1884, when he was 48, his throat began to bleed. At first it was diagnosed as "clergymen's sore throat" and treated as such. But as the bleeding continued, the malady was recognized for what it was: cancer. Medical attention was immediately sought and eminent *vaids*—practitioners of Indian traditional medicine— were consulted. They prescribed their remedies but Ramakrishna showed no improvement. Next homeopaths were asked in. For a time one Dr. Mahendra Lal Sarkar became Ramakrishna's physician. At this time the saint lived in Cossipore Gardens, in a two-storied building, with three rooms below and two above. Ramakrishna occupied the hall in the center of the upper story. To the right of the hall was an open terrace where the master, as he was known, sometimes sat or walked.

The seriousness of the Master's illness soon became known and it was held by his adoring disciples that he, surely, could cure himself. They kept pressing him to do so, "for our sake, at least." On one occasion, the Master was clearly annoyed. "Do you think that I have been undergoing this suffering voluntarily?" he asked them. "I do wish to recover. But how is that possible? It all depends upon the Mother." Narendranath pressed further. "Then please pray to her for your recovery. She cannot but listen to you." "It is easy for you to say so" replied Ramakrishna, "but such words I can never utter."

But the disciples would not take no for an answer. "All right," he promised Narendranath, "I shall try to do so if I can." A few hours later, Narendranath reminded the Master of his promise and wanted to know what had come of his prayer to the Mother. "I said to her" replied Ramakrishna, "I cannot eat anything for this pain. Please so arrange that I may eat a little. She showed you all and said, 'Why, you are eating through so many mouths.' I was ashamed and could not utter another word." The pain kept increasing. The bleeding would not stop. But Ramakrishna was serene through the passing weeks. Yet another distinguished homeopath of Calcutta, Dr. Rajendra Lal Dutta was called in.

On December 23, 1885 Ramakrishna evidently had given up hope himself. "My task of teaching" he told his disciples, "is almost finished—I can no longer instruct people. The whole world I see to be nothing but the Lord. I sometimes think: whom shall I teach?"

By the beginning of 1886, though, he was feeling better. One day, he was walking through the spacious garden when he fell into a state of semi-consciousness. He had to be carried back to the house. By now his body was worn almost to a skeleton. He hemorrhaged continuously. Eating was difficult, not impossible. Through all this, the Master maintained his serenity and went about his daily routine. "Pain," he told those who inquired about it, "is unavoidable, so long as there is form." On another occasion he said: "Spirit and matter sometimes borrow from each other. When the body is ill, the spirit thinks it is ill."

The hot and dreary months of May, June and July 1886 passed, each day bringing fresh pain and suffering. About eight or nine days before the end finally came, Ramakrishna asked one of his devotees, Yogin, to read to him from the Bengali Almanac the dates from the 25th *Shravana* (August 9). Yogin did as he was asked and read until he came to the last day of *Shravanan*, Sunday, August 15. The Master then made a sign that he did not want to hear any more. He must have had a premonition of impending death. Now he became restless. His pulse was irregular. On August 15, a little before dusk, the Master felt great difficulty in breathing. In the evening he complained of hunger. Attendants gave him a little liquid food, but he could swallow very little of it. They washed his mouth and carefully laid him on the bed. Two attendants fanned him. All was quiet, except the gentle swish of the fans in the hot and humid Calcutta air.

Suddenly the Master fell into *samadhi* (induced unconsciousness). The body became stiff. The attendants waited since this was not an uncommon thing. Some time after midnight Ramakrishna regained consciousness and said that he was exceedingly hungry. He was helped to sit up and took a full cup of porridge without visible discomfort. "I feel refreshed" he told his relieved attendants. Narendranath, who was still with him now suggested that the Master should go to sleep. At this, Ramakrishna, in a clear voice, uttered the name of Kali and slowly lay down. Seeing him comfortable, Narendranath, who was himself weary, went downstairs to rest.

Suddenly, at two minutes past 1 a.m. a shudder passed through the Master's body, making the hair stand on end. His eyes became fixed on the tip of his nose and the face was lit up with a benign smile. Again he had entered *samadhi*. There was little the attendants could do but keep watch. Early in the morning, the doctors were summoned. At 8 a.m. Col. Vishwanath Upadhyaya arrived, found the body still warm and began to rub the spine. There was no response. About noon time, Dr. Mahendra Lal Sarkar came and observed that life had passed out only half an hour before. At 5 p.m. the body was dressed in ochre cloth, decorated with sandal paste and flowers, taken to Cossipore Burning Ghat and cremated.

WILLIAM SHAKESPEARE: "Forbear to dig the dust enclosed here."

William Shakespeare who wrote so much and so eloquently about his heroes has so little written about his own death. He died on April 23, 1616 when he had just completed his fifty-second year. By modern standards, he died middle-aged. At the beginning of 1616, however, no one could have guessed that the poet's end was so near, though his strength was failing. Shakespeare himself said he was, in the conventional phraseology of those times, "in perfect health and memory" as a prelude to writing his will.

The will had been readied by a solicitor, Francis Collins, and was due to be signed by the poet on January 25, but it was, for the time, laid aside. Shakespeare was passing through some sad times. His younger daughter, Judith, had married at the age of 32, a man four years her junior. He was a younger son of Shakespeare's close friend of middle life, Richard Quiney, but the marriage had been solemnized during Lent when ecclesiastical law prescribed that a license should be obtained before the performance of the rite. The wedding had taken place before a license was obtained and for failure to explain the omission as demanded by the Bishop's Consistory Court at Worcester, a decree of excommunication had been issued. Shakespeare was obviously distressed over this.

About this time, two old friends, Michael Drayton and Ben Jonson, called on the poet at Stratford and the three together, who had many things in common "had a merry meeting." We have it, on the dubious authority of one John Ward who was Vicar of Stratford in Charles II's time and who compiled a diary of local gossip, that Shakespeare "it seems drank too hard." In any event he contracted a fever which resulted in the death of the poet.

That is all that history tells us of the last days of the world's greatest dramatist, and it is a very sketchy account indeed. Shakespeare was never known as much of a toper, though in his younger days he may have had a fling or two, as indeed one record explicitly states. What is possible is that with two close and dear friends at hand, he may have tried to drown some of his sorrow at his daughter's plight with "sherris sack." But that by itself could hardly have produced the fever to which he fell a victim. According to Sir Sidney Lee, who has written the poet's biography, Chapel Lane, which ran beside the poet's house, was known as a noisome resort of straying pigs and that the insanitary atmosphere may likely have prejudiced the failing health of the distinguished neighboring resident.

The fever dragged on. During the month of March, it got to be worse. Shakespeare had his will drafted earlier in January revised and he signed it on March 25, in the presence of five neighbors, Francis Collins, the solicitor, Julius Shaw, Hamnet Sadler, Robert Whatcote and John Robinson. There is no record of what happened in the days that followed. On April 17, Shakespeare's only brother-in-law, William Hart was buried in the parish churchyard. That must have come as a blow. If the poet's illness got worse, it is not recorded. Nor have we much information on what he said or did between April 17 and April 23, when he died.

It was his birthday and if he was conscious, he must have known that. Two days later, on Thursday, April 25, he was buried inside Stratford Church, in front of the altar, not far from the northern wall of the chancel. The grave was made seventeen feet deep—with purpose—and on the gravestone were carved the lines the poet himself had ordered:

> Good friend, for Jesus' sake forbeare
> To dig the dust enclosed heare;
> Bleste be the man that spares these stones,
> And curst be he that moves my bones.

It would seem strange that so great a poet should have so prosaic a thought engraved on his tombstone. But he had reason enough. Impinging on the northern wall of the chancel stood the charnel-house or "bone house" where, according to a universal custom, the bones dug from neighboring graves were piled in heaps. The scandal of such early and irregular exhumation was a crying grievance throughout England in the seventeenth century, as Sir Sidney Lee notes, and no doubt it was to guard against such unseemly profanation that Shakespeare gave his instructions regarding the inscription. It has been stated that had not the curse threatened him, the Sexton would not have hesitated in course of time to remove Shakespeare's dust to the "bone house." As it was, the poet was buried inside the Church, and it speaks for his local repute that he enjoyed the supreme distinction of a grave before the altar. It was never opened, not even to receive his wife and daughters although they expressed a desire to be buried in it. In due time his wife was buried in a separate adjoining grave on the north side of his own.

The name of Shakespeare's wife had been omitted from the first draft of his will, but in the final draft signed on March 25 and witnessed by five friends she received his "second best bed with the furniture." She received nothing else. It is not clear whether Shakespeare so acted to show his disdain for his wife for whom he apparently bore no great love. One theory has it that probably her ignorance of affairs and the infirmities of age (she was then past sixty, being older than her husband) combined to unfit her in the poet's eyes for the control of property and it is possible that

Shakespeare thought it would be "an act of prudence" to commit his wife to the care of his elder daughter who had inherited some of his shrewdness.

ST. FRANCIS OF ASSISI: "And Death is our sister; we praise Thee for Death!"

St. Francis of Assisi—born Francesco Bernardone in the small town of Assisi, in Italy—who renounced wealth and power for a life of poverty is one of the most loveable of saints.

On Saint Mathias's Day, 24th February, 1209, when he was 27, Francesco was praying in a little chapel called the Portiuncula (The Little Portion, the Small Holding) when he heard the celebrant reading the Gospel of Matthew, the story of Christ's instructions to his Apostles: "Heal the sick, raise the dead, cleanse lepers, cast out demons . . . take no gold, nor silver, nor copper in your belts, no bag for your journey, nor two tunics, nor sandals, nor a staff." Francesco felt the words were addressed to him. With the literalness of the unlettered, he cast away his shoes, his purse and his staff. He kept only his tunic, replacing the belt by a triply knotted rope (that every Franciscan wears to this day) and from then on his course of life was determined by direct communication with the divine. At that instant, one may say, a saint was born.

The rest of his life, till 1226 (when he was 44) Francesco did his administration to the sick and the poor. His saintliness became a byeword in the towns and villages through which he passed. They called him the Fool of God. Francesco was opposed to all possessions, but he possessed two trained sheep, a crow, a hawk and a wolf he had tamed. He hated killing but was not averse to enjoying a good steak. He was a delightful mixture of contradictions. He loved birds, especially. And he loved nature fully. He performed miracles. There seemed to be nothing odd about it at all. It was the way Francesco was. But there was nothing that he could do to his own suffering. That he bore patiently. So close was he to birds, that on one occasion, a swarm of birds—wood pigeons, crows, rooks—assembled on a tree to hear his sermon and at the end bowed their heads reverently. When he arrived at Mount La Verna to take temporary abode there amidst the trees, the birds in the area congregated to give him a tumultuous welcome. Once a monk brought him a rabbit that had been caught in a snare. "Come here little brother hare" said Francesco, "why did you let yourself be caught?" The hare ran up to Francesco and buried its head in the saintly breast. He would throw freshly caught fish back into the water again with an admonition never to get caught again. He gave bees honey to sustain them in winter and told the cicadas to sing God's praise. And they sang.

In the end he contracted acute eye trouble which blinded him. Stricken as he was, he now wrote poetry and in this he was the forerunner of Dante. The beauty of his *Cantico di Frate Sole* (Canticle of Brother Sun) commonly known in English as *The Song of the Creatures* is a hymn of praise that has few equals:

> *Altissimo omnipotente bon Signore,*
> *tue so le laudi li gloria e l'onore e onne benedizione...*

> Most high and most holy, most powerful Lord,
> Whom with honor and blessing and praise we acclaim,
> No man can be worthy to utter the word,
> The Name of thy Name!

In the winter of 1225-1226 Francesco spent his days in Reiti, in one of its hermitages. His eyesight was nearly gone. Now, in addition, he had dropsy. His hands and feet were already bleeding with stigmata. He longed to go home to his Portiuncula, but the summer heat was great and it was decided to remove him to a mountain hermitage of Bagnara. There he dictated letters to other brother friars and also wrote his Testament.

As summer waned, Francesco was brought down from his mountain retreat to the Bishop's palace of Assisi where he was guarded night and day. A doctor was fetched to treat him. Francesco wanted to know how long he would live. After some prevarication the doctor said that the disease was incurable and Francesco might die at the end of September or on the fourth of October. Francesco was overjoyed. Raising his hands, he cried: "Welcome, Sister Death!"

He called for Brothers Leo and Angelo, his companions, and bade them sing "The Canticle of the Creatures." As they concluded, he told them he had another stanza for them:

> And Death, is our sister, we praise Thee for Death,
> Who releases the soul to the light of Thy gaze;
> And dying we cry with the last of our breath
> Our thanks and our praise.

Francesco joined them in the singing, but they thought this was rather unseemly. But Francesco told them not to worry. "Since I have received this revelation (of death) I have been so filled with joy that I can no longer weep. And so I sing and I shall sing to God's honor, for He has given me the benefit of His grace and the assurance that I shall share in the bliss of Paradise."

Francesco took farewell of his friends and friars but now insisted that he would prefer to die in the holy discomforts of the Portiuncula. So thither he was taken. Here, lying on the floor, he dictated letters, one to the Lady Chiara, another to the Lady Giacoma dei Settesoli, his loving patroness in Rome. Happily, before the letter was even completed, Lady Giacoma and her two sons arrived in Assisi. On Saturday, October 3, 1226 Francesco was near to death. He asked his physician to announce the arrival of Sister Death. "She will open for me the door of life," he explained. Now, following his instructions, the Franciscan Brothers laid on a coarse cloth spread on the ground and sprinkled him with dust and ashes. His voice was heard to mutter faintly the 142nd Psalm:

> I cry with my voice to the Lord,
> With my voice I make supplication to the Lord,
> I pour out my complaint before Him,
> I tell my trouble before Him.
> When my spirit is faint, Thou knowest my way!

Then he struggled to sing once more his "Canticle of the Creatures." But his voice failed. He died singing the praise of death. A spectator said: "He had the look of a smiling saint." The Lady Giacoma took him in her arms. At that moment, it is said, a great swarm of larks assembled, long filling the air with welcoming music. And a friar averred that he saw Francesco's soul, a blazing star, borne on a white cloud to heaven.

SIGMUND FREUD: "A little island of pain floating on a sea of indifference."

The last days of Freud, father of psychoanalysis, were full of suffering. He was 83 when he died (May 6, 1856-September 23, 1939) but almost all his life he seemed to have been preoccupied with thoughts of death. In 1907 he was certain that he would die in February, 1918. "The superstition that my life is due to finish in February, 1918" he told his friend Ferenczi, "often seems to me quite a friendly idea . . . there is nothing strange in a man of my years noticing the gradual decay of his person."

Such thoughts persisted. In 1936, when he had just passed his 80th birthday, he remembered that both his father and his half-brother Emmanuel had died when they were approaching 81 and he was convinced that the same would happen to him. His 81st birthday came and went, but now Freud began to fear that he would die at the age of 95 as his mother had done seven years earlier! Had Freud died at age 81, perhaps it would have been just as well; he would have been spared much humiliation and suffering.

First was the humiliation of being expelled from his own country and his own home. The Nazis took over Austria on March 12, 1938. *"Finis Austriaw"* Freud entered in his personal diary that evening, mournfully. Three days later, on March 15, a gang of Nazi storm troopers broke into his home at Berggasse 19 and took away 6,000 shillings and the passports of his entire family. A week later, on March 22, the thugs returned again, and this time ransacked the house.

Freud's life was in danger. Now some of his friends and admirers intervened. Pressures were put on the Nazi government by Princess Bonaparte, U.S. Ambassador to France, William C. Bullit and President Franklin Roosevelt himself to let Freud go. On June 15, 1938, Freud landed at Dover, England, with his personal library and his collection of antiques—but not his savings. He had been forced to leave behind his four sisters—Rosa Graf,

Dolfi Freud, Marie Freud and Paula Winternitz, all of whom were over 70. In a few months Freud lost them all. The Nazis had them gassed and cremated.

Freud was now 82; he had earlier two painful operations for cancer. Now, in England, he was forced to undergo yet another, and third, operation. A biopsy showed a further malignancy which the surgeons diagnosed as "inoperable, incurable cancer." Roentgen ray treatment was prescribed on a daily basis, but was not of much help. The weeks were borne in almost continuous agony. "Since my operation in September" he wrote to Hanns Sachs in March 1939, "I have suffered from uninterrupted pains in the jaw which didn't cease after a fragment of the bone had been expelled." It was bad enough during daytime; but nights were worse. He wrote to Princess Bonaparte: "The radium has once more begun to eat in, with pain and toxic effects and my world is again what it was before—a little island of pain floating on a sea of indifference."

Yet his mind was clear; on occasion he would decline to take pain-killing drugs, arguing, no doubt quite rightly, that he preferred to think in torment than not to be able to think clearly. Above all he wanted to think clearly. He had work to do. Despite the pain which was excruciating most of the time, Frued managed to conduct four analyses daily, until a few weeks before his death. He finished his book *Moses and Monotheism* under the most difficult physical circumstances. He continued to work on *The Outline of Psychoanalysis* but was not to complete it.

It was an amazing example of mind over matter. Freud was constantly refining his material. His biographer Giovanni Costigan says: "Nowhere is there any sign of staleness or of tedium, nor any indication that the book was written in a period of great physical pain during an illness from which there could be no escape but death. *The Outline of Psychoanalysis* has all the verve and confidence of youth. It gives no indication of being the work of an old and dying man."

Freud was not given to self-pity, but he was also a man without any illusions. On his 80th birthday he told a friend: "How a man of 80 feels is not a matter of conversation!" To an American visitor he remarked: "There is an old saying that there is no virtue in youth. But it is just the opposite which is true. Young people are the only ones with virtue. The older you get, the worse you become. Women are especially awful in old age, but men are not much better!"

He refused to be awful. He will endure suffering stoically. His mouth was distorted by pain but Freud manfully continued to work on *The Outline of Psychoanalysis*. We get some idea of the torment that he must have been undergoing from the manuscript. It ends abruptly in the middle of a sentence. Freud must have doggedly persevered until pain would not let him work any more.

Four days before his death, Freud received his friend Ernest Jones. He was under heavy sedation, so much so that he could barely open his eyes. He recognized his visitor, though, and raised his hand, unable to utter a word. Then he dropped it with a "highly suggestive gesture" which Jones interpreted to mean, "Farewell, the rest is silence." The manner of Frued's dying, wrote Stefan Zweign, "was no less a moral feat than his life."

Freud died just before midnight on September 23, 1939. By then the second world war had begun. He had earlier written to Marie Bonaparte: "I hope you will soon console yourself over my death and let me go on living in your friendly recollections—the only kind of limited immortality I recognize!"

ALBERT EINSTEIN: "The end comes some time; does it matter when?"

To be interested in life and maintain a healthy curiosity about the nature of the universe till the very end, irrespective of vicissitudes, is the hallmark of the truly great. Among them is Albert Einstein.

He was born on March 14, 1879 and died in 1955, at the age of 76. At the age of 26 he postulated the special theory of relativity but the mathematical expression of that theory had to wait until 1950, when he was 71! It took another two years for him to announce completion of work on his unified field theory which attempts to explain gravitation, electromagnetism and sub-atomic phenomena in one set of laws. Genius, he might well have said, is ten per cent inspiration and ninety per cent perspiration.

When, at the age of seventy, he had provided a new theory to the riddle of the universe that was to replace the one he had provided at age 50, he knew even then that experimental evidence was not easy to find. To an inquirer, he characteristically answered: "Come back in twenty years' time!"

Even if he could not provide the answer, he was sure someone else would. "The important thing is not to stop questioning" he told a friend. "Curiosity has its own reason for existence. One cannot help but be in awe when one contemplates the mysteries of eternity, of life, of the marvelous structure of reality. It is enough if one tries merely to comprehend a little of this mystery each day. Never lose a holy curiosity!"

What did his personal curiosity do to help him understand the mystery of the universe? Did he believe in a God? "I cannot accept any concept of God" he told Prof. William Hermanns, "based on the fear of life or the fear of death or blind faith. I cannot prove to you that there is no personal God, but if I were to speak to Him, I would be a liar."

Then what did he believe in? His reply was clear. "I believe in the brotherhood of man and the uniqueness of the individual. But if you ask me to prove what I believe, I can't. You try to be true but you could spend a whole lifetime without being able to prove them. The mind can proceed only so far upon what it knows and can prove. There comes a time where the mind takes a higher plane of knowledge, but can never prove how to get there. All great discoveries have involved such a leap." Until 1945, when he was 66, he enjoyed indifferent health, but it was in no sense crippling. He had suffered periodically from stomach cramp, nausea and vomitting but that year his doctors decided that an operation was necessary. He recovered from it, though it was noticed that he had considerably weakened. Three years later, a second operation was deemed necessary and this time the surgeons found an aneurism in the main artery. When, two years later, he was re-examined, it was found that his condition had worsened. From 1950 on, Einstein knew that time was running out on him. He was not particularly bothered. When it was first discovered that he had an aneurism and warned that unless he took care his aorta might burst, he had dismissed it brusquely, saying: "Let it burst!" All he was interested in was work. As early as 1942 he had written to an old Jewish friend: "I am an old man, mainly known as a crank who doesn't wear socks. But I am working at a more fantastic rate than ever and I still hope to solve my pet problem of the unified physical field . . . "

That was as true in 1942 as it was in 1955. Honors were coming to him, thick and fast, but he kept both his humor and sense of proportion. He was offered the presidentship of Israel. He rejected the offer, saying "I know a little about nature and hardly anything about men!" At his seventieth birthday celebrations, fellow scientists arranged for a meeting during which a series of papers on his own subject were read. He sat through the meeting and when asked if he had found them tiring, he replied: "They would have been tiring if I had understood them!" He was sceptical even about his own findings and wrote to one scholar: "There is not an idea of which I can be certain. I am not even sure that I am on the right road!" Maybe, he thought, God could be "a little malicious!"

On April 11, 1955, he received the Israeli Ambassador Abba Eban to discuss Israel. On that same day he also heard from the philosopher Bertrand Russell in the matter of the nuclear arms race. He was excited at the prospect of doing something to maintain world peace. On April 12 he was in pain. But he refused to have his doctor called. He was planning to make an Independence Day broadcast for Israel and he worked on the draft. On April 13 he was still in pain but he received the Israeli Consul who had come from New York to his home in Princeton. He went over the draft with Consul Reuven Dafni. Dafni left by midday but the strain was too much. He collapsed in midafternoon. Now the doctor was quickly summoned. The patient was given an electrocardiogram, fixed up in a bed and given morphia injections to kill the pain. The diagnosis was a small leakage of blood from a hardened aorta, but the doctor found Einstein "very stoical." More specialists were brought from New York who suggested operation. An operation, it was put to Einstein, gave him a 50 per cent chance of survival. Without the operation, his chances of survival were minimal. Einstein declined the operation. He was "violently opposed" to the surgery. To Helen Dukas, his housekeeper, he said philosophically: "The end comes some time; does it matter when?"

He had asked his doctors how long death would take and had been truthfully told that it might come in a moment, or could take hours, even days. It did not faze him. He was taken to the hospital and when he arrived there and began to feel better, his first request was for his spectacles; then he wanted some writing material. He had work to do and time was of the very essence.

At the hospital his step-daughter Margot, who herself was in hospital, was wheeled in to see him. Einstein joked with her, told her she looked better—while he himself seemed to be in great pain—and Margot later said that Einstein faced his own death with "complete superiority." He talked with perfect calm, even with slight humor about the doctors and was waiting for his end as if for an expected "natural phenomenon."

On the day of his death, Hans Albert and Otto Nathan came to visit him. With the former he discussed science. With his friend Nathan, he discussed politics and the danger of German re-armament. He was relaxed and late in the afternoon, Dr. Dean, his physician, even felt that the aneurism might be repairing itself, as was quite possible. But Einstein complained of pain toward evening and was given another injection. At 11 p.m. Dr. Dean came round to check and Einstein was sleeping peacefully.

Soon after midnight, the nurse on duty, Alberta Roszel, noticed a difference in Einstein's breathing and quickly called for assistance. With the aid of another nurse Miss Roszel cranked up the head of the bed, so the patient could breathe more easily.

Einstein was muttering in German, a language neither nurse knew and there was no way they could understand him. Then suddenly he took two deep breaths. It was all over.

AURANGZEB: "I came alone and I go as a stranger."

Aurangzeb, last of the great Moghuls, who came to the throne after imprisoning his own father and killing his brothers and who, at the height of his conquests ruled as much of India as no one since the time of Chandragupta Maurya, died, at age 88, a hated and despised man.

He had fought and won battles. He had waged great campaigns; he had led armies in the battlefield such as had not been seen before. But in a life of religious bigotry that was notable for unmentionable cruelty, Aurangzeb had mostly made enemies, not friends. In his last years he had conquered two far off kingdoms, those of Bijapur and Golconda, later captured the Maratha chief Shambhuji; but the Marathas were not themselves easily suppressed. Sniping Maratha guerillas lay in wait wherever Aurangzeb marched or halted.

So many and so prolonged were the wars that Aurangzeb waged, that the Moghul Empire was getting bankrupt. Everyone was sick of war, except the aged emperor himself. "So long as a single breath remains in this mortal life" he told his Grand Vizier, "there is no release from labor."

The years and the wars were taking a huge toll. But Aurangzeb kept pushing on and in 1705, when he was a ripe 86, he wound up his last military campaign with the seige of an insignificant fortress called Wagingera, not far from Bijapur City. It was now time to return to imperial Delhi, seat of the Moghal capital. The homeward march began, but as Aurangzeb reached Devapur, on the Krishna river in Bijapur province, he fell violently ill. The emperor's journey had to be halted. He stayed in Devapur from April to October 1705. In October the camp was broken up and Aurangzeb and his retinue once again were on the move, with the emperor being carried in a palanquin. On January 20, 1706, the caravan reached Ahmednagar. Here Aurangzeb was to spend his last, miserable year.

There was no one with him near and dear. His rebel son, Akbar, had died in Persia in 1704; two years earlier, his poetess daughter Zebun-nissa had died in Samugarh prison. Now, in 1706 came news of the death of his sister Gauharara Begum. Life was bleak and joyless. His only companion was his spinster daughter Zinat-un-nissa and his last wife Udipuri Mahal, reputedly a Georgian slave girl he had appropriated from his brother Dara Shikoh's entourage. But Aurangzeb was a lonely man, indrawn and concerned with death.

Early in February, 1707 Aurangzeb fell ill for the second time, running high fever. He would not easily give up. Five times a day, for three days, he insisted on saying public prayers. His nobles suggested that to ward off evil influences, he make a gift of an elephant and a valuable diamond, but such suggestions he dismissed as smacking of Hindu practices he despised. Nevertheless he recommended that the court send four thousand rupees (the price of the beast) to the chief *Qazi* for distribution to the poor. And should he die, he further commanded, "carry this creature of dust quickly to the first burial place and consign him to the earth without any useless coffin."

That was the voice of the puritan in Aurangzeb. The great Moghul would have none of the pomp associated with the burial of monarchs. To his son Azam he wrote:

> I came alone and I go as a stranger. I do not know who I am, nor what I have been doing. The instant which has passed in power has left only sorrow behind it. I have not been the guardian and protector of the empire. Life, so valuable, has been squandered in vain. God was in my heart, but I could not see Him. Life is transient, the past is gone and there is no hope for the future . . . I fear for my salvation, I fear my punishment. I believe in God's bounty and mercy, but I am afraid because of what I have done . . . .

He wrote a similar letter to another son, Kam Bakhsh.

> Soul of my soul, I am going home. I grieve for your helplessness, but what is the use? Every torment I have inflicted, every sin I have committed, every wrong I have done, I carry the consequences with me. Strange that I came into the world

with nothing, and now I am going away with this stupendous caravan of sin . . . I have sinned terribly and I do not know what punishment awaits me . . . .

Meanwhile, Aurangzeb made preparations for his death. He would divide his empire among his sons to prevent a bitter war of secession, and to avoid "fighting between armies and . . . slaughter of mankind."

He wrote a will. In it he said that a sum of four rupees and two annas—the price of the caps he had sewn in his lifetime—be spent on his death shroud and another sum of three hundred and five rupees which he had earned copying the Koran, be distributed to fakirs. He wanted no ostentation. He was to be buried bareheaded, the coffin covered with white cloth, but no canopy and no musicians.

Bitterness still ruled his heart as his days drew near. Said his testament: "Never trust your sons, nor treat them during your lifetimes in an intimate manner; because, if Emperor Shah Jehan had not (favored) Dara Shikoh, his affairs would not have come to such a sorry pass. Ever keep in view the saying, 'The word of a king is barren.' "

February 21 came. Aurangzeb said his morning prayers and returned to his sleeping quarters, but quickly fell into a trance of compulsive prayer. He continued to tug at his rosary, his stiffening fingers pressing desperately at bead after bead. His lips were mumbling the Creed but no one heard the words. For one moment, this once mighty monarch hovered between here and eternity. At eight o'clock the movement of the fingers stopped. The rosary fell silent. Aurangzeb was dead. He had died, as he always wanted, on a Friday, the Moslem Sabbath.

They took him to his grave, which had been completed during his lifetime, and buried him. A red stone slab, three yards long, two yards wide and a few inches keep marks the spot. There is no inscription on it. *"Tabula rasa"* comments his biographer Waldemar Hansen, "for the last of the great Moghals."

LENIN: "I have now finished liquidating my affairs and can depart in peace."

An extraordinarily strong-willed person was Lenin who created the Bolshevik Party and was the brain behind the November Revolution. He was the founder of the Soviet Union as we know it. His will power is legendary. After his death, when an autopsy was made, a German specialist present later said that Lenin's brain had shrunk in its material composition to about one quarter of the normal size of the cerebral mass. And the surgeon who did the autopsy, Professor Rozanov, wrote: "When we opened him up we found a massive sclerosis of the cerebral vessels and sclerosis only. The amazing thing was not that the thinking power remained intact in such a sclerotic brain, but that he could live so long with such a brain."

Lenin had three strokes before he finally died, but he recovered after the first two, to everyone's surprise. His health had begun to deteriorate toward the end of 1921 and by the beginning of 1922 he was having severe headaches and had spells of vertigo. When his physicians assured him that these were minor ailments brought about by overwork, he firmly told them: "No, I feel this is the first sign." The leading medical specialists of Russia and Germany who examined Lenin at first thought that Lenin might be suffering from metal poisoning because of a bullet that remained in his body as a result of attempted assassination in 1918. An operation was performed and the bullet extracted. But that did not seem to help matters greatly.

Early in May, 1922, Lenin suffered his first stroke that left him without the ability to speak or move. He was nursed by his sister Maria and his wife Krupskaya who taught him to write with his left hand and to articulate words aloud. He recovered and by May 28 he was seeing close associates. By July Lenin was fully on his feet and his improvement was so great that on October 2, 1922 he was able to return to Moscow from his home in Gorki. Though the doctors did not permit him to work long hours, he took the risk of appearing at the Fourth Congress of the Comintern and to address the gathering, though he often fumbled for words.

In the second half of November the same year, Lenin started complaining of headaches and insomnia again and by November 25 had been ordered to take "absolute rest." Visitors were practically barred, but Lenin read a great deal. He also tried to back-track on some of the policies that had been initiated in the first flush of Bolshevik victory.

In December, 1922 Lenin suffered a second stroke, more grievous than the first. He was again ordered to take total rest, but that was foreign to his nature. He wrote articles on the role of the cooperatives in the Soviet economic system, wondering whether "we could do for the start (of cultural development) with some genuine bourgeois culture." On December 12 he sat at his desk for the last time and dictated letters. To Stalin, he wrote: "I have now finished liquidating my affairs and can depart in peace. There remains only one circumstance which disturbs me very strongly—that I cannot take part in the Congress of the Soviets . . . " He also developed a toothache and he referred to it in a brief note he sent to the Politburo expressing his worry about the future of minorities in the Soviet Union: "I am" he said, "declaring a war not for life, but to the death, against great Russian chauvinism. As soon as I rid myself of my damned tooth, I shall eat it with all my strength. One must absolutely insist that the United Central Executive Committee be presided over in turn by a Russian, a Ukranian and a Georgian and so on. Absolutely.

But he knew that his end was nearing. He dictated his testament on December 25 and 26, and in a postscript added on January 4, 1923, he evaluated the various Bolshevik leaders. Stalin, he said, "is too rude and this fault, entirely supportable in relation to us Communists, becomes insupportable in the office of General Secretary." Therefore, he said he proposed to the comrades "to find a way to remove Stalin from that position and appoint to it another man who in all respects differs from Stalin only in superiority, namely more patient, more loyal, more polite, more attentive to comrades, less capricious, etc. . . . "

Lenin was infuriated with rudeness shown by Stalin to Krupskaya, Lenin's wife, and in a letter sent to Stalin on March 5 he demanded an apology if he was not to sever relations between them. But fate now took a hand. That very day, Lenin's condition took a turn for the worse. And on March 9, he suffered his third stroke. He could hardly speak and had to convey his feelings by the inflexion of his voice and by gestures. Even the word "revolution" he could not utter and each syllable would be repeated two or three times. But as before, Lenin's will prevailed. By October he was on his feet again. On October 10 he again left Gorki for Moscow, and went to his office in the Kremlin and there, reportedly, walked around his desk in silent contemplation.

But his illness caught up with him. A damaged brain was acting up. To cheer him up, he would be taken on sleigh rides or by car into the countryside when the weather was good. On December 24 his wife even set up a Christmas tree and called in the peasants. Lenin looked cheerful.

On January 20, 1924 Lenin felt unwell, out of sorts and complained, as was his wont for some months, of headache and loss of appetite. The next morning he awoke with the same feeling and refused food and had to be persuaded to have a small breakfast. At dinner time he ate very little. After dinner he lay down to rest. Suddenly those around him noticed that his breathing was heavy and irregular. At 6 p.m. on January 21, 1924, a severe attack set in. Lenin lost consciousness. His face grew deathly pale and his breathing became more labored. His temperature rose rapidly. Then hemorrhage of the brain occurred, resulting in paralysis of the respiratory organs. Within fifty minutes of the attack, Lenin breathed his last. He was 54.

MAHATMA GANDHI: "Short-lived is the spring in the garden of the world."

The last days of Gandhi were full of sadness and foreboding. Everywhere around him he saw the collapse of the values he had cherished: Hindu-Muslim unity, peace and brotherly love. Bloody riots had torn the countryside and refugees were streaming across the land bringing with them a legacy of hatred. His prayer meetings in Delhi were well attended, but occasionally one heard cries of *"Gandhi murdabad"*—Death to Gandhi—and it sent a chill through his admirers and followers.

Toward the end of January, 1948, while he was addressing a prayer meeting at Birla House, a slab of guncotton was exploded. There was no panic, but his grandniece, Manubehn threw herself at his feet, clasping them with all her strength. Gandhi pacified her. The man who exploded the guncotton, Madanlal Pahwa, was quickly apprehended, but it had become clear that there was a conspiracy to murder the Mahatma. Gandhi himself seemed conscious of it. Two days after the explosion, he told Manubehn: "I am greatly depressed and so you should keep up my courage. You have acquitted yourself well. As I said yesterday at the prayer meeting, I wish I might face the assassin's bullets while lying on your lap and repeating the name of Rama with a smile on my face. But whether the world says it or not—for the world has a double face—I tell you that you should regard me as your true mother. I am a true Mahatma."

He continued to receive visitors. On the morning of January 29, he received Jayaprakash Narayan, the socialist leader. Later, that same morning, Indira Gandhi called on him with her four year old son Rajiv and with them came Nehru's sister Krishna Hutheesing and Padmaja Naidu, daughter of an old colleague of his, Sarojini Naidu. Gandhi teased them by saying: "So the princesses have come to see me!" More visitors, less exalted, called on him, some bringing their complaints, some to bitterly attack him for trusting Muslims. One group told him: "You have done enough harm! You have ruined us utterly! You ought to leave us now and take up your abode in the Himalayas!"

The incident disturbed him enough for him to make a reference to it in his evening prayer meeting. "I seek my peace amid disorders" he said. Later that evening he had a fit of coughing and he looked very tired. He seemed to be laboring under a feeling of oppression. The violence around him that he had all his life opposed now seemed to engulf him. "How can we look the world in the face?" he asked in despair. And he recited the words of the Urdu poet, Nazir: "Short lived is the spring in the garden of the world, enjoy the brave spectacle while it lasts." He told Manubehn, who was massaging his head with oil: "If I were to die of a lingering disease, or even from a pimple, then you must shout from the housetops to the whole world that I was a false Mahatma. Then my soul, wherever it might be, will rest in peace. If I die of an illness, you must declare me to be a false or hypocritical Mahatma, even at the risk of people cursing you. And if an explosion takes place, as it did last week, or if someone shot at me, and I received his bullet in my bare chest without a sigh and with Rama's name on my lips, only then should you say that I was a true Mahatma."

On the last day of his life Gandhi woke up at his usual time, 3:30 a.m. to face a heavy day. He was full of forebodings. When Manubehn asked him what prayer she should chant for him, he asked for one of his favorite songs:

> Whether weary or unweary, O man, do not rest,
> Do not cease your single-handed struggle.
> Go on, and do not rest.
>
> The world will be dark and you shall shed light on it,
> And you shall dispel the darkness around.
> O man, though life deserts you, do not rest.

He went through his file of correspondence, expressing annoyance that a letter he had written the previous day had been misplaced. He then took a short stroll in the garden, had a massage and then took a bath. When Manubehn went to prepare some cough lozenges, he called her back, saying: "Who know what is going to happen before nightfall or even whether I shall be alive? If at night I am still alive, you can easily prepare some then."

He breakfasted at 9:30 a.m., had a discussion with his secretary, Pyarelal, saw a host of visitors, but strangely seemed indecisive. To one of his secretaries, he said: "Bring me my important papers. I must reply to them today because I may not be alive tomorrow." This was the fourth or fifth time he had hinted of his approaching death. He must have had premonitions of what was awaiting him. In the afternoon he had his abdominal mudpack and dictated some letters. He received a French photographer who presented him with an album of photographs. He gave an interview to Margaret Bourke-White, the photographer for Time-Life. He saw Sardar Vallabbhai Patel, the Deputy Prime Minister, to persuade him to reconcile his differences with Prime Minister Jawaharlal Nehru. When he was interrupted by Manubehn who came to say that two Congress leaders from distant Kathiawar had come and wanted some minutes with him, he replied: "Tell them they can talk to me during my walk after the prayer meeting, if I am still alive." No one took that remark seriously.

Sardar Patel left and he took some food after the tiring talks and by then it was past five o'clock and he was late for his prayer meeting. It distressed him because he prided himself on being punctual. Manubehn picked up his spectacle case, rosary, notebook and spittoon that accompanied him to a prayer meeting and with Manubehn on one side and Abhabehn on the other, on whom he relied, Gandhi walked briskly towards the garden of Birla House, hurrying to make up for lost time.

The journey was a short one and did not take more than three minutes. Striking a light note, Gandhi told Abhabehn, who had served him supper, that she had been serving him "cattle fare." Abha retaliated by saying Ba (Mrs. Gandhi) used to call it "horse fare." Somewhat amused, Gandhi replied: "Is it not grand of me to relish what no one else cares for?"

As he moved forward the crowd made way for him. He took two or three more steps amid the crowd, his hands folded in the traditional Indian *namaskar* to greet the people, smiling, when it happened. A man wearing a khaki jacket over a green pullover brusquely pushed his way past Manubehn that sent the spittoon, spectacle case and rosary flying out of her hands and bent low as if in obeisance before the Mahatma. Such incidents were not uncommon and Manubehn addressed the man. "Bhai" (brother) she said, "Bapuji (Gandhi) is already late for prayers. Why are you bothering him?" She had hardly spoken the words when three shots rang in quick succession. The first shot struck Gandhi in the abdomen, near the navel; the second and third shots struck him in the chest. "Hey Ram! Hey Ram!" said Gandhi as he tumbled, his hands still folded, his cry to God whom he had always revered. Over his white woolen shawl, blood trickled.

There was panic. The assassin in the khaki jacket, who was later identified as Nathuram Vinayak Godse, was overpowered and rushed to a nearby police station. But in the Birla House garden there was no doctor. From Gandhi's chest wounds blood continued to flow. Quickly he was carried to his room and laid on the floor. By then he was dead. He had died instantaneously.

He had wanted to live to be 125 years; he died when he was slightly over 78, on January 31, 1948. India was then barely five months independent.

LEO TOLSTOY: "So this is the end! And it's nothing . . . "

Lev Nikolayevitch Tolstoi, as the Russians knew him, was born in 1828, spent his youth like that of other Russian nobles, in army service, in dissipated pleasure, siring a bastard in the process. But his soul-searching and desire for social reform were early expressed by his attempt to create a school for serfs. After his marriage in 1862, he retired to his family home Yasnaya Polyana where he wrote his great works, *The Cossacks, War and Peace* and *Anna Karenina*, the last a moral tragedy set against the background of St. Petersburg society. About 1876 he underwent a "conversion" to belief in Christian love, non-resistance to evil and the simple faith of the peasants and soon attempted to give away all his property.

It created complications. Tolstoy continually saw himself in a false position, because he was eating well when the peasants were starving, because he lusted when he thought desire was enslaving his body. He had proclaimed the necessity for chastity in marriage, but even when he was 63, he continued to desire his wife Sonya, whom he tried to ignore to her annoyance and gathering anger. He seldom spoke to her of his plans, did not share his work with her, upbraided her grossly in front of the children and went out of his way to avoid her. In his eyes, she personified two dreadful sins: lust and cupidity. If he wanted to get rid of his possessions, she wanted to keep them. She was jealous of his friends, especially of Chertkov, his agent and literary executor. It was affecting Tolstoy to the point that his physician prescribed separation with his wife.

His writings had come to offend both Church and State in Russia and in Moscow and St. Petersburg people were saying that the "thirteenth apostle" as he came to be known, would soon be confined to his estate or sent abroad or even locked up in the Suzdal monastery. He wrote *The Kingdom of God is Within You* which was to be the keystone of his entire ethical structure. It was prohibited by the Russian censor.

He was inconsistent, like all saints past. He preached universal love but made his wife miserable. He preached poverty, but could not escape the life of the rich. He preached forgetfulness, but recorded his every moral twinge. He sought fusion with God and wasted much of his life in domestic bickerings. He had contempt for fame, but was not above currying celebrity.

But the struggle was too great for him to bear. Finally, one early morning, on October 28, 1910, when he was 82, he left his wife and family to go to some distant village where he had friends, to live with them. To his wife he left a note: "My departure will cause you pain and I am sorry about that; but try to understand me and believe that I could not do otherwise. My position in the house is becoming—has already become—intolerable. Apart from everything else, I cannot go on living in the luxury by which I have always been surrounded and I am doing what people of my age very often do: giving up the world, in order to spend my last days alone and in silence. Do understand this, I beg of you and do not come rushing after me even if you should learn where I have gone . . . " He added: "I thank you for the 48 years of honorable life you spent with me and I ask you to forgive all the wrongs I have done to you . . . . " In his escape from home, he was accompanied by his doctor Makovitsky and his daughter Sasha.

First they took a train, traveling by second class and later third class. In the third class compartment filled with smoke, he was recognized and drawn into conversation. After they had traveled for some hours, they got down at a station and went to a nearby monastery where they were welcomed. Not far from the monastery was a convent where Tolstoy's sister Marya lived as a nun and he called on her for a happy reunion.

After two days, the party again left, taking a train to Rostov-on-Don. On the train he developed fever. His teeth chattered. Sasha later wrote: "For the first time I felt that we had no house, no home. We were in a smoke-filled second class railroad car with strangers all around us, and not a single corner in which to lay a sick old man." Tolstoy tried to soothe his worried daughter. "Courage Sasha" he said, "everything is fine."

But it was not. Perhaps the exposure to the autumn chill had affected him. They decided to get off at the next stop, a small station called Astapove. He had grown weak and had to be helped to get down. There was no hotel in the town, so the station master, who had recognized Tolstoy, offered the travelers his own small cottage, set in a little garden. The living room was cleared, a small iron bed installed and Tolstoy was helped to lie down. Next morning Tolstoy had a telegram sent to his friend Chertkov: "All yesterday passengers saw me leave train in weak condition. Fear publicity. Going on. Make arrangements" it said. He told his daughter, who had now become his nurse: "God is that infinite whole of which man is conscious of being a finite part. Man is His manifestation in matter, space, time." He wrote a farewell letter to his children Tanya and Sergey.

Chertkov soon arrived at Astapove. So did his son Sergey who had been informed by a newspaperman of his father's whereabouts. Soon his wife, too, was to arrive though denied admission to his presence. Sonya, Tolstoy's wife, was furious as usual at having been left behind. She poured out a torrent of reproach against her husband, affirming he was a monster. Members of his family now tried to make it comfortable for Tolstoy, but his response was: "But the peasants (*muzhiks*), you know how they die!"

On the morning of November 4, he whispered: "I think I am dying; maybe not." He was asked not to try to think. But he replied: "How can I not think? I must, I must think!" A day earlier, he had written in his diary: "Difficult night. Two days in bed with fever . . . . And here is my plan. *Fait ce que dois, adv . . .* It is all for the good of others and mostly for my own." (The French saying which he did not complete, *fais ce que dois, advienne que pourra* meant, "do as you must, come what may.") He kept mumbling: "Seek, keep seeking . . . " When he could not write, his fingertips made writing motions.

On November 5, his condition grew worse. He told his son Sergey: "I cannot seem to go to sleep. I am still composing. I am writing. Everything moves on smoothly to the next." The next day, he was feeling no better. As his daughter Sasha tried to help fix his pillow, he told her: "I just wanted to advise you to remember that there are in the world many people beside Lev Tolstoy and you are looking only at this one Lev!"

By now there were six doctors in attendance on him. He told Tanya: "So this is the end! And it's nothing . . . " They thought the end had indeed come. He was given an injection of camphor in oil. Oxygen was brought for him to inhale. For a moment Tolstoy regained his consciousness. His son Sergey heard him say: "Ah, what a bother. Let me go somewhere, where nobody can find me. Leave me alone . . . " Tolstoy was still trying to run away in his mind.

Suddenly he shouted like an angry peasant. "Clear out . . . got to clear out." Toward the evening of November 6, 1910, his condition perceptibly worsened. The blue spots came to his ears, lids, nails. He was given more oxygen. But now Tolstoy wanted none of this. He whispered: "This is all foolishness. What's the point in taking medicine?" By now he was muttering, the words coming slowly out. "The truth . . . I care a great deal . . . How they . . . " The muttering stopped. At five minutes past six in the morning of November 7, life finally ebbed out of his body. Dr. Makovitsky leaned over and gently closed the eyes of the illustrious dead.

ANNE BOLEYN: "Acquit yourself of your charge for I have long been prepared."

Anne Boleyn was born in 1503 or just as possibly 1504. The exact date is not recorded. She was beheaded in 1536 at the behest of King Henry VIII whom she had married against the wishes of his people. She was 33.

The times were such that death by beheading raised no eyebrows. In fact, after the news was announced, King Henry arranged a joust to celebrate the event. She was a dark-haired beauty, the daughter of Sir Thomas Boleyn, Earl of Wiltshire and Ormonde and Lord Privy Seal, besides. No commoner, she. When Henry saw her, it was practically love at first sight. He was still married to Katherine of Aragon whom he wanted to divorce because she gave him no male heir. Katherine had had seven pregnancies, all of which had ended either in miscarriages or in dead children.

But he was hoping to get an annulment of the marriage, so he could marry Anne. He would write passionate love letters to her. In September, 1528 he wrote: "I would you were in my arms, or I in yours, for I think it long since I kissed you." When the marriage finally took place on January 25, 1533, it was Henry's hope that Anne at least would provide him with an heir. He was still in love with her. The King "cannot leave the concubine for an hour," wrote his Ambassador to Charles V of France.

She was not the handsomest of women, as the newly appointed Venetian Ambassador described her. "She is of middling stature" he wrote, "with a swarthy complexion, long neck, wide mouth, bosom not much raised and in fact has nothing but the King's great appetite and her eyes which are black and beautiful." Anne, too, had three miscarriages. But quite early in the marriage, Henry seemed to have tired of her. There was too much gossip about Anne. In Oxford, a drunken midwife was called before a magistrate for describing the queen as a "whore and a bawd."

Historians are not quite sure whether indeed she was

licentious. But Henry's ministers were anxious to depict her as one, so that they could get rid of her. Henry seemed agreeable. He wanted a son and Anne could not provide him with one. Now his minister, Cromwell, stepped in. There had been elaborate spying within the King's court. Evidence finally was produced of Anne's alleged adultery and incest. Four courtiers, including her own brother, were arrested. Anne was first ordered to stay in her room. She was then taken to the Towers. On May 13, the queen's household was broken up. Two days later she was tried before the Privy Council and a jury.

Cromwell read out the charges. For three years or more, he said, the queen, "despising her marriage and entertaining malice against the King and following daily her frail and carnal lust, did falsely and traitorously procure by base conversations and kisses, touchings, gifts and other infamous incitations, divers of the King's servants to be her adulterers . . . " The charges were grim and if proven, death was the only punishment.

Anne stoutly denied incestuous relations with her brother, Lord Rocheford. Her denial of other charges were no less vehement. But the Privy Council and the jurors would hear none of her pleas of innocence. She was pronounced guilty of "incest, adultery and high treason." The Council proceeded according to form. Did she have anything to say to the findings? Anne replied briefly and courageously. "I am ready for death" she said, "I regret that of innocent persons." But the King was absolutely sure that he had been infamously betrayed by the very women for whom he had defied the Holy See and convulsed his kingdom. In the Towers, Anne received the Sacrament for the last time. She also kept up her courage. On May 18, 1536, Sir William Kingston, her warder, wrote to Cromwell: "I have seen many men, and also women, executed and they have been in great sorrow and, to my knowledge, this lady hath much joy and pleasure in death."

The time for the execution had been fixed for 9 in the morning. It had, however, to be postponed. When Sir William went to Anne to apologize, she said: "Master Kingston, I hear I shall not die before noon—and I am very sorry, therefore, for I thought to be dead, and past my pain." Sir William quickly assured her that there would be no pain and the execution was "so subtle." Anne replied with almost clinical detachment: "I heard say that the executioner was very good—and I have a little neck." She laughed.

When the time came Sir William again approached her and said: "Madam, the hour approaches—you must make ready." But she was ready. She answered: "Acquit yourself of your charge—for I have been long prepared." An executioner from France had been specially brought for the job, a man who was known for the swiftness with which he despatched the victim. Now, properly masked, he met Anne before the scaffolding and said, kneeling before her: "Madam, I crave your Majesty's pardon—for I am ordered to do my duty." Anne came forward and said: "Willingly," and gave him his fee of twenty pounds.

A large throng had assembled to see the beheading. To this she now addressed herself. "Good Christians" she said, and her voice, at first feeble, rose in strength as she continued, "I am come hither to die, for according to the law and by the law, I am judged to die and therefore will I speak nothing against it. I am come hither to accuse no man . . . . And thus I take my leave of the world, and of you all, and I heartily desire you all to pray for me." She then removed her cape; she also took off her coif, replacing it with a linen cap. Her eyes were bound. The executioner asked her to kneel down and say her prayers. She was guided gently to the block. She knelt down, taking care to fold her gown about her feet and said: "To Jesus Christ I commit my soul. O Lord, have mercy on me. To Christ I commend my soul. Jesu, receive my soul."

"Bring my sword" ordered the executioner. Anne placed her head on the block. There was a sharp hissing noise, the sword cutting through the air in one swift stroke. It sufficed. Anne's bloodied head rolled on the straw below. The executioner quickly picked up the severed head, held it aloft for all to see that the job had been done, as well as justice. At that moment, cannon sounded from the battlements. And an official called out: "So perish all His Majesty's enemies."

IVAN TURGENEV: "Me? I don't worry about death; it disappears in the slav mist."

Turgenev, the poet and writer, died of cancer of the spine. He was a little short of his sixty-fifth birthday. A huge man who would stand out in any company, his last days were full of suffering, bravely borne.

He was born on October 28, 1818 and died on September 3, 1883 and was thus a contemporary of some of the great literary figures of his age: Flaubert, Henry James, Emile Zola, Guy de Maupassant, Tolstoy. Though he was of Russian origin, he lived a great deal in France where he found himself most at home. Indeed, the man for whom he had the greatest regard and affection was none other than Flaubert.

His attitude towards religion remained much the same during the last years of his life. "From my observations during the past few years" he wrote to the novelist, Pissemsky in 1876, "I have become convinced that depression, melancholia and hypochondria are nothing but fear of death. There is no radical cure for it, but there are palliatives!" He added: "If, as you write, religious feelings have become more and more predominant in you, then I can only congratulate you on this invaluable acquisition; it is an infallible remedy, but it is not accessible to everybody!" In his poem "Prayer," Turgenev wrote that man always prayed for a miracle. "Every prayer comes down to the same thing, namely, O Lord, make it so that twice two should not be four!"

Sceptic he was. In another of his poems in prose, "Nature," that he wrote in November, 1879, he made nature say: "All creatures are my children and I take care of them in the same way and destroy them in the same way." He was a great traveler, but in 1871 he finally installed himself in Paris and two years later he had made Bougival, near St. Germain, his regular summer resort. In Paris he could meet his literary friends and have quiet lunches in a private room at his favorite restaurant. After the tables were cleared, there was always discussion and on one occasion, records Alphonse Daudet, the talk veered to death. What, Turgenev was asked, did he think of it? "Me? he replied, "I don't worry about death. No one in Russia worries over the spectre of death; it remains distant, it disappears in the slav mist."

Though he lived in France, he visited Russia frequently enough and when he was there in February 1889, he fell in love with a young woman, Savina, then only 25. He wrote to her: "You have become something in my life from which I shall never part." She was then engaged to someone else, but Turgenev was smitten. He entered his 63rd year, quite extraordinarily fit and full of optimism for the future. The last story he had written was a great success; his obsession with death had left him and he was conducting a mildly flirtatious correspondence with Savina.

On May 3, 1882 Turgenev wrote to Polonsky that he was suffering from a special kind of angina, which his doctors said was *cardialgia nevralis*. He had severe pains. He could not stand on his own feet for more than 2 minutes at a time or sit in a chair for more than a quarter of an hour. His condition began to worsen. He had to have morphine injections to kill the terrible pain. He described his condition in three poems: *"Patridges, Nessum Maggier,"* "Delore" and "Caught Under a Wheel," all in June, 1882 with philosophical detachment. But movement was hard. The physicians had to devise an iron frame in which his bed could be fitted, so he could be raised or lowered. In August of that year, he started a journal and called it "My Death Roll" and entered his day-to-day agony in it. He wrote to Tolstoy asking for a copy of the latter's *Confession* and told the older man that he will never get angry with anyone because "only young men who imagine that they know everything get angry and I shall be 64 soon." He put on a brave air. He wrote to Polonsky that while he has been ill, things could have been much worse. "After all," he said, "I could have been deprived of my eyesight or of the use of my legs. And now I can even work."

That was a bit of exaggeration. Turgenev was confined to bed most of the time in pain. But he was not the one to lose heart. To his physician, Dr. Bertenson, he wrote: "Charles XII lay in bed for 18 months, though there was nothing wrong with him. And he did not mind! So why should I?"

He returned to Paris on November 17, still in pain. In January, 1883 he was operated on for the removal of a neuroma in the abdomen. Months passed. He had heard that Tolstoy had given up writing. At the beginning of July he wrote to the sage of Yasnaya Polyana to return to literature and to tell him how glad he was to be his contemporary.

A fortnight before his death, Maupassant came to call on him. By then Turgenev had suffered enough and the pain was hard to bear. Turgenev for once lost his control which he had exercised so admirably and asked his friend to get him a revolver, so he could put an end to his torment. It was a sad moment for Maupassant.

Two days before his death, he lost consciousness. He was beyond help. His family and friends watched him, his gaunt body thinned, fighting for very life. Shortly before his death, on September 3, 1883, he seemed to come out of his deep coma for some fleeting seconds. "Come nearer, nearer" he was heard saying. "Let me feel you all near me. The moment of parting has come. Goodbye, my darlings."

VOLTAIRE: "Farewell, my dear Morand. I am dying."

Voltaire, who was born in 1694, not only lived in the Age of Reason, for all practical purposes, he was the personification of that age. In the last twenty-five years of his life, his disciples ranged from the humble to Frederick II of Prussia, and other princes. His outstanding virtues were persevering courage, high intelligence, an inconceivable capacity for work and what one writer has called "a surpassing literary art of persuasion." He was a turbulent man.

Ill health dogged him most of his life, but that did not prevent him from waging his battles against superstition and the Church. He was not godless; he believed in "natural religion" but not in organized church which he wanted to dispense with. He was not an atheist and argued against the materialist-atheistic of his times. What Voltaire objected to most was the intolerance of religion, the imposition of a single faith, the denial of freedom of thought. He wanted a mind unfettered. He wrote prodigiously. A good part of his middle years he devoted to historiography and though, as in *The Age of Louis XIV,* he was remarkably objective, only two of his histories survive as literature.

His poetry was not of any great caliber either. They are read now in anthologies, examples of the conventional and the didactic. But it was for his poetry and in his tragedies in verse that he first won a European reputation. He published work under 150 pseudonyms and made quite a small fortune, which enabled him to have freedom of movement. A Frenchman, he spent most of forty years in exile from Paris.

In 1759, when he was sixty-five, he established himself at Ferney, on the Swiss border and issued his famous war cry: *"Ecrasez l'infame"*—stamp our infamy! It is something of a tribute to his durability that some of the biggest challenges that he met were after he was sixty. Indeed, in his eighty-third year he was still able to say: "I write in order to act!"

Though he had no particular quarrel with monarchism as an institution, in *Republican Ideas,* written in 1765, he advocated the town meeting form of self-government and went so far as to seek seats for workers on the Grand Council of the Republic of Geneva. He showed his sympathy for workers in even more concrete terms: for Geneva's watchmakers and stocking weavers who had been driven out by their employers he built a village and erected factories on his estate.

Voltaire returned to Paris in February, 1778, "wrapped up" as he characteristically wrote "in eighty-four years and eighty-four maladies." His journey was a triumphal procession and the four remaining months of his life in Paris were an apotheosis. Crowds were constantly at his door; he was even able to totter to a gala performance of *Irene,* one of his last, if feeble, works.

On May 12, 1778, as he was out walking, he told his niece, Madame Denis, that he was feeling ill and would return home. He went straight to bed. He had developed high fever. His condition grew worse. By the time his doctor could be called, there seemed little to do. On May 16 he revived a little, but he was exhausted and had to be kept alive by spoonsful of jelly.

A day before he fell ill, on May 11, Voltaire had written: "Whoso fears God, fears to sit at ease." He was not afraid of God. And he had no desire to save his soul, despite the opportunings of priests and friends. The Abbe Gaultier had tried, on February 20, only to be dismissed as "a good fool." A few days later, Abbe Martin similarly called on Voltaire and insisted that the sceptic should make confession then and there.

"I have come for that. I shall not move an inch."

"From whom do you come, M. l'Abbe?" Voltaire had asked.

"From God Himself," came the reply.

"Well, well, sir," retorted Voltaire, "and your credentials?"

When, on February 25, while dictating in bed, he had a sudden, violent fit of coughing and broke a blood vessel, his friends had again called a priest. But Voltaire, turning to those around him had bade them remember that he had fulfilled "what thy call here one's duties." Yet he was pressed to show that he was not godless, little use though he had for the church and its princes. On February 28, 1778, Voltaire wrote, clearly and firmly, his real faith: "I die adoring God, loving my friends, not hating my enemies and detesting superstition. February 28, 1778. Voltaire."

And he proved it toward the end. At six o'clock on May 30, de Tersac approached Voltaire, as he lay dying and said in a loud voice, as if to arouse the philosopher: "Jesus Christ!" Voltaire was up to it. Rousing a little from his stupor, he made a motion with his hand. "Let me die in peace."

Ten minutes before he died, he took the hand of his friend Morand and said: "Farewell, my dear Morand. I am dying." He never spoke again. At a quarter past eleven, on the night of May 30, 1778, in his 84th year, died Francois Marie Arouet Voltaire, the greatest of all guerilla fighters for man's freedom.

THOMAS MORE: "I pray you, see me safe up . . ."

Sir Thomas More, author of *Utopia*, English statesman and humanist, saint and martyr in the Roman Catholic Church was beheaded, like Anne Boleyn after him, on charges of treason. He was then 57.

Robert Bolt called him "a man for all seasons." Indeed he was. He faced political tensions at home, the pressure of international crises abroad and the friendships of kings and emperors. He was a lawyer's lawyer, a judge's judge, a diplomat's diplomat. But none of these availed him when his time came.

At first there were successes. He was made the High Steward of the universities of Oxford and Cambridge—and this in the age of Erasmus. He wrote a history of Richard III which subsequently was to influence Shakespeare who wrote a play of the same title. He was the King's ambassador and played a major role in negotiating peace between the Emperor Charles of Spain and King Francis of France. He was knighted and finally succeeded Cardinal Wolsey as Lord Chancellor of England, the second highest rank in the realm, next to the King himself. He was loyal to his king. "If my head could win him a castle in France" he once told his family, "it would not fail to go." But it was not the castle in France that finally caused his head to fall but the King's wish to get a divorce from his first wife, Katherine of Aragon.

When the Pope gave a negative answer to King Henry's request for a divorce, Henry decided he could ease the matter by declaring himself the supreme head of the Church in England. This was an issue of conscience for Sir Thomas. One by one the yes-men in the realm had agreed with King Henry in his bid to be the head of the church as well. First the universities agreed to the idea. Then Parliament approved the action. Finally the clergy—with the exception of John Fischer of Rochester, who died for his belief—took the oath of allegiance and the oath of divorce. Sir Thomas waited. The day following, he resigned his office as Chancellor.

This was asking for trouble. So far he had been loyal to the king; now he had been loyal to his conscience which told him that the King was wrong. Compromise he would not; nor would he seek cheap popularity. He was in grave trouble. He had a large family to take care of and there was no money in the house. When the bishops presented him with a princely collection of over $350,000 for his past services, he refused it. He would not accept conscience money.

There were other temptations. Three of his bishops invited him to be their guest at the coronation of Anne Boleyn; he declined the honor. But every minute of his life was a living condemnation of King Henry and the monarch was inwardly seething with anger. Here was a man who had thrown away the second most powerful job in the country, openly disagreed with the universities, the clergy, the bishops, the parliament, all for a point of conscience. It was ridiculous.

Then the inevitable happened. Sir Thomas was placed on trial. His response to the judges was a summary of his lifelong integrity. "You must understand, sir, that in things touching conscience, every true and good subject is more bound to have respect for his conscience and to his soul than to any other thing in all the world besides." He told them: "I do nobody any harm. I say no harm. I think no harm, but wish everyone well. And if this be not enough to keep a man alive in good faith, then I long not to live!" It was a challenge.

Here was a man who was not afraid to die, but was clearly afraid to fall in his own estimation. The trial wore on; but it was becoming increasingly clear that he would have to face the ultimate sentence: death by beheading. Evidence of disloyalty was hard to get. When a certain unhappy character, Richard Rich, perjured himself to fabricate a suspicious conversation with More, Sir Thomas replied: "My Lord, if I were not a man who did not regard an oath, I needed not, as is well known in this place, at this time or in this case, to stand here as an accused person. And, if this oath of yours, Master Rich, be true, then I pray that I never see God in the face which I would not say were it otherwise to win the whole world." Brave words, from an extraordinarily brave man.

During his long months of imprisonment in the Tower of London, More meditated and prayed that he would be granted the strength to bear his burden. Henry commuted the sentence of disembowelment to beheading. Sir Thomas joked that he hoped such kingly kindness would not be extended to many of his other friends.

On the day he was to be beheaded, he was led to the scaffold, still cheerful and still urbanely courteous to his guards. He leaned on the lieutenant of the guard as he climbed the scaffold. "I pray you" he told the unhappy guard, "see me safely up. As for my coming down, let me shift for myself." Ghoulish humor, but it also showed the caliber of the man.

Arriving at the top, somewhat out of breath, Sir Thomas embraced the thoroughly embarrassed executioner, paid him the customary gold coin and asked him to spare his beard, which he put outside the block, saying that certainly his beard had committed no treason to be so unceremoniously cut off! Asked whether he had anything to say, Sir Thomas asked the assembled people to pray for him in this world and he would pray for them elsewhere. Then, in a magnificent gesture, he asked the people to pray earnestly for the King, that it might please God to give the king good counsel, protesting that he died the king's good servant, but God's first. And then the axe fell. It was the year 1535.

MUHAMMAD: "Have I accomplished my mission?"

We do not know the date of the Prophet's birth; we know that in A.D. 622 he emigrated to Medina from Mecca and that he died there in 632. It is surmised that he was born around 570, into the tribe of Koreish, that he first married Khadija, a wealthy widow, that he was forty when he had visions, that he fought with Mecca which, however, fell to him in 630 without a fight. Victory over Mecca came under conditions such as make this historic event, as one historian put it, "one of the kind which brings honor to the human race."

The Prophet entered the city without striking a blow, overturned the idols in the Ka'bah. Truth has come, he proclaimed, error is scattered. He returned to Medina.

In 632 Muhammad returned to Mecca with 90,000 pilgrims to perform rites that had become fixed in Islam: the taking of the simple pilgrim dress of the *ihram* and the entry into the state of taboo, the seven circumambulations at two different paces, round the Ka'bah of Abraham, the veneration of the Black Stone, the running between the hills of al-Safa and al-Marwah in memory of Hagar and Ishmael, the standing at the foot of Mount Arafat, the sermon (on the 9th) on Mount Arafat, the rapid descent to Muzdalifa towards nightfall, the stoning of the three pillars called demons, the sacrifice of sheep and camel and the ending of the taboo by the cutting of the hair and the nails. That became the pilgrimage of farewell.

Muhammad preached himself on Mount Arafat. He exhorted the Arabs to remain united in Islam after his death, proclaimed the reciprocal rights and duties of married couples, the abolition of usury and the blood feud and the fixing of the year at twelve lunar months without solar correction. He warned the people to be kind to one another, to treat their wives tenderly and to keep faithful to the Lord. He spoke with a sense of urgency, with the urgency of a man who knew his days were now numbered, that if he had anything important to say it had better be there and then. "O Moslems," he said, "remember that all Moslems are brothers unto one another. You are one." And he continued, as the faithful listened to him in wrapt attention. He reminded them of their years together and the work of God that had led them. Finally, he threw up his arms towards heaven and said: "O Lord, I have delivered my message and accomplished my mission." And he told the assembled: "Today I have made perfect your religion; I have fulfilled my grace upon you and I am pleased that your faith should be Islam." There was, it is said, thunderous rumbling in the sky. From several thousand throats came the affirmative reply.

Muhammad then left the pilgrims and went alone to the

cemetery where Khadija lay. He felt her call upon him now, louder than ever before. She was the first of the faithful and first confidante of his great plan. Now, as his time seemed to come, he would go to her for one last visit and say his prayers. It comforted him. All night he lay down beside Khadija's grave, wrapped in an old gray blanket, remembering the past. Next morning he woke up, and walked back to the pilgrims' camp, prayed, washed and having eaten, set out for Medina.

There was just one final task to do, to lead the faithful in a campaign against the Romans in Syria. He appointed Osama, the twenty-year-old son of his adopted son Zaid and Baraka, the slave who had nurtured Muhammad as a child and baby. The Byzantines had to be pacified and he knew that this would be accomplished. Muhammad was sure of what was to come and a great peace came upon him.

The day after the army marched away, Muhammad awoke feeling weak and sick. He did his ablutions and said his prayers but he staggered in the mosque. Fatima, his wife, heard of it and came running, only to be told that she had nothing to worry. In his illness, Muhammad sought the house of Aisha, most dear to him of his living wives. Here he lay, his fever rising, his mind, however, still lucid. They put cold cloths on his brow to bring the fever down, gave him sweet water and juices to drink, but the illness would not go.

On the fourth day of his illness he went to the mosque and prayed and addressed the assembled. His voice was weak, but his spirit seemed unconquerable. But there was humility in his last words which few heard, so gently were they whispered. "The Lord has offered this servant" said Muhammad, "the choice between this life and that which is nigh unto Him and the servant has chosen that which is near the Lord."

Abu Bakr, who was standing nearby, heard and tears flowed down his careworn cheeks. Muhammad smiled at him and praised him. To those still lingering in the mosque, he said the next day Abu Bakr would be leading the prayers because the Prophet was too weak. He returned to the home of Aisha to rest.

Next morning—it was June 8, 632—13 First Rabi of the year XI, Muhammad was well enough to come to the mosque to pray, though Abu Bakr still led the congregation in prayers. He spoke, but his voice was weak and could not carry. For the last time he left and returned again to Aisha's home where she immediately settled down to nurse him.

Slowly, the fever arose. Muhammad began to mumble. Those who heard him felt as if Muhammad was already in the presence of the Lord and his angels. Then, suddenly, his face took on a rapt expression. His body relaxed as if the great struggle was at last over. There was a gentle smile on his face. It was over. Stilled was the voice of Allah.

DAG HAMMARSKJOLD: "And I begin to know the map and to get my bearings."

Dag Hjalmar Agne Carl Hammarskjold—Dag Hammarskjold, for short—was born, the youngest of four brothers, on July 29, 1905, in Jonkoping, Sweden and died in the jungles of far-away Africa on September 17, 1961. He was 56.

As Secretary General of the United Nations, it had fallen to his unenviable lot to negotiate a settlement in the Congo which had then become the cockpit of international intrigue. Tensions had been mounting not merely in the Congo but in other areas of the world as well. To be Secretary General of the world body was no bed of roses. Hammarskjold was under fire, it seemed, from all sides. A bachelor, he must have felt lonely and beset in those times of stress. In his diary, *Markings*, we get an idea of what was going on in his mind: a mixture of determination, resignation, fatigue, loneliness and a growing faith. The entry for Whitsunday, 1961 is an example:

> I don't know who—or what—put the question. I don't know when it was put. I don't remember answering. But at one moment I answered yes to someone or something. From that moment stems the certainty that existence is meaningful and that therefore my life, in submission, has a goal. From that moment I have known what it means "not to look back" to "take no thought for the morrow."

> Led through the labyrinth of life by Ariadne's thread of the answer, I reached a time and a place where I knew that the way leads to a triumph which is a fall and to a fall which is a triumph, that the price of one's effort in life is defamation and the depths of debasement the only exaltation open to man. After that, the word courage had lost its meaning since nothing could be taken from me.
>
> As I continued along the way I learned, step by step, word by word, that behind every saying in the Gospels stands one man's experience. Also behind the prayer that the cup might pass from him and his promise to drink it. Also behind each of the words from the Cross.

That was on Whitsunday. On August 24 he made what was to become his last entry into his diary:

> The seasons have changed
> And the light
> And the weather
> And the hour.
> But it is the same land.
> And I begin to know the map
> And to get my bearings.

Hammarskjold wanted to create "poetry by action." The concept, originally put to him by an explorer friend of his, Sten Selander, fascinated him. Though he was a man of deep contemplation, Hammarskjold also was a man of action and in the case of the Congo, he decided to put in his own personal diplomacy. He would go to the Congo himself and talk to President Moise Tshombe.

Fighting was taking place in Katanga, a U.N. Force had been sent there and the events in that unhappy state were being avidly followed all over the world, more and understandably so at the United Nations. Hammarskjold was anxious to stop the fighting and he was being informed by the military that it would soon be over anyway. His representative, Mr. O'Brien, had been instructed that he spare no effort to find Tshombe and impress on him the necessity to compose his differences with the Congolese Central Government. And Hammarskhold himself arrived to use his personal prestige in the Congo and landed at Ndjili, the Leopoldville airport, on September 13, 1961. Hammarskjold was greeted on arrival by the Prime Minister, Adoula, the Vice Prime

Minister, Gizenga, Colonel Mobutu and Justin Bomboko, the Foreign Minister. It was a united cabinet that had come to receive him and Hammarskjold was pleased. He inspected a Guard of Honor with Adoula and later went into conference with his staff.

On September 15, Hammarskjold, who had originally planned to return to New York to report to the U.N. Security Council, decided not to return but instead to try to consolidate the U.N. position and at the same time find a way to end the fighting. But he had to talk to Tshombe, the Katanga rebel, who was holding out. The mercenaries hired by Tshombe were constantly attacking the U.N. troops and threatening "total war." Hammarskjold felt that in the circumstances, a meeting with the Katanga leader was both essential and urgent.

Near midnight on September 16, Tshombe offered to meet Hammarskjold's representative O'Brien the next day in Rhodesia. Hammarskjold, however, decided that he himself would see Tshombe and that this could be done at a place called Ndola. And he sent word to that effect to the Katanga leader. Tshombe's reply came on the morning of September 17. He was agreeable to meet with Hammarskjold, he said, agreeing, in principle, to an immediate cease-fire, on condition that the U.N. should cease all troops movements and be confined to their camps. At 2 p.m. on the same day, word came to Hammarskjold that Tshombe had chartered a plane and was taking off for Ndola in less than an hour. The Secretary General decided that, in the circumstances, he too would rush to Ndola to keep his appointment.

He had at his disposal a DC-6B, the *Albertina* which had returned that morning from Elizabethville. He did not expect to stay at Ndola more than a day and decided that he did not need to take with him more than his briefcase. Everything else he left behind him at Leopoldsville. That included his purse, his checkbook, a key ring, a typed copy of an article he had written for the Yearbook of the Swedish Tourist Association, a copy of the first twelve typed pages of his translation into Swedish of Martin Buber's *Ich und Du*, and a book he had been reading, Thomas a

Kempis' *Imitation of Christ*. His own briefcase contained, apart from his personal effects, a small extra copy of the U.N. Charter, a small English edition of the New Testament and Psalms, Rainer Maria Rilke's *Duineser Elegien* and *Die Sonette an Orpheus* and an English edition of *Ich und Du*. Besides, he carried a writing pad, a book he had recently bought, Jean Giono's *Noe* of which the pages had not yet been cut, a map of New York State and some notes.

Hammarskjold's party arrived at Ndjili shortly after 4:30 p.m. local time. Some business was transacted and messages read. The plane took off again at 4:51 p.m. into an overcast sky. Some four hours later, at 8:02 p.m. GMT, the *Albertina* called the Salisbury flight information center and gave its expected time of arrival at Ndola as 10:35 p.m. GMT (or 12:35 a.m. local time). Half an hour later, it reported its position at a point over the southern end of Lake Tanganyika. Asked for its flight plans, the aircraft informed the Ndola tower that it would give its future intentions after it had landed. At 11:35 p.m. local time (9:35 p.m. GMT) the *Albertina* informed the Ndola tower that it would arrive at twenty minutes after midnight (10:20 p.m. GMT) and at ten minutes after midnight (10:10 p.m. GMT) it further intimated the tower that the airfield lights were in sight and that it was descending. The tower radioed that the aircraft should report when it reached 6,000 feet and this message was acknowledged. That was the last thing heard of it.

The plane flew over the airfield at a height of 2,000 feet (6,000 feet above sea level) with its navigation lights and flashing anti-collision beacon on the high tailfin switched on. Then nothing more was heard of it. Preparing to land, the *Albertina* had lowered its wheels and flaps and while making a turn, brushed the treetops nine and a half miles west of the airport, cutting a long swathe in the forest. The crash occurred at 10:11 p.m. GMT.

Anticipating the arrival of Hammarskjold, the Associated Press had already sent a dispatch from Ndola saying that the Secretary General and Tshombe had met for more than an hour and the *New York Times* had published the report. At that time

Hammarskjold's body was lying on its back, near a small shrub. He had been thrown clear of the wreckage and, alone among the victims, was not burned at all! He had suffered a fractured spine. Several of his ribs had been broken, so also a thigh bone and his breastbone. He might have lived for a few painful moments after the crash but the internal hemorrhage had been severe. Death must have come mercifully quick. When the search party finally found him, his hand was clutching a tuft of grass and his face, says his biographer, Brian Urquuhart, was "extraordinarily peaceful."

NAPOLEON: "France ... Armee ... Tete d'armee ... Josephine!"

Napoleon was born on August 15, 1769, the son of a Corsican and died on May 5, 1821, a prisoner on the island of St. Helena, not yet 52. In between he became an emperor and left a string of victories and two major defeats behind him. The final defeat at Waterloo was the beginning of the end. A frightened England saw to it that the Emperor was exiled to distant St. Helena and here he arrived on October 17, 1815 and there he lived for almost six years before the end came.

Those six years were the most miserable for Napoleon. To be confined to a rock for a man who had raised armies and won glory was degradation enough. His English warden, the governor of the island, sought to make matters worse for the Emperor by inflicting minor insults on him. Napoleon survived them. He spent his time dictating memoirs, talking to those who had cast their lot with him and had joined him in voluntary exile. The Emperor who once had palaces at his disposal had two rooms to live in, each about fourteen feet by twelve and ten feet high. The bedroom had a threadbare carpet, muslin curtains, a fireplace, painted wooden chairs, two small tables and a sofa. It also had a little camp-bed that Napoleon had used at Austerlitz, hung with green silk curtains, a silver lamp and on the washstand, a magnificent set of silver ewers and basins. But the rooms were infested with rats.

The Emperor's party consisted of three counts and one baron, two valets and dependents—in all forty. By the end of six years, their number had been reduced by half. Napoleon refused to see the governor whom he despised. One attempt resulted in Napoleon and the governor having an argument over the cost of the establishment. On the second occasion, Napoleon refused to see him and told his servant: "Tell him he can bring his executioner's axe, if he likes. But if he wants to enter my room, he must do so over my dead body. Give me my pistols!"

Napoleon read a great deal; he also received visiting travelers. He took an active interest in the working people. He had great sympathy for a gardener, a Malay slave. "Poor devil" Napoleon remarked to a companion one day, "snatched from his family, torn from his home, robbed of himself, sold into slavery! If a captain did it, he was a villain; but if the crew combined to seize poor Tobias, they were hardly responsible. Wickedness is always individual, never collective. Joseph's brethren could not make up their minds to kill him, but Judas betrayed his master!"

He was considerate towards his attendants. Once when his doctor had a fainting fit, Napoleon personally attended on him. On another occasion, when he was out riding, he saw a farmer ploughing the land. The Emperor dismounted, took the handles of the plough, and with incredible speed drove a perfectly straight furrow over a long distance. When he finished it, the Emperor awarded the astounded farmer a gold coin.

He blamed no one for his fate. "No one but myself can be blamed for my fall. I have been my greatest enemy." he said for the record. To visiting Englishmen he would say: "It is not a handful of nobles or rich men that makes a nation, but the mass of the people." Of his own hopes and dreams he was always explicit. "I wanted to found a European system, a European code of laws, a European court of appeal; there would have been but one people throughout Europe!" In a moment of remarkable candor, he said, "Taking it all in all, what a ballad my life has been!" But he was ill most of the time. He complained of stomach pains "like the stab of a pen -knife." He stayed in bed when the agony became unbearable. "I have got so fond of my bed that I would not exchange it now for a throne" he told his attendants. "What a pitiful creature I have become! I, who hardly ever needed sleep, pass my days in lethargy. It seems a desperate resolve merely to open my eyes. Often enough, I used to dictate on different topics to four secretaries at once. In those days I was Napoleon!"

His valet reported one day that a comet had become visible. The Emperor remarked: "That was the sign before the death of Ceasar." But when his doctor pointed out that no comet, in fact, had been seen, Napoleon dismissed it by saying: "Well, people die without comets!"

As the years passed, so did the loyalty of the men who had come with him. During the last four weeks of his life, Napoleon saw a new exodus. Napoleon told his faithful valet, Marchand: "If this goes on much longer, no one will be left here but you and me. But you will look after me till the end and will then close my eyes for me."

His strength on the decline, Napoleon made one last appeal for help. He wrote to Pauline, dearest of his relatives, in the third person: "The Emperor earnestly hopes that Your Highness will acquaint influential Englishmen with his situation. He is dying on this dreadful rock, forsaken by all. His death struggle is terrible." In the middle of April, 1821, he dictated his last will and testament to Montholon. A beautiful document. "I am dying before my time" he dictated, "murdered by the English oligarchy and its hired assassins." He made various, and princely, bequests. He had to have the dictated will given to him to be rewritten in his own hand, for authentication. As his executors, he appointed three, one of them his humble valet. "The services he has rendered me are those of a friend" wrote the Emperor.

There was advice to his son not to seek to avenge the father's death, but to reign in peace. "I was obliged to daunt Europe by arms; in the present day the way is to convince her by reason" he wrote. "Let him do by general consent what circumstances forced me to work for by force of arms . . . . Let the kings listen to reason; Europe will no longer provide matter for maintaining international hatreds . . . ." This was a conqueror speaking.

Once the effort at writing the will was over, he was relaxed. He told his entourage: "When I am dead, each of you will have the sweet consolation of returning to Europe. You will see again, the one his relatives, the other his friends; but for my part, I shall meet my brave warriors in the Elysian Fields. Yes, Kleber, Desaix, Duroc, Ney, Murat . . . ."

On April 21, a fortnight before the end, Napoleon sent for his Corsican priest and gave him instructions on what to do after his death. "You will set up your altar at my bedside and will say Mass with the usual ceremonies until I am under ground." For days now, Napoleon had not been shaved and he looked unkempt. He had terrible racks of gastric spasms, one worse than the other, until he was left moaning and groaning under the cumulative pain. Often he dozed in between these spasms, and dreamt of Josephine.

On April 29, Napoleon had a feverish night. Yet he dictated two drafts, one dealing with the utilization of Versailles and the other with a reorganization of the National Guard. But instead of directing them to any official he merely writes: "First Dream" and "Second Dream" on them. Then he says, like a man relieved: "I feel so wonderfully well now. I could go for a thirty-mile ride." But next day he sinks into a delirium which was to last till he died.

There was a moment of lucidity even during those last five days, when Napoleon again was issuing orders. "When I lose consciousness, you must on no account admit an English doctor . . . You will remain true to my memory . . . All my laws and all my actions were based upon the strictest principles . . . ."

The next day Napoleon was babbling, his mind wandering amid the memories of youth and of Corsica. Marchand, faithful to the last, took down the Emperor's words. "I leave to my son my house in Ajaccio with its outbuildings . . . ." Still in a delirium, Napoleon then called for his fallen comrades: "Desaix, Massena! Victory is ours! Quick! Forward! We have them . . . ."

The next day, the priest went in to see Napoleon who had spent a terrible night. He was still in delirium and Montholon heard him say: *"France! . . . Armee . . . Tete d'armee . . . Josephine!"* Those were his last words. Next moment, however,

Napoleon seemed to be possessed. With an energy that amazed everyone afterwards, Napoleon sprang out of his bed, grappled Montholon, and brought him down to the floor. He had to be rescued by Archambaud, who hearing the noise, came rushing toward Napoleon's bedroom to witness the strange sight. There was no way of knowing what enemy the Emperor was trying to strangle in this, his last fight.

The rest of the day he lay breathing quietly. He seemed to ask for water, which he could barely drink. They held a sponge of moist vinegar to his lips. Outside there was a storm and at five in the evening, two trees were uprooted by a fierce gale. Only two men were present, a count of the old French nobility and a humble man of the people, a valet, to watch over the Emperor's bedside. At that point, Napoleon went into the throes of prolonged rigor. There were no signs of pain. Napoleon's eyes were widely open, staring into vacancy. The death rattle was in his throat. As the sun sank into the sea, his heart stopped beating.

MARTIN LUTHER KING JR.: "Free at last, free at last, thank God Almighty, I'm free at last!"

For a Civil Rights champion, Martin Luther King Jr. was ridiculously young when he was killed by an assassin. He was born in Atlanta on January 15, 1929. His death occurred on the balcony of a Memphis motel on April 5, 1968. Between these two days he had helped usher in a civil rights revolution that was to change the racial situation in the United States. And it was done through acceptance of non-violence as the lever of change.

The years, of course, were by no means easy. Indeed, they were very hard on him. He had to suffer abuse, one attempt on his life, imprisonment and police brutality. He survived them until that final moment. He was not afraid of death. "If a man hasn't found something he will die for" he once had said, "he isn't fit to live." His work took him to America's cities where his leadership was so much in demand. He had achieved national leadership; his work had won him a Nobel Prize. "I accept the

Nobel Prize" he had said at the ceremony in Oslo, "at a moment when twenty-two million Negroes of the United States of America are engaged in a creative battle to end the long night of racial injustice . . . . " That was what it was all about: a creative battle, and he was both the general and the foot soldier, making innumerable forays into enemy territory, facing tear gas and police beatings.

There were moments of glory, as when he addressed a mammoth gathering in front of the Lincoln Memorial when he closed a tear-bringing peroration with a call for freedom to ring:

> When we let freedom ring, when we let it ring from every village and every hamlet, from every state and every city, we will be able to speed up that day when all God's children, black men and white men, Jews and Gentiles, Protestants and Catholics, will be able to join hands and sing in the words of that old Negro spiritual, "Free at last; Free at last! Thank God Almighty, we are free at last!"

In a strange manner, Martin Luther King was to gain his "freedom."

The powers of evil—the killers of his dream—were getting active. There was violence in the air. White supremacists had accepted his challenge. As in many cities, in Memphis too, a march had been planned. But Martin learned that the city had been granted a federal court injunction against demonstrations. That meant that no march or demonstration could be held in Memphis. He was determined that one shall be held, though. He told his friends: "We are not going to be stopped by mace or injunctions." "We stand by the First Amendment. In the past, on the basis of conscience, we have had to break injunctions and if necessary we may do it. We'll cross that bridge when we come to it."

The threats of the judiciary left Martin unmoved. It was suggested to him, however, that the proposed date could be moved further in order to facilitate better organization of labor.

He had been living in fear. According to his friend, Andy Young, Martin had developed the disturbing habit of looking about him as though any moment he expected to be shot. He needed some boosting for his occasionally sagging spirit. He was asked to address the black community that had gathered at Mason

Temple. He accepted the invitation. Toward the end of his sermon, he referred to threats against his life. One could not dismiss rumors, he said, out of hand. "Well, I don't know what will happen now," he went on, "but it doesn't really matter with me now. Because I've been to the mountain top. I won't mind." Of course, he said, he would like to live long, like everybody else. "Longevity has its place. But I'm not concerned about that now. I just want to do God's will. And He's allowed me to go up to the mountain. And I've looked over and I've seen the promised land." He continued, his baritone voice ringing through the chamber: "I may not get there with you, but I want you to know tonight that we as a people will get to the promised land. So I'm happy tonight. I'm not worried over anything. I'm not fearing any man. 'Mine eyes have seen the glory of the coming of the Lord.' "

That was on a Wednesday. Most of Thursday, Martin spent in room 306 of the Lorraine Motel, planning the coming Monday's demonstration. Opposite the motel was a seedy transient hotel from where an assassin was soon to do his dastardly job. But Martin could not possibly have known about it.

Shortly before 6 p.m. a chauffeur for a prominent black mortician arrived at the Lorraine to drive Martin to the home of a supporter. Martin was ready, but could not find his tie. His friend Ralph Abernathy pointed it out to him and Martin quickly picked it up, knotted it around his neck and was teasing his would be host's wife about her talent to cook "soul food." Then, for reason that only the fates know, he pushed aside the plate glass sliding door and stepped outside onto his balcony. Perhaps he wanted to get a breath of fresh air. Perhaps he thought he would step outside as Ralph took time to sprinkle himself with his favorite toilet water. Others joined Martin on the balcony. In the courtyard below were the chauffeur Jones, Jesse Jackson, Andy Young and Ben Branch, a local musician. "So you know Ben?" Jesse asked. "Yes" replied Martin, doing a superb job of appearing to slide into a mood of folksy comradeship, "Ben, be sure and sing 'Precious Lord, Take My Hand.' " After the dinner there was to be another church rally and Ben was to sing there.

So Martin added, as an afterthought: "Sing it real pretty." Jones, who was listening, meanwhile shouted to Martin to wear his top coat, because it was getting to be chilly. "Okay" said Martin, "I will."

He had hardly said those words when a shot rang in the air and it hit Martin. He fell, with one leg caught in the balcony railing. Blood was gushing through a facial wound. Ralph bent down, shock registered on his gaunt face, saying: "Martin, Martin, it is Ralph." But Martin would not answer. He was dead. He was free at last. Thank God Almighty, he was free at last from man's hatred.

OLIVER WENDELL HOLMES: "If I were dying my last words would be: 'Have faith and pursue the unknown end.'"

The story of Justice Oliver Wendell Holmes, his biographer, Catherine Drinker Bowen has written, is the story of his country. That is only a partial commentary on one of the greatest judges the United States has ever had. His judgments to this day are worth quoting. He was called the Great Dissenter.

He lived up to a ripe old age. He was born in 1841; he died in the same month he was born, March, in the year 1935. He was then 94.

Death came like a friend, not an enemy, which seems a fitting tribute to a man who all his life was ready for his end. He had once said: "To have done what lay in you to do, to say that you have lived and be ready for the end . . ." When death finally came, it found him ready.

A few weeks before he died, he had remarked to his secretary: "Why should I fear death? I have seen him so often. When he comes he will seem like an old friend." And he has added: "If the good Lord should tell me I had only five minutes to live, I would say to Him, 'All right, Lord, but I'm sorry you can't make it ten.'" And on still another occasion he had said: "If I were dying my last words would be: 'Have faith and pursue the unknown end.'"

It was inevitable that a man who lived up to the age of 94

would have his thoughts. But it is not so inevitable that these thoughts would be so pleasant. Holmes drove through life and to his death in a horse and carriage. He had resigned from the U.S. Supreme Court at the age of 91, with little fanfare. On the day he resigned, he went to the Supreme Court as usual, delivered a majority opinion, reading it—and this should have told the Court what to expect—in a faltering, thickened voice and took his noon recess as usual. When the Court rose at 4:30 p.m. he got his hat and coat, walked over to the Clerk's desk and quietly said: "I won't be down tomorrow." That was it.

That night, he sat down and wrote his resignation to the President. To his own colleagues, he sent a note: "My dear brethren," he wrote, "you must let me call you so once more. Your more than kind, your generous letter touches me to the bottom of my heart. The long and intimate association with me who so command my respect and admiration could not but fix my affection so well. For such little time as may be left for me, I shall treasure it as adding gold to the sunset." The newspapers had said of him: "Justice Holmes makes of old age a pleasure, something to look forward to."

On his ninetieth birthday, the nation had paid him grateful tribute. There were speeches, symposia. Holmes' turn had come to reply. "In this symposium" Holmes told his listeners, "my part is only to sit in silence. To express one's feelings as the end draws near is too intimate a task." And then he added: "But I may mention one thought that comes to me as a listener-in. The riders in a race do not stop short when they reach the goal. There is a little finishing canter before coming to a standstill. There is time to hear the kind voices of friends and to say to one's self: 'The work is done.' But just as one says that, the answer comes: 'The race is over, but the work never is done while the power to work remains.' The canter that brings you to a standstill need not be only coming to rest. It cannot be while you still live. For to live is to function. That is all there is in living. And so I end with a line from a Latin poet who uttered the message more than fifteen hundred years ago: 'Death plucks my ear and says, Live—I am coming.' "

Death came quietly. On the afternoon of February 23, 1935 Holmes went out for a drive. Next morning he had caught a cold. Holmes went to bed sneezing; the sneeze turned out to be a cough and from that it progressed to pneumonia. Holmes was not dismayed, though he knew he was dying. He lay quietly, joking with the nurses when he had the strength. He dismissed attempts at coaxing him to eat, to have stimulants. "Lot of damn nonsense" he said, grumbling. He wasn't afraid. Lord, he had had his share of the good life. He was a soldier during the Civil War; a judge in Massachusetts, a judge of the U.S. Supreme Court. Life, he had once said, was action and passion. He had all that. What more was there to live for? Even his darling wife had died before him. With Fanny Holmes dead, Justice Holmes had half a life taken away from him.

Now he himself faced death. The days passed. Came March. In his long white iron bed Holmes lay, breathing heavily, his eyes closed. In the adjoining room, doctors consulted, knowing that the end could not be too far away. On the fifth of March, late in the afternoon, newspapermen saw an ambulance stop outside his home. An oxygen tent was seen being carried in. Holmes opened his eyes, saw the huge, unwieldy contraption wheeled to his bed and on to cover him. He made a movement. The doctors heard him say clearly: "Lot of damn foolery."

But the doctors were only doing what they thought needed to be done. But even they knew their limits. At 2 in the morning they had realized that the moment had come. Quietly, the oxygen tubes were taken away. Holmes continued to breathe, slowly, slowly, his eyes closed. It was a picture of a man totally at peace with himself and his God. Outside in the March gardens, wet branches were creaking under the melting snow of the winter. Soon Spring would come.

The doctors watched. The minutes ticked, measure by measure. The doctors never quite knew when the great Judge died. He had departed so quietly, with no sign of any struggle that it was hard to tell when he was gone.

GENERAL TOJO: "Although I now depart I shall return to this land."

The Second World War was over. Japan had been defeated—and humiliated. General MacArthur had arrived in Tokyo and ordered the Stars and Stripes to be flown in full view of the Imperial Palace. What would the Americans do to Premier Hideki Tojo, who had led his country to defeat?

Tojo stayed at his modest home in Setagaya beseiged by correspondents and photographers. His wife was worried as to what would happen to him. He asked her to leave the home and take her maid with her. Mrs. Tojo was afraid he might commit suicide. "Take care of yourself, please" she begged, "please take care of yourself." Tojo merely grunted.

The maid left. Now the American Military Police surrounded the house. They wanted him to come out. An officer shouted: "Tell this yellow bastard we've waited long enough. Bring him out!" But Tojo had other plans. His doctor had carefully made a chalk mark on his chest where the heart was and now, his wife away, he shot himself with a .32-calibre Colt. When the arresting party heard the shot, it rushed in, followed by a reporter of *The New York Times*. Major Paul Kress, leader of the party, called out: "Don't shoot." Tojo hardly heard him. He collapsed in a chair, his shirt stained with blood. It was 4:27 p.m. But he had not died instantly, as he had thought. He called for water, which was brought him. He drank it and called for more. At 4:29 p.m. his lips began to move. "I am very sorry it is taking me so long to die" he murmured. The Americans standing over him now showed no sympathy.

His voice gathering strength, Tojo said: "I am very sorry for the nation and all the races of the greater Asiatic powers. I would not like to be judged before a conqueror's court. I wait for the righteous judgment of history." Tojo explained that he wished to commit suicide "but sometimes that failed." On this occasion it had failed though Tojo had shot himself in the exact spot that his doctor had marked for him. But the bullet had missed the heart. As he was placed in am ambulance to be whisked to a hospital, he told the medic: "I did not shoot myself in the head because I wanted the people to recognize my features and know I was dead." In the hospital he told General Eichelberger, who had come to see him, "I am dying, I am sorry to have given so much trouble." "Do you mean tonight or for the last few years?" asked General Eichelberger, cynically.

But Tojo lived, to be tried as a war criminal. On November 12, 1948, he was sentenced to death. While he was in prison he had become a changed man. He had taken to religion. As John Toland recounts it, in his excellent book *The Rising Sun*, a few hours before his execution, Tojo told Dr. Shinso Hanayama, a Buddhist priest, that he had much to be thankful for. His body would soon become part of the soil of Japan; his death would be not only an apology to the Japanese but a move toward peace and the rebuilding of Japan. It was time that he died, as he was getting old. It was better to die than to spend the rest of his days in prison, a victim of worldly passions. And, finally, it was a joy to die in the knowledge that he would be reborn in Amitabha's paradise.

Tojo wrote his final testament. He told the Americans not to alienate the feelings of the Japanese or infest them with communism. He apologized for the atrocities committed by the Japanese military and urged the American authorities to show compassion and repentance toward the civilians of Japan. He also predicted that a third world war was bound to break out because of the conflicting interests of the United States and the Soviet Union. The battlefields, he said, would then be Japan, China and Korea. It was therefore the responsibility of the Americans to protect a helpless Japan. The testament closed with two poems:

> Although I now depart I shall return to this land,
> As I have yet to repay my debt to my country.
> It is time for farewell; I shall wait beneath the moss,
> Until the flowers are fragrant again in the islands of
>   Yamato (Japan).

On December 22, 1948, three days before Christmas and in

his 64th year, Tojo silently walked up the thirteen steps to the gallows with dignity. Just after midnight, the trap was sprung.

JOHN, DUKE OF MARLBOROUGH: Never fought a battle he did not win.

Neither power, nor fame, nor glory is a defence against sickness, unhappiness and misery. That is the message of the life of John, First Duke of Marlborough, of whom it is said that his military successes were unmatched even by Napoleon. Marlborough, it was said by Churchill, "never fought a battle he did not win, nor besiege a fortress he did not take." It brought him glory, but at the same time it brought him the attention of his enemies, as well as dishonor and exile.

There has been no question in the minds of historians that Marlborough was one of the greatest soldiers of all time, if not the greatest. The Duke of Wellington, no mean soldier himself, was once asked what he thought of Napoleon and Marlborough. Who was the greater general? "I used always to say" replied Wellington, "that the presence of Napoleon at a battle was equal to a reinforcement of forty thousand men. But I can conceive nothing greater than Marlborough at the head of an English army."

Marlborough led victorious allied forces against the threat of tyranny in Europe. It was his great program to counter the French bid for hegemony under Louis XIV. Churchill has said that Marlborough was "not only the foremost of English soldiers, but in the first ranks among statesmen of our history; not only that he was a Titan, but he was a virtuous and benevolent being."

It was this man who had brought glory to England who was unceremoniously dismissed by his queen and practically sent into exile. When he appeared before his queen, nobody "hardly took notice of him." He stood alone among his enemies. The queen convened a meeting of her cabinet and the following decision was taken:

> Being informed that an information against the Duke of Marlborough was laid before the House of Commons, by the

> commissioners of the public accounts, her Majesty thought it fit to dismiss him from all his employments, that the matter might undergo an impartial investigation.

So much for the fruits of victory. This was not all. One of his daughters died of what was then called "pleuretic fever" and that was a blow to the soldier. He and his wife Sarah gave way to deep depression. They retired to their country estate and here the headaches and giddiness that had always dogged him culminated in a paralytic stroke. He was robbed of both sense and speech.

It took him six months to recover; happily his political fortunes had changed. Queen Anne had died, her successor had welcomed him back and he had been restored to his post as Captain General. But now family affairs plagued him. His two surviving daughters would not get along with their mother and treated her undutifully and cruelly. In his old age, this distressed Marlborough greatly. His old enemies were still active. Envious of Sarah they accused her of a plot to dethrone the King and to his deep chagrin he was summoned by his own son-in-law to receive the monstruous accusation against his wife. It would have broken a man of lesser stature.

And yet there is this story told of him. One day he was pacing, with failing steps, the enormous rooms of Blenheim Palace that, in his old age, he had set himself to build, and stood at one point in front of a portrait of his hanging on the walls. Long he stood and intently contemplated it. Then he turned away with the words: "That was once a man!" Clearly, the times had taken their toll of Marlborough.

Then, in early June 1722 he had more paroxysms and had to be confined to bed. His reason remained unclouded but his strength was beginning to deteriorate rapidly. One would have thought that at least in these circumstances, the family differences would be muted. But his illness only made matters worse between his wife and daughters. The day before he died, there was a scene between mother and daughters. She was not sure they should come to see him, but they did. When Sarah entered the room where her husband lay, the daughters would not talk to her. It must have pained the loving father no end.

Sarah then suggested that some prayers be offered. When they were over she asked her husband if he heard them well. Sarah was pleased to hear from him that not only had he heard the prayers but that he had joined in them. A little later he went into a coma and lay thus for some hours. He died with the dawn on June 16, 1722 in the seventy-third year of his age. That was the only battle he fought—and lost.

Churchill, in his biography of Marlborough, writes: "The span of mortals is short, the end universal; and the tinge of melancholy which accompanies decline and retirement is in itself an anodyne. It is foolish to waste lamentations upon the closing phase of human life. Noble spirits yield themselves willingly to the successively falling shades which carry them to a better world or to oblivion."

However, for all the unhappiness that his family brought him in the closing years of his life, Marlborough would have been happy to note that to the end of her life, his wife, as in the past, remained loyal to his memory. After the Duke's death there were not suitors lacking to propose to her. At sixty-two she was still remarkably handsome. One Lord Coningsby begged her to marry him, but she put him aside gently. Another suitor, the Duke of Somerset, himself a very rich man, also pressed his affection. To him she replied in a letter now famous: "If I were young and handsome as I was" she wrote, "instead of old and faded as I am, and you could lay the empire of the world at my feet, you should never share the heart and hand that once belonged to John, Duke of Marlborough."

SWAMI VIVEKANANDA: "When men are once trained it is essential that their leaders leave them."

Swami Vivekananda, who founded the Ramakrishna Mission and took the message and meaning of Hinduism to the Western world, had once prophecied that he would not live up to be forty. He died on July 4, 1902, six months before the target he had set for himself.

His health had been deteriorating for some time. As early as August 27, 1901 he had written to a disciple, Mary Hale: "I am a dying man; I have no time to fool in . . . I now do nothing—except try to eat and sleep and nurse my body the rest of the time." Knowing that he was ill, his disciples had come pouring in from the far corners of the world toward the last two months of his life. They were all individually received, encouraged and asked to go on with their mission.

He began to divest himself of important responsibilities. "How often" he said, "does a man ruin his disciples by remaining always with them. When men are once trained, it is essential that their leader leave them, for without his absence they cannot develop themselves." On another occasion he had said similar words. "Plants always remain small under a big tree."

His life in the last eight weeks continued in this strain. He remained indifferent to world events where once he was full of passion. "I can no more enter into outside affairs" he said matter of factly, "I am already on the way." On another occasion he put it in even more blunt terms. "You may be right; but I cannot enter any more into these matters. I am going down to death." He might have said that he was going out for an evening walk, for all the casual way he spoke of his impending end.

Sometimes, though, he was less explicit. To Miss McLeod he wrote on May 15, 1902: "I am somewhat better, but of course far from what I expected. A great idea of quiet has come upon me. I am going to retire for good—no more work for me. If possible, I will revert to my old days of begging."

His guru, the saint Ramakrishna, had said that Vivekananda, his mission completed, would refuse to live with his physical body and would merge forever into *samadhi*—from which there was no return, if once he realized who he was. A brother monk one day asked him casually: "Do you know who you are?" "Yes, I now know!" came the shocking answer. The monk quickly dropped the subject.

It was known among the Swami's disciples that he had

received the grace of Siva—the power to will his death at a time determined by him. So, one day, when Vivekananda asked for the Bengali almanac—Sri Ramakrishna before him had similarly asked for one—there was apprehension. It was as if the Swami was trying to make up his mind which would be the best day for him to depart the worldly scene. Indeed, three days before he actually attained *mahasamadhi*—the total self-extinction—Vivekananda pointed out to Swami Premananda a particular spot on the monastery grounds where he wished his body to be cremated.

On July 2, 1902, a Wednesday, the Swami fasted. It was *ekadasi*, the eleventh day of the moon and fasting was customary on the day. His English woman disciple, Sister Nivedita called on him for advice. He referred her to other Swamis in the monastery, but insisted on serving her the morning meal. When she had finished, Indian style, he insisted on pouring water on her hands and to dry them with a towel. Sister Nivedita remonstrated. "But Swamiji, " she said, "it is I who should be doing these things to you, not you to me!" Vivekananda replied gravely: "Jesus washed the feet of his disciples!" Later, Sister Nivedita recorded that she almost felt like saying: "But that was the last time!" but that the words froze on her lips.

Vivekananda himself did not appear sad or grim. Few made any real effort to engage him in conversation and if they did, they would talk about his pet animals or his garden experiments, or books, or absent friends. But there seemed to be something luminous about him. Everyone felt his presence. Came Friday. Vivekananda rose very early, went to the chapel, alone, shut the windows and the doors, contrary to his habit and meditated for three hours. As he came out, he was heard to sing a hymn in praise of Kali, the goddess he worshipped. Mother, he called her.

> I hardly know who Mother is,
> Though I have pondered all my life:
> Now Purusha, now Prakriti,
> And now the Void, She seems to be.

Then, almost in a whisper, as if speaking to himself, he said: "If there were another Vivekananda, then he would have understood what this Vivekananda has done! And yet—how many Vivekanandas shall be born in time!"

To his disciples he expressed a desire to worship Kali the next day and asked some of them to get ready the necessary articles for the ritual. Next, he asked Swami Suddhananda to read a passage from the *Yajur Veda* and the commentary of a well-known scholar. He disagreed with the commentary and suggested a better interpretation be provided without himself going into the details.

There was no way in which anyone could have guessed that the end was approaching. He sat with his fellow monks for what turned out to be his last meal, bantered with them and as one last act of service gave a three-hour lecture on Sanskrit grammar to the novices. In the afternoon he invited Swami Premananda for a long walk during which he discussed his plans to start a Vedic College in the monastery.

"What will be the good of studying the Vedas?" teasingly asked Premananda.

"To kill superstition," replied the Swami.

The walk had mellowed him. Back in the monastery he spoke feelingly about the rise and fall of nations. "India is immortal" he told the monks, "if she persists in her search for God. But if she goes in for politics and social conflict, she will die."

Then Vivekananda spoke to each of the assembly in turn. That was a moment of tenderness to one and all. Soon the chapel bell rang the seven o'clock call for evening worship. Quietly, with a word that none should disturb him, he went to his own room for an hour's meditation. Then he called one of his disciples in and asked him to open all the windows and fan his head. Without a word, he lay down and a silence enveloped the room. The disciple continued to fan the Swami. Minutes passed and not a word was uttered. It was presumed that Vivekananda was either sleeping or gone into deep meditation and in any event it was not for the disciple to break either by word or deed.

At the end of an hour, says Swami Nikhilananda in the Swami's official biography, Vivekananda's hands trembled a little and he seemed to take a deep breath. There followed a shattering silence. The Swami again took a similar deep breath. "His eyes became fixed in the center of his eyebrows, his face assumed a divine expression and eternal silence fell."

The Great Ecstacy took place at ten minutes past nine at night. It was July 4. In his beloved United States, they were celebrating Independence Day. Afterward, the disciple recorded that he had noticed 'a little blood' in the Swami's nostrils, about his mouth and in his eyes. It was as it was said in the Yoga scriptures.

But such is hope that the brother disciples now gathered around him started to chant his name, hopefully to bring him back to consciousness. Physicians were sent for, artificial respiration tried, to no avail. At midnight, the great leader was pronounced dead.

THOMAS JEFFERSON: "I go to my Father's; I welcome the shore . . . ."

Thomas Jefferson, President of the United States, wrote his own epitaph, selecting what he considered the three most important achievements of his life. "Here was buried" the epitaph reads, "Thomas Jefferson, author of the Declaration of American Independence, of the Statute of Virginia for Religious Freedom and Father of the University of Virginia." No man could have done more.

Jefferson was born on April 2, 1743 and died eighty-three years later, on July 4, 1826, for the author of the Declaration of Independence, significantly on Independence Day itself. Philosopher, scientist, statesman and distinguished in all three spheres—and a whole lot more—Jefferson was not enamoured of power. When he relinquished his presidency and returned to his home in Monticello, he wrote to a friend, Pierre du Pont, that at last he felt free.

"Never did a prisoner released from his chains'" he wrote, "feel such relief as I shall on shaking the shackles of power. Nature intended me for the tranquil pursuits of science, by rendering them my supreme delight. But the enormities of the times in which I have lived, have forced me to take a part in resisting them and to commit myself on the boisterous ocean of political passions. I thank God for the opportunity of retiring from them without censure and carrying with me the most consoling proofs of public approbation." No truer words were said.

He had left Washington, the capital of the New World, on March 11, 1809 and he was to live another seventeen years as a country gentleman, tending his estate, taking delight in growing things, boasting of being in the saddle from dawn till dusk. He renewed old friendships; he entertained lavishly. He corresponded with scientists all over the world. He remained President of the American Philosophical Society until 1815. In his retirement he studied local Indian languages, worked on building his grand palace at Monticello, compiled what came to be known as the Jefferson Bible. At the ripe age of 74 he embarked on the project of his heart's desire, the founding of the University of Virginia.

When it was opened in March 1825, a year before his death, he had naturally to be its first rector! There he was, inviting young students to dine with him and converse with him on the mysteries of the universe. It was a sight for the gods. There never seemed to be a dull moment. Scholars were badgering him for information and narratives on the Revolution and who better could they have sought than the author of the Declaration of Independence? He was 77 when he started writing his memoirs though, halfway through, he was remarking: "I am tired of talking about myself!"

Others were not and he was continually receiving visitors, writing to friends, consoling them in their times of trouble. When Abigail Adams died, her heart-broken husband, the great John Adams, was turning to Jefferson. "While you live, I seem to have a bank at Monticello on which I can draw." And draw he did.

He was active at 81, riding a thoroughbred called Eagle, despite his rheumatism. It has been said that he could have gone on like this for many more years except that tragedy had begun to strike his home. One of his favorite granddaughters, Anne, had contracted a bad marriage and was suffering from it to Jefferson's distress. Then, as 1826 dawned, he was to lose Monticello itself— Monticello on which he had lavished so much attention. Debts piled upon debt. A friend, for whom he had signed a promissory note, betrayed him to the tune of $20,000—the news almost killed him and for several days his family actually thought he was dying. Ruin faced the great statesman.

For most of February, 1826 Jefferson was bedridden, suffering from an acute form of diarrhea. Now he knew he was dying. He wrote a particularly touching letter to his friend, James Madison. "You have been a pillar of support through life. Take care of me when dead and be assured that I shall leave with you my last affections." On March 16 he made his will. Thereafter he steadily went downhill.

Late in June came an invitation from the Mayor of Washington to join the citizens of the young capital in a celebration of the fiftieth anniversary of American independence. Fifty years had passed and, as Jefferson glumly noted, of that "host of worthies," as he called them "who joined us on that day, in the bold and doubtful election we were to make for our country, between submission or the sword" only he, and John Adams and Charles Carroll, still survived.

In his letter to the Mayor declining the invitation, he nevertheless expressed a beautiful hope. "May the day be to the world," he wrote, words now flowing like pearls on a string, "what I believe it will be . . . the palpable truth, that the mass of mankind has not been born with saddles on their backs, nor a favorite few booted and spurred, ready to ride them legitimately, by the grace of God . . . . Let the annual return of this day forever refresh our recollection of these rights and an undiminished devotion to them."

Two days before he died, on July 2, he called his family to his bedside and spoke to them briefly about the virtues of honest and truthful lives. Later in the day he summoned Martha Randolph and handed her a small casket, in which he had placed a sheet of paper on which he had written in still firm and clear a hand, his very special goodbye:

> Life's visions are vanished, its dreams are no more
> Dear friend of my bosom, why bathed in tears?
> I go to my Father's: I welcome the shore
> Which crowns all my hopes or which buries my cares.
> Then farewell, my dear, my lov'd daughter, adieu!
> The last pang of life is in parting from you!
> Two seraphs await me long shrouded in death;
> I will bear them your love on my last parting breath.

On the third of July Jefferson slept throughout the day only to wake up in the evening, about seven o'clock. By his side were his faithful grandson Jefferson Randolph and Nicholas Trist, husband of his granddaughter Virginia. He stirred. "This is the fourth of July" he noted, but had to be reminded that it wasn't. It was the third. At 9 p.m. his doctor came to administer some medicine, but Jefferson wanted none of it. "No, doctor, nothing more" he said, his voice still clear and distinct.

He was getting restless. He sat up in bed, leaned forward as if in a gesture of writing. He was delirious. "The Committee of Safety must be warned" he mumbled. In the corner, a grandfather clock ticked the minutes away. At 11 p.m. Jefferson looked at Trist, asked, his voice a bare whisper: "This is the 4th?" Trist pretended as if he had not heard. Afraid Jefferson was dying and even more afraid to tell a dying man an untruth, Trist was miserable. Jefferson repeated the question. Mutely, Trist nodded assent. "Ah!" he heard Jefferson sigh, as if satisfied with the knowledge that he had seen the fiftieth anniversary of his beloved Republic arrive.

Now others joined Trist and Randolph at the great leader's bedside. Jefferson fell into a disturbed sleep. The midnight hour struck. Conscious or not, Jefferson had realized his desire. At 4 a.m. on the morning of July 4, Jefferson stirred and called for Burwell, one of the slaves he had freed in his last will and testament. He did not speak again. On the noon of July 4, fifty minutes past meridian, Jefferson ceased to breathe. Trist, standing nearby, closed Jefferson's eyes. A few hours later, in Braintree, Massachusetts, Jefferson's old friend, John Adams, was also to die, in the belief that Jefferson was still living. Adams' last words were: "Thomas Jefferson still survives!"

POPE JOHN XXIII: "All days are good for being born, all days are good for dying."

Angelo Guiseppe Roncalli, born poor on November 25, 1881 died Pope on June 3, 1963 aged 82, loved, honored and worshipped, not just because he was a Pope, but because he loved his fellow man.

He had been elected Pope much to his own surprise. "I tremble and am afraid" he had told the Cardinals. Asked how he would wish to be called, he had said in Latin: *"Vocabor Johannes"* I will be called John. There had been twenty-two other Popes by that name. So he became John XXIII.

Nearly all the twenty-two, John XXIII said, in explaining why he had chosen the name "had a brief pontificate." He was hinting that he, too, might not last long. When he was elected in October, 1958, he was already 77. In five years he had made the Papacy a well-loved institution all over the world. Even the Soviet leader Kruschchev, to whom John had sent a peace medallion, was proud to own it.

He was an innovator, a humanist, and above all, a humanist. He loved mankind and lived to serve it. He knew he did not have many years to live. "I feel like Saint Martin" he said on the eve of his fourth year as Pontiff, "who 'neither feared to die nor refused to live.'"

His illness that resulted in his death began around the time of his 80th birthday, November, 1961. In his private journal he wrote: "I notice in my body the beginning of some trouble that must be natural for an old man. I bear it with resignation, even if it is sometimes rather tiresome and also makes me afraid it will get worse. It is not pleasant to think too much about this; but once more I feel prepared for anything." He had stomach cancer. His mother had died of cancer. So had a brother and four sisters. He must have known that his time had come.

On the eve of his 82nd birthday, he told a group of visitors: "We are entering our eighty-second year. Shall we finish it? All days are good for being born, all days are good for dying."

His doctors had told him that he had "gastropathic condition." "That is because I am a Pope. Otherwise you would call it a stomachache" he told them jokingly. When rumors started that he was on his deathbed he remarked: "Tell them the Pope still lives. And there is no reason to bury him before he dies!" Throughout 1962 John knew he was wasting; he had become perceptibly weaker. One evening he was told that he had a tumor. "A tumor?" repeated John. *"Ebbene,* very well, let God's will be done. But don't worry about me because my bags are packed. I'm ready to go!"

On the night of Tuesday, November 27, John had a massive intestinal hemorrhage. His secretary, Capovilla, had to rush to get the doctor in attendance. Coagulants, blood plasma, morphine were administered and by the next morning, the bleeding had been brought under control. A public audience, scheduled for the day, however, had to be cancelled. On Sunday, John was on his feet and appeared at his study window and told the cheering gathering below: "Good health, which threatened to leave us, is returning—has returned." The people cheered. Their affection deeply moved John. He wept.

His bags were packed, he had said, but he kept working. He worked on *Pacem in Terris*—Peace on Earth; he wrote a long letter to his peasant family among whom he was born. He addressed it to Zaverio, his eldest brother. "My eighty years of life completed tell me, as they tell you, dear Savero, and all the members of our family, that what is most important is always to keep ourselves well prepared for a sudden departure, because this is what matters most: to make sure of eternal life, trusting in the goodness of the Lord who sees all and makes provision for all . . . "

He had always been kind. Now he seemed even more considerate to those around him. He kept urging Capovilla to get more rest "or you will go off before your boss." When he learned that many in the parish of Sotto il Monte, his birthplace, wanted to come to see him, he bantered: "Well, tell them to come quickly. Are they waiting until I am dead?"

On April 30, 1963 he suffered another hemorrhage. But

with all the peasant strength in him we weathered that storm. On May 20 Cardinal Stefan Wyszynski of Poland came to see him and it was suggested to him by Capovilla that he could see the visiting Cardinal in his bedroom. "We haven't come to that yet!" said John purposefully and walked to the library for the meeting. As the Cardinal was leaving, he expressed the hope that he would see the Holy Father in September, at the next session of the Vatican Council. John smiled. "In September" he remarked, "you will either find me here, or another. You know, in one month they can do it all—the funeral of one Pope, the election of another." Graveside humor. But it was the humor of a man who was not afraid to die.

After that he had three successive hemorrhages. Yet the body held. On the night of May 29 he had yet one more hemorrhage. This time the cancerous mass burst the intestines and flooded the abdominal lining with poison: peritonitis. What John always spoke reverently of as Sister Death was now close by. For four more days John suffered. He lay in his bed, spent and gaunt, his huge frame shrunken. His solace was the ivory crucifix on the wall opposite his bed which he was happy to see "with the first glimpse in the morning and the last one at night."

On May 30, Mazzoni, his physician called. "Holy Father," he addressed John, "you have asked me, many times, to tell you when the end was near, so you could prepare." Mazzoni could barely continue. John, lying majestically in bed, was smiling, though. "Yes," he said, "don't feel badly, doctor. I understand. I am ready."

Capovilla, his secretary was in tears, kneeling by John's bedside. "Courage, my son" John said softly, "I am a bishop and I must die a bishop, with simplicity but with majesty and you must help me. Go, get the people together." He called for his confessor.

After his confession and last communion, he received the holy oil of Extreme Unction. *"Ut unum sint"* (that they may be one) he repeated again and again, the words of Jesus after the Last Supper.

Now the Cardinals came in and the Monsignori to witness the passing away of the Pope. His family was summoned. He embraced his brothers and sole living sister. "I am happy because in a little while I shall see our mother and father in heaven" he told them. "Pray."

On Sunday, June 2, his temperature rose to 104 degrees. He called his doctor. He wanted to give his physician something to remember him by. Fumbling, he found his fountain pen. "Take it" he told Mazzoni, "it is nearly new!" By then Mazzoni was crying. He called his faithful secretary Capovilla. "I am sorry to have kept you from your mother such a long time" he apologized. "Promise me when this is over that you will go to see her."

On Monday, June 3 they removed his false teeth so that the doctors could better administer oxygen. John lost consciousness. In the evening, Cardinal Luigi Traglia, John's vicar for Rome, celebrated an outdoor Mass for those thousands who had come to St. Peter's square knowing that John's death was imminent. Prayers were said and the soft murmur of prayer hung in the air like incense. A little before eight Cardinal Traglia spoke the traditional words of dismissal: *"Ite missa est."* "Go, the Mass is ended." At that same moment, in his dimly lit bedroom, John breathed his last.

HENRIK IBSEN: "Soon I shall go into the great darkness."

Henrik Ibsen, the great Norwegian dramatist (1828-1906) died at the age of 78, physically a broken man. Most of his life he had been in good health and he was still in good health as the twentieth century dawned. He was then 72.

He had been proud of never having consulted a doctor, but he was getting to be frail. In January, 1900 he wrote a note to his doctor, Christian Sontum. "I can no longer permit myself" he said, "to parade in your files as an unreliable debtor from the last century. And since you take no steps to take what is due to you, I must take the matter into my own hands and presume to send you the enclosed trifle as compensation for your trouble and time.

The rejuvenation you have caused I could not repay with its weight in gold. A Happy New Year to you and yours!"

All his great work had already been written: *Peter Gynt, The Pillars of Society, A Doll's House, Hedda Gabler, When We Dead Awaken*. By the turn of the century Ibsen had established himself as one of the outstanding figures in modern world theater. Now, in the evening of his life, illness struck him.

In April, 1900 he was writing to an admirer that he had been ill for five weeks and that his doctors had forbidden him to write. But he was in good cheer. On August 11, he wrote to his niece, Anna Stousland, that she may certainly call him her "Sun God" because "all the fire of my youth still burns in me." But in the autumn of the year his health was beginning to lose again. The next year he had a stroke that virtually made him unable to walk. It was summer and he would have loved to take his regular constitutional. He complained to the daughter of his physician: "I cannot walk, you know, but they can carry me." He mellowed. One friend who saw him in 1902 described him as "brilliant as ever" though "an extraordinary mildness pervaded his manner, supplanting his former sternness."

In the spring of 1903 Ibsen had a stroke, his second. It practically crippled his hand. He tried to write with his left hand, practicing every day. He sadly remarked to his wife: "Strange that I, who was once quite a dramatist, now have to learn to write the alphabet." It was painful.

On February 14, 1904 Ibsen shakily pencilled a word of thanks to his doctor, Dr. Bull. It took him, Dr. Bull later told his son, three days to scribble "Tak," the Norwegian word for thanks. But he was still putting on a brave front. In an interview he gave to *Verdens Gang* he said that there was "nothing much wrong" with him just then. "I just have to be careful."

But the stroke was not without its effects even on his speech. He had difficulty in formulating words, sometimes used the wrong ones and had to have someone to interpret him, much to his annoyance. It pained him, this master of words, now to have his words interpreted for him. But when he spoke of his friends, his eyes would sparkle. Yet the old man lingered on. One January night in 1905 he was heard to cry in his sleep: "I'm writing! And it's going splendidly!" His frustrations were being expressed in his sleep. His helplessness continued to increase. He could not lift a piece of paper and place it on the table. It hurt him deeply.

One day a friend and regular visitor, Christopher Brunn, tentatively brought up the subject of Ibsen's relations with God. Ibsen went red in the face, as if he had been asked a most personal question. Angrily he replied: "Leave that to me!" Ibsen was now afraid his wife would die before him. "If you die before me" he told her, "I shall die five minutes later." And no doubt he meant it. His son Sigurd was constantly with him to keep him company. One evening Ibsen told him: "Soon I shall go into the great darkness." That evening, his daughter-in-law afterwards wrote, was "a beautiful memory."

Ibsen's 78th birthday came and went, but he was still showing great resilience. He was weak and from May 16 could not even stand and lay stretched on his bed. Often in a coma, he occasionally uttered a word or two indistinctly and incoherently. On May 22 he opened his eyes, pressed his physician's hand and muttered: "Thank God!" A little later his nurse heard him say: *"Tvertimod!"* (On the contrary!) There was no way of knowing what was going on in his mind as he lay hovering between life and death. In a moment of clarity, Ibsen looked up at his wife who was sitting by his bed and said to her: "My dear, dear wife, how good and kind you have been to me." Nothing more was said. On May 23, at 2:30 p.m. the end came. Ibsen was dead.

GOETHE: "Light, more light!"

Johann Wolfgang von Goethe (1749-1832) poet, dramatist, novelist—a universal genius if there was one—whose life was despaired at birth (his mother was in pangs for three days) lived like Voltaire and Isaac Newton, into his eighties. If he had a difficult birth, his death was no less difficult. But he had lived long and age had taken its toll before death took its.

Of few it can be said, as it can be said of Goethe, that he knew himself and had no illusions about his greatness. Goethe freely acknowledged to a friend in an interview, that he owed a great deal to the world around him. "The greatest genius" he said, "would not get very far if he attempted to find everything within himself. What would become of a genius if one were to deprive him of the gift of using everything that comes to hand, of taking the marble to build his house from here, the bronze from there?" And he asked, as though looking at himself from a distance: "Who am I? What have I created? I have taken and absorbed everything that I have heard and observed. My works have been nourished by thousands of the most diverse natures, fools and wise men, clear heads and dullards." And to another, he said: "My work is that of a composite being, and it bears the name Goethe."

He was not, then, the ivory tower intellectual. Indeed until the very last days of his life, he maintained an active interest in natural science, mineralogy and even astronomy. He even took time to send a note to the observatory in Jena to ask it to make preparations for observing the comet expected in 1834. And he kept writing. There was optimism in what he wrote. *"Kein Wesen kann zu nichts zerfallen!"* —No being can decay to nothingness, he wrote in his last great poem, his legacy.

A Virgo—he was born on August 28—he spent his last few months putting his affairs in order. There was the question of disposing his estate, his collections and the posthumous works. These he attended to, with customary methodicalness. Then, one day in March, 1832, with a cool and sharp spring wind blowing, he went out for a drive. As it happened to Voltaire, he caught a chill and returned home to be ordered to bed. Later, his doctor, Dr. Vogel, recorded what followed.

Goethe did not die easily. He was afraid of death, and he fought it tenaciously. At the slightest sign of improvement his hopes would rise and he would ask his servant what day of the month it was. When told it was March 22, he said: "Ah, that means spring has begun and we can recover quicker!"

He had great belief in the curative property of the open air. He asked his physician not to give him any more medicine because movement in the open air would soon restore his strength. The doctor knew otherwise. Two days before Goethe's death, the doctor had been summoned in the early hours of the morning to check on his distinguished patient. What Dr. Vogel saw was a piteous sight. Later he recorded what he saw:

> A piteous sight awaited me. The aged man, who had long been in the habit of moving only very sedately, was in the grip of a terrible fear and agitation which drove him at one moment to bound into bed, where he vainly tried to find relief through constant changes of position, and at the next to jump up into the armchair at his bedside. The pain, which became more and more localized in his chest, forced alternate groans and loud screams from the tortured man. His features were distorted, his face ashen, his eyes, sunk deep in their livid sockets, were dulled and feeble; in his look was the most hideous fear of death. The whole ice-cold body ran with sweat, his pulse, unusually frequent, quick and hard, was barely perceptible; the abdomen was very swollen, his thirst agonizing . . . ."

Goethe had contracted catarrhal fever which had turned into pneumonia. That was ultimately to result in failure of the heart and lungs. But Goethe kept struggling. He continued to dream till the end. He spoke in his dreams. "Observe the lovely woman's head—with its black locks in magnificent coloring against the dark background!" It was as if his mind was working on a new book whose theme was evolving in bits and pieces. He was no longer able to speak; so he would lift his hands, as he always used to, while dictating. Only now words failed to come out. They stayed in his head.

Yet Goethe struggled. Tired, his hands fell. But the mind, that great mind that had produced some of the greatest literature in the world, would not rest. He was hunched in his armchair and his fingers kept tracing letters on the coverlet round his knees. The last letter, according to his friends, that he drew was a large W, which his biographer has said could be taken for the first letter of Goethe's given name, Wolfgang, or "in keeping with his last great thoughts on world literature and the mutual understanding of mankind, of World." There is, in addition, the legend that as Goethe lay dying, he said: "Light, more light!" But he died at noon, the hour of his birth, on March 22, 1832, when there was light around, though the shutters were closed. Possibly it was his last effort to see the world around him.

The beginning and end of his life were brought together in a small symbolic detail: his coffin was placed on the old Goethe bridal rug, belonging to the Goethe family, which had been used at the child Goethe's christening in the Katharinenkirche at Frankfurt over eight decades ago.

In the last poem that he had written, on his arrival at Wiesbaden, he had closed it with the symbol of death in flames:

Keine Ferne macht dich schwierig,
Kommst geflogen und gebannt
Und zuletzt, des Lichts begierig,
Bist du Schmetterling verbrannt.

Aware of neither toil, nor distance,
As thou fliest on, decoyed,
Till yielding to the flame's insistence,
Butterfly, thou are destroyed.

So it might have been said of Goethe, though "destroyed" is a harsh word and Goethe still lives among us.

AKBAR: In greatness lies no trust.

Akbar the Great (1542-1605) the third and greatest of the Mughal Emperors, died a sad and embittered man. His last years were tormented. One by one those whom he trusted and who had given him unstinted devotion and loyalty had died. First it was Raja Bhagwandas and later Raja Todermal who both died in 1589. They were followed in August 1593 by Shaikh Mubarak, who had been a pillar of strength to Akbar in his religious innovations. In 1596, Shaikh Faizi upon whom Akbar had bestowed the title of Poet Laureate died after a prolonged illness. Akbar was desolate.

Of his three sons Salim, Murad and Danial, he was singularly unfortunate. Both Murad and Danial were inveterate drunkards. So was their heir-apparent, Salim. Worse, Salim had developed an unquenchable thirst to ascend his father's throne, even when Akbar was alive. As early as 1591 there had been rumors that Akbar had been poisoned by his son when the emperor had an attack of colic. "Baba Shaikhji," Akbar is said to have exclaimed at that time, "since all this Sultanate will devolve on thee, why hast thou made this attack on me?" The very thought must have saddened him grievously.

But Prince Salim was unrepentant. He had been suspecting—wrongly as it turned out—that Akbar was showing preference for his younger son Murad. Happily for the Mughal dynasty and unhappily for Akbar himself, Murad died in a town in the Deccan of delirium tremens caused by excessive drink, in May of 1599. And Danial similarly died of drinking but after 40 days of struggle in April, 1604. If the deaths of two sons in such ignoble circumstances brought tragedy into the royal household, it brought joy in Prince Salim's camp. At last he could think of no other claimnant to the Mughal throne. Not that he had not schemed and rebelled before this. His insolence knew no bounds as his actions showed. Stationed in Allahabad, he had had coins in gold and copper struck in his name and he had the additional impudence to send some of them to Akbar's court!

Akbar had to put up with all this, and worse. Abul Fazl, trusted among Akbar's nobles, was then in charge of the imperial interests in the Deccan and when he heard of Prince Salim's disloyalty had advocated strong action against him. Abul Fazl further had decided to come personally to Delhi to press his pleas. But he made a mistake. Prince Salim had heard of Fazl's coming and had ordered one of his henchmen, Bir Singh, the Bundel chief of Orchcha, to waylay Fazl and kill him. Moving through Bundel territory without an adequate guard, he was set upon and murdered by Bir Singh's men. Fazl's head was then severed and sent to Prince Salim, who with unconcealed glee had it thrown "into an unworthy place." The news reached Akbar. It was an insult that he could not tolerate.

But the rebel was his own eldest son and heir apparent. There was no getting away from the fact. His nobles would not accept the idea of placing Akbar's grandson, Khusrau, in direct line of succession. So after repeated attempts, some superficial reconciliation had to be effected. Emperor and Heir Apparent were finally to meet in public, with Akbar bestowing on his errant son the right of succession by placing his own headwear on the head of Prince Salim. But the palace was ripe with intrigue.

Nevertheless Akbar sought to preserve an outward semblance of reconciliation with his son. But his worries were telling on him. His iron constitution showed signs of weakening. On September 21, 1605, he was struck with an attack of dysentery. The illness worsened. The emperor was no longer able to give the customary *darshan* or sit in the *jharoka*. On Saturday, October 22, Father Xavier and his colleagues presented themselves at the palace to administer the last consolations of their religion to Akbar in the belief that his time had come and that he would want to die a Christian. They had to return when they learned that Akbar was in good spirits and apparently not so critically ill as was rumored.

But Akbar's condition worsened. Prince Salim, who till then had been sulking in his own apartments refusing to see his dying father, now thought it expedient to call on the sire. Akbar was slowly sinking and could hardly talk. But he was still conscious and indicated by signs that Salim should put on the royal turban and the imperial sword of Humayun which always hung at the foot of the royal bed. Akbar then asked his son to show himself outside the palace so the waiting crowd assembled in the courtyard could know that he had been duly invested with power.

Between October 22 and 27 Akbar fought a losing battle with death. He was conscious some of the time, but if he said anything, it has not been recorded. The end came on October 27, in the early hours of the morning, when only a few trusted friends were at his bedside. The great Moghul had lost his final battle.

The obsequies were hurried and simple. His blessed spirit, according to his Sunni faith, had to be released at once from its human fetters and hastened to ultimate peace. No time was to be lost. A gap was pierced in the wall of Agra Fort which the dead emperor had himself built. Through this aperture the body of Akbar was borne on the shoulders of his rebel son, Salim, now become Emperor Jehangir, and some of the courtiers. The few dear friends who were with Akbar in his last moments formed themselves into a small procession and followed the dead king to the sepulchre at Sikandra, three miles away. Not a shot was heard, not a funeral note as they hurried the corpse to its burial place.

It is said that those present at his bedside, worried by their monarch's eclectic religious proclivities in his lifetime tried soberly to remind him of Allah and the Prophet Mohammad. It is also said that though he tried several times to oblige them by uttering the name of the One God, no sound came forth. He may have died, according to one source, a pantheist. However, when the Adilshahi Sultan of Bijapur asked the Jesuit Botel, who had spent several years at Agra and Bijapur, whether the emperor had died a Christian, the reply was: "Sire, I would to God it had been so, but he kept us deluded with such hopes and died in your sect of Muhammad."

ISAAC NEWTON: "Only a boy playing on the seashore . . . ."

It is something of a shock to remember that Isaac Newton (1642-1727) of whom Pope wrote: "Nature and nature's laws lay hid in night, God said, Let Newton be, and all was light" was born so diminutive and feeble that two women who had been sent out to bring medicine for the just-born child did not expect to find him alive on their return. At birth Newton indeed was so small that his mother later told him he might have been put into a quart mug.

He was born on Christmas Day, the year Galileo died and at school he was no better than any other healthy normal boys of his age. That he grew to become "an ornament of the human race" as the inscription on his tomb in Westminster Abbey rightly says, remains a subject for mortals to rejoice as the inscription again correctly enjoins. During his eight decades Newton demonstrated the motions and figures of the planets, the paths of the comets and the tides of the ocean, the different refrangibilities of the rays of light, discovered the calculus and the theory of gravity and revolutionized mathematics. It is said in a charming quartrain in "The Irish Schoolmaster":

> Sir Isaac Newton was the boy
> That climbed the apple tree, sir;
> He then fell down and broke his crown
> And lost his gravity, sir.

But Newton had rightly made his name by discovering the law of gravity. When he was 84 years old, he told a friend, Stukeley, how he discovered it:

> It was occasioned by the fall of an apple, as he sat in a contemplative mood. Why should that apple always descend perpendicularly to the ground, thought he to himself. Why should it not go sideways or upwards, but constantly to the earth's centre? Assuredly, the reason is, that the earth draws it. There must be a drawing power in matter: and the sum of the drawing power in earth must be in the earth's centre, not in any side of the earth. If matter thus draws matter, it must be in proportion of its quantity. Therefore the apple draws the earth, as well as the earth draws the apple . . . . "

By then Newton, though intellectually alert, was physically on the decline. Indeed, from the age of 80, his vigor had been declining. In 1722 he showed signs of serious illness. Two years later, in August, 1724 it was diagnosed as stone in the bladder. It was a painful condition and, in the absence of operational techniques, a suffering to be quietly borne. He was advised by his physician, Dr. Mead, to take life more leisurely and to avoid too much travel. Newton was then president of the Royal Society and Master of the Mint, positions that demanded much from the old man. But authorities were most loth to let Newton resign, and it was decided to give him assistance in the person of a Deputy President.

In January, 1725 Newton suffered from congestion of the lungs, a common complaint in those days during winter, when it was easy to catch a cold. He decided to leave London and go to Kensington village. But by February 28, 1727 he felt well enough to return to the city to preside over a meeting of the Royal Society on March 2. It was probably a mistake. When he returned to Kensington on March 4, he was in great pain. Newton showed some improvement by the middle of the month and was able to read and talk to his physician. On the evening of March 18, however, there was a grave relapse and Newton fell into a state of unconsciousness from which he never recovered. All throughout the next day he lay slowly dying and life ebbed out of his body in the early hours of March 20, 1727.

Newton, for all his genius, had a modest estimate of his own capabilities. He once wrote:

> I do not know what I may appear to the world; but to myself I seem to have been only a boy playing on the seashore, and diverting myself in now and then finding a smoother pebble or a prettier shell than ordinary, whilst the great ocean of truth lay all undiscovered before me.

The world, of course, has a better appreciation of Sir Isaac. In the ante-chapel of Trinity College, Cambridge are memorial statues to some of the illustrious sons of the college: Francis Bacon, Lord Tennyson, Lord Macaulay, among others. At the head of the line, alone is Newton's statue with the simple inscription:

NEWTON
qui genus humanum ingenis superavit
Who surpassed all men of genius

GEORGE GORDON BYRON (1788-1824): "But I have lived, and have not lived in vain."

A famed fortune teller in Scotland had told Byron, when he was a boy, that he should beware of his 37th year. Byron recounted this story to his physician, Dr. Millingen, and when charged with superstition replied: "To say the truth, I find it equally difficult to know what to believe in this world and what not to believe."

Byron died in his 37th year in the town of Missolonghi, in Greece. He had gone to Greece, romantic that he was, to fight for her independence. His days of writing poetry were over; here he was in Missolonghi, seeking to organize the people which he often found a totally hopeless task. He fell ill. He went into mental depression. One day in February, 1824, Dr. Millingen told him that if he changed his lifestyle he might get back his lost vigor, he replied impatiently: "Do you suppose that I wish for life? I have grown heartily sick of it and shall welcome the hour to depart from it . . . " What Byron hated above all was to die in bed of torture or terminate his life like Swift—"a grinning idiot!"

Throughout February, Byron went about his work of military organization with the true zeal of the man with a mission. He had his ups and downs, but he seemed determined not to allow his physical weakness to govern his life. To those around him he seemed as if he was living constantly at the edge of his physical and mental strength. There were days of excitement as when he forced a Turkish seige to be lifted. But these were momentary. The sands of time were running out on the poet turned hero. He had grown thin and more irritable. He was frequently angry over trifles.

Early in the second week of April, after he returned home from a ride, he was seized with a shuddering and complained of fever and rheumatic pains. He told the friend who was attending on him that he was suffering a great deal of pain. "I do not care for death; but these agonies I cannot bear." He could not leave Missolonghi because of a storm that was raging unabatedly. He hated medicine and he could not stand the thought of being bled by leeches—a common remedy for most illnesses in those days. Doctors would suggest it and he would resist the idea with all his might. He would say to those who would advise some blood-letting that "he knew well that the lancet had killed more people than the lance." He would have none of it.

But his illness persisted and on three occasions he let the doctors have their way. He had earlier suggested as an alternative that the physicians go search for an old and ugly witch in the town so "she may examine whether this sudden loss of my health does not depend upon the evil eye." Byron hoped that the witch might devise some means to dissolve the spell. The plan was given up.

He seemed to have forebodings of death, but spoke of it with a good deal of composure. Dr. Millingen recorded: "I did not hear him make any, even the smallest, mention of religion." Once Byron was heard to remark: "Shall I sue for mercy?" There was a pause. Then Byron added: "Come, come, no weakness! Let's be a man to the last . . . ."

The taking of blood barely helped. Byron had given up hope. "Come, you are, I see, a damned set of butchers. Take away as much blood as you will; but have done with it." The relief to Byron was little, if any. Byron's pulse was steady, but he complained from time to time of a numbness in his fingers. He was frequently in delirium. But in his lucid moments he would express his opposition to bleeding. Sometimes he talked so wildly, that it was decided to remove the stiletto and pistols from his bedside.

By April 17, Dr. Millingen and other physicians attending on the poet had begun to have serious apprehensions as to how long Byron might last. They gave him some China bark, water and wine to allay his thirst and applied two blisters on the insides of his thighs—which tells us of the state of medicine in those days—because Byron would not allow anyone to see his club foot.

On the 18th he was delirious and very ill still. One last effort was made to apply leeches at Byron's temples; two pounds of blood were thus extracted. For a while the poet grew calm but that was more due to weakness than to improved health. By mid-afternoon all hope of his recovery was given up. Around Byron the servants had begun to cry. Byron called Dr. Millingen to give him some last minute instructions. "Your efforts to preserve my life will be vain. Die I must; I feel it. Its loss I do not lament; for to terminate my wearisome existence I came to Greece. My wealth, my abilities, I devoted to her cause. Well, there is my life to her. One request let me make you. Let not my body be hacked or be sent to England. Here let my bones moulder. Lay me in the first corner without pomp or nonsense."

The lamentations while he was still dying annoyed Byron. Half smiling, he said in Italian: *"Oh questa e una bella scena!"*

Then swiftly he became delirious again talking of mounting a breach in an assault. He spoke half in English, half in Italian: "Forwards . . . forwards . . . courage . . . follow my example . . . don't be afraid . . . ." His assistants watched him. One of them, Parry, loosened the bandage round Byron's forehead. The poet kept saying:" *Ah Christi, Ah Christi"* in Italian. When the bandage was loosened Byron started to shed tears. Parry said: "My Lord, I thank God, I hope you will now be better; shed as many tears as you can, you will sleep and find ease." Byron replied: "Yes, the pain is gone, I shall sleep now."

He sank into an uneasy slumber. But soon he was awake again and talking incoherently, but sometimes lucidly. Parry sat with him and held his hand. Byron expressed himself sometimes in English, sometimes in Italian. He mentioned names and also sums of money. "Poor Greece, poor town, my poor servants" he muttered at one time. Then: "Why was I not aware of this sooner?" And again: "My hour is come—I do not care for death— but why did I not go home before I came here?"

Still later he said: "There are things which make the world dear to me *(Io lascio qualche cosa di caro nel mondo.)* For the rest, I am content to die!" As Byron grew delirious, his orders became more and more incomprehensible. The physicians, meanwhile, had concocted another purgation, this time a mixture of senna, three ounces of Epsom salts and three of castor oil. Byron got out of bed a little before six in the evening to relieve himself. "The damned doctors" he cursed, "have drenched me so that I can scarcely stand." That was the last time he was out of bed. On Sunday, April 18, 1824, his attendant heard him say: "I want to sleep now." Those were his last words. He seemed so still, the doctors made one last attempt to apply leeches to his forehead at the temples. By now Byron was in a comatose condition, oblivious of the ministrations of his determined physicians.

For the next twenty-four hours he hardly moved. On the evening of the 19th, his servant Fletcher saw Byron open his eyes and then shut them, but without any signs of pain. "Oh, my God" said Fletcher, sure of what he saw, "I fear his Lordship is gone."

The doctors took his pulse. One of them said: "You are right; he is gone." At that moment, it was later reported, there was the most awful thunder storm ever witnessed in the area. The Greeks said it was heaven's sign that a super man had died.

Unconsciously, Byron had written his own epitaph in his great poem "Childe Harold" more evocative than any words said about him then or after:

> But I have lived, and have not lived in vain;
> My mind may lose its force, my blood its fire,
> And my frame perish even in conquering pain:
> But there is that within me which shall tire
> Torture and Time, and breathe when I expire;
> Something unearthly, which they deem not of,
> Like the remembered tone of a mute lyre . . . .

JOHN KEATS: "Lift me up for I am dying—thank God it has come!"

John Keats, of whom it has been said that few poets have equalled his dazzling achievement, died deplorably young. He was born in 1795; he died in Rome in 1821. He was then not yet 26. At the beginning of February, 1820, when he was four months short of twenty, he returned home from town late at night, staggering. His friend, Charles Brown, thought Keats was drunk, but quickly realized the young poet was ill.

Sent to bed, Keats hardly struck his pillow, when he coughed and spat a drop of blood on the white sheet. "Bring me a candle, Brown" whispered Keats. He looked steadfastly at that single drop of blood and then said: "I know the color of that blood; it is arterial blood. I cannot be deceived in that color; that drop of blood is my death warrant. I must die."

Then he coughed some more; and yet some more. And more blood came, as if he was vomitting. It was in his throat, in his mouth, it was suffocating him. A doctor was summoned. Keats lay limp in bed, exhausted. For most of two months he was bed-ridden or moving forlornly around the house. He had not written poetry for months now. In late June, 1820, he had another hemorrhage. He was miserable. He wanted to die.

His friends persuaded him to go to sunny Italy, then, as now, an attraction to the British. He had to have someone to accompany him. The artist, Joseph Severn, agreed to go with him. There was an element of urgency to the trip. Keats' life was at stake. On September 17 Keats, together with Severn, boarded the *Maria Crowther* and made for southern Europe. Keats had dark thoughts of death. He wrote to Browning: " . . . is there another life? Shall I awake and find this all a dream? There must be. We cannot be created for this sort of suffering."

It took all of three weeks to reach Italy. Keats was continuously ill and throwing blood. In the Bay of Naples the party had to wait ten days to fulfil quarrantine regulations. They went ashore on Keats' birthday. He was then twenty-five. In Rome, the friends took rooms at the bottom of the famous Spanish Steps in the Piazza di Spagna. Keats rested but he had now no illusion of what was coming. To Brown he wrote: "I have an habitual feeling of my real life having past and that I am leading a posthumous existence."

Things went steadily downhill. On December 10 he coughed two cupfulls of blood and was in delirium for a full twenty-four hours. In the following nine days he had five more hemorrhages. It was terrifying. Keats begged Severn to let him kill himself, but was dissuaded.

There were letters from home, from his beloved Fanny, but they remained unopened. Keats had lost interest in life. All he could hope for was release, blessed release from incessant suffering. Often he shivered, his teech chattered uncontrollably and he broke into cold sweat. He discussed with Severn about what should be done when he died. He would be buried in the Protestant cemetery in Rome and the stone above him would carry a simple legend: "Here lies one whose name was writ on water." And in the grave itself, the letters from Fanny would be placed.

All of December and the January and February following, Severn watched Keats with fraternal care and affection. Then the end came. On Friday, February 23, 1821, around four o'clock in the afternoon Severn heard himself called. Keats was calling for him. "Severn, Severn, lift me up, for I am dying. I shall die easy; don't be frightened. Thank God it has come!"

Severn rushed to his friend's bedside, took the young poet in his strong arms and waited. Severn was still holding Keats tightly when the poet died. In his "Ode to a Nightingale" he had written:

> Darkling I listen; and for many a time
> I have been half in love with easeful death,
> Call'd him soft names in many a mused rhyme,
> To take into the air my quiet breath;
> Now more than ever seems it rich to die,
> To cease upon the midnight with no pain . . .

PERCY BLYSSHE SHELLEY: "Nor other trace I find, But as of foam after the ocean's wrath, is spent upon the desert shore."

Shelley, Keats and Byron—they lived about the same time— all died young. Byron was 37, Keats 26, Shelley (1792-1822) not even 30, when they died. But they left behind them a legacy that is one of the most precious in English poetry.

Shelley was the rebel of the three. From Oxford he was expelled because of his pamphlet *The Necessity of Atheism*. He then eloped to Scotland with his sister's schoolmate, Harriet Westbrook. Three years later he eloped again, this time with Mary Wollstonecraft Godwin.

He spent the summer of 1816 in Switzerland where he struck his friendship with Byron. Soon after came the first tragedy in Shelley's life: Harriet committed suicide. He then married Mary Godwin. In 1818 they went to Italy, where he composed the greater part of his poetry. He was drowned on July 8, 1822 while sailing in the Bay of Spezia.

That, in brief, is his life, though volumes have been written about his poetry. His political philosophy, interestingly enough, long inspired radical thinkers when his reputation is based on his poetry. But Shelley, early, had defected from his respectable middle class and the cumulative effect was to force him further and further away from his father, the people he grew among and the cultural background into which he had been born. By the time his life was cut short, one month before his thirtieth birthday, he was in every sense an exile from the land of his birth.

Byron had become a hero because of his exploits in Greece, but Shelley, for all the lyric grace of his poetry, long remained in disrepute and obscurity. When news of his death was published in the London papers, an article in the *Courier* began with this unkind remark: "Shelley, the writer of some infidel poetry has been drowned; now he knows whether there is a God or no."

Byron, who knew of Shelley's reputation, wrote after his friend's death, to Tom Moore in London: "There is thus another man gone about whom the world was ill-naturedly, and ignorantly and brutally mistaken." According to one of Shelley's biographers, the Noble Lord himself had been guilty of compounding it.

The death should not have happened. On the day before Shelley's planned departure by boat to Genoa, the poet was seeing "spirits" and was alarming the whole house. Asked to explain, Shelley said he had two visions: one was of two figures covered with blood who staggered into his room and supporting each other shouted: "Get up, Shelley, the sea is flooding the house and it is all coming down." Shelley did not sail to Genoa the next day as planned, but stayed back to calm down his wife Mary.

On July 1, Shelley, Captain Roberts and Williams and a boat boy sailed for Livorno and docked at half past nine in the evening and spent the night on the boat. After quarantine cleared them in the morning they went ashore where Shelley met with Byron, and the Leigh Hunts and had a happy reunion. Differences between Byron and Hunt were smoothened out by Shelley to some degree. The three poets were together for the best part of a week, having gone to Pisa and returned. On July 8, Shelley decided to return to his own home. The heat was overpowering and obviously a prelude to a real thunder storm. Shelley ignored the weather. The *Don Juan* was waiting and Shelley jumped down onto the deck, wearing his familiar double-breasted reefer jacket, white nankeen sailor's trousers and black leather boots. He had Hunt's copy of Keats poem doubled back in the jacket pocket. The ship cast off and about two in the afternoon drew out of the harbor and hoisted full sail to catch the gathering winds. His friend Trelawny waved him goodbye and watched the boat with a spy glass as it headed out to sea. Captain Roberts was now getting anxious. Low clouds were ominously gathering on the horizon to the west as he saw the *Don Juan* disappearing into a thickening haze. Then the expected storm came up rapidly from the southwest and broke at about half past six. Summer squalls like this were not uncommon or unfamiliar to the local Italian *feluccas* who quickly ran for safety into Livorno harbor. One of the Italian captains reported having sighted the *Don Juan* in heavy seas. The Italian captain knew that the *Don Juan* could not make it and bore down upon it with offers of help, suggesting that crew and passengers should abandon the boat and come aboard his ship. Shelley would have none of it. "No" came his astounded answer. The waves were running mountain high and one crashed heavily over the boat which still had full sails. One of the Italian sailors, experienced in these matters took out a horn and addressed himself to Shelley's crew: "If you will not come on board, for God's sake reef your sails or you are lost!" Williams, who was traveling with Shelley, reportedly made an effort to lower the sails, but Shelley, for no understandable reason, stopped him from doing so, whether out of ignorance of sailing expertise or just a sudden desire to get drowned. Not long afterwards the *Don Juan* went down into the Gulf of Spezia, some ten miles west of Via Reggio, under full sail.

The bodies of the boat's passengers, including that of Shelley were eventually washed up along the beach between Massa and Via Reggio ten days after the storm. The exposed part of Shelley's arms and face had been entirely eaten away and he could only be identified by what he wore and by the copy of Keat's poems found in his breast pocket. The problem was what to do with the bodies. Quarantine laws were complicated and for the time being at least the only solution was to bury the bodies in the sand with quick lime.

Shelley's body, now all but decomposed and eaten up by

the fish and the lime was dug up again, after permission was obtained, placed in a portable iron furnace and cremated on the beach itself in the presence of Leigh Hunt, Byron and some local militia and fishermen. Much later Shelley's ashes were collected and buried in the Protestant cemetery in Rome after having remained for several months in a mahagany chest in the British Consul's wine cellar.

In his "The Mask of Anarchy" he had written about the chariot, the chariot of life under which people would be crushed, evoking, simultaneously, a great storm wave thundering through the sea. The lines seem appropriate for his own death:

> Yet ere I can say where—the Chariot hath
> Past over them; nor other trace I find
> But as of foam after the ocean's wrath
> Is spent upon the desert shore . . . .

QUEEN CHRISTINA: "Sibyl has told the truth; that was what I was thinking."

Queen Christina, daughter of Gustavus Adolphus of Sweden who became queen when she was six years old but abdicated in favor of her cousin in 1654 when she was twenty-eight, was mistaken for a boy when she was born. Adolphus would have liked to have a son as his successor, as any King would, but his queen having had several miscarriages before, he was pleased to have any issue at all. When the child was brought to him by his sister, Adolphus said: "Sister, I am content, I pray God that He will preserve her. She should be clever, since she has deceived us all!"

Christina was not pretty; her mother thought she was "ugly" for a girl. It was perhaps that thought that subconsciously contributed to her determination not to marry. It was this, in part, that no doubt was responsible for her abdication. She left Sweden in men's clothes, entered the Catholic Church and settled in Rome. Her later attempts to regain the Swedish throne failed.

For a queen, she was surprisingly indifferent to her appearance. She looked very much like a peasant woman. In April, 1688, when she was 62 years old, she was described by a French traveler who saw her as being "very small of stature, exceedingly fat and corpulent." And her complexion, voice and face, the traveler said, "are those of a man."

Indeed, she wore a man's knee-length *justaucorps* (a shirted coat) of black satin, buttoned all the way down and a very short black skirt revealed a pair of men's shoes. In her old age Christina would say that on a par with the ancient monuments, she was one of the sights of Rome. In her last days, she had hoped to return to Sweden and was making preparations to go but toward the end of 1688 she seemed to have some presentiment that she really had not long to live.

She ordered what was for her an extraordinary dress of white silk embroidered with flowers and trimmed with golden fringe. The dress had been got ready for her by Christmas and on Christmas Eve she tried it on in front of two mirrors under the admiring gaze of her maids, the Passaglia sisters. As Christina was putting the dress on, in walked a wise woman called Guila, who was a story teller and something of an alchemist. So turning to Guila, Christina said: "Looking at this dress makes me think of important things; I will soon wear it. Sibyl, do you divine in what ceremony?"

The old woman replied with a perfectly straight face: "Your pardon, Madam, but Your Majesty will be buried in that dress not long from now!" There were shocked words of protest from the Passaglia sisters, but Christian said softly: "The Sibyl has told the truth; that is what I was thinking."

Came the New Year and Christina made a short trip to southern Italy and returned but shortly afterwards she had a fainting fit and fell ill and it was said that she suffered from erysipelas, probably owing to the swelling of her legs. But she developed high fever and was almost given up for lost, but she recovered, though not for long. In April, 1689, almost a year after she had made her special dress, she fell in a paroxysm and was unconscious for a few days, with occasional bouts of lucidity during which she confessed and was able to respond to the prayers in the office for the dying. At six o'clock in the morning of April 19, 1689, Christina breathed her last.

In her will Christina had said that her dead body should be shrouded in white and buried in the Church of the Rotonda and forbade any funeral pomp, but her wishes were denied her. She was laid to rest in a crypt in St. Peter's. She was a remarkable woman who patronized writers and artists and as a queen had invited Descartes to her court. One of her contemporaries said of her: "She freely followed her own genius in all things and car'd not for what anybody said." That would have pleased Christina most to hear.

GOGOL: "The ladder! Quick, pass me the ladder!"

Who would have thought that Gogol, the playwright who gave us the rib-tickling *Inspector-General* would die the kind of death he did? He was ridiculously young when he died. He was born in 1809 and died in 1852, when he was 43. He was so thoroughly Russian in his thinking and his upbringing that, perhaps his death was the only kind of thing he could have attained.

Gogol was the true believer, and very much the man of his Russian times. And he seemed to be a man of premonitions. When the sister of a poet friend of his died in 1852, he himself felt nudged toward the precipice. He had a premonition that his time, too, has come. After seeing the young woman in a coffin, he said: "Nothing could be more solemn than death; life would lose all its beauty if there were no death."

To a friend he wrote: "Ask God to make my work conscientious and to find in me, some degree, however tiny, of worthiness to sing the hymn of heavenly beauty." To elevate himself to that degree of "worthiness" he started to read pious books, prayed, fasted, ever to make himself a fit receptacle to God. He was making penance of a high order. He had a spiritual guide, a certain Father Matthew, whose letters he carried in his pockets wherever he went. It was Father Matthew's desire to save

Gogol's soul rather than to save Russian literature. Father Matthew thought that Gogol often wrote profane literature. In consequence, Gogol had stopped writing. His concern was more for his soul. He fasted, ate little and only when absolutely necessary during many days and that too, holy bread and a glass of water, perhaps a few spoonfuls of borscht. He went to church frequently, confessed and took communion, prostrated on the ground and wept. He was worried about the nature of his writings. On February 10, 1852, he summoned Count Tolstoy, his friend, and told him that the Count on Gogol's death should turn over all his writings to the Metropolitan of Moscow so that the supreme ecclesiastical authority could decide just what should be made public and what should be left out. "Whatever he finds useless, let him ruthlessly strike it out!" said Gogol. Tolstoy bluntly refused.

One evening, at the home of Count Tolstoy, Gogol tried to burn some of his notes and manuscripts for the second part of *Dead Souls*. They were the work of many years—now confined to the flame. When Tolstoy was summoned, Gogol told him: "See what I have done! I wanted to burn some things and I have burnt a lot. How powerful is the Evil One!" Tolstoy could say nothing but words of comfort for his crazy friend. "It's a good sign" he said, "You've burned manuscripts three or four times already, only to do better next time. Besides, you must remember what you've written!" That seemed to comfort Gogol.

In the ensuing days he sank into lethargy. "Everyone has to die; I am ready; I will die" he told a visitor, appropos of nothing. Tolstoy summoned a doctor but Gogol solemnly said that he abandoned himself to the will of God. He wrote his will. To the doctor he said, "Leave me alone!" and he would not answer any questions. But Gogol's mysterious illness continued. More doctors were summoned, but the patient was uncooperative. "Ought we to abandon the case?" was the question. One decision was to feed him by force. Gogol was groaning. "What are they doing to me, my God!" he cried as his doctors worked on him. "They are pouring cold water on my head! Thy don't listen to me,

They don't see me; they don't hear me! What have I done to them? Why are they tormenting me? What do they want from me, miserable me? What can I give them? I have nothing!" The physicians withdrew, but one of them stayed back to apply leeches to his nose and the fat things clung to his nostrils, gorging blood. Gogol yelped: "You mustn't. Take the leeches away! Get the leeches out of my mouth!" The treatment was as terrible as the mysterious disease. Plasters were put on Gogol's extremities, ice on his head and he was fed with a mixture of marshmallow root and cherry-laurel water. Gogol was dying.

When the doctor left, Gogol lay on his side, exhausted. His pulse was weak and his breathing began to be congested. He asked for something to drink. He was given some broth. He took a swallow, then his head dropped back. He fell semi-unconscious. His friends watched over him far into the night. Around 11 p.m. he was heard to mutter a loud cry: "The ladder! Quick! Pass me the ladder!"

The ladder had been in Gogol's mind for a long time. In the final chapter of his *Selected Passages from My Correspondence with My Friends* he had written: "God alone knows, but perhaps, because of this unique desire (love of one's fellow man, through God) a ladder stands ready to be thrown down to us from heaven, and a hand is outstretched toward us, to help us mount in one bound." Now, in his last moments, he was desperately seeking that ladder and that hand by the wavering light of the vigil lamp. But there was no ladder coming down to him. So Gogol would have to reach up to it. He was semi-conscious now and he made one brave attempt to get up. But his legs would not carry him. The body had no power of motion. He was dizzy. Watching his attempt to get up, Dr. Tarasenkov and a servant helped Gogol into an armchair but he could no longer hold up his head. It dropped like that of a newborn baby.

Now his body was turning cold. His feet indeed had turned icy. Dr. Tarasenkov slid a hot-water bottle under Gogol's feet, but it had no effect. Cold sweat started pouring down Gogol's face. Blue circles appeared under his eyes. The administrations continued.

Towards midnight, the doctor gave Gogol a dose of calomel and placed hot loaves of bread around his body. Gogol began to moan again. His mind wandered quietly, all night long. "Go on!" he whispered, "Rise up, charge, charge the mill!" He was incoherent. This went on for some time. But as time passed, he grew weaker, quieter, his breathing calmed down. At eight in the morning of February 21, 1852 he breathed his last.

One of Russia's greatest writers thus died. In death he was honored. "Gogol is dead" Turgenev wrote. "What Russian soul could not be smitten by those words? Our loss is so cruel and so sudden that we cannot yet accept it." But Gogol had no use for words, as he had no use for worldly goods. When he died, a list was made of his earthly belongings. It included a gold watch that had once been Pushkin's, a black woolen overcoat with a velvet collar, two old black woolen frock coats, three well-worn pairs of linen trousers, four old cravats, two sets of underclothes and three handkerchiefs. No money, no jewels, no important papers. His was the wardrobe of a pauper.

But in his will he had written: "Everything I possess, I bequeath to my mother and sisters. The servants who have waited on me must be rewarded. Give Yakim his freedom .... There is no door but the one we were shown by Jesus Christ. Whoever tries to reach heaven by any other route is a scoundrel and a thief!" And then he had added: "If you do not become as little children, you will not enter into the kingdom of heaven!"

H. G. WELLS: "Here I am with one foot in the grave and the other kicking out at everything!"

H. G. Wells, the social satirist, the novelist, the father of science fiction, so to speak, the historian, the futurist, in the end came to religion. He made one of his characters, Mr. Britling, say: "Religion is the first thing and the last thing, and until a man has found God, and been found by God, he begins at no beginning, he works to no end."

But if he had found faith in God, he had lost faith in man.

Toward the end of his life, he committed his thoughts in *Mind at the End of Its Tether:*

> The Truth remains that today nothing stands in the way to the attainment of universal freedom and abundance but mental tangles, egocentric preoccupations, obsessions, misconceived phrases, bad habits of thought, subconscious fears and dreads and plain dishonesty in people's minds—and especially in the minds of those in key positions. That universal freedom and abundance dangles within reach of us and is not achieved, and we who are citizens of the future wander about this present scene like passengers on a ship overdue, in plain sight of a port which only some disorder in the chartroom prevents us from entering. Though most of the people in the world in key positions are more or less accessible to me, I lack the solvent power to bring them into unison. I can talk to them and even unsettle them, but I cannot compel their brains to see.

But while he despaired, he continued to write. His unceasing mind would not stop. From 1937 to 1939 he went on writing novels like *You Can't Be Too Careful*. When the war came in 1939, he must have realized how right he was, that though he had a vision of a World Order, he lacked the power to convey that vision to the people in key places.

He wrote a new work: *All Aboard for Ararat* which came out in 1940, one year after the war in Europe started. It was a lively dialogue between Mr. Noah Lammock and the Lord God, who calls unexpectedly, as one might well imagine, expresses some sympathy for Mr. Lammock (an alter ego for Mr. Wells) in the failure of his mission in life. God also admits to having some difficulty with his adversary, the devil, who has been getting hold of physicists and mathematicians. "Well, I ask you!" says Lord God to Mr. Lammock, "they come along now declaring that space is *finite!*" And Mr. Lammock expresses sympathy for God's predicament.

But Wells is a man who clearly—and after a lifelong toil—has come to the end of his tether. When a friend, Sir Richard Gregory, called on him, Wells told him: "Here I am with one foot in the grave and the other kicking out at everything!" There was so much to kick. Religion, bigotry, indifference, nationalism and dogma of all kind. Wells would have liked so much to overthrow them. But he had become desperately ill and his strength was ebbing.

From 1944 onwards he had been ill and he knew that his time was up. He had lived to see the atom bomb dropped over Hiroshima and a new world indeed being born in its frightful glare. He was asked to comment on it: "This," he had said, "can wipe out everything—good and bad—in this world. It is up to the people to decide which."

He was home one day and his nurse was around. He was moving around in his room. It was still afternoon. It was summer, August 13, 1946. Suddenly he decided he would send his nurse away. What impulse moved him to do so will forever remain a mystery. The nurse left. Ten minutes later, he was dead. He died alone, suddenly, quietly, unattended. He was 80.

ABRAHAM LINCOLN: "Well, it is only a dream, Mary, let us say no more about it!"

Do dreams foretell the future? In the case of Abraham Lincoln, one did. A few days before his assassination, Lincoln had a dreadful dream. He had retired very late, after waiting for dispatches from the war front. As he later recounted the dream to his friends and his wife, Mary, he could not have been long in bed when he fell into a slumber and began to dream.

In the dream he felt a death-like stillness about him. Then he began to hear subdued sobs, as if a large number of people were weeping. He left his bed and wandered downstairs at the White House. There too he heard the sobbing but the strange part of it was that there were nowhere any mourners to be seen. Lincoln went from room to room, but while he heard the pitiful sounds of crying, there was no one in sight. The rooms seemed lighted; Lincoln could recognize familiar objects. But where were the people? What could be the meaning of all this? Lincoln kept moving along until he came to the East Room where he was to receive the biggest surprise. There before him was a catafalque, on which rested a corpse wrapped in funeral vestments. There was a guard at arms, surrounding it. And there were people thronging.

Curious, Lincoln asked: "Who is this dead in the White House?" And one of the soldiers said: "The President. He was killed by an assassin!" At this there was a loud burst of grief from the people and the sound awoke the dreaming Lincoln.

When Lincoln stopped recounting his dream, Mrs. Lincoln was aghast. "That is horrid" she replied, "I wish you had not told it. I am glad I don't believe in dreams, or I should be in terror from this time forth." Lincoln tried to soothe her. "Well, Mary" he said, "it is only a dream. Let us say no more about it and try to forget it." Mr. Lincoln himself seemed to have been deeply perturbed by that dream. In conversation with a friend some time afterwards he quoted from *Hamlet*: "To sleep, perchance to dream! Ay, there's the rub!" and he repeated with a strong accent the last three words.

On another occasion he said: "Well, let it go. I think the Lord in His own good time and way will work this out all right. God knows what is best." On the morning of April 14, 1865 Lincoln called for a cabinet meeting. His mind still seemed to dwell on his dream. The President told his cabinet that he had a peculiar dream the previous night, one that had occurred several times in his life. He had a vague sense of floating—floating away on some vast expanse toward an unknown shore. Colleagues offered explanations, one of which Lincoln wryly accepted.

The cabinet meeting was over by noon. Lincoln decided he would take a drive with Mrs. Lincoln and with no one to accompany them. He spoke to her of the future. "Mary" he said, "we have had a hard time of it since we came to Washington, but the war is over and with God's blessing we may hope for four years of peace and happiness and then we will go back to Illinois and pass the rest of our lives in quiet." That evening, as they had planned, they went to the theater.

The theater was Ford's and the play *Our American Cousin*. The day happened to be Good Friday, but it was not treated as very sacred in America, besides which, the President was fond of the theater which was one of his few means of recreation. But his decision had set a whole chain of action moving.

John Wilkes Booth, a Confederate sympathizer, had first plotted to abduct Lincoln, but the plan had failed. Around noon of April 14, he learned that Lincoln was to attend the theater and decided that he would now kill the President. He made out a statement for his reasons to commit the murder. He carefully laid out his plans and he had accomplices to assist him in his dastardly act. He knew how to approach the presidential box and he had a horse waiting for him to take him away, once the deed was done.

The President was delayed. There had been unexpected visitors to see him and when he and his party went to Ford's the play was already on. But courtesies and protocol had to be maintained. The band struck "Hail to the Chief," the actors ceased playing, the audience rose to greet the President and Lincoln bowed to acknowledge the cheering. Then they all sat down.

Meanwhile, Booth had gone to a neighboring saloon, taken a stiff drink of brandy, and entered the theater. He showed a card to the servant in attendance and made his way toward the presidential box. Hate and brandy had done their trick and Booth now entered the box with a pistol in one hand and a knife in the other. Security had been lax; this was unexpected. Major Rathbone, sitting close by, sprang to grapple with Booth as he put the pistol to the President's head. He received a savage knife wound for his troubles. Booth shot, then rushing forward, he vaulted to the stage in a high leap that only a trained athlete could have managed. However, his spur, which he was still wearing, was caught in the flag that draped the front of the box and Booth fell, broke his leg, but rose instantly and still brandishing his knife shouted: *"Sic semper tyrannis!"*

The audience was in a turmoil. "Stop him!" went the cry, as Booth scampered across the stage and out of sight. Again went the cry: "He has shot the President" and before the words died, two or three men jumped upon the stage in hot pursuit. But Booth had carefully planned his mission and escaped into the night— though he was later discovered in a barn after much hysterical searching and shot.

The President was quickly carried across the street from the theater to the house of a Mr. Peterson, stripped of his clothes and laid on a bed. His features were calm and striking. But soon his right eye began to swell and that part of his face became discolored.

A little before seven the next morning, Lincoln's death struggle began. He bore himself well, but on two occasions gave way to overpowering grief and sobbed aloud. Then the sobbing stopped. Lincoln turned his head and leaned on the shoulder of Senator Summer. Breathing now came slowly; at 22 minutes past seven, it wholly stopped. He was 56.

THOMAS ALVA EDISON: "Life hereafter? I do not know!"

Thomas Alva Edison, the great inventor who brought us electric light and the telephone, among other things, died in 1931, aged 84, full of honors. He had over 1,300 patents to his credit and he was a genius. He was known as the man who repelled darkness, which was true. Because of him, mankind could work longer in the night and do more efficiently. He made the industrial revolution take giant leaps.

But as the years came to an end, his body tired, he would absent himself for longer and longer intervals from his laboratory at Menlo Park. During the last two years, it seemed, only his will power kept him going. He ate next to nothing. He stayed in bed or sat in an easy chair at home, though in close touch with his colleagues and co-workers. He took an active interest in scientific affairs. When he met Colonel Charles Lindberg, he insisted on being taken to see how he took off and landed at an airport. "The aviators tell me" he said, "that they must find a means to see through the fog. I have an idea about it." He was always full of ideas.

On August 1, 1931, he had a sudden sinking spell and lay at the point of death. He could not take any food at all; he rallied for a while, but soon realized that he was getting weaker and began to lose interest in life. Friends, like Henry Ford, called on him to comfort him.

By October, he was slipping badly. The man who thought no moment could ever be wasted was now constantly in a state of semi-sleep. Doctors came and went. He was both difficult and courageous. He wanted to know what was being prescribed to him and why. He asked for microscopes and the slides prepared of his several blood tests. He wanted to know how the "campaign" to preserve him was going.

One who ministered to him asked, albeit indelicately, what he thought of a life hereafter. "It does not matter" he replied in a low voice, "no one knows."

In the early days of October, 1931 word went round that Edison may not have long to live. His mind became befogged at last, his eyes dimmed. He would be placed in a chair, all wrapped up, facing one of the tall windows of his bedroom, overlooking a great sweep of lawn and beyond a group of beech trees.

Once Mina Edison asked him: "Are you suffering?" "No, he replied, gently, "just waiting." He was waiting for death. On another occasion, Mina heard him say: "It is very beautiful over here."

He was then the world's most famous man and with word that he is sinking, newspaper reporters came to maintain a death watch. Edison's room was kept in the dark at night, with a nurse sitting by the patient. Edison's friends and associates, especially in the last days, waited in a hall below. Some of them had kept a similar vigil in happier days as when they had wanted to find out for how many hours the scientist's carbon filament lamp would live. That was 52 years ago. Now Edison's son, Charles, would periodically go to his father's room and return to tell his friends: "The light still burns."

Edison sank slowly, imperceptibly. On October 17, his pulse dropped steeply. In the early morning hours of Sunday, the 18th, at 3:24 a.m. the lights in his room went on; the end had come.

There was no suffering; hardly any pain. An old man who had worked hard all his life died peacefully in his sleep. It would be the kind of death many would wish for, but seldom get.

SAMUEL JOHNSON: "I have prayed that I may render my soul to God unclouded."

Another man to die a peaceful death, surrounded by his friends, was Samuel Johnson, the lexicographer—Dr. Johnson, made famous by Boswell.

Samuel Johnson was 75 when he died in 1784; he had lived a full life, by any account, seen so many sources of happiness gone and now, in the evening of his life, he seemed ready to meet death.

To his old friend, Burney, he wrote: "I struggle hard for life; I take physic and take air. My friend's chariot is always ready. We have run this morning twenty-four hours and could run forty-eight more. But who can run this race with death?" Autumn came. Johnson, who was living in the countryside, wanted to return to London. To a friend he wrote: "The town is my element. There are my friends and there are my amusements. Sir Joshua told me long ago that my vocation was to public life and I hope still to keep my station, till God shall bid me go in peace." So to London he went, but with new forebodings of death. His letters in the last two years of his life are full of frank avowal of his fear. "Death, my dear" he wrote to Lucy Porter, "is very dreadful; let us think nothing worth our care but how to prepare for it. What we know amiss in ourselves let us make haste to amend and put our trust in the mercy of God and the intercession of our Saviour." His fear, it seemed, was not so much of death itself, but of the judgment after death.

In the last week of his life, he burnt many of the letters he had received. On Sunday, December 5, 1784, Johnson took the sacrament in company with a large number of friends. He was concerned about many of them. He requested three things of Sir Joshua Reynolds: to forgive him thirty pounds which he had borrowed of him; to read the Bible and never to use his pencil on a Sunday. Sir Joshua readily acquiesced.

When his physician, Dr. Warren, asked him whether he was feeling better, Johnson replied: "No, sir; you cannot conceive with what acceleration I advance towards death." But his mind remained clear. Once, when Dr. Brocklesby was attending on him, Johnson burst out in the words of *Macbeth*:

> Canst thou not minister to a mind diseased,
> Pluck from the memory a rooted sorrow,
> Raze out the written troubles of the brain,
> And with some sweet oblivious antidote
> Cleanse the full bosom of that perilous stuff
> Which weighs upon the heart?

It was quite an outburst. Dr. Brocklesby, himself a literate man, replied in the next verse of the play:

> Therein the patient
> Must minister to himself.

Johnson got the point. "Well applied" he said, "That's more than poetically true."

Johnson trusted Brocklesby. He wanted to know, truthfully, how long he had to live. Did he have a chance of recovery? Brocklesby hesitated and asked if Johnson was prepared to face the truth, whatever it might be. Reassured that Johnson was ready, Brocklesby said that only a miracle could save his life. "Then" said Johnson, "I will take no more physic, not even my opiates; for I have prayed that I may render up my soul to God unclouded."

Whatever the terrors of death, Johnson wanted to face them with a clear mind and a clear conscience. His reward, says his other biographer, John Wain, was great. In his last days from whatever source it came, he was granted mercy. He was often loquacious. To some friends gathered around him, he sermonized. "You see the state in which I am," he told one group, "conflicting with bodily pain and mental distraction; while you are in good health and strength, labor to do good, and avoid evil, if ever you hope to escape the distress that now oppresses me." Then he added: "I had, very early in my life, the seeds of goodness in me; I had a love of virtue and a reverence for religion; and these, I trust, have brought forth in me fruits for repentance; and, if I have repented as I ought, I am forgotten."

His concern was for repentance, for a happy after-life. "At

these times" he would say, "I have had such rays of hope shot into my soul, as have almost persuaded me that I am in a state of reconciliation with God." On December 5, with a mind at peace, he wrote his last prayer:

> Almighty and most merciful Father, I am now, as to human eyes it seems, about to commemorate for the last time, the death of Thy son Jesus Christ, our Saviour and Redeemer. Grant, O Lord, that my whole hope and confidence may be in His merits and in Thy mercy; forgive and accept my late conversion, enforce and accept my imperfect repentance; make this commemoration (of) Him available to the confirmation of my faith, the establishment of my hope, and the enlargement of my charity and make the death of Thy son Jesus effectual to my redemption. Have mercy upon me and pardon the multitude of my offences. Bless my friends, have mercy upon all men. Support me by the grace of Thy Holy Spirit in the days of weakness and at the hour of death and receive me, at my death, to everlasting happiness, for the sake of Jesus Christ.

On December 13, Johnson had a visitor. She described herself as a Miss Morris, daughter to a "particular friend of his." She insisted on seeing Johnson because she wanted to ask for his blessing. She followed Johnson's servant to the patient's room. And while he tried to explain who the visitor was and what she wanted, Johnson's almost helpless body turned over in the bed. He looked at her and said: "God bless you, my dear." Those were his last words. His breathing ceased, quietly and with no disturbance. It was some minutes before it was realized that he had died. It was so peaceful a death.

JOSEPH STALIN: This is the bulletin of a dying man.

Stalin, the man before whom a whole nation quaked, in his time the most powerful, died a pitiful death, holed up in a bare room in his dacha.

On February 28, 1953, Stalin invited Malenkov, Beria, Bulganin and Krushchev, four of his habitual guests, to dinner at his dacha in the evening. From all accounts, he was in excellent spirits. The dinner itself was long, well supplied with drinks and meat. Stalin loved the simple but full peasant fare. With his companions he was full of pranks and jokes. And he could drink others under the table. The dacha was his home, his headquarters, the place where he lived and enjoyed to be most. The place was furnished somberly and by any modern standards it was ugly. A large table, chairs, a few armchairs, a sideboard—and here and there a beautiful rug. And for long winters, there were many fireplaces. When he went to sleep Stalin did so in a small, low-ceilinged room which held only a narrow bed and a night table. Except for the dark oak panelling on the wall, everything in that room was severe and bare "as in the consulting room of a public dispensary." When food was served, it was served in plenty. It was spicy; so was the conversation. Wines and vodka flowed in torrents. That had been so in the past. That was so on February 28.

The party lasted until dawn, when finally Malenkov and company returned to their own nearby dachas to get some sleep. Came March 1. The men had awakened, and were waiting to be called again. It was unusual for Stalin not to call them back for more talk and more drinks. Stalin apparently was not yet up. And there always were instructions never to disturb him when he was asleep.

Stalin's daughter Svetlana called that afternoon but failed to reach her father. An officer on duty told her: "There's no movement right now!" which meant that the dictator was in his small room, out of touch with the world and wanting it to be so. Stalin had the habit of turning night into day and day into night, sleeping when he could sleep, for hours at a time, always well guarded. There were times when he would not remove his garb, but would merely take off his heavy shoes and warm himself under a blanket.

Came nightfall and Stalin was not up still. Guards began to get worried. There were telephone calls to Malenkov, Beria, Krushchev and Bulganin to come around at once. Something, the guards guessed rightly, was wrong. This was not like Stalin. All four rushed out of their dachas to where Stalin lived. All was ghostly quiet. The men waited. Stalin had not ordered dinner. There were no precedents. Finally, around 3 a.m., it was decided to walk up to his door to see what had happened. And when they did, they found Stalin, still fully dressed, lying on a rug, in a deep, abnormal sleep.

Old intimates of Stalin were now sent for, Voroshilov and Kaganovich. Then the most reputed doctors were ordered to rush to Stalin's bedside. Their diagnosis was clear. Stalin had become a hopeless invalid and it was most probable that he would die soon.

Svetlana, Stalin's daughter, was finally told on March 2 and when she arrived, she found her father in a coma and Krushchev and Bulganin in tears. Beria was moving around, peering at Stalin once in a while, his eyes revealing nothing. Sitting beside her father for whom she had no especial liking, she took his left hand, the one that still moved, and kissed him. Then she too retired while the six members of the Presidium present organized guard duty, taking turns two at a time, both to keep an eye on the doctors and to prepare for the future. Already two factions were forming in the Soviet top hierarchy: that of Malenkov and Beria on the one side and of Krushchev and Bulganin on the other.

There were brief spells when Stalin would open his yellow eyes without really regaining full consciousness. Then everyone would rush to his side, trying to find out what the great leader had to say, if anything. At such moments, Beria would multiply his demonstrations of devotion to Stalin, but when the sick man lapsed into unconsciousness again, the dreaded police chief would indulge in sneers and insults. The place was being turned into a nightmare for the rest.

On the fourth day, doctors noticed an improvement in Stalin. He regained consciousness and a nurse gave him a small drink out of a spoon. Stalin raised his good arm and pointed at the wall to a bad reproduction of a picture of a young girl feeding milk to a lamb. He tried to smile, but the smile would not come. At this point he went into death throes. He was suffocating. There was little that the doctors could do as they watched his face turn almost black and his features become unrecognizable for lack of oxygen. Stalin was fighting his last fight and he seemed to know it.

There was one last moment of agony. Stalin opened his

eyes, took in everyone in one long and furious glance and then raised his hand as though pointing at something high up or just as possibly, bringing down a curse. Then it was over. A communique issued over the signature of eight professors of medicine said: "On March 5, at 21:50, the cardiovascular and respiratory insufficiency became accentuated and Joseph Vissarionovich Stalin died."

For three days before, radios had been given short bulletins about his condition. He had been struck by a cerebral hemorrhage which had attacked vital areas of his brain. He had lost consciousness; his right arm and leg had been paralyzed. He had lost his power of speech. The most powerful man had been left powerless by one stroke. As they listened to the litany, everywhere people had said: "This is the bulletin of a dying man."

And then death came, after much struggle on Stalin's part, but still, mercifully.

CHINGHIS KHAN: "My children the end is near for me . . . . "

Chinghis Khan, also known as Genghis Khan, probably the bloodiest monarch in all history, who brought to heel the whole Ch'in empire of northern China, overran Turkestan, Transoxonia and Afghanistan and led an empire stretching from the China Sea to Dnieper and, in his times, was known as the Conqueror of the World. He died in 1227, aged 65, a terror to the end.

He only knew how to kill. And his orders to his soldiers, when he sought the Tanguts in his last foray, for instance, was "As many Tanguts as you can take are yours to do as you please with!" The Tangut king had refused to accept Chinghis Khan's overlordship. He could take the consequences.

The depradations of the Mongols, led by Chinghis Khan were, as always, ghastly. Whole populations were put to death and no one was spared. The fields were covered by human bones. The Tanguts were an agricultural people but the Mongol nomads had no use for them. The Mongols had no other conception of life, except a nomadic one and settled communities were looked upon merely as raiding grounds. So it turned to pass that in his closing years, Chinghis Khan was engaged in destroying the Tanguts. The year was 1227.

But now sickness was taking its toll on him. A year earlier, while on a chase, he had had a fall from his horse. The horse reared and threw him. When he was picked up, he must have suffered internal injuries. He complained of sharp intestinal pains. And he had high fever. But pain was not going to stop him from his punishing attack on the Tanguts. Yet, he was mortal and as the year went by, he knew his time was coming. It was time, too, to settle who should succeed him.

His eldest son—he was allegedly a bastard—had died in the province of the Aral in February, 1227. Of his other three sons, Jaghatay was away, commanding a reserve army. Chinghis Khan therefore summoned his other two sons, Ogodei and Toluy, who were campaigning in his own vicinity. When they called on him, he received them alone. "My children, " he told them, "the end is near for me. Aided by the Eternal Heaven, I have conquered for you an empire so vast, that from its center to its bounds is a year's riding. If you would retain it, hold together, act in unison against your enemies, concert to further the fortunes of your followers. One of you must occupy the throne. Ogodei shall be my successor. Respect this choice after my death and let Jaghatay, who is not here, make no trouble."

But he was too much of the soldier to let it go at that. There were still lands to be conquered and the King of Gold, the Mongol's hereditary enemy, still held his stronghold retreat at Honan with its seemingly impregnable capital. To his sons Chinghis Khan taught strategem, outlining a last plan of campaign that was to be executed and was indeed executed six years after the Khan's death—and quite successfully.

But even on his deathbed, Chinghis Khan was intent on exacting his full tithe of vengeance from the last of the Tanguts. This was an obsession with him. When the citadel of the Tanguts falls, he told his sons and officers, all men and women, "fathers and mothers" to the last generation, were to be exterminated. As funeral sacrifices, he demanded, the dead Tanguts should be offered to him. "During my repast, declare to me: to the last man they have been exterminated! The Khan has eliminated their race!" And so it was done.

To one man, his faithful Tolun-cherbi, who, the year before had helped him to his feet after that fateful fall from the horse and had advised him to give up a hapless expedition, he was grateful and kind. "It was you, Tolun" said Chinhis Khan, "who after my hunting accident were concerned about my condition, you who wanted me to get proper care taken in time. I did not listen to you, I came to punish the Tanguts for their venomous words. All the king of the Tanguts has brought us, his moveable palace, his dishes of gold and silver, take it. I give it to you!"

Nevertheless Chinghis Khan found it hard to take leave of the world. In his final hour, according to his chronicler, Chinghis Khan reflected on his life and on what he had achieved, with a sense of nostalgia, envy and melancholy. "My descendants will go clothed in gold-embroidered stuffs; they will feed on the choicest meats; they will bestride superb steeds and press in their arms the most beautiful of young women. And they will have forgotten to whom they owe all that . . . . "

Chinghis Khan died on August 28, 1227 and was buried in the mountains of the eastern Kansu, under a mantle of cedars, pines and larch trees. The Khan had himself chosen the site of his grave, on the flank of one of the heights of the Burqan-qaldun massif, a mountain sacred to the ancient Mongols. The last journey of Chinghis Khan was as terrifying as any of his journeys when he was alive and leading armies. As his funeral cortege passed, his escort slew as they went any stranger they came across, along with his horse and oxen. It was an old Altaic custom. As they killed, the escort declared: "Go to serve our master, the Khan, in the hereafter!"

The theme of Chinghis Khan's last journey is the subject for one of the most magnificent poems in Mongol literature. Amid the lamentations of the army, is the address of one of the Mongol generals: "Have you gone, my lord, soaring like a falcon?" But the Lord was gone; and so, years later, was his empire; gone like other empires before and after, dust unto dust.

GEORGE WASHINGTON: "I am just going. Have me decently buried...."

George Washington died after a brief illness, nobly borne; he quickly realized that he was dying and took his impending death philosophically and with stoicism. On the morning of December 12, 1799 he had gone out for a ride around his large farm, inspecting, as was his wont, the cattle sheds, the trees and the state of his estate. He had been in the open for five long hours.

It had snowed, and when the General returned home, his hair was wet, though he had been protected by a large overcoat. To all outward appearances, he was hale and hearty as ever. The next day the cold worsened and the snowing which had started the previous night continued. Washington developed a sore throat. He should have stayed at home, but he did not feel too bad and so decided to go out again to mark some trees he wanted cut down. When he returned, his hoarseness had increased. It was suggested to him that he should take something to help his throat but he said that he did not take anything for a cold but preferred to "let it go as it came."

The cold turned into fever and around three in the morning, Washington woke up his wife Martha to tell her he felt ill. He breathed with difficulty and could scarcely speak. Mrs. Washington quickly summoned the General's aide, Tobias Lear, to tell him of the master's condition. A mixture of molasses, vinegar and butter was offered to Washington in the hope it could clear his throat, but he could not swallow it. Each effort to do so brought on a spasm. At the same time, an overseer, Mr. Rawlins, had also been summoned to administer blood letting. Rawlins was most uncomfortable as he began his unhappy task, but Washington told him not to be afraid. When the incision was made, the General said: "The orifice is not large enough," though the blood flowed rather freely. Washington pressed for more.

Still there was no change in the General's condition. A soft cloth soaked in sal volatile was wrapped round his neck and his feet were bathed in warm water. It was past eight in the morning and there was no change. The General decided he would get up and so he was dressed. By 9 a.m. two doctors had arrived and they diagnosed the illness as "inflammatory quinsy" and put a blister of cantharides on the General's throat in the hope of drawing the inflammation to the surface. A second bleeding was done. Washington was able to inhale from a steaming kettle of vinegar and water, but could not gargle. When he tried to let a mixture of sage tea and vinegar run down his throat, he again almost suffocated.

At this point a consultation was summoned. At three in the afternoon, Dr. Dick arrived and it was again decided that the General should be bled—standard practice for those times. A dose of calomel and tartar emetic was also prescribed. Washington was now in deep distress in his breathing. He kept asking what the time was. He had been put in bed and had to summon all his strength just to turn and had to be helped to do so.

Finally he asked for his wife, Martha. At his request, she brought to him two wills he had made, one of which he asked to be burnt. The other he gave to the care of his wife. Lear was by the General's side all the time. To him Washington said: "I find I am going, my breath cannot continue long; I believed from the first attack it would be fatal; do you arrange and record all my late military letters and papers; arrange my accounts and settle my books, as you know more about them than anyone else . . . . " It was all very matter of fact; no sentiment, no fear of death, no worry about either the past or the future.

In the late afternoon he was helped onto a chair, so he could sit up. The doctors were standing by him. To them, he said in a strained voice: "I feel myself going. I thank you for your attention. You had better not take any more trouble about me; but let me go off quietly; I cannot last long." Again the acceptance of finality, without fuss, without apparent distress. The consultants left the room. Lear laid Washington on the bed again, now counting the minutes as they ticked by. Medical skill had failed. Yet the doctors were reluctant to give up. About 8 p.m. they were back and giving blisters to the general's legs and feet and soft poultices of wheat bran to his throat. Nothing, however, changed. Washington was still restless and with the help of Lear, moved his position; but there was neither sigh nor word of complaint from his lips. Around 10 at night, Lear noticed that the General wished to speak and leaned close in an effort to catch what was being said. The words were slightly blurred. "I am just going" Washington said, "Have me decently buried and do not let my body be put into a vault in less than two days after I am dead." Lear nodded, unable to speak and fighting to keep back his tears. Washington looked at him directly and asked: "Do you understand me?" Lear answered: "Yes sir." Washington spoke once more. "'Tis well."

Mrs. Washington was keeping vigil by the foot of the bed. A little after ten, the General's breathing became much easier and he lay quietly. Lear still held his hand. Then, unexpectedly, Washington withdrew it to feel his own pulse. There was a change in his countenance. Washington's fingers slipped from his wrist and lay limp by his side. Doctor Craik laid his hand gently over Washington's eyes. There was no flicker. "Almost as if he realized that everything was now in readiness for his last command, George Washington withdrew in the presence of Death." It was a supreme study in self-control.

BENITO MUSSOLINI: "Shoot me in the chest!"

Benito Mussolini (1883-1945) the Fascist leader who ruled Italy with an iron fist, was captured by the Partisans after the collapse of the German army during World War II and shot in North Italy. It was a pathetic end to a dictator. With him was his mistress, Claretta Petacci, who too was killed. She had refused to leave him, telling his captors: "My life will be nothing once he is dead. That is all I am asking, to die with him."

The order that Mussolini should be shot had come from the partisan headquarters since there was a fear that the American army might want to have him collected first. The cry was: *Fatelo fuori* (Finish him off!). Mussolini had been lodged in a house along with Claretta and now the partisans came to fetch him. As their leader, Audisio, entered the room, he greeted Mussolini: "I've come to liberate you!" He wanted to lull the Duce's suspicions and Mussolini, moved, replied: "I'll give you an empire!" But Mussolini knew quite well that his time had come.

The partisans had strict instructions: there were to be no stage effects, no historical sentences, just execution. And that was how it was going to be. Mussolini was ordered into a car, along with Claretta. She sat in the back seat holding Mussolini's hand and both of them were strangely tranquil. They were driven down to a predetermined spot where Audisio read out the death sentence to the Duce. "By order of the High Command of the Volunteer Freedom Corps, I have been charged to render justice to the Italian people!" he said. Claretta began to scream: "You can't kill us like that. You can't do that!" she cried out. Audisio warned her. "Move aside, or we'll kill you first!"

Audisio's hand moved to his machine gun. It had jammed. Cursing, he tore his revolver from its holster. But the trigger clicked drily. Audisio turned to his assistant, Moretti and said: "Give me your gun!" It was a long barrelled French machine-pistol, 7.65 D-Mas model, bearing a tricolor ribbon. While this was going on, Mussolini unbuttoned his grey-green jacket, as if he was willingly preparing to be shot. His words came distinctly. He told his executioner: "Shoot me in the chest!" But even as Audisio fired, Claretta tried to seize the gun barrel and in the melee, it was she who fell first, shot through the heart, a sprig of flowering creeper in her hand.

Audisio backed away and then, at three paces, he fired two bursts, nine shots in all, at Mussolini. Four struck the dictator in the descending aorta; others lodged in the thigh, the collar bone, the neck, the thyroid gland and the right arm. Mussolini fell down, dead. It was April 29, 1945.

Now the mountain pass around where the execution took place began to be filled as word went round that Mussolini had been shot to death. The bodies of Mussolini and Claretta had been hung by their boots to the girders of a bombed-out filling station. Someone had placed a sceptre in Mussolini's hand and his head lay propped on Claretta's white blouse. But now came a scene of savagery that was unprecedented.

One man darted to aim a savage kick at Mussolini's head and give it a hideous crunch. People began to dance round the dangling corpses. A woman fired five shots into the dictator's body—one for each of the sons she had lost in the Duce's war. Another ripped off his shirt, fired it. Some women spread their skirts and urinated over Mussolini's upturned face. The bodies were cut down. The people trampled the corpses, blind with the hatred of years. Finally came orders from Partisan headquarters: "This has got to stop!"

Once again the bodies of Mussolini and Claretta were hoisted to join with some other bodies of Fascists who had been executed. The screams of execration gradually began to cease. Now there was only silence and awe "as if it was God's will and this was the end." "Imagine" a woman was heard to say, staring at Claretta, "all that and not even a run on her stockings."

There was joy in the Allied camp. When news of Mussolini's death was conveyed to Churchill, he told some dinner guests he was entertaining: "The bloody beast is dead." To his Chief of Staff, General Bedell Smith, General Dwight Eisenhower said: "God, what an ignoble end. You give people a little power and it seems like they can never be decent to human beings again!"

The Partisan Command later expressed a sense of shame at the manner in which the bodies of Mussolini and Claretta were dishonored. "The insurrection is dishonored" said one of its leaders. He was told: "History is made that way—some people must not only die, but die in shame."

The question turned as to what to do with the bodies. A poor man's morgue had been found. So came the final orders: "Take him there. Have him guarded by partisans and let nothing more happen to him, because it is over now. Let no more harm come to that man—no more harm at all!"

ADOLF HITLER: "It is all finished; death will be a relief for me. I have been betrayed . . ."

Adolf Hitler, the Nazi dictator of Germany, committed suicide in his bunker on April 30, 1945, a few days after his 56th birthday. It was a gruesome event. The Second World War was coming to its inexorable end. German war power was finished. The Russians and the Allies were closing in on Berlin, the nation's capital. There was nothing for Hitler to do but wait for his end.

He had been living with his mistress, Eva Braun. Now he decided to marry her. There was the question of who should conduct the marriage ceremony. Herr Goebbels, the Propaganda Minister, remembered that he had been married by a certain Walter Wagner, a justice of the peace. Soldiers were sent to locate this official and to bring him to Hitler's headquarters. It was done. A marriage certificate was produced, particulars filled in. In the bunker underground, surrounded by friends, Herr Hitler was asked by Wagner: "My Fuehrer, Adolf Hitler, are you willing to take Fraulein Eva Braun as your wife?"

"I do" said Hitler.

"Fraulein Eva Braun, are you willing to take our Fuehrer, Adolf Hitler, as your husband?" she was asked in turn.

"I do" said Eva Braun.

"Since both of the betrothed have declared their intentions" said Herr Wagner, "I declare that this marriage is legal in the eyes of the law."

Documents were now signed. A wedding banquet was held the same evening, April 29, 1945. Eva Hitler, giddy with champagne, was being toasted by everybody. Hitler too, sipped champagne and reminisced. He spoke about Goebbel's own wedding day. "That was a happy day" he said, "it is all finished." Then he added: "Death will be a relief for me. I have been betrayed and deceived by everyone."

The marriage had taken place the day before Hitler had decided to commit suicide. He wrote a private testament in which he explained why it was that he had decided to marry at this late stage of his life. And in the final paragraph he said: "My wife and I choose death to avoid the disgrace of defeat or capitulation. It is our wish to be cremated immediately in the place where I have done the greatest part of my work during the course of my twelve years' service for my people."

There were other things in the testament he had said that could not possibly have been carried out, like bequeathing possessions to his native town of Linz. But he ordered that the former Reichsmarschell Hermann Goering be deprived of all his rights and replaced by Grossadmiral Doenitz as President of the Reich. Hitler also dismissed Himmler.

By then it was about 4 a.m. in the morning of April 29. Hitler and Eva went to bed. They slept fitfully. The next day, they woke around 11 a.m. and Hitler was washed, shaved and in full uniform when he attended the usual midday conference. The position was totally hopeless. The Russians were advancing; German ammunition was running low. Hitler told his pilot, Han Baur, that the Russians surely knew where he was and would try to smoke him out. "The consequences would be unimaginable if they captured me alive!" he said.

Death had to be quick. He had been originally supplied with poison phials by Himmler but Hitler was not sure they were genuine. He wanted to have them tested. Professor Haase was summoned and it was decided that one phial would be tried out on Hitler's favorite wolfhound, Blondi. The dose was administered. "Death" Professor Haase reported, "was very nearly instantaneous." Hitler could not bring himself to watch the poisoning of his favorite dog but he took good care to see the dead bitch. Blondi had pups and the latter were still clinging to their mother's teats when they were shot one by one. Then they were buried in the garden.

That night Stockholm Radio announced that Mussolini had been killed. Hitler heard the news but did not seem especially distressed. He had his own death on his mind. Around midnight, Hitler began to issue hysterical orders to the Ninth Army. But the reply he received was clear. Berlin was now beyond saving. This meant that Hitler's own death could no longer be infinitely delayed if he wanted to avoid capture. Nevertheless he delayed his decision. Men clung to hope, even when all hope was lost. He had intended to shoot himself at 2:30 a.m. and he gave orders that those who wished to take a final leave-taking should line in the corridor. About twenty people, mostly women, came to say farewell to Hitler. Accompanied by Bormann, the dictator walked gravely along the line, shaking hands, saying nothing. His eyes were glazed, his color a deathly white and he was trembling. If anyone spoke, he did not seem to hear. Words no more meant anything to him.

Once the eerie reception was over and Hitler went into his own quarters, the people who had come for the farewell broke into unrelieved joy! They lit cigarettes, sang, played phonograph records, joked and spoke in loud voices. Hitler had finally to send word that the noise should stop and the people should disperse.

On the last day of his life, Hitler slept well for a few hours and awoke refreshed. For the first time in life he had nothing to do; no orders to give, no decision to take. And the Russians were within a hundred yards of the underground bunk and only a couple of ruined streets separated them from the man who had brought war and ruin upon Europe. At 2:30 p.m. Hitler took lunch with his two secretaries and his vegetarian cook. Eva was not hungry and stayed in her own room tending to her thoughts. The lunch consisted of a dish of spaghetti with light sauce and was over in a few minutes. There was nothing said.

Even as he was having his last meal, orders had gone to collect 200 liters of gasoline to be placed inside the bunker. Now the last act was to follow. Out of his bunker came Hitler and Eva, the latter wearing a dark blue polka-dot dress, nylon stockings and Italian-made shoes. She was completely self-controlled. She embraced the women and smiled at the men who kissed her hand. Hitler shook hands mechanically with everyone and said nothing at all. It was his last farewell.

Then Hitler and Eva turned into a small room that had been kept ready for them. At that point, Magda Goebbels came running to the door screaming that there still was hope and that Hitler must not commit suicide. She demanded to see Hitler. The door to the room was slightly opened and the guard asked Hitler whether he would receive Mrs. Goebbels. Hitler replied: "I don't want to see her." The door was closed. Outside the guard waited. Moments passed by. Hitler and Eva sat on a couch in the small room, twelve feet long and nine feet wide. If they said anything to each other in their last moments, they could not possibly have been recorded.

By and by a barely perceptible smell of gunpowder drifted out of the room. The guard, Otto Guensche, and another man, Heinz Linge, now opened the door and found Hitler and Eva still on the couch. Hitler had a small hole, the size of a German silver mark, in the right temple and blood was slowly trickling down his cheek. Eva had bitten the phial of potassium cyanide and her head was nestling against Hitler's shoulders. In dying she had flung out her arm and overturned a vase of flowers on the table in front of her. Yet she looked very composed, as though she were sleeping. On the floor just below Hitler's right hand, lay his 7.65 Walther pistol that he had used to shoot himself. No sound had been heard. The pistol must have been muffled when it was used.

Goebbels was summoned and he entered the room to be followed by Artur Axmann, the leader of Hitler Youth who had been fighting in the streets and could not come for the last farewell. Bormann came too. A picture was taken of the dead people and then Linge wrapped the dictator's body in a blanket and carried it up the four flights of stairs leading to the Chancellery Garden, followed by Bormann who carried Eva. The bodies were placed in a shell hole and a moment later gasoline was poured over them. Within ten minutes of their death, Hitler and Eva's bodies were burning in a windy, blustery afternoon, the blue flames fluttering menacingly in the skies. The flames were kept burning for more than two hours to make sure that nothing remained of the man and his wife. Around 11 p.m. on April 30, 1945 their ashes were scooped up and buried in another part of the same garden. Such was their end.

LUDWIG VAN BEETHOVEN: "Applaud, my friends, the comedy is finished!"

Beethoven, creator of the great symphonies, died at the age of 57, having written some of his greatest music beset with deafness. His last compositions, after 1817, were written when he was totally deaf, including *Missa Solemnis*, the *Ninth Symphony* and the last five string quartets. When he died on March 27, 1827, his reputation had already been firmly established. He belonged to the gods.

His last years were full of toil and trouble. His expenses had been heavy, his income not commensurate. His nephew, Karl, was a source of unhappiness. The boy even had attempted suicide. Beethoven's suffering over that incident was indescribable. "The blow bowed down the proud figure of the composer and he soon looked like a man of seventy."

His health began to deteriorate. He became restless and quarrelsome. From his home in Germany he decided to go to Vienna in December, 1826. The weather was cold; he was not sufficiently well dressed. He contracted pneumonia, though later he jested about it with a friend. *"Wir irren allesamt nur jeder irret anderst"* he wrote. (We all of us err, but each of us errs differently). But doctors had to be called. On top of penumonia, Beethoven developed dropsy and had to be operated upon, without benefit of anaesthesia. His humor did not desert him; he was tapped and when the tube was inserted into his stomach and water spurted out, Beethoven told the doctor: "Professor, you remind me of Moses striking the rock with his staff!" The doctor replied: "You bore yourself like a knight!"

Beethoven bore his burden stoically but seemed to have suffered premonitions of death, in spite of being assured by his physicians that he will recover. On January 3, 1827 he drafted his will, leaving his nephew Karl all his property. He felt that he could not possibly have a long time to live.

Friends kept calling on him. From one friend in London he received a delightful present, forty volumes of Handel's works.

Beethoven long wanted to possess them. He had said Handel "is the greatest, ablest composer that ever lived. I can still learn from him!" On another occasion he said of Handel: "To him I bow my knee!" To read Handel's scores, even in a sick bed was for Beethoven a joy not to be exceeded. That gift of Handel's volumes might have done a lot of good to cheer Beethoven up.

On February 27 his friend Schindler wrote to say that "the noble patient thought himself already saved and wanted to work on his tenth symphony, which he was allowed to do to a small extent." To Schindler himself, Beethoven wrote: "Miracles! Miracles! The learned gentlemen (the doctors) are both defeated. Only through Malfatti's science shall I be saved!"

But Beethoven continued to have anxieties about his financial affairs. "Doctors, surgeons, everything has to be paid" he complained. He asked for help from friends in London who readily obliged by sending him 100 pounds at once. Beethoven acknowledged it, saying that he considered the money "as a relief sent him from heaven." His cares seemed to vanish overnight. Over and over again, Beethoven was heard to say about his London admirers: "May God reward them all a thousandfold!" His friends elsewhere rallied, too. From Vienna they sent him regular gifts of fruit and drink. He received a gift of a print of Haydn's birthplace. Beethoven, childlike, showed the print to a visitor and said: "See this little house? In it so great a man was born!" He kept a correspondence with his own publisher. He promised to write a new symphony specially for his London friends, sketches for which he had got ready. But he was rapidly weakening.

A week before his death he had visits from two distinguished men, a composer and a pianist. To the pianist, Hummel, Beethoven said: "I have been lying here for four months—one must lose patience in the end!"

He had written a will before; again, on March 23, 1827 he signed another, drawn in a simple form. He told a friend, Herr von Breuning: *"Plaudite amici comoedia finita est."* It was said in his favorite sarcastic-humorous manner, at the departure of his doctors, as though to imply that there was really nothing more that could be done. The doctors and he were engaged in a joke, no more.

And then came the day. It was five o'clock on the afternoon of March 27, 1827. There was a sudden flash of lightning which garishly illuminated the death-chamber. Then there was an accompanying thunder clap. At this startling, awful peal of thunder, as if the very heavens were waiting for Beethoven, the dying man suddenly raised his head and stretched out his right arm majestically. One who was in the room, Herr Huttenbrenner, later described the movement as one "like a general giving orders to an army!" It was all over in an instant. The arm sank down. Beethoven fell back; he was dead. The heavens at that moment claimed him as their own.

The Roman Catholic Church awarded him the privilege of its most solemn and ceremonial rights to which he had been averse all his life, though it is true that as he lay dying he had accepted Extreme Unction and thanked the priest for bringing him comfort. And he received a magnificent funeral.

VICTOR HUGO: "Here it is a battle between day and night!"

When Victor Hugo (1802-1885) died at the ripe age of 83, he had already become a legend. People venerated him. In 1881, Mme. Daudet saw him dining and later wrote about him: "Aged, a little isolated, a little deaf, the master sits enthroned with the silence of a god, the moments of absent-mindedness of a genius on the verge of immortality."

He looked an old stonemason, with much refined courtesy. He knew death was coming and was more than willing to meet it halfway through. Once, walking with a young admirer along the pont d'Iena, he stopped to see the flaming sky and exclaimed: "How splendid it is! My child, you are going to see that for a long time. But I myself shall soon see an even grander sight. I am old, I am going to die. I shall see God. To see God, and talk to Him, what a great thing that will be! What shall I say to Him? I often think about it. I am getting ready for it!" Later he wrote: "I am going to close my terrestrial eyes but my spiritual eyes will remain open, wider than ever!"

On February 26, 1882 a group of his admirers presented him with a fine bronze of Moses. Hugo replied: "My dear friends, I thank you. I gratefully accept your gift. I expect nothing more for myself except one great gift: this great gift, this eternal gift, is death and I await it with a pious heart." For Hugo, this gift was not extinction but the beginning of a new life. When someone assured him that everything ends for the soul after this world, he answered: "That may be for your soul, but I know that mine is eternal." He was so positive of it that it called for no argument.

He made no attempt to hide his age or the ravages of time. He continued his old habits of taking a cold water bath every morning until his physician told him not to. He could never get accustomed to an overcoat which he considered a needless burden. He never carried an umbrella. He would go for long drives on the upper deck of an omnibus, until the conductors began to recognize him.

Then his mistress died and with her a great part of Hugo died. She had been his mistress for fifty years and she had been faithful to him as he to her. In 1881 he had written to her: I possessed you freely, you who are beauty, you who are grace, you who are the woman of your century. May the day be greater than ever, my beloved. I love you, I possess you, I bless you, I adore you!" Such was his passion. It was a total immersion of his personality with hers. As he had put it: "I do not understand anything without you or beyond you. I ask that your life should be my life, that your death should be my death, that your eternity be my eternity."

On August 2, 1883, Hugo made a codicil to his will. He wrote: "I give 50,000 francs to the poor. I want to be taken to the cemetery in their hearse. I refuse prayers of all the churches. I ask for a prayer from every soul. I believe in God!" Hugo may not have believed in the Church, but he firmly believed in God. He was not irreligious.

September that year he had a visit from a pastor, Gustave

Gabre. They talked about religion. Hugo told the pastor: "I believe profoundly in God and in the human soul. Yes, I believe in God with all the power of my soul. There is nothing useless in the world and the whole world would be useless if there were not a divine thought which presided over all . . . . " As they were taking leave, Gabre volunteered the hope that God would grant Hugo a long life and a happy old age. "Oh" he replied, "my life is long enough, I am eighty one and a half; but since my early childhood nothing has shaken my faith. I am waiting, with confidence, for the moment when I appear before God, before Infinity!"

The weeks rolled by. Honors kept pouring in. They meant nothing to Hugo who had seen them all. Now he was waiting for Time, the Reaper. One month after his mistress had died, he had written: "I shall soon be with you again, my beloved!" If there was one thing, above all, that he wanted, it was to be united with her again in eternal silence.

In 1885 Hugo's eighty-third birthday was celebrated with a banquet at the Hotel Continental in Paris. But he was a tired old man. It was too much for him. He begged to be let off. As he was about to reach home, he grasped the hand of his host, apologetically and said: "I am too old for these celebrations." On Friday, May 15, 1885 Hugo was found to be suffering from a lesion of the heart and from congestion of the lungs. He was put to bed and he stayed there till the end. On May 22, Friday, he sent for his grandchildren. It was six in the morning. He brought out his hand from under the bedsheet and kissed them slowly, with tears on his lips. But his eyes were smiling as if he alone now held the secret of afterlife. The sun was peeping through the windows and everything seemed so peaceful.

Around seven in the morning, the agony began. He seemed to be murmuring lines of poetry. *"C'est ici le combat du jour et de la nuit!"* He seemed radiant. His eyes were fixed but there was no sign of pain. But the death rattle was grievous to those who heard it. It was at first a raucous sound like that of a sea on the pebbled shore, then the sound grew fainter, then it ceased. It was twenty-seven minutes past one. Beyond noon.

Word had gone round and in the streets at least five thousand people were waiting for the news. A quiet lamentation filled the air. And the funeral became the celebration of an immortal.

QUEEN ELIZABETH: "Who should succeed me but a king . . . "

Queen Elizabeth I (1533-1603) under whom Britain became a great nation, died at the age of 70, enjoying power and prestige to the very end. Indeed, very considerable were her achievements in the last years of her life. The nation had recovered from a dark period of economic distress and she, as well as her courtiers, knew it. She was in total command. As Lord Cecil would put it: "I know not one man in this kingdom that will bestow six words of argument to reply, if she deny it."

She ruled firmly and where possibly, wisely. "I have ever used to set the last judgment day before mine eyes and so to rule that I shall be judged to answer before a high judge" she once wrote. To be a king, she thought, was "a glorious title" but "to be a king and wear a crown is a thing more glorious to them that see it than it is pleasant to them that bear it. For myself, I was never so much enticed with the glorious name of a king or royal authority of a queen, as delighted that God hath made me His instrument to maintain His truth and glory . . . . "

She considered herself only a woman and an unworthy one at that. She did not attribute anything to herself. Everything was the doing of Providence. "For, I, Oh Lord, what am I, whom practices and perils past should not fear?" Throughout Christendom, she was coming to be regarded as a kind of phenomenon, the woman of wit and intelligence, a stateswoman who commanded political and military triumphs. Ballad singers called her "the great lioness." She led a healthy life. She took frequent and vigorous exercise. She was seldom absent from her duties because of illness. And yet she never feared death. She said so often, and obviously meant it. And she showed no curiosity whatsoever about what would happen to her when she ceased to exist. She was willing, when the audit and the judgment came to let the record speak for itself. She had played her part; let others play theirs.

But age was telling. Once before she had a major bout with smallpox; she had survived. She had an ulcer on her leg, above her ankle, that made her wobble at times. But though she had excellent doctors by the standards of the day, she seemed disinclined to accept their services. Throughout her life she disliked taking medicine in any form. She had extraordinary physical resilience, like her father.

Troubles arose in the kingdom. There was the Essex uprising and the execution of Essex. She did not give the event another thought. A queen has no time for the past; she must look into the future.

The year 1602 was the final full year of her life. She was reasonably content and by and large in good health. She was seen at one court wedding dancing gaily and at another there was "singing, dancing and playing wenches." Early in 1602, when she was 69, she entertained the Orsini Duke of Bracchiano and to show that she is not so old as some would have her, danced both measures and galliards in his presence. She took great pleasure in the ball and music and told her courtiers that in her youth she danced very well. Indeed, she would dance by herself, sometimes when alone in her private quarters. Late in August, 1602, she rode ten miles and then went out hunting on the same day, tiring enough for anyone, let alone a 69-year-old woman. On September 26, she was seen by the Duke of Stettin walking in her garden, "as briskly as though she were 18 years old."

And so the days passed. But by the autumn of 1602 those who watched her saw that her health was quietly fading, though not dramatically. In October she had to be reminded what were the duties of various courtiers who had come to pay their respects to her. It was not that her authority was declining, but her strength. She was still active. On January 1 and 6, 1603 she saw plays performed at Whitehall. Later that same month she set out for Richmond and broke journey en route to have dinner with an old friend.

But her health was getting to bother her. Not any one thing, but several factors. A combination of insomnia, cold, rheumatism and sadness. She received a Venetian Ambassador and addressed him in Italian, a language in which she was very fluent, though she told him: "I do not know if I have spoken Italian well; still, I think so, for I learnt it when I was a child and believe I have not forgotten it." Towards the end of February, 1603 she seemed to have guessed that death was tugging at her. She withdrew into herself. When Sir Robert Carey, brother of the Lord Chamberlain, of whom she was very fond, called on her to wish her good health, she took him by his hand, wrung it hard, and said: "No, Robin, I am not well." She indeed seemed to have been in a sorry plight.

For nearly a fortnight she continued to suffer quietly. She was restless; she complained of a great heat in the stomach and a continual thirst which obliged her to take something continuously to sip. She refused medicine "notwithstanding all the importunities of her counsellors and physicians." She said she knew her own strength and constitution better than they and that she was not in such danger as they imagine. She was told to get into bed. There was a flash of the old imperial fire. The word "must" she said, is not to be used to princes! To Nottingham she said: "My Lord, I am tied with a chain of iron about my neck, I am tied, I am tied and the case is altered with me."

She seemed to recover, relapse again. It was a form of bronchitis or pneumonia and it was gradually setting in. She would relapse into silence for a couple of hours; she was seen holding her fingers continually in her mouth, her eyes open, lying on her couch in her day clothes. On March 21 she was finally persuaded to undress and go to bed. She was fed some hot broth, but began to lose her speech.

The next day with Nottingham on her right, Egerton on her left and Cecil at the foot of her bed, Elizabeth indicated that James of Scotland should succeed her. "Who should succeed me but a king . . . who, quoth she, but our cousin of Scotland?" The next day, her last, still unable to talk, she made the sign of a crown, as if to emphasize what she meant.

For two days she had lain in her bed, speechless, very pensive and silent, her eyes fixed upon an object at a time, many hours together; there were no signs of fear in those eyes nor of a memory wandering. When the Archbishop came in to offer prayers she hugged his hand, as if pleased.

About three in the morning of March 24, a Thursday, Elizabeth died, peacefully, as Manningham wrote: "mildly like a lamb, easily like a ripe apple from the tree." That night it rained heavily.

MARIE CURIE: "I want to be left in peace."

There is something about the deaths in the Curie family that is poignant and painful. Though Marie Curie herself died old (1867-1934), her husband Pierre died a tragic death in an accident in which his head was crushed. A daughter, Irene, who had been exposed to massive amounts of radiation, died of leukemia; Irene's husband, Fred, also died because of exposure to radiation.

Atomic science was then at its earliest stage and the Curies were pioneers. But Pierre's death was inexcusable. It was over in a matter of seconds. Only one or two people actually saw it—and it was gruesome to behold. On Pont Neuf, in Paris, a cart driver was egging a pair of horses along in tight rein when he had to stop to let a tram pass in front of him. He then moved along at a steady pace down the right-hand lane of the Rue Dauphine with a load of military uniforms. Then it all happened in a flash. On the other side of the street, a horse cab was passing; from behind it a man in a black suit appeared and came right in the path of the horse cart with no warning. The asphalt was wet, the man slipped and fell under the first horse; he tried to grab it, whereupon the horse reared, making matters worse. The driver tried to put on the brakes, but the horse pulled and the man in black fell between two straining animals and the moving cart's front wheels. The left rear wheel hit and smashed the head of the man. The man was Pierre Curie, the scientist, husband of Marie.

There was no more futile a death in the history of science

than that of this young scientist, cut down in the prime of life. Pierre Curie was one who always desperately wanted to believe in some spiritual phenomenon that could be brought into the realm of the measurable. In one of his earliest letters to his wife, Marie, he had written: "I must confess that these spiritualism phenomena intrigue me a great deal. I think that there are things in these questions which touch closely on physics." Pierre's death took a great toll on Marie's life. Now she had to plod her own path, without his guidance and leadership and inspiration. She put her heart and soul in her work.

But she was not just a workaholic. She enjoyed physical exertion. She swam whenever she could and boasted to her children of the three hundred yards she still could manage in her late fifties with her respectable and stately breast stroke. She could even be vain at times and quite capable of standing in front of her mirror and inviting her daughters to admire her slim figure.

It is remarkable that with all the exposure she had to radiation, she should have survived so long. But by the time she was 65, the wear and tear had begun to show. Her face was worn out, she had become anemic. One day, early in 1932, as she was walking in her laboratory, she slipped and fell. She had to be picked up, greatly shaken and in pain. She had thrown her right arm out in a gesture of self-protection and she had broken her right wrist. The wrist was quickly placed in a cast; but the wound would not heal easily. She tried to shrug it off as of no moment. But she had to confine herself to bed now for long periods.

There were other signs of infirmities. Radiation burns on her fingers were getting to be more sore and she was never entirely free from pain. To cap it all, she had a maddening drumming in her head, which seemed to center itself on her eyes and ears.

In December, 1933 she was again gravely ill, but this time from a large gallstone in her bladder. She was given the option of an operation or a strict diet. She chose the diet; she wasn't going to be on an operation table, if she could help it.

She had the satisfaction of seeing her son in law and daugher get a Nobel Prize in 1935—the third to go to the Curie family. When Joliot and Irene presented her the first sample of an artificially radioactive isotope in a little glass tube, they watched her face light up. But as she held the tube, they also noticed how badly burned by radium her hands were.

By the winter of 1935 it was clear that Marie Curie was really ill and that her condition was worsening. In the weeks that followed, her spirits rose and fell and it was recommended that she be placed in a sanatorium. Her condition had been originally presumed to be tuberculous. But an examination of Marie's lung X-rays clearly showed pernicious anemia. There was nothing left to be done but to await the end. Eve Curie, the younger daughter, had to rush out into the corridor to cry so that her mother should not see her.

Marie did not even have the strength in her last days to hold a thermometer firmly in her hands. She found speech exhausting. Her conversation became more and more feeble. At times it was incoherent. Her daughter Eve would sit by her side, trying to communicate. Marie would mumble: "I can't express myself properly." "What are you going to do to me?" Then one day, with Eve still by her bedside, she said: "I want to be left in peace." Those were her last words.

LORD NELSON: "Now I am satisfied. Thank God I have done my duty."

The last hours of few who have fought and been killed in battle have been chronicled at greater length than those of Horatio, Lord Nelson, Admiral of the Fleet. Nelson fell at the Battle of Trafalgar, to become an English naval hero at the age of 47. The defeat of the combined Spanish and French fleets off Cape Trafalgar in 1805 decisively established British naval supremacy for many decades to come.

Nelson was aboard his flagship, the *Victory* when personal disaster struck him. He was pacing up and down a 20 foot stretch of the quarter deck when a ball hit him from up front. Nelson collapsed, trying to support himself with his left, and only, arm.

He was bleeding profusely. Captain Hardy came running over to him and solicitiously asked, though he should have at once known better: "I hope you are not severely wounded, my Lord?"
"They have done for me, at last, Hardy," Nelson replied in agony.
"I hope not" replied Hardy, more out of hope than knowledge.
"Yes" said Nelson, "my backbone is shot through."

Nelson was quickly picked up and ordered to be taken to the cockpit at once. As he was being carried, Nelson, anxious that word should not pass that the Admiral himself had been struck down, managed to use his one arm to take out a handkerchief and place it over his face so that no one would recognize him. It was a futile gesture. Several wounded men recognized Nelson from the decorations on his coat and the cry went up that he had become a casualty.

The naval battle was then going on at full speed and there was then no saying what the outcome would be. 32-pounders were crashing in a frightful din on the decks and the smell of gunpowder and burnt flesh and the cries of the wounded mingled with the sound of waves pounding and sails crashing everywhere.
"Who is that carrying me?" asked Nelson.
"Beatty, my Lord, and Burke" he was told by his surgeon.
"Ah, Mr. Beatty, you can do nothing for me. I have but a short time to live; my back is shot through" said Nelson.

The surgeon, assisted by Captain Hardy, his steward, Henry Chevalier, and his personal valet, Gaetano Spedito, began to undress Nelson to take care of the wound. Nelson looked at Dr. Scott and said in a weak voice: "Doctor, I told you so. Doctor, I am gone." There was nothing that the surgeon could do but try to make Nelson as comfortable as possible in the circumstances of total carnage. The wounded were being constantly brought down and the decks were splattered with blood and broken limbs. Nelson was placed on a purser's mattress with his back against the ship's side. The woods shivered as cannonballs hit the rafters and Nelson's body shivered with the rafters.

Just then a midshipman, one Westphal, who was bleeding in his head, was brought along and placed next to Nelson. The man was bleeding so badly that he needed something to hold the wounds before they could be attended to. In the general confusion, the orderlies picked up a coat and pressed it on the poor man. It was Nelson's. Chevalier and Spedito were hovering round Nelson. Burke kept fanning the Admiral, massaging his chest to help circulation. Nelson had turned deathly white as a result of loss of blood.

Convinced that he would die within a few minutes, Nelson's thoughts turned to his famous mistress, the Lady Hamilton. "I have to leave Lady Hamilton, and my adopted daughter Horatia, as a legacy to my country" he was heard to murmur. Meanwhile, Beatty was getting ready with his surgical instruments in the vain hope of extracting the ball from where it had lodged. It had plunged deep into Nelson's chest and was expected to be lodged in his spine. Nelson kept repeating: "I am confident my back is shot through." He was asked to say how he felt about body sensations. "I feel a gush of blood every minute within my heart" he replied, in clinical detail. "I have no feeling in the lower part of my body . . . breathing is very difficult and gives me very severe pain about the part of the spine I am sure the ball has struck for I felt it break my back."

They propped him up, half lying, half sitting as that seemed to be the only posture in which he felt most comfortable, his back against a thick oak frame which groaned every time a 32-pounder hit the ship, which was frequent. Lanterns, with their flickering candles, cast eerie shadows on the walls. Surgeons were flitting from patient to patient, trying to help one wounded after another, as they were rushed to the infirmary. There were faint cheers from decks above. "Why are they cheering?" Nelson wanted to know. He was told "another enemy ship has sunk, my Lord."

He seemed pleased. He asked for a drink and for someone to continue to fan him. He was told the enemy was being decisively defeated and that he would surely live to rejoice in victory. But Nelson was not the one to be fooled. "It is nonsense, Mr. Burke" he gasped, "to suppose I can live: my sufferings are great, but they will soon be over." Told not to despair, he added: "Ah doctor, it is all over, it is all over!"

The battle, meanwhile, was being fought with great vigor. Still conscious, Nelson summoned Captain Hardy. "Well, Hardy, how goes the battle? How goes the day with us?"

"Very well, my Lord. We have got twelve or fourteen of the enemy's ships in our possession."

"I hope none of our ships have struck, Hardy."

"No, my Lord, there is no fear of that."

"I am a dead man, Hardy, I am going fast; it will be all over with me soon. Come nearer to me . . . "

As Hardy bent down, Nelson told him: "Pray let my dear Lady Hamilton have my hair, and all other things belonging to me."

A couple of hours had passed since the time Nelson was first hit and now Beatty again came forward to see what he could do for the Admiral. Nelson ordered him out to help those who needed it most, "for you can do nothing for me." Soon Nelson complained that all power of motion and feeling below his breast were gone and that he knew that it was all over. Beatty told him, truthfully: "My Lord, unhappily for our country, nothing can be done for you."

Nelson was lost in his own thoughts. He was speaking almost to himself: "I know it, I feel something rising in my heart which tells me I am gone." He was heard mumbling: "Oh *Victory, Victory*, how you distract my poor brain!" and then: "How dear life is to all men!" His breath was coming in short measure now and he was gasping. The pain apparently was unbearable. "It continues so severe" he told Beatty, "that I wish I was dead!" "Yet" he added, "one would like to live a little longer too."

Again his mind would wander. They heard him say: "What would become of poor Lady Hamilton if she knew my situation." Yet another hour passed. It was suggested to the dying Admiral that perhaps Admiral Collingwood should take charge of the direction of affairs. The suggestion had been delicately put that he was dying and should name the next chief. At that Nelson seemed greatly offended. Trying vainly to straighten himself up, as if he was about to take full command, Nelson said: "Not while I live, I hope, Hardy!" It was the strongest rebuke he could make to his lieutenants.

The effort to raise himself was too much and Nelson sank back, exhausted. Around him men stood in awed silence. Presently Nelson bestirred himself. He addressed himself to Hardy and said: "Don't throw me overboard, Hardy."

"That would not be done," he was promised.

"Then you know what to do; and take care of my dear Lady Hamilton. Hardy . . . kiss me, Hardy." As Hardy knelt down, Nelson whispered: "Now I am satisfied. Thank God I have done my duty."

The *Victory's* log recorded that day: "Partial firing continued until 4:30 when a victory having been reported to the Right Honourable Lord Viscount Nelson, he then died of his wound."

WILLIAM BUTLER YEATS: "Cast a cold eye, on life, on death. Horseman, pass by."

William Butler Yeats, poet, mystic, dreamer of dreams, died at the ripe old age of 74, wondering, as he wrote in one of his poems, "what then?"

> All his happier dreams came true
> A small old house, wife, daughter, son,
> Grounds where plum and cabbage grew.
> Poets and wits about him drew.
> "What then?" sang Plato's ghost, "What then?"

This was a man who asked questions. Was happiness enough as a goal, an aim, in life? In his old age he interested himself in Eastern philosophy, in the ancient wisdom of the Upanishads. He made friends with an Indian mystic and spent many days with him. He and Shri Purohit Swami collaborated on a translation of the Upanishads and his mind was full of India, while his body was suffering from dropsy.

It was a fulfilled life, with little to spare by way of anger. He wrote *The King of the Great Clock Tower* and showed it to

Ezra Pound. Pound called it "putrid." But it was acted most successfully at the Abbey Theatre and Yeats asked notices of the play to be sent to Pound, saying: "I may confound him! He may have been right to condemn it as poetry, but he condemned it as drama. It has turned out the most popular of my dance plays."

He was getting on in years. In February, 1935, when he was 70, he collapsed and had to be confined to bed for some time. But his productivity did not diminish. In November, 1935 he published *A Full Moon in March*. He went to Majorca for a rest cure as much as for collaborating with his Indian mystic friend. He wrote much, slept little, often getting up in the morning at four to work at proof sheets. His industry was indefatigable. He also continued to write poetry. The last book of verse that Yeats wrote and saw through the press was *New Poems*. His lines were simple, majestic and evocative.

> Picture and book remain
> An acre of green grass
> For air and exercise.
> Now strength of body goes,
> Midnight, an old house
> Where nothing stirs but a mouse
> . . . .
> Grant me an old man's frenzy.

There were other lines, reminiscent of *Dark Night of the Soul*; or of Gogol's call for a ladder to go up to heaven:

> Now that my ladder's gone
> I must lie down where all ladders start,
> In the foul rag-and-bone shop of the heart.

He spent half the summer of 1938 in England, but like most perceptive men who realize that their time has come, Yeats too was preparing for the event. His last public appearance was in August, 1938 at the Abbey Theatre. On January 4, 1939 he wrote to Lady Elizabeth Pelham: "I know for certain that my time will not be long. In two or three weeks . . . . I will begin to write my most fundamental thoughts. I am happy, and I think, full of an energy, of an energy that I had despaired of . . . . When I try to put all into a phrase, I say: 'Man can embody truth, but he cannot know it.' I must embody it in the completion of my life. The abstract is not life and everywhere draws out its contradictions. You can refute Hegel, but not the Saint or the Song of Sixpence." He was feeling so happy, he said, that he had given up reading detective novels and was deep in poetry again.

What a happy end to a man! On January 26, 1939, friends saw him. His speech was wandering. The next day he had bouts of pain and breathlessness which was relieved by morphia. He died on January 28 at two in the afternoon, a man at peace with himself. At his suggestion, the tombstone carried the following lines:

> No marble, no conventional phrase
> On limestone quarried near the spot.
> By his command these words are cut:
> Cast a cold eye,
> On Life, on Death.
> Horseman, pass by!

HENRY DAVID THOREAU: "One world at a time."

Henry David Thoreau, author of *Walden*, one of the most delightful books on nature and man's relation to it, died at a comparatively young age. He was just 45. He was born in Concord, Massachusetts, on July 12, 1817 and died on May 6, 1862. When he died, his sister Sophia said: "I feel as if something very beautiful had happened—not death."

His contemporary and friend, Ralph Waldo Emerson, turning away from Thoreau's newly-filled grave murmured: "He had a beautiful soul, he had a beautiful soul." Thoreau's fame rests on his monumental work *Walden*, which he wrote during the two years he spent alone in a cabin by the side of its waters. His other works include *A Week on the Concord and Merrimack Rivers, The Maine Woods* and *Cape Cod*. Thoreau was one of America's earliest naturalists, if not ecologists. He was almost universally loved. Gandhi considered him his teacher on the strength of Thoreau's essay "Civil Disobedience."

Thoreau had been keeping indifferent health during the last two years of his life and was coughing a great deal. In mid-September, 1961, he could not gather the strength even to make a brief journey outside his home. On November 3 he made his last entry in the journal that he kept so faithfully for many years. Later that month, a friend who saw him recorded that he appeared "much wasted." He had a flush in his cheeks and an ominous brightness in his eyes, signs of tuberculosis. Another friend, Theo Brown who saw him about the same time wrote: "He seemed to be in an exalted state of mind for a long time before his death." In mid-March, 1862, Thoreau dictated a letter to yet another friend, Myron Benton. He said: "You ask particularly after my health. I suppose that I have not many months to live; but, of course, I know nothing about it. I may add that I am enjoying my existence as much as ever, and regret nothing." Earlier in February Thoreau had written an essay which he had entitled "The Higher Law" which was subsequently called "Life Without Principle" and published in 1863—after Thoreau's death.

As the weeks passed by, his friends recorded their love and respect for Thoreau in many ways. Bronson Alcott, writing in the April issue of *Atlantic* described Thoreau as "purely a son of nature. I know of nothing more creditable to his greatness than the thoughtful regard, approaching to reverence, by which he has held for so many years some of the best persons of his time" said Alcott. Daniel Ricketson was to write: "Truly you have not lived in vain—your works, and above all, your brave and truthful life, will become a precious treasure to those whose happiness it has been to have known you . . . . " And yet another friend, Sam Staples, wrote to Emerson after calling on Thoreau, saying: "Never spent an hour with more satisfaction. Never saw a man dying with so much pleasure and peace." Indeed, Thoreau was singularly at peace with himself and the world. Almost till the last he was writing. When Grindall Reynolds called on him and found him working on a manuscript, Thoreau looked up cheerfully and with eyes twinkling, remarked: "You know it's respectable to leave an estate to one's friends!" As late as 13 days before his death he was still trying to rouse himself for work. His friends were most solicitous and their devotion greatly touched Thoreau. Total strangers were sending him messages wishing him recovery.

Thoreau once remarked: "I should be ashamed to stay in this world after so much had been done for me. I could never repay my friends."

Ill as he was, he never once complained. On the contrary, he seemed to be full of cheer. To a friend who tried to console him somewhat undiplomatically by saying: "Well, Mr. Thoreau, we must all go," Thoreau replied, "When I was a very little boy I learned that I must die, and I set that down, so, of course, I am not disappointed now. Death is as near to you as it is to me." He retained his sense of humor. When his aunt Louisa asked him if he had made his peace with God, Thoreau replied: "I did not know we had ever quarrelled, Aunt." A friend, Parker Pillsbury, visited Thoreau just a few days before the end came and casually asked: "You seem so near the brink of the dark river, that I almost wonder how the opposite shore may appear to you." Thoreau answered: "One world at a time."

On May 4, Thoreau was visited by Alcott and Channing. They returned again the next day and found Thoreau very weak, but obviously not suffering and definitely cheerful. Thoreau talked pleasantly, as if he had not a care in the world. Alcott, then a venerable old man, kissed Thoreau on his brow before taking leave. Later Channing commented on it. "It seemed to me an extreme unction, in which a friend was the best priest."

By then Thoreau must have realized that he did not have long to live and asked that one of his close friends, Edmund Hosmer, be called. As Hosmer was ready to leave after seeing Thoreau he was presented with one of Thoreau's books. On May 6, about seven in the morning, Thoreau began to get restless. A local judge had come to see him arriving with a bouquet of hyacinths. Thoreau smelled them and said he liked them. He was still self-possessed. A little after 8 a.m. he asked to be raised up in his bed. His mind was still full of ideas about the papers he was planning on Main Woods and his last words were "moose" and "Indian." As his mother, sister and aunt watched him, his breathing grew fainter and fainter and without the slightest struggle, as if he was going gently into the good night, he died at nine o'clock.

A man who was ever at peace with himself, died peacefully.

All of Concord honored him. More than 300 of the town's four hundred school children walked in the funeral procession. Afterwards, Louisa May Alcott wrote: "It seemed as if nature wore her most benignant aspect to welcome her dutiful and loving son to his long sleep in her arms. As we entered the church yard, birds were singing, early violets blooming in the grass and the pines singing their softest lullaby. . . . "

WOLFGANG AMADEUS MOZART: "Did I not say I was writing the Requiem for myself?"

Wolfgang Amadeus Mozart, who gave the world some of its most heavenly operas, *Idomeneo, The Marriage of Figaro, Don Giovanni, Cosi fan tutte, Die Zauberflote* (The Magic Flute) and music to be remembered (No. 39 in E Flat, No. 40 in G minor and No. 41 in C were written in the space of three months) died at the age of 35 in absolute poverty. He was trying to finish his Requiem Mass when he died. Surely Shelley must have had someone like Mozart in mind when he wrote:

> . . . . a gentle trace
> Of light diviner than the common sun
> Sheds on the common earth, and all the place
> Was filled with magic sounds woven into one
> Oblivious melody . . . .

Mozart dealt with magic sounds indeed. *Eine kliene Nachtmusik* remains one of the world's most popular instrumental pieces. His string quartets rank with the greatest. He also wrote sonatas and concertos, though operas held his greatest interest. The world listened to him, but left him practically penniless. As he lay dying, he told his sister-in-law: "I have the taste of death on my tongue. I *taste* death; and who will support my dearest Constanze if you do not stay with her?"

His last illness started in an uncommon way. On November 21, 1791 he had gone to a favorite restaurant, the Silver Serpent, in Vienna. He was listless and tired and went to a rear room and threw himself wearily in a chair. When a waiter came by he ordered some white wine, very unusual for him, because he always asked for beer. The waiter brought the wine, but Mozart seemed uninterested. The proprietor of the restaurant came around and casually remarked: "You look like a very sick man, Herr Kapellmeister!" Mozart indeed was sick and perhaps he knew it. The proprietor, Herr Josef Deiner, was trying to engage Mozart in conversation when the latter suddenly felt very ill. He pressed his lips together, gripped the edge of the table and staggered to his feet. "Josef" he told the proprietor, "I've got a chill . . . that's queer. I'm going home. You drink my wine . . . and come to my house tomorrow." Mozart gave the waiter a coin and staggered to his home. He could hardly manage the one flight of stairs.

When Herr Diener called at Mozart's home the next day, Mozart was in bed and was in no position to discuss anything with his friend. "Not today, Josef" he said gently, "today we have to do with doctors and apothecaries . . . and death!" Mozart had been concerned with death for quite some time. The previous December Haydn had called on him and the two spent a day together. When the time came to part, Mozart burst into tears and said: "We are taking our last farewell in this world." His parting with another friend, Lorenzo, was just as grim. Lorenzo had been trying to persuade Mozart to go to London, but Wolfgang was unwilling. He claimed to have his hands full with a long opera. "Oh, finish it there" Lorenzo remarked, "or don't finish it. We can always write a better one."
Mozart was adamant. "No, dear friend. Now I am thinking only of this German opera, this Zauberflote—and then, and then . . . "
"Yes?" replied Lorenzo, inquiringly.
"Of death." Mozart replied.

Now he was confined to bed with kidney trouble and in agonizing pain. Artists who were playing his operas started calling on him to tell him how the performances went. In the evenings Mozart would try to follow: "Now the first act is over . . . now comes the great Queen of the Night!"

One Sunday afternoon he asked to be propped up with pillows and motioning those who had called on him to sit around his bed gave them the *Lacrimosa* to sing. Mozart himself tried to join in, but could hardly make his voice heard. His face twisted in a painful grimace and he burst into tears. His wife's sister Sophie arrived the same evening and Mozart told her: "I have the taste of death on my tongue—I taste death; and who will support my dearest Constanze if you do not stay with her?" Later he said: "Did I not say I was writing the Requiem for myself?"

He never could complete it. He was too ill. Constanze, his wife, sent for a doctor, but he was at the theater and did not come until very late. When he arrived it became clear to him there was no hope. Nevertheless he ordered cold compresses to be applied to Mozart's head in a futile last minute gesture. It did not work. Mozart began to shudder violently. Soon after, he fell unconscious. Those around heard him break into an occasional delirious cry. Once they saw him raise his hand as if holding something and then puff out his cheeks as if trying to blow a trombone. Constanze, her sister Sophie and a friend, Sussmayr knelt at the bed, repeating prayers for the dying. Around midnight Mozart tried to raise himself, opened his eyes, but sank again. He turned his face to the wall.

The three by his bedside waited. About one o'clock on the morning of December 5, Mozart died. He was given a pauper's funeral—this man who enriched the world of music. His body was confined in a mass grave. When, 17 years later, an attempt was made to locate it, it was learned that the grave had been dug up seven years earlier to make way for other bodies. We remember Mozart by his music now, not by a mere tombstone.

SUMMING UP

A remarkable feature of the biographies of the fifty odd men and women whose last days have been examined in the previous pages is that, barring the lives of acknowledged saints and men of God, so little is known or recorded of the spiritual and religious convictions they held. It is as if it was presumed that not their understanding of God but their understanding of men that is more important. The fifty odd men and women were chosen at random, from out of a hat, as it were, with no preconceived notions about how their deaths may turn out to be, though the last days of Krishna, Buddha, Christ, Mohammad, Socrates seemed natural ones to be examined.

One suspects that if instead of this random set, one had chosen another set—Sebastian Bach, Honore de Balzac, Johannes Brahms, Albert Camus, Cervantes, Cezanne, Chekov, Chopin, Dante, Doestovsky, Ralph Waldo Emerson, Paul Gauguin, Handel, Hayden, Hemingway, Franz Kafka, Soren Kierkegaard, Leonardo da Vinci, Guy Maupassant, Michaelangelo, Montaigne, George Orwell, Marcel Proust, Pushkin, Rembrandt, Renoir, Mark Twain, Wagner, Walt Whitman, Wren—one would not have gotten a more meaningful appreciation of their lives in terms of God. It could be a shortcoming not of their lives, but those of their biographers.

And yet even the sketchy knowledge we have of the men and women whose last days provide us an inkling into the nature of their convictions and the steadfastness of their faith indicate that no matter when their lives occur on the time-scale of history, their reaction to the knowledge of their impending death is not time-bound. In other words, insofar as we can contemplate their existence, they might have lived in any period of history.

This is the reason why their lives were not taken up in any particular order, chronological or otherwise. Human beings do not fall into neat categories. Courage, decency, fear of God or love of Him, or any other human attribute are not incremental in terms of time or circumstance. Cicero could cheerfully lay himself down and let his head be chopped off as in their time did Anne Boleyn or Thomas More. History, then, is not a vertical slab of time, with the years marked off as temperature on a thermometer, but a boundless, infinite field, with fallen men and women lying everywhere freed of the constraints of measurement.

If this is acceptable—and that is the only valid conclusion we can come to—then certain other conclusions seem inescapable. One is that man is continually restating an earlier condition, attesting to the theory propounded by Freud (*Beyond The Pleasure Principle*) of the instincts of living organic matter.

"The child," wrote Freud, "never gets tired of demanding the repetition of a game . . . he wants always to hear the same story instead of a new one, insists inexorably on exact repetition and corrects each deviation which the narrator lets slip by mistake. According to this" said Freud, "an instinct would be a tendency in living organic matter, impelling it towards reinstatement of an earlier condition, one which it had abandoned under the influence of external disturbing forces . . . . The rudimentary creature would from its very beginning not have wanted to change, would, if circumstances had remained the same, have always merely repeated the same course of existence . . . . It would be counter to the conservative nature of instinct if the goal of life were a state never hitherto reached. It must be rather an ancient starting point, which, the living being left long ago and to which it harks back again by all the circuitous paths of development . . . . the goal of all life is death."

What does this signify? Whether it is what Feud intended to say or not, it is hard not to derive the conclusion that Frued, in fact, is hinting that death is not the end of man, but the beginning of the repetition of man, in his many and continuing phases. The idea bears further examination. In his essay on Nirvana (*Some Turns of Thought in Modern Philosophy*) Santayana seems to agree with the thesis that there surely is a past life for each of us. Discussing the law of karma, Santayana wrote:

> We are born, it says, with a heritage, a character imposed, and a long task assigned, all due to ignorance which in our past lives has led us into all sorts of commitments. These obligations we must pay off, relieving the pure spirit within us from its accumulated burdens, from debts and assets both equally oppressive . . . . When life is understood to be a process of redemption, its various phases are taken up in turn without haste and without undue attachment . . . the point is to have expressed and discharged all that was latent in us . . . .

If this is true, then death cannot possibly hold any terror. In fact, death should not hold any terror nor the event itself be an occasion for sadness. For one thing we might ask ourselves what other end there can possibly be. As Santayana put it, an invitation to the dance is not rendered ironical because the dance itself cannot last forever. The transitoriness of things is essential to their physical being and not at all sad in itself. It becomes sad only by virtue of a sentimental illusion, which makes us imagine that they wish to endure and that their end is always untimely. Death, if it must be said, is never untimely. If the law of karma has any relevance at all, it means that from the moment we are born, our lifespan has been predetermined and there is nothing that we can possibly do about it except to accept it as inevitable. The relapse of created things into nothing, then, should be considered as no violent fatality, but something naturally quite smooth and proper, weaving life and death together into the texture of a more comprehensive destiny.

The crux of the problem is our ignorance of what is meant by the comprehensiveness of our destiny. We equate long life with prospects of fulfilling a destiny, when, for all one knows, what we call destiny was more likely fulfilled in a short span of time. If Keats had lived longer, would he have surpassed himself? Or, for that matter, Shelley or Byron? They all died young and yet it is hard to imagine that any one could have improved on his own work; in fact, our knowledge that their lives were so short add not only poignancy to their art but a special relevance as well, that may have been denied if the poets had lived long and laborious lives.

To equate a long life with the full flowering of our destiny is one of the fundamental errors that man is prone to make. In the first place—as has been argued in an earlier context—how is one to define the right time to die? The biblical definition of the full life is three score years and ten—seventy years. That Methusellah lived a multiple of that span without having significantly added to the wisdom and knowledge of mankind should be argument enough that time has no meaning in assessing life.

The Upanishad says: *Kurvanneveha karmani jijivshet shatam samah*: In the midst of activity alone wilt thou desire to live a hundred years. The stress, it is well to remember, is not on the length of time but on the intensity of activity. One can live for a hundred years and not feel that one has lived that long; time has no relevance except in terms of intensity of feeling which can only come as a reflection of activity, and an activity, moreover, that is outward bound.

For as Rabindranath Tagore has so eloquently put it, it is the very characteristic of life that it is not complete in itself. It must come out. Its truth is in the commerce of the inside and the outside. For even if man does nothing external to him, his body is fully employed with its own inside activity. Its heartbeat must not cease, it must continue without interruption; every organ is fully employed; cessation of any activity means illness and ultimately death.

But surely life is more than internal activity? By its very nature life has to seek external activity to complete itself. And what is true of the body, says Tagore, is even more true of the soul. It cannot live on its own internal feelings and imaginings. It is ever in need of external objects—as Tagore sees it, in need of Brahma, God.

In other words, man, to fulfill himself—complete itself, as it were—has to relate himself to God. He has to abide in God within as well as without. *Maham brahma nirakuryyam ma ma brahma nirakarot.* Brahma has not left me, let me not leave Brahma. And how is this to be achieved? *Yadyat karma prakurvita tadbrahmani samarpayet.* Whatever works thou doest, consecrate them to Brahma. It is the same philosophy of the Gita, stated in different terms.

In examining the lives of men and women and their deaths, the overwhelming fact that is striking is that those who seemed to have fulfilled their lives with utter selflessness died the happiest deaths. Such is the death of George Washington, who was remarkably composed to the last to the point of checking on his own pulse rate to the end. But Washington is the exception, not the rule. For if there is another fact that is endlessly striking, it is that so few knew the art of dying. For dying, like living, is an art and if only most of us mastered the art of dying as much as we seek to master the art of living, there would be many more happy deaths.

The fact of the matter, however, is that the art of living is not different from the art of dying; in fact, the one flows into the other, and cannot be separated one from the other. He who has mastered the art of living has already mastered the art of dying; to such, death holds no terrors.

In his work *Sadhana*, Tagore has dealt at considerable length on this subject. Those who have mastered the art of living are the *rishis*. And who are they?

> *Samprapyainam rishayo jnanatriptah*
> *Kritatmano vitaragah prashantah*
> *te sarvagam sarvatah prapya dhirah*
> *Yuktamanah sarvamevavishanti.*

> They who have attained the supreme soul in knowledge were filled with wisdom, and having found him in union with the soul were in perfect harmony with the inner self; they having realized him in the heart were free from all selfish desires, and having experienced him in all the activities of the world, had attained calmness. The rishis were they who having reached the supreme God from all sides had found abiding peace, had become united with all, had entered into the life of the universe.

The same has been said in the Bible: "I am the way, the truth, and the life; no man cometh unto the Father but by me." To know the way is all. It is the gift of surrender.

Of all things in life, to surrender to a higher being is the hardest; man's ego is perpetually a stumbling block. It requires extraordinary strength to be able to accept God, not theoretically, not in times of crises, but as a way of life at all times. Tagore serves to remind us of this in *Gitanjali*. Death and everlasting life runs as a silver thread throughout the work. "Thou hast made me endless, such is thy pleasure. This frail vessel thou emptiest again and again and fillest it ever with fresh life." "This little flute of a reed thou hast carried over hills and dales and hast breathed through it melodies eternally new . . . Ages pass and still thou pourest and still there is room to fill." "Death, thy servant is at my door. He has crossed the unknown sea and brought thy call to my home. The night is dark and my heart is fearful—yet I will take up the lamp, open my gates and bow to him my welcome. It is thy messenger who stands at my door."

To those of us living, the last days of the great should provide something more than prurient interest. It may sound like a cliche, but neither power, nor glory, nor riches, nor fame bring happiness in the end. It may be argued that neither does poverty or lack of power. The point is that not externals matter as much as the way they are used. Power is not necessarily a barrier to happiness and peace of mind; Queen Elizabeth I was perfectly at peace with herself in her last moments; Aurangzeb was not. It says something about the use of power by these two powerful sovereigns.

In the end it is not what we take from society but what we give to it that alone is relevant. A good life may not promise a painless end, but it surely will make for a peaceful end. Pain has nothing to do with goodness. Ramakrishna Paramahansa, one of India's great saints, died of cancer of the throat. When he was asked how he would explain this, he gave the obvious answer. Where there is form, there is pain, there is suffering. Ramakrishna's inner self was totally at peace; it was his external self that was being ravaged.

There is no way in which most of us can escape pain. Pain is inherent in life. To pray for a painless end, in the circumstances, is to pray for the impossible. What one may pray for is a peaceful end and that should be within the reach of most of us. Napoleon was struggling to the very end, we know not what inner demons possessed him. Vivekananda willed his death; it was a most beautiful way to go.

The fact of the matter is that to die a peaceful death, one must accept death gracefully. To deny death its final conquest is to invite a suffering of a special kind. Death is not evil. It is a friend to be welcomed with open arms. Victor Hugo understood it. Yeats appreciated it. Voltaire had no difficulty in taking death to his bosom. And Pope John, that most loveable of Popes said any day was good to die, as any day was good to be born. And since there is no way in which we can abolish death, why don't we accept its inevitability with courage if not joy?

One does not have to believe in any theory about life after death to be able to die with a song on one's lips and a prayer in one's heart. But it is nevertheless interesting to speculate on the nature of death, as did Santayana. I find his speculation quite charming:

> The end of life might be the beginning of another, if the Creator had composed his great work like a dramatic poet, assigning successive lines to different characters. Death would then be merely the cue at the end of each speech, summoning the next personage to break in and keep the ball rolling. Or, perhaps, as some suppose, all the characters are assumed in turn by a single supernatural spirit who, amid his endless improvisations is imagining himself living for the moment in the particular solar and social system. Death in such a universal monologue would be but a change of scene or of meter, while in the scramble of a real comedy it would be a change of actors. In either case, every voice would be silenced sooner or later and death would end each particular life in spite of all possible sequels.

Werner von Braun, one of the great scientists of our times, believed in God. Waiting patiently to die—he was suffering from cancer—he wrote an 85-page paper to the synod of the Lutheran Church of America in which he confessed to his faith. It is a touching document. He expressed himself troubled that many scientists could not visualize god. "What strange rationale" he asked, "makes some physicists accept the inconceivable electron as real while refusing to accept the reality of God on the ground that they cannot conceive Him? One cannot be exposed to the law order of the universe without concluding that there must be a divine intent behind it all. Speaking for myself, I can only say that the grandeur of the cosmos serves only to confirm my belief in the certainty of a creator. The better we understand the intricacies of the universe and all its harbors, the more reason we havef found to marvel at God's creation."

The universe truly continues to mystify scientist and layman. If we look at the constellation of Orion, for instance, and find the star Rigel, we discover that it is a "blue supergiant" burning with the luminosity of 40,000 suns! The sun itself, is no great shakes as a star, as stars go. It is a garden variety of star, a so-called fifth magnitude star the like of which there are literally millions! Moreover, instead of being in the galactic center of the Milky Way, it is located on the periphery. The galaxy of which the sun is a part is one of a "local cluster" of galaxies—there are millions of such clusters—and the light from our closest neighboring galaxy takes 2 million years to reach us. It is an awful thought. It almost confirms what has been said in the Bible: The fool hath said there is no God. One suspects that if God did not exist we must invent him to explain the wonder and mystery of the expanding universe.

Tagore had a proper appreciation of the place of man in the scheme of things and a truly relevant attitude toward death. "In the playhouse of infinite forms I have had my play and here I have caught sight of him that is formless." How so much like Santayana! Or again: "In one salutation to thee, my God, let all my senses spread out and touch this world at Thy feet." There is total surrender here. No resistance, no anger, no frustration. Just acceptance. And that final invocation in the *Gitanjali*: "Like a flock of homesick cranes flying night and day back to their mountain nests, let all my life take its voyage to its eternal home in one salutation to Thee." With such thoughts, one might well ask with Henry Francis Lyte: "Where is death's sting? Where, grave, thy victory?"

BIBLIOGRAPHY

Self-knowledge (Atmabodha): Swami Nikhilananda, New York, Ramakrishna-Vivekananda Center.

The Mystics of Islam: Reynold A. Nicholson; Routledge & Kegan Paul Ltd., London.

Indian Philosophy: S. Radhakrishnan; The Macmillan Co., New York.

A Sourcebook in Indian Philosophy: ed. S. Radhakrishnana and Charles A. Moore; Princeton University Press, Princeton.

The Reconstruction of Religious Thought in Islam: Sir Mohammad Iqbal; Oxford University Press, London, 1934.

The Tibetan Book of the Dead: W. Y. Evans-Wentz, Causeway Book, New York.

The Integral Philosophy of Sri Aurobindo: ed by Haridas Chaudhuri and Frederic Spiegelberg; George Allen and Unwin Ltd., London.

Reincarnation: An East-West Anthology: Compiled and edited by Joseph Head and S. L. Cranston; The Julian Press, Inc., New York.

The Koran: Translated with notes by N. J. Dawood, Penguin.

Great Dialogues of Plato: Translation by W. H. D. Rouse; The New American Library, Inc., New York.

The Judaic Tradition: Texts edited and introduced by Nahum N. Glatzer; Beacon Press, Boston.

Moses Maimonides: The Guide for the Perplexed: Translated by M. Friedlander; Dover Publications, New York.

Dark Night of the Soul: St. John of the Cross; translated by E. Allison Peers; Image Books, Doubleday & Co., New York.

The Question of God: Protestant Theology in the 20th Century; Heinz Zahrnt; Harcourt, Brace, Jovanovich, New York.

A History of Christian Thought: Paul Tillich; edited by Carl Braaten, Simon and Schuster, New York.

A Histroy of Western Philosophy: Bertrand Russell; Simon and Schuster, New York.

The Ocean of Theosophy: William Q. Judge; Theosophical University Press, Pasadena, California.

A Handbook of Christian Theology: A Meredian Book: New American Library, New York.

Death, the Riddle and the Mystery: Eberhard Jangel; The Westminster Press, Philadelphia.

Live Until You Die: Randholph Crump Miller; United Church Press, Philadelphia.

The Tarjuman al-Quran: Maulana Abul Kalam Azad; Asia Publishing House, Bombay.

The Rationalists: Translations by John Veitch, R. N. M. Elwes and George Montgomery; Doubleday & Company, New York.

Introductory Readings in Philosophy: Marcus Singer and Robert Ammerman; Charles Schribners Sons, New York.

Sri Aurobindo or the Adventure of Consciousness: Satprem; Harper & Row, New York.

Twentieth Century Book of the Dead: Gil Elliot; Charles Schribners Sons, New York.

Death: The Final Stage of Growth: Elisabeth Kubler-Ross; Prentice-Hall, Ind., Englewood Cliffs, New Jersey.

The Meaning of Death: Edited by Herman Feifel; McGraw Hill Book Co., New York.

Life and Teachings of Sri Madhwacharya: C. M. Padmanabhacharya; Sri Palimar Mutt, Dudupi.

Man Is Not Alone: Abraham Joshua Heschel; The Noonday Press, New York.

The Saviors of God: Nikos Kazantzakis; Simon and Schuster, New York.

Man's Search for Meaning; Viktor E. Frankl; Beacon Press, Boston.

Prolongevity: Albert Rosenfeld, Alfred A. Knopf, New Yrok.

Man in the Universe: W. Norman Brown, University of California Press, Berkeley.

Tragic Sense of Life: Miguel de Unamuno; Dover Publications, Inc., New York.

Chance and Necessity: Jacques Monod; Vintage Books, New York.

The Spirit of the East: The Sirdar Ikbal Ali Shah; E. P. Dutton & Co., New York.

The Kabir Book: Robert Bly; Beacon Press, Boston.

The Only Dance There Is: Ram Dass; Anchor Press, Doubleday; New York.

Living and Dying: Robert Jay Lifton and Eric Olson; Praeger Publishers, New York.

Buddhist Sutras: Trans. by T. W. Rhys Davids; Dover Publications, Inc., New York.

The Philosophy of the Upanishads: Paul Deussen, Dover Publications Inc., New York.

The System of the Vedanta: Paul Deussen, Dover Publications Inc., New York.

The Upanishads: Trans by Max Muller; Dover Publications, Inc., New York.

The Way of All the Earth: John S. Dunne; The MacMillan Company, New York.

Many Mansions: Gina Cerminara; The New American Library Inc., New York.

Life After Life: Raymond A. Moody Jr., Mockingbird Books, Inc., Atlanta.

Buddhism for the West: Dorothy C. Donath; McGraw Hill Paperbacks, New York.

The Secret of the Golden Flower: Trans. by Richard Wilhelm, Causeway Books, New York.

Labyrinths: Jorge Luis Borges, New Directions Publishing Corporation, New York.

Vedanta for the Common Man: ed by Christopher Isherwood, New American Library, New York.

The Perennial Philosophy: Aldous Huxley; Harper & Row, New York.

The Mahabharata: Chakravarti V. Narasimhan, Columbia University Press, New York.

Einstein: The Life and Times: Ronald W. Clark; Avon Books, New York.

St. Francis of Assisi: Morris Bishop, Little, Brown, and Co., Boston.

A Life of William Shakespeare: Air Sidney Lee, Dover Publications, New York.

Buddha: His Life and Teachings: Paul Carus and Nyanatiloka; Crescent Books, New York.

Sigmund Freud: A Short Biography: Giovanni Costigan, The Macmillan Company, New York.

Life of Sri Ramakrishna: Advaita Ashrama, Calcutta.

Cicero: Elizabeth Rawson, Allen Lane, London.

Cicero: D. R. Shackleton Bailey, Charles Scribner's Sons, New York.

The Nature of Alexander: Mary Renault, Pantheon Books (Random House), New York.

The Holy Bible

The Peacock Throne: The Drama of Mogul India: Waldemar Hansen, Holt, Rinehart and Winston, New York.

Lenin: A Biography: David Shub, Penguin Books, London.

The Life and Death of Mahatma Gandhi: Robert Payne, E. P. Dutton & Co., New York.

Tolstoy: A Life of My Father: Alexandra Tolstoy, Harper & Brothers, New York.

Tolstoy: Henry Troyat, Doubleday & Co., New York.

The Challenge of Anne Boleyn: Hester W. Chapman, Coward, McCann & Georghegan, Inc., New York.

Turgenev: A Life: David Magarshack, Faber & Faber, London.

The Life of Voltaire: S. G. Tallentyre, Loring & Mussey, New York.

The Voice of Allah: Edwin Hoyt, The John Day Company, New York.

Muhammad and the Islamic Tradition: Emile Dermenghem, Harper & Brothers, New York.

Vivekananda: The Yogas and Other Works: Chosen with a biography by Swami Nikhilananda, Ramakrishna-Vivekananda Center, New York.

Marlborough: His Life and Times: Winston Churchill, Schribner's New York.

Hammarskjold: Brian Urquhart, Alfred A. Knopf, New Yrok.

Yankee From Olympus: Catherine Drinker Bowen, Little Brown & Co, Boston.

Napoleon: Emil Ludwig; Modern Library, New York.

The Rising Sun: John Toland; Random House, New York.

King: A Critical Biography: David L. Lewis; Penguin Books, Baltimore.

The Man from Monticello: An Intimate Life of Thomas Jefferson; Thomas Fleming; William Morrow and Company, Inc., New York.

Ibsen: A Biography: Michael Meyer, Doubleday & Co, New York.

I Will Be Called John: A biography of Pope John XXIII. Lawrence Elliott; E. P. Dutton & Co., New York.

Akbar: J. M. Shelat; Bharatiya Vidya Bhavan, Bombay.

Queen Christina: Georgina Masson; Sphere Books, Ltd., London.

Divided Soul: The Life of Gogol: Henry Troyat, Minerva Press, New York.

Goethe: His Life and Times: Richard Friedenthal; The World Publishing Co., New York and Cleveland.

Sir Isaac Newton: H. D. Anthony; Abelard-Schuman Ltd., London, New York.

Byron: A Portrait: Leslie A. Marchand; Alfred A. Knopf, New York.

Keats and His World: Timothy Hilton; The Viking Press, New York.

Shelley, The Pursuit: Richard Holmes, E. P. Dutton & Co., New York.

Queen Christina: Georgina Masson; Martin Secker & Warburg, London.

H. G. Wells: His Turbulent Life and Times: Lovat Dickson; Atheneum, New York.

The Lincoln Reader: Paul M. Angle, Rutgers University Press, New Brunswick.

Edison: A Biography; Mathew Josephson, McGraw Hill Books, Co., New York.

Samuel Johnson: A Biography: John Wain, The Viking Press, New York.

The Life of Samuel Johnson: James Boswell, Doubleday & Co., New York.

The Death of Stalin: Georges Bortoli; Praeger Publishers, New York.

Conqueror of the World: The Life of Chinghis Khan: Rene Grousset, The Orion Press, New York.

Washington: Richard Harwell; Charles Schribners Sons, New York.

Duce!: Richard Collier; The Viking Press, New York.

The Life and Death of Adolf Hitler: Robert Payne; Praeger Publishers, New York.

Beethoven and the Age of Revolution: Frida Knight; International Publishers, London.

Marie Curie: Robert Reid, Saturday Review Press, E. P. Dutton & Co., New York.

Elizabeth I—A Biography: Paul Johnson, Holt, Rhinehard & Winston, New York.

Victor Hugo: Joanna Richardson, St. Martin's Press, New York.

W. B. Yeats: Joseph Hone, St. Martin's Press, New York.

Decision at Trafalgar: Dudley Pope, J. P. Lippincott, & Co, Philadelphia and New York.

Some Turns of Thought in Modern Philosophy: Five Essays: George Santayana, Charles Schribners Sons, New York.

Death and After: Annie Besant, The Theosophical Publishing House, Adyar, Madras.

A Book of Life: Martin Gray, The Seabury Press, New York.

Sadhana: The Realization of Life: Rabindranath Tagore; Omen Communications, Inc., Tucson, Arizona.

Mozart: Marcia Davenport, Charles Scribner's Sons, New York.

The Days of Henry Thoreau: A Biography: Walter Harding; Alfred A. Knopf, New York.

The Celebration of Life: A Dialogue on Immortality and Infinity: Norman Cousins, Harper & Row, Publishers, New York.

Death as a Fact of Life: David Hendin; W. W. Norton & Co., Inc., New York.

Death: An Interdisciplinary Analysis: Warren Shibles; The Language Press, Whitewater, Wisconsin.

Death: Current Perspectives: Edwin S. Schneidman; Mayfield Publishing Co., Palo Alto, California.

Book of Wisdom: Swami Rama; Himalayan International Institute, Honesdale, Pennsylvania.

Life Here and Hereafter: Swami Rama; Himalayan International Institute, Honesdale, Pennsylvania.

Only In America: Harry Golden, The World Publishing Co., New York.

Islam: Abdul Haq Ansari et al; Punjab University, Patiala.

The Spirit of Islam: Ashfaque Husain; Asia Publishing House, Bombay.

Existentialism, Religion and Death: Walter Kaufmann, New American Library Inc., New York.

The Way of the Sufi: Idries Shah, E. P. Dutton & Co., New York.

The Religions of Man: Huston Smith; Harper & Row, Publishers, New York.

The Theory and Practice of Meditation, edited by R. Ballentine, The Himalayan International Institute, Honesdale, Pennsylvania.

Freedom from the Bondage of Karma: Swami Rama; Himalayan International Institute, Honesdale, Pennsylvania.

Yoga and Psychotherapy: The Evolution of Consciousness: Swami Rama, et al.; Himalayan International Institiue, Honesdale, Pennsylvania.

Sri Aurobindo: Centenary Volumes 10 to 29; Sri Aurobindo Ashram, Pondicherry.

Index

A

Addison, Joseph, 65
Akbar the Great, death of, 253-256
Aldrich, Thomas B., 66
Alexander, death of, 176-178
Ali, Anaeer, 96-97
All Men are Mortal, 124-125
antaratman, 11, 12
archetypes, 63
Archetypes and Collective Unconscious, 63
asana, 13
astral body, 57-59
Atharva Veda, 135
atman, 10, 11
Augustine, 106, 107, 115
Aurangzeb, death of, 193-195
Aurobindo, Sri, 68-73
avidya, 51-52

B

Bardo Thodol, 53-55
Barth, Karl, 118-120
de Beauvoir, Simon, 124-125
van Beethoven, Ludwig, death of, 296
Bhagavad Gita, 15-18, 21
Binyon, Lawrence, 128
Boleyn, Anne, death of, 206-208
Booth, John Wilkes, 276
Brahma Sutras, 131
Brahman, 10-11, 17
Brahmarandhra, 135-136
von Braun, Werner, death of, 324
Brihadaranjaka Upanishad, 19
Browning, Robert, 140
Bryant, William Cullen, 126
Buddha, 45-47
  death of, 163-165
Byron, George Gordon, death of, 258

C

Calvin, John, 110-112
Carducci, 137
Cato, 65
Cayce, Edgar, 33-36
Cerminara, Dr. Gina, 33-36
Chandogya Upanishad, 11, 20
Charvaka, 22-25
Chikhai Bardo, 53-54

Chomjid bardo, 54
Christianity, 105-109
  and destiny, 110-112
  and immortality, 109
  and justification by faith, 114-115
  and sacraments, 115-116
  and sin in Catholicism, 112-114
Christina, Queen, death of, 267-269
Churchill, Sir Winston, 237
Cicero, death of, 168-170
creation, Judaism, 91-93
Curie, Marie, death of, 304-306

D

Dali, Salvador, 63
Dark Night of the Soul, 120
death, Jewish attitude of, 93-95
  legends of, 3-10, 16-17
devachan, 59-60
dharana, 14
dharma, 16
dhyana, 14
DNA, 139
Dryden, John, 126
dualism, 37
dying, art of, 321-325

E

Edison, Thomas Alva, death of, 277
Einstein, Albert, death of, 189-193
Eleazor, 93-94
Elizabeth, Queen, death of, 301-304
Esfandiary, F. M., 141
Esoteric Buddhism, 57

F

faith, 118, 120
fana, 102-103
finitude and infinity, 122-123
Four Noble Truths, 47-50
Francis of Assisi, death of, 184-186
Frankl, Victor E., 145-147
Franklin, Benjamin, 67
free will, 87-91
Freud, Sigmund, death of, 187-189

G

Gandhi, Mahatma, death of, 198-202

Gaon, Saadia, 88
Garfield, Dr. Charles, 30
Gita, see Bhagavad Gita
Gitanjali, 322-323, 325
Goethe, Johann, death of, 250-253
Gogol, death of, 269-272
Golden, Henry, 131-132
grace, 108, 119-120

H

Hammarskjold, Dag, death of, 219-223
Henley, William E., 65
Heschel, Joshua, 133-134, 142
Hindu philosophy, 43
History of Christian Thought, 111
Hitler, Adolf, death of, 292-295
Holmes, Oliver Wendell, 66
  death of, 230-232
Hugo, Victor, 64
  death of, 298-301
Huxley, Aldous, 61-62

I

Ibsen, Henrik, death of, 248-250
ignorance, 50-52
Indian Thought & Its Development, 64
Intellectual Autobiography, 64
Ishopanishad, 56
Islam, 95-97
  and destiny of man, 97-100
  and heaven and hell, 100-102
  and Sufism, 102-105
Iqbal, Sir Mohammad, 97-100

J

Jain philosophy, 38-41
Jefferson, Thomas, death of, 241-244
Jesus Christ, 138
  death of, 170-176
jiva, 38-39, 43-45
John, Duke of Marlborough, death of, 235
John XXIII, Pope, death of, 245-248
John of the Cross, St., 120
Johnson, Samuel, death of, 279-281
Jovenal, 127
Judaism, 84-87
  and creation, 91-93
  and death, 93-95
  and free will, 87-91
Judge William Q., 57-60
Jung, C. G., 62-63
Juniper, F., 141

K

Kabir, 147-148
Kali, 134-135
Kamath, personal philosophy of, 129
karma, law of, 21, 36-40, 55

Katha Upanishad, 7, 17, 21
Kaufmann, Walter, 83
Kazantzakis, 143-144
Keats, John, 28
  death of, 262-264
Khan, Chinghis, death of, 284-287
King, Martin, death of, 227-230
Kipling, Rudyard, 65
Koran, 96-102
kosha, 43-44
Krishna, Lord, death of, 161-163
Kubler-Ross, Dr. Elisabeth, 25, 146-147

L

Last Poems, 72-73
Lenin, death of, 196-198
life after death, 25-31
Life After Life, 29
Life Here and Hereafter, 31
Lincoln, Abraham, death of, 274-277
lokas of the astral man, 59
  of the jiva, 43-44
  of the soul-complex, 54-55
lokayata, doctrine of, 22-25
Lucian, 126
Luther, Martin, 113-114

M

Madhava, Sri, 130-131
Madhva, 37
Mahabharata, 134, 147
  and death, 3-5
Maimonides, Moses, 86, 88-93, 133
Man Against Mortality, 141
Man Is Not Alone, 134
Man's Search for Meaning, 145
Mandukya Upanishad, 15
Many Mansions, 33
Masefield, John, 64-65
maya, 55-57, 148-149
meditation, and subconscious, 32
  Buddhist, 49
metempsychosis, see rebirth
Midrash Yetzirat ha-Velad, 86
Modena, Leone, 84-85
moksha, 18, 19
Monod, Jacques, 21-25
Moody, Dr. Raymond, A., 29-30
Moor, George Foot, 60-61
More Lives Than One?, 32
More, Thomas, death of, 214-216
Mozart, Wolfgang, death of, 315-317
Muhammad, 95-96
  death of, 216-219
Mundaka Upanishad, 12, 19-20
Murray, John Middleton, 61
Mussolini, Benito, death of, 289-291
McGinley, Phyllis, 144-145

N

Nachiketa, 7-10
Napoleon, death of, 223-227
National Institute Mental Health, 33
Nelson, Lord, death of, 306-310
New Poems, 311
Newton, Isaac, death of, 256-258
nidanas, 49-50
nirvana, 40-41
Nivedita, Sister, 239
niyama, 13
non-dualism, 37

O

Only in America, 131-132
Osiris, 80-81
Osis, Dr. Karlis, 30-31

P

Paul the apostle, 107-108
The Perennial Philosophy, 61-62
Pittinger, W. Norman, 107
Plato, 165-166
pranayama, 13
pratyahara, 13-14
Prolongevity, 139
Pryor, Barbara, 25-27
purusha; 10

Q

qualified non-dualism, 37
Question of God, the, 119

R

Radhakrishnan, Dr., 19-20, 40, 51, 55
Raja Yoga, 14, 103
Rama, Swami, 31, 32, 35
Ramakrishna Paramahansa, death, 178
  on Swami Vivekananda, 238
Ramanuja, 37-38
rebirth, 18-21, 32-35, 60-70
reincarnation, see rebirth
Ritchie, Dr. George, 27-29
The Rising Sun, 234
Rosenfield, Albert, 139-140
Rumi, 99, 104

S

sacraments in Christianity, 115-116
Saint Watching, 144-145
salvation in Christianity, 117-118
samadhi, 14
Sankara, 37
Santayana, 319-320
Sarvadarshanasangraha, 23
Sarvasiddhantasangraha, 23

Satapatha Brahmana, 18
Satprem, 71-73
Satyavan, and Savitri, story of, 5-7
The Saviors of God, 143-144
Schweitzer, Albert, 63-64
Shaagat Arya, 84-85
Shakespeare, William, 126, 181-184
Shelley, Percy Blysshe, death of, 264
Sidpa bardo, 54-55
sin, 122-123
Sinnett, A. P. 57
Socrates, 74-79, 127, 140, 165-168
The Song of the Creatures, 185
sookshma sharira, 43-44
Stalin, Joseph, death of, 281-284
sthoda sharira, 43-44
Sufism, 102-105
Svetasvatara Upanishad, 11, 22
Synesius, 80

T

Tagore, Rabindranath, 321, 322, 325
Talmud, 86, 88
Tennyson, Lord, 137
Tertullian, 126
Thanatopsis, 126
theosophy, 57-60
Thoreau, Henry David, death of, 312
Three Venerations, 52
Tibetan Book of the Dead, 53-55
Tillich, Paul, 111, 113, 122
Tojo, General, death of, 233-235
Toland, John, 234
Tolstoy, Leo, death of, 202-205
Tragic Sense of Life, 137
transubstantiation, 116
Trent, Council of, 112
Turgenev, Ivan, death of, 290-211
turiya, 15

U

Unamuno, Miguel de, 137, 138-139, 142
Upanishads, 7, 11, 12, 15, 17, 19, 56, 320

V

Vedanta philosophy, 37
Vivekachudamani, 37
Vivekananda, Swami, 14-15, 237-241
Voltaire, death of, 211-213

W, X, Y, Z

Washington, George, death of, 287
Wells, H. G., death of, 272-274
Whitman, Walt, 66-67
yama, 13-14
Yama, Lord of Death, 5-10
Yeats, William Butler, death of, 310-311
Zahrnt, Heinz, 119
Zoroastrianism, 81-83

BOOKS PUBLISHED BY THE HIMALAYAN INSTITUTE

Living with the Himalayan Masters	Swami Rama
Yoga and Psychotherapy	Swami Rama, R. Ballentine, M.D., Swami Ajaya
Emotion to Enlightenment	Swami Rama, Swami Ajaya
A Practical Guide to Holistic Health	Swami Rama
Freedom from the Bondage of Karma	Swami Rama
Book of Wisdom	Swami Rama
Lectures on Yoga	Swami Rama
Life Here and Hereafter	Swami Rama
Marriage, Parenthood and Enlightenment	Swami Rama
Meditation in Christianity	Swami Rama, et al
Superconscious Meditation	Pandit Usharbudh Arya, Ph.D.
Philosophy of Hatha Yoga	Pandit Usharbudh Arya, Ph.D.
Yoga Psychology	Swami Ajaya
Foundations of Eastern & Western Psychology	Swami Ajaya (ed)
Psychology East and West	Swami Ajaya (ed)
Meditational Therapy	Swami Ajaya (ed)
Diet and Nutrition	Rudolph Ballentine, M.D.
Theory and Practice of Meditation	Rudolph Ballentine, M.D. (ed)
Science of Breath	Rudolph Ballentine, M.D. (ed)
Joints and Glands Exercises	Rudolph Ballentine, M.D. (ed)
Yoga and Christianity	Justin O'Brien, Ph,D.
Inner Paths	Justin O'Brien, Ph.D. (ed)
Faces of Meditation	S. N. Agnihotri, Justin O'Brien, (ed)
Sanskrit Without Tears	S. N. Agnihotri, Ph.D.
Art and Science of Meditation	L. K. Misra, Ph.D. (ed)
Swami Rama of the Himalayas	L. K. Misra, Ph.D. (ed)
Science Studies Yoga	James Funderburk, Ph.D.
Homeopathic Remedies	Drs. Anderson, Buegel, Chernin
Hatha Yoga Manual I	Samskrti and Veda
Hatha Yoga Manual II	Samskrti and Judith Franks
Philosophy of Death and Dying	M. V. Kamath
Practical Vedanta of Swami Rama Tirtha	Brandt Dayton
The Swami and Sam	Brandt Dayton
Chants from Eternity	Institute Staff
Thought for the Day	Institute Staff
Spiritual Diary	Institute Staff
Himalayan Mountain Cookery	Martha Ballentine
The Yoga Way Cookbook	Institute Staff